Prague

THE ROUGH GUIDE

There are more than eighty Rough Guide titles covering
destinations from Amsterdam to Zimbabwe

Forthcoming titles include
China • Jamaica • New Zealand • South Africa
Southwest USA • Vienna • Washington DC

Rough Guide Reference Series
Classical Music • The Internet • Jazz • Rock Music • World Music

Rough Guide Phrasebooks
Czech • French • German • Greek • Italian • Mexican Spanish
Polish • Portuguese • Spanish • Thai • Turkish • Vietnamese

Rough Guides on the Internet
http://www.roughguides.com/
http://www.hotwired.com/rough

Rough Guide Credits

Text Editors:	Amanda Tomlin and Catherine McHale
Series Editor:	Mark Ellingham
Editorial:	Martin Dunford, Jonathan Buckley, Samantha Cook, Jo Mead, Alison Cowan, Annie Shaw, Paul Gray, Vivienne Heller, Sarah Dallas
Online:	Alan Spicer (UK), Andrew Rosenberg (US)
Production:	Susanne Hillen, Andy Hilliard, Judy Pang, Link Hall, Nicola Williamson, Helen Ostick
Cartography:	Melissa Flack, David Callier
Finance:	John Fisher, Celia Crowley, Catherine Gillespie
Publicity:	Richard Trillo, Simon Carloss (UK), Jean-Marie Kelly, Jeffrey Kaye (US)
Administration:	Tania Hummel

Acknowledgements

Special thanks to David Charap, for friendship and the Nuselské schody, Mira for her Serbian cakes and hospitality, Luboš for the loan of his flat and Lenka for putting up with me, Petr, Pavla and Zdeněk for Brno breaks, Kate, Nat, Nancy, Dave, Stan, Josh, Gren, Juliet and Bal and Gunk in Wetherby.

Thanks also to the following people who contributed to the production of this book with their letters and comments: Cathy Aitchison, Allison Bartlett, W. Burkinshaw, David Carlisle, Barbara Challenor, J. Chamberlin, Rebecca and Robert Cherny, Rosemary Creeser, Kay Donaghue and Roger Feakins, William Donaldson, Sue Downes, Peter Driscoll, Denise Dutton, Catherine Farr, Irena Forstová, Mark Graham, Mark Gutteridge and Anton Gabszewicz, J. Harrington, Ian Jenkins, Simon Johnson, Khalil Nasrallah, Alison Noble, Anna-Louise and Stephen O'Toole, Pauline Peacock, Eamon Quinn, Jan Rance, Derek Robinson, Marian Seager, Anil Seth, Richard Shaw, Stephanie Smith, Clive Staines, Sue Stanbury, Paul Stronge and Julie Heslop, Stephen Taylor, Jack Tykal, B.L. Underwood, William Walker, Jane Wiltshire.

And thanks to all those at **Rough Guides**, in particular Amanda Tomlin, Catherine McHale, Susanne Hillen, Nicola Williamson, Judy Pang, Melissa Flack, and Derek Wilde for proofreading.

This edition published in 1995 by Rough Guides Ltd, 1 Mercer Street, London WC2H 9QJ.
Reprinted in January 1997.

Distributed by the Penguin Group:

Penguin Books Ltd, 27 Wrights Lane, London W8 5TZ.

Penguin Books USA Inc, 375 Hudson Street, New York 10014, USA.

Penguin Books Australia Ltd, 487 Maroondah Highway, PO Box 257, Ringwood, Victoria 3134, Australia.

Penguin Books Canada Ltd, 10 Alcorn Avenue, Toronto, Ontario, Canada M4V 1E4.

Penguin Books (NZ) Ltd, 182–190 Wairau Road, Auckland 10, New Zealand.

Previous edition published in the US and Canada as *The Real Guide Prague*.

Printed in the United Kingdom by Cox & Wyman Ltd (Reading).
Typography and **original design** by Jonathan Dear and The Crowd Roars.
Illustrations throughout by Edward Briant.
Maps by Judit Ladik.

Prague

THE ROUGH GUIDE

Written and researched by
Rob Humphreys

With additional research by
David Charap

THE ROUGH GUIDES

Contents

Maps

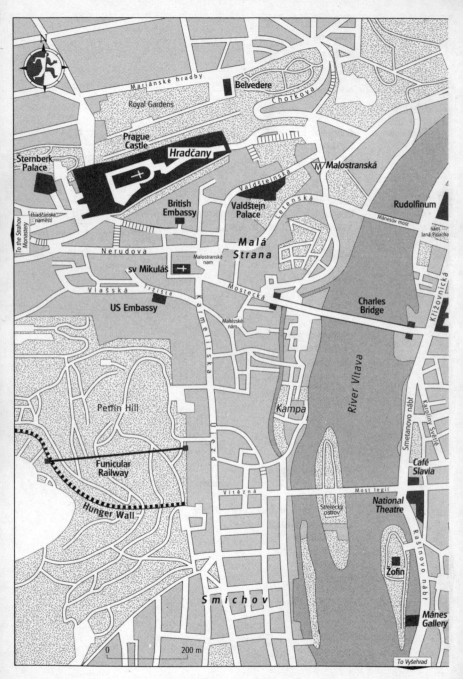

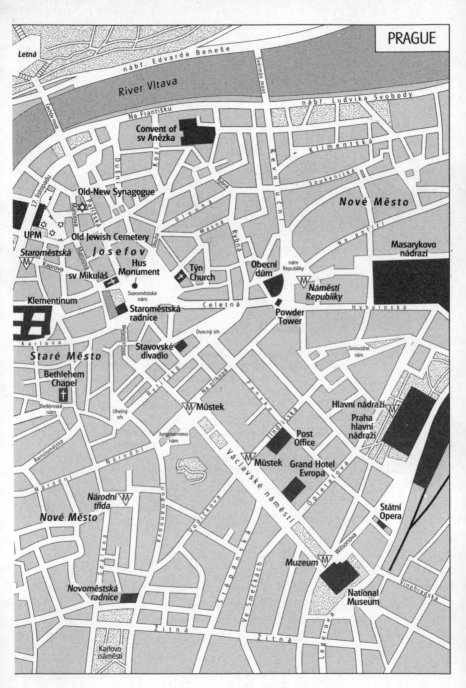

MAP OF PRAGUE

Help Us Update

We've gone to a lot of effort to ensure that this new edition of *The Rough Guide to Prague* is up-to-date and accurate. However, things are changing at an extraordinary speed in Prague – every hotel, restaurant and bar in the country has changed hands since 1989 and the current economic instability means that many will do so again in the future. Any suggestions, comments or corrections would be much appreciated. We'll credit all contributions, and send a copy of the next edition (or any other Rough Guide if you prefer) for the best letters.

Please mark letters "Rough Guide Prague Update" and send to:
The Rough Guides, 1 Mercer Street, London WC2H 9QJ, or
The Rough Guides, 375 Hudson Street, 3rd Floor, New York NY 10014.

Introduction

P rague (Praha to the Czechs) is one of the least "Eastern" European cities you could imagine. Architecturally, and in terms of city sights, it is a revelation: few other cities, anywhere in Europe, look so good – and no other European capital can present six hundred years of architecture so completely untouched by natural disaster or war. Culturally, it is closer in many ways to Paris than Moscow, and after four decades of Soviet-imposed isolation the city is now keen to re-establish its position as the political and cultural centre of *Mitteleuropa*.

One of Prague's most appealing characteristics is that its artistic wealth is not hidden away inside grand museums and galleries, but displayed in the streets and squares. Its town-planning took place in medieval times, its palaces and churches were decorated with a rich mantle of Baroque, and the whole lot has escaped the vanities and excesses of postwar redevelopment. Prague's unique compactness allows you to walk from the grandeur of the city's castle district, via a series of intimate Baroque lanes, across a medieval stone bridge, through one of the most alluring central squares on the continent, and end up sipping coffee on Wenceslas Square, the modern hub of the city, in under half an hour.

As well as having a rich history, Czechs have been at the forefront of European **culture** for much of the modern era. Before World War I, Prague boasted a Cubist movement second only to Paris, and, between the wars, a modernist architectural flowering to rival Bauhaus. Today, its writers, artists and film directors continue to exert a profound influence on European culture, out of all proportion to their numbers.

The city's recent history has attracted the attention of the west like no other capital in the former eastern bloc. The 1968 **Prague Spring** captured the imagination of a generation, with an explosion of cultural energy which, for a moment, made the "third way" between communism and capitalism seem a real possibility. Then, in the messy, sometimes bloody, upheavals of 1989, Czechoslovakia, and in particular Prague, outshone the rest with its unequivocably positive "Velvet Revolution". True to its pacifist past, the country shrugged off forty years of communism without so much as a shot being fired.

The exhilarating popular unity of that period, and the feeling of participating in history itself have now gone, perhaps forever. Few Czechs continue to talk about the events of 1989 as a "revolution". Disorientation at the speed of change, the break with Slovakia, and the first real taste of western vices in the capital have taken their toll. Economically, too, the country is going through some difficult times. Ninety percent of state-owned property has been "restituted", that is given back to its pre-1948 owners in various states of disrepair. Foreign companies have bought up huge slices of Czech industry for a song and the traditional heavy industrial base has shrunk considerably.

Walking the streets of the city centre, you'd be forgiven for thinking otherwise. But then Prague is in a privileged position vis-à-vis the rest of the country – as the place where the majority of the country's new businesses and corporations have made their head offices, and, of course, thanks to its potential for attracting western tourists. The feeling in much of the rest of the country is that Prague has prospered at the expense of other cities and regions. Which is not surprising, given that it is something like seven times the size of any other city in Bohemia, all the government ministries are based here, and it's where all the big decisions are made.

That's not to say that Prague doesn't have more than its fair share of problems. Its recent mini-boom may have brought crowds of tourists and hordes of, mostly American, expats, but it has done little to improve life for much of the city's population. The western-ized shops and restaurants in the centre, with their glitzy window-dressing, are out of reach for most Praguers. Racial tensions, suppressed under the police state, have surfaced once more, with a spate of skinhead attacks on the city's considerable Romany and Vietnamese communities, which the police seem powerless and/or unwilling to prevent. Prostitution is endemic in Prague, thanks to the large number of western businessmen visiting the capital and the drastic drop in living standards. The lifestyle gulf between Party and non-Party members has been replaced by the western malaise of rich and poor. There's nothing new in this, but it does serve as a sobering footnote to the city's glowing image in the west.

Prague is also trying to come to terms with its more distant past. Both the forced, and frequently violent, removal of the German minority and the virtual extinction of the Jewish population had a marked effect on the city, but were never discussed openly under the previous regime. Much of the current retrospection is positive, a cultural rediscovery of the cosmopolitan interwar period, when the city was ethnically far more diverse. There is also the extremely sensitive matter of the events of the last war: the degree of collaboration with the Nazis and of acquiescence in the fate of the Jews. These are issues that need to be addressed if the city is to break free from the monocultural straitjacket which makes it stand out amongst the multicultural capitals of the west.

When to go

Lying at the heart of central Europe, Prague has a continental climate: winters can be bitterly cold, summers correspondingly scorching. The best times to visit, in terms of weather, are late spring and early autumn. Summer in the city can be pretty stifling, but the real reason for avoiding the peak season is that it can get uncomfortably crowded in the centre – finding a place to eat in the evening, let alone securing a room, can become fraught with difficulties. If you're looking for good weather, April is the earliest you can expect at least some sunny days, October the last warm month. If you don't mind the cold, the city looks beautiful in the snowy winter months.

Prague average daily temperature & rainfall

	Jan	Feb	Mar	April	May	June	July	Aug	Sept	Oct	Nov	Dec
Min °C	-5	-4	-1	3	8	11	13	13	9	5	1	-3
Max °C	0	1	7	12	18	21	23	22	18	12	5	1
mm	18	18	18	27	48	54	68	55	31	33	20	21

The Basics

Getting There from Britain

By far the most convenient way to get to Prague is **by plane**. From London, it takes just under two hours (compared with more than 24 hours by train), and there are at least four daily direct flights from London throughout the year.

By Plane

Both *Czechoslovak Airlines* (*ČSA*) and *British Airways* (*BA*) run two daily **scheduled flights** from London to Prague. *BA*'s cheapest standard ticket is an **Apex** return, which currently costs £265 in high season (June–Aug, Christmas & Easter) and £235 in low season (Sept–May, except Christmas & Easter); expect to pay around £15 more for a weekend flight. *ČSA* sometimes offers much cheaper promotional deals, bringing the price down to around £165 return (low season), £195 in high season, but extra restrictions may apply. *ČSA* also flies three times a week from Manchester to Prague for £195 (low season) and £225 (high season). The usual Apex fare restrictions apply to all these fares: reservations must be made at least fourteen days in advance and there's a refund of fifty percent on tickets cancelled before the fourteen-day deadline. Tickets are valid for three months and can be booked direct from either airline or through most high-street travel agents.

   Discounted flights to Prague now feature in most of the "bucket shop" adverts of the various London freebie magazines, *Time Out*, *The Evening Standard* and the quality Sunday papers, where return fares, usually on *ČSA*, can be bought for as little as £130. You could also try specialist agents, such as *Campus Travel* or *STA* (see box overleaf for details). Note, however, that in peak season discount flights are often booked up weeks in advance. It might also be worth considering flying to a neighbouring European city like Berlin, Munich or Vienna, for which return fares can be as little as £100 – again, you'll find the cheapest fares in the sources quoted above.

Package Deals and City Breaks

Several tour operators offer simple flight and accommodation **package deals** to Prague, which for a short trip can often be better value than travelling independently. *ČEDOK* offers a city-break, with a return flight from London and two nights' accommodation for around £255 high season, £200 in low season. *Travelscene* offers a three-day/two-night citybreak including flights and accommodation for £265. With these packages, there's no compulsion to go on any organized tours once you're there. A list of the main agents can be found in the box overleaf.

By Train

From London to Prague takes just under 24 hours by train. Trains leave Victoria station daily at around 8am, arriving in Prague the following morning. The main route is **by ferry to Ostend**, then by train via Brussels, Cologne, Frankfurt and Nuremberg, entering the Czech Republic by the Schirnding/Cheb border crossing. You'll have to change at Cologne in the early evening (you may also have to change at Frankfurt). It's a good idea to reserve a seat in advance in summer; you may also want to reserve a **couchette** for the final, overnight leg of the journey from Cologne or Frankfurt (around £12 one way).

Tickets and Passes

A **standard rail ticket** from London (bookable through some high-street travel agents or at London's Victoria Station) will currently set you back £220 return: tickets are valid for two months and allow one stopoff en route.

Airlines

British Airways	☎ 0181/897 4000
Czechoslovak Airlines (ČSA)	☎ 0171/255 1898

Agents and Operators

Bohemian Promotions
61 Mere Road,
Erdington,
Birmingham B23 7LL   ☎ 0121/373 9107
*Offers a full range of
accommodation in Prague.*

Bridgewater Travel
217 Mouton Road,
Mouton Village,
Manchester M30 9PA   ☎ 0161/707 8547
*Accommodation and
package deals.*

Campus Travel (Eurotrain)
52 Grosvenor Gardens,
London SW1   ☎ 0171/730 3402
541 Bristol Rd,
Selly Oak, Birmingham   ☎ 0121/414 1848
39 Queen's Rd,
Clifton, Bristol   ☎ 0117/929 2494
5 Emmanuel St,
Cambridge   ☎ 01223/324283
53 Forest Rd,
Edinburgh   ☎ 0131/668 3303
166 Deansgate,
Manchester   ☎ 0161/273 1721
13 High St,
Oxford   ☎ 01865/24206
*Student/youth travel specialists;
branches also in YHA shops and
universities around Britain.*

ČEDOK
49 Southwark St,
London SE1   ☎ 0171/378 6009
*Former state-owned tourist
board; flights, accommodation
and package deals.*

Czech Travel Ltd
Trinity House,
1 Trinity Square,
South Woodham Ferrers,
Essex CM3 5JX   ☎ 01245/328647
*Rooms and flats for rent
in Prague.*

Czechbook Agency
Jopes Mill,
Trebrownbridge,
Near Liskeard,
Cornwall PL14 3PX   ☎ 01503/240629
*Cheap private and self-catering
accommodation in Prague.*

Czechdays
89 Valence Road,
Lewes BN7 1SJ   ☎ 01273/474738
Cheap rooms in Prague suburbs.

Czechscene
1 Thon Lea,
Evesham,
Worcestershire WR11 6TN   ☎ 01386/442782
*B&B and self-catering flats
available in Prague.*

Kingscourt Express
15 Balham High Road,
London SW12 9AJ   ☎ 0181/673 7500
*Coach tickets and
accommodation in Prague.*

Martin Randal Travel
10 Barley Mow Passage,
London W4 4PH   ☎ 0181/994 6477
*Specialist cultural guided
tours of Prague.*

STA Travel
86 Old Brompton Rd,
London SW7   ☎ 0171/937 9921
117 Euston Rd,
London NW1   (personal callers only)
25 Queen's Rd,
Bristol   ☎ 0117/929 3399
33 Sidney St,
Cambridge   ☎ 01223/66966
28 Vicar Lane,
Leeds   (personal callers only)
36 George St,
Oxford   (personal callers only)
75 Deansgate,
Manchester   ☎ 0161/834 0668
*Independent travel and discount
flight specialists; offices also at
universities of Birmingham, London,
Kent and Loughborough.*

TK Travel
14 Buckstone Close,
London SE23   ☎ 0181/699 8065
*B&B and self-catering
apartments for rent in Prague.*

Travellers' Czech Ltd
203 Main Road,
Biggin Hill,
Kent TN16 3JU   ☎ 01959/540700
*Private accommodation in,
and packages to, Prague.*

Travelscene
11–15 St Ann's Rd,
Harrow,
Middlesex HA1   ☎ 0181/427 4445
*Two-night breaks and
upwards in Prague.*

A better-value option for under-26s is the discounted **BIJ** ticket, available from *Eurotrain* or *Wasteels*. This can be booked for journeys from any British station to any major European station; it's valid for two months and allows unlimited stopovers along a pre-specified route (which can be different going out and coming home). The current return fare from London to Prague is £168 (via Ostend).

If you're planning to visit Prague as part of a more extensive trip round Europe, it may be worth purchasing an **InterRail pass** (currently £249 a month, if you're under 26 or over 65; £269 a month if you're not). InterRail passes are available from British Rail or travel agents; the only restriction is that you must have been resident in Europe for at least six months. The pass entitles you to free travel on most European rail networks (including Czech railways), as well as half-price discounts in Britain and on the Channel ferries.

By Bus

The cheapest way to get to Prague is by **bus**. There's a direct service from London to Prague which runs daily except Mondays in summer (three times a week only in winter), leaving from Victoria bus station at around 7pm (3pm on Sat) and arriving around 24 hours later at the city's main bus terminal, Florenc. It is operated by *Kingscourt Express*, who has offices in London and Prague; tickets currently cost £85 return for those under 26, £90 for those over 26 (roughly £5 less for both in low season).

Eurolines (an offshoot of *National Express*) also runs bus services to Prague, departing from London on Mondays and Fridays at 9.30am (daily July–mid-Sept); tickets currently cost £58 single and £89 return, with a youth fare of £52 single and £84 return, for those under 25. Times and frequencies are liable to change, so always check first. Address and telephone numbers for both these operators are in the box below.

The journey is long but quite bearable – just make sure you take along enough to eat, drink and read, and a small amount of Belgian and German currency for coffee, etc. There are stops for around fifteen minutes every three hours or so, and the routine is broken by the Ramsgate–Ostend ferry (included in the cost of the ticket).

By Car

Driving to Prague is not the most relaxing option – even if you're into non-stop rally motoring, it'll take the best part of two days – but with two or more passengers it can work out relatively inexpensive. The quickest way of taking your car over to the continent is to drive to the **Channel Tunnel**, where *Le Shuttle* operates 24 hours a day, carrying cars, motorcycles, buses and their passengers between Folkestone and Calais. At peak times, services run every fifteen minutes, making advance bookings for the 35-minute journey unnecessary; during the night, services run hourly. Return fares between May and August cost £280–310 per vehicle (passengers included), with discounts in the low season.

Cheaper cross-Channel options are the conventional **ferry** or **hovercraft** links between

Train Information		**Kingscourt Express**	
British Rail European Travel Centre		15 Balham High Road,	
Victoria Station,		London SW12 9AJ	☎0181/673 7500
London SW1	☎0171/834 2345		
Eurotrain		**Cross-Channel Information**	
52 Grosvenor Gardens,		**Hoverspeed**	
London SW1	☎0171/730 3402	Dover	☎01304/24001
Wasteels		London	☎0181/554 7061
121 Wilton Rd,		**Le Shuttle**	
London SW1	☎0171/834 7066	Information and ticket sales	☎01303/271100
		P&O European Ferries	
Bus Information		Dover	☎01304/203388
Eurolines		London	☎0181/575 8555
National Express,		**Sally Line**	
164 Buckingham Palace Rd,		Ramsgate	☎01843/595522
London SW1	☎0171/730 0202	London	☎0181/858 1127

Dover and Calais, and Ramsgate and Dunkirk. **Fares** vary enormously with the time of year, month and even day that you travel, and the size of your car. The Dover–Calais run, operated by *Stena Sealink* and *P&O*, starts at about £130 return for a small car and two adults, rising to £250 in high season. *Sally Lines* charge slightly less for the longer Ramsgate–Dunkirk crossing: from £120 return in low season and £180 in high season. The cheapest *Hoverspeed* route is Folkestone–Boulogne, which costs around £140 return in low season and starts at £225 in high season.

The most direct route from northern France to Prague is via Lille, Brussels, Cologne, Frankfurt and Nuremberg, entering the country at the **Waidhaus–Rozvadov** border crossing: a distance of over 1000km. Another possibility is to head east from Cologne through Hessen via Erfurt and Chemnitz, and enter at the **Reitzenhain/Pohraniční** border crossing. Note that if you want to travel on any motorways within the Czech Republic, you'll need authorization in the form of a *dálniční známka*, which costs 400kč, and is available from all border crossings and most post offices.

Getting There from Ireland

There are no direct flights from anywhere in Ireland to Prague. The cheapest way of getting there is usually to fly to London, then pick up a connecting flight or package from there (see *Getting There from Britain*, p.3). Discount travel agents, such as *USIT*, may be able to organize both flights.

There are numerous daily flights **from Dublin to London**, operated by *Ryanair*, *Aer Lingus* and *British Midland*; the cheapest is *Ryanair*, which costs from around IR£50 return to Luton or Stansted, though the price of the bus and underground journeys across London may make the total cost greater than *Aer Lingus* or *British Midland* IR£75 fares to Heathrow. **From Belfast**, there are *British Airways* and *British Midland* flights to Heathrow for around £95, but the cheapest service is with *Jersey European* from Belfast City airport to Gatwick or Stansted for £70 return.

Airlines in Ireland	
Aer Lingus	
Dublin	☎01/705 6565
Belfast	☎01232/245151
2 Academy St,	
Cork	(no telephone calls)
Aeroflot	
Dublin	☎01/679 1453
British Airways	
Belfast	☎0345/222111
in Dublin contact *Aer Lingus*	
British Midland	
Dublin	☎01/283 8833
Belfast	☎0345/554554
Jersey European	
Belfast/Exeter	☎0345/676676
Ryanair	
Dublin	☎01/677 4422

Travel agents and tour operators		Group & Educational Travel	
USIT		11 South Anne St,	
19–21 Aston Quay,		Dublin 2	☎ 01/671 3422
O'Connell Bridge,		**Joe Walsh Tours**	
Dublin 2	☎ 01/679 8833	8–11 Baggot St,	
Fountain Centre, College St,		Dublin	☎ 01/676 8915
Belfast BT1	☎ 01849/324073	**Thomas Cook**	
Budget Travel		118 Grafton St,	
134 Lower Baggot St,		Dublin	☎ 01/677 1721
Dublin 2	☎ 01/661 1866		

From Dublin you can slightly undercut the plane's price by getting a *Eurotrain* ticket to London, but from Belfast you'll save nothing by taking the train and ferry instead of a plane.

Alternatively, you could opt for a **package tour** with an operator such as *Thomas Cook*, who offer a seven-day trip to Prague for around IR£675.

Getting There from USA and Canada

The quickest and easiest way to reach Prague from the US or Canada is **to fly**. One of the most convenient options is *Czechoslovak Airlines* (*ČSA*), who flies non-stop out of New York (four times a week in summer, two in winter), Montreal (twice weekly throughout the year) and Chicago (once a week).

In addition, the major carriers offer dozens of one- and two-stop flights from any number of North American gateways via major European cities. Nevertheless, flights from North America are still comparatively expensive, and you may be better off buying a cheap transatlantic flight to London or Frankfurt and making your way to Prague overland by train, bus or car (see p.5 for details).

To save any hassle, and sometimes even money, you may want to consider some form of package tour – names and addresses of agents specializing in travel to Prague and details of some of the various options are given below. Unless specified otherwise, prices quoted are for round-trip tickets and include all applicable taxes.

Flights from the US

If you're flying to Prague from the US (or Canada, for which see below), bear in mind that high season lasts from mid-June to the end of August, plus a two-week spell over Christmas; the rest of the year cheaper low season fares operate.

Airlines serving Prague		Canada	☎1-800/555-1212
Air France		**KLM**	
USA	☎1-800/237-2747	USA	☎1-800/374-7747
Canada	☎1-800/667-2747	Canada	☎1-800/361-5073
American		**Lufthansa**	
USA only	☎1-800/433-7300	USA	☎1-800/645-3880
British Airways		Canada	☎1-800/563-5954
USA	☎1-800/247-9297	**SAS**	☎1-800/221-2350
Canada	☎1-800/668-1059	**Sabena**	
ČSA		USA only	☎1-800/955-2000
USA	☎1-800/231-0856	**TWA**	
Canada	☎1-800/561-5171	USA only	☎1-800/892-4141
Delta		**United**	
USA	☎1-800/241-4141	USA only	☎1-800/538-2929

Flying out of New York or Chicago, the **non-stop** service offered by *ČSA*, which costs under $800 for a low-season Apex ticket, rising to $1100 in high season, is probably your best bet.

Starting from other US cities, airlines offering **flights to Prague** include *Delta* (via Frankfurt and Vienna), *Lufthansa* (via Frankfurt), *SAS* (via Copenhagen), *TWA* and *KLM* (via Amsterdam) and *American* (via London or Zürich). **Apex fares**, which usually need to be booked at least 14 days in advance, are pretty much identical whichever airline you choose, with low-season rates starting at around $600 from New York, $800 from West Coast cities; in high season fares rise to $900 from the East Coast, $1100 from the West.

Full-time students and anyone under 26 can take advantage of the excellent deals offered by *Council Travel*, *STA* and other **student/youth travel agents**. These fares are for flights on major carriers like *British Airways* or *Air France*, and even in the peak season cost as little as $700 from the East Coast and $950 from the West Coast. A further advantage to these student fares is that they allow you to **stop over en route** for little or no extra charge, something you can't do on an Apex ticket.

If you don't meet the student/youth agents' requirements, you can still save some money by buying your tickets through a **discount agent**, which deals in blocks of tickets offloaded by the airlines, and often offers special student and youth fares and a range of other travel-related services such as travel insurance, rail passes, car rentals, tours and the like. If you travel a lot, **discount travel clubs** – organizations which

specialize in selling off unsold seats for bargain rates – are another option. The annual membership fee may be worth it for the benefits such as cut-price air tickets and car rental (addresses are listed in the box below).

If you're flexible about your travel plans, or have waited until the last minute to buy your ticket, you can pay as little as $440 from New York, $660 from Los Angeles or Seattle for a low-season return, through a **seat consolidator**. For the best prices, scan the ads in the back pages of the Sunday travel sections of *The New York Times* or your local paper, and phone around. Note, however, that these tickets are basically impossible to change once you've paid for them, so be sure about your dates and ask about the routing of the flight – many involve lengthy lay-overs and multiple changes of plane.

Flights from Canada

Getting **flights from Canada to Prague** is no problem. *ČSA* flies non-stop twice a week from Montreal for around CDN$1000 high season, CDN$750 low season, though it can be difficult to arrange an inexpensive connection from else-where in the country. Outside Montreal, your best bet is *Lufthansa*, who fly more or less daily from several major Canadian cities to Prague via Frankfurt. Fares from Toronto start at CDN$1000 low season, CDN$1200 high season; from Vancouver you can expect to pay around CDN$1250 (low season) or CDN$1550 (high season). For **students** and those **under 26** it's worth trying *Travel Cuts*, who can sometimes find cheap youth flights.

Flights via Europe

Since direct flights to Prague are usually more expensive than flights to other European cities, it may be worth your while to fly to another country and make your way overland from there. Munich, Berlin, Frankfurt and Vienna are the closest major European cities to Prague: *Lufthansa*, for example, offers return fares to Berlin from the East Coast for around $550 low season, rising close to $900 high season. From there you can reach Prague by train in well under twelve hours.

"**Open-jaw**" **fares** provide more flexibility, enabling you to fly into one city and out of another. For example, you can fly with *Lufthansa*, from San Francisco into Berlin, then out of Prague two weeks later, for around $1200 in peak season; $900 low season. A similar flight from New York costs under $1000 even in peak season. See "Getting There from Britain", on p.3,

for a more complete rundown of trans-European options.

Eurail Passes are not valid in the Czech Republic, but if you're visiting Prague as part of a more extensive tour of Europe, they may be worth considering. The all-country pass, which you must purchase before you leave for Europe, allows unlimited free travel on the railways of sixteen western European countries (plus Hungary); for under-26s the cost is $398 for 15 days and $578 for one month; over-26s must buy a first class pass at $498 for 15 days and $798 for one month. North Americans of all ages are also eligible for a **Czech Flexipass**, which costs $69 and is valid for five days first class train travel in any fifteen within the Czech Republic. However, since Czech trains are exceptionally cheap, the pass will almost definitely not pay for itself.

Discount Agents, Consolidators and Travel Clubs in North America

Council Travel
205 E 42nd St,
New York, NY 10017 ☎ 1-800/743-1823
Nationwide US student travel organization with branches (among others) in San Francisco, Los Angeles, Washington DC, Austin, Seattle, Chicago and Minneapolis.

STA
48 E 11th St, Suite 805,
New York, NY 10003 ☎ 1-800/777-0112
Worldwide specialist in independent travel with branches in the Los Angeles, San Francisco and Boston areas.

Travel Cuts
187 College St,
Toronto, ON M5T 1P7 ☎ 416/979-2406
Canadian student travel organization with branches all over the country.

New Frontiers/Nouvelles Frontières
12 E 33rd St,
New York, NY 10016 ☎ 1-800/366-6387
Sherbrooke East, Suite 720,
Montreal, H2L 1L3 ☎ 514/526-8444
Discount travel firm with branches in Los Angeles, San Francisco, Montreal and Quebec City.

Discount Travel International
Ives Bldg, 114 Forrest Ave, Suite 205,
Narberth, PA 19072 ☎ 1-800/334-9294
Discount travel club.

Encore Travel Club
4501 Forbes Blvd,
Lanham, MD 20706 ☎ 1-800/444-9800
Discount travel club.

Interworld Travel
800 Douglass Rd,
Miami, FL 33134 ☎ 305/443-4929
Consolidator.

TFI Tours International
Head office: 34 W 32nd St,
New York, NY 10001 ☎ 1-800/745-8000
Consolidator, with other offices in Las Vegas, San Francisco, Los Angeles.

Travac
Head office: 989 6th Ave,
New York, NY 10018 ☎ 1-800/872-8800
Consolidator and charter broker, with another branch in Orlando.

Travelers Advantage
3033 S Parker Rd, Suite 900,
Aurora, CO 80014 ☎ 1-800/548-1116
Discount travel club.

Travel Avenue
10 S Riverside, Suite 1404,
Chicago, IL 60606 ☎ -800/333-3335
Discount travel agent.

UniTravel
1177 N Warson Rd,
St Louis, MO 63132 ☎ 1-800/325-2222
Consolidator.

Package Tours

Since the situation regarding tourism is still very changeable, along with everything else in the former Eastern Bloc, **travel agents specializing in Eastern Europe**, such as *East-West Travel* and *Czech & Slovak Travel Service*, are excellent sources of up-to-date advice, as well as being the best way to find out about any other cheap flight deals that might be available. *East-West Travel*, for example, offers an eight-day package to Prague from New York for $799 low season and $1099 high season, including flight and accommodation. Other **package tour** companies worth consulting are *Fugazy International*, who offers week-long flight and accommodation deals from the East Coast for around $1100, and *ČEDOK*, the old state tourist monopoly, which still has the broadest range of all-inclusive tours. A list of specialist travel agents is given in the box below.

Specialist Agents in North America

ČEDOK
10 E 40th St,
New York, NY 10016 ☎212/689-9720

Czech & Slovak Travel Service
7033 Sunset Boulevard Suite,
Suite 210,
Los Angeles, CA 90028 ☎213/389-2157

East-West Travel
10 E 39th Street,
New York, NY ☎212/545-0737

ETT Tours
198 Boston Post Rd,
Mamaroneck, NY 10543 ☎1-800/551-2085

Fugazy International
770 US-1,
North Brunswick, NJ ☎1-908/828-4488

Globus Gateway
92-25 Queens Bvd,
Rego Park, NY 11374 ☎1-800/221-0090

Pilgrimage Tours & Travel
39 Beechwood Ave,
Manhasset, NY 11030 ☎1-800/669-0757

REI Adventures
1700 45th St East,
Sumner, WA 98390 ☎1-800/622-2236

Unique World Travel
39 Beechwood Ave,
Manhasset, NY 11030 ☎1-800/669-0757

Getting There from Australia and New Zealand

There are no direct flights from Australia or New Zealand to Prague, so many people choose to travel **via London**. There are, however, alternative stopover points in Europe, and these are often available at economical fares. Whichever route you choose, most airlines can add a Prague leg onto an Australia or New Zealand to Europe ticket. Bear in mind that high season from Australia is basically mid-November to mid-January; low season runs from mid-January to March and again from September to mid-November; shoulder season is March to August.

Czechoslovak Airlines (*ČSA*) flies twice a week from Bangkok and Singapore to Prague, with connecting flights from Sydney to Bangkok or Singapore on *Qantas* for A$1800 (low season), A$2100 (shoulder season) and A$2200 (high season). However, the cheapest fare is with *Aeroflot*, who flies from the east coast to Prague via Moscow for A$1700 (low season) and A$1900 (high season). From other cities in Australia, *Qantas* can ferry you to Singapore, where you connect with *Aeroflot* for Prague via Moscow, which costs A$1800 (low season) and

Airlines in Australia and New Zealand

Aeroflot
Sydney   ☎ 02/233 7911
no NZ office.

KLM
Sydney   ☎ 02/231 6333 or 008 222 747
no NZ office.

Air France
Sydney   ☎ 02/321 103
Auckland   ☎ 09/303 1229

Lufthansa/Air Lauda
Sydney   ☎ 02/367 3800
Auckland   ☎ 09/303 1529

Alitalia
Sydney   ☎ 02/247 7836
Auckland   ☎ 09/379 4457

MAS
Sydney   ☎ 02/231 5066 or 008/269 998
Auckland   ☎ 09/373 2741

British Airways
Sydney   ☎ 02/258 3300
Auckland   ☎ 09/367 7500

Qantas
Sydney   ☎ 02/957 0111 or 236 3636
Auckland   ☎ 09/303 2506

Czechoslovak Airlines (*ČSA*)
Sydney   ☎ 02/247 6196
no NZ office.

Thai
Sydney   ☎ 02/844 0999 or 008 221 320
Auckland   ☎ 09/377 3886

Garuda
Sydney   ☎ 02/334 9900
Auckland   ☎ 09/366 1855

United
Sydney   ☎ 02/237 8888
Auckland   ☎ 09/307 9500

NOTE: ☎ *008 numbers are toll free, but only apply if dialled outside the city in the address.*

Discount and specialist agents

Accent on Travel
545 Queen Street,
Brisbane   ☎ 07/832 1777

Adventure World
73 Walker Street,
North Sydney   ☎ 02/956 7766
8 Victoria Avenue,
Perth   ☎ 09/221 2300

Anywhere Travel
345 Anzac Parade,
Kingsford, Sydney   ☎ 02/663 0411

Brisbane Discount Travel
360 Queen St,
Brisbane   ☎ 07/229 9211

Budget Travel
PO Box 505,
Auckland   ☎ 09/309 4313

Discount Travel Specialists
Shop 53, Forrest Chase,
Perth   ☎ 09/221 1400

Eastern European Travel Bureau
75 King Street,
Sydney   ☎ 02/262 1144

Eastern European Travel Centre
343 Little Collins Street,
Melbourne   ☎ 03/600 0299

Flight Centres
Circular Quay,
Sydney   ☎ 02/241 2422
Bourke St,
Melbourne   ☎ 03/650 2899
National Bank Towers,
205–225 Queen St,
Auckland   ☎ 09/309 6171
Shop 1M, National Mutual Arcade,
152 Hereford St,
Christchurch   ☎ 09/379 7145
50–52 Willis St,
Wellington   ☎ 04/472 8101

Russia and Eastern Europe Travel
Floor 1, Room 8, 2 Hindmarsh Square,
Adelaide   ☎ 08/232 1228

STA Travel
732 Harris Street, Ultimo,
Sydney   ☎ 02/212 1255 or 281 9866
256 Flinders St,
Melbourne   ☎ 03/347 4711
Traveller's Centre, 10 High St,
Auckland   ☎ 09/309 9995
233 Cuba St,
Wellington   ☎ 04/385 0561
223 High St,
Christchurch   ☎ 03/379 9098

A$2000 (high season), or with *ČSA* for a direct, but slightly pricier, flight to Prague.

There are any number of European airlines, who fly to Prague via their own home bases (see box for airline numbers). Some of the better-value fares include *KLM* via Amsterdam (A$2090 low season/A$2640 high season), who throw in coupons for four single flights within Europe with the price of the ticket; *Alitalia* via Rome (A$1930 low season/A$2230 high season); *Lufthansa* via Frankfurt (A$2100 low season/A$2260 high season) and *Qantas/BA* via London or other European hub cities (A$2245 low season/A$2450 high season).

There are very few options **from New Zealand**, and they all involve combinations of airlines to take you via Asia or the US to a European hub city, and thence to Prague. The best deal is *Qantas* to either Los Angeles, Singapore or Bangkok, where you connect with *Alitalia* to Prague via Rome; fares start at NZ$2260 low season and rise to NZ$2700 high season.

A slightly pricier option, but one which gives more flexibility is a **round-the-world ticket**. Fares from Sydney via Asia and Europe and back to Sydney start at around A$2000 low season, A$2500 high season. One which includes Prague is *BA*'s Global Explorer ticket allowing six stop-overs anywhere (South America excluded) in the *Qantas*, *BA* or *USAir* network; it currently costs A$2270 or NZ$2840.

Red Tape and Visas

British, Irish, US and most EU nationals need only a **full passport** to enter the Czech Republic for up to three months, though the passport itself must be valid for at least six months beyond your return date. Officially they are supposed to notify the local police within thirty days of their arrival, though few people do. At the time of writing, Canadian, New Zealand and Australian citizens still need a **visa** (valid for thirty days), available from a Czech embassy or consulate – the process takes no more than two days and costs $30 or equivalent – but check your nearest Czech consulate for the latest information (addresses are listed below).

To stay longer than three months, you either need a really good excuse, or a residence permit

Czech Embassies and Consulates

Australia
169 Military Rd,
Dover Heights,
Sydney, NSW 2030 ☎ 02/371 8877

Austria
Penzingerstrasse 11–13,
1140 Vienna ☎ 1/894 3741

Belgium
152 Avenue A. Buyl,
1050 Brussels ☎ 02/647 5898

Canada
541 Sussex Drive,
Ottawa,
Ontario K1N 6Z6 ☎ 514/849-495

France
15 Avenue Charles Floquet,
75343 Paris ☎ 47 34 29 10

Germany
Wilhelmstrasse 44,
10117 Berlin ☎ 030/229 4027

Ireland
Confederation House,
Kildare St,
Dublin 2 ☎ 01/671 4981

New Zealand
16A Tiverton Crescent,
New Plymouth ☎ 07/751 0719

UK
28 Kensington Palace Gardens,
London W8 4QY ☎ 0171/243 1115
Visa hotline ☎ 0891/171267

USA
3900 Spring of Freedom St, NW,
Washington DC 20008 ☎ 202/363-6315

Foreign consulates and embassies in Prague are listed on p.231.

(*občanský průkaz*), which is difficult to obtain unless you're studying here or have a job (and, therefore, a work permit). If you need a residence permit, you'll have to fill in the application form known as *povolení k pobytu*, which you can only get by going in person to the second floor of the Úřad práce, Zborovská 11, Smíchov (Mon & Wed 8am–4pm, Thurs 8am–noon). Then go to the head passport office at Olšanská 2, Žižkov, Prague (you'll need to be there when it opens at 7.30am on Mon–Fri). You should bring with you your passport, your work permit, a 1000kč stamp (*kolek*) and a letter from the owner of the property you're staying in.

Many people avoid this bureaucratic nightmare – which can take up to six months – by simply leaving the country for a few days when their time runs out and getting a new date upon re-entry, but the legality of this is somewhat doubtful, and the Prague police are clamping down on foreigners working or staying here illegally.

Customs allowances into the Czech Republic are 200 cigarettes or 100 cigars, 1 litre of spirits and 1 litre of wine. Remember that you are not permitted to import or export Czech currency over the value of 100kč. Allowances when taking goods from the Czech Republic into EU countries are 250 cigarettes, 2 litres of wine and 1 litre of spirits. These allowances may change in the future, though, so if in doubt, check with customs before you leave for Prague.

Health and Insurance

No inoculations are required for the Czech Republic. Health standards are coming under increasing criticism, however. With much of the country blighted by decades of ecological abuse, there have been well-founded criticisms about the quality of the water, milk, meat and vegetables. More specifically, if you have respiratory problems,

avoid coming to Prague during the winter months when sulphur dioxide levels in the city centre regularly reach three or four times World Health Organisation safety levels (see box below).

Travel Policies

Reciprocal arrangements between the Czech Republic and most EU countries (including Britain and Ireland) mean that you're entitled to free emergency medical care, with a charge only for imported drugs and certain specialized treatments. Citizens from other countries should have their own health insurance, and even EU residents would be well advised to take out their own health policies, rather than rely on Czech state medical care.

For everyone, some form of **travel insurance** is pretty much essential, enabling you to claim back the cost of any treatment and drugs and covering your baggage/tickets in case of theft. **In Britain**, travel insurance schemes are sold by all travel agents. *ISIS* policies, originally designed for students but now available to all comers, are available from any of the youth/student travel companies listed on p.4, and offer comprehensive insurance covering medical expenses, theft and baggage loss for £20 for two weeks/£35 for a month. Alternatively, try specialist, low-priced firms like *Endsleigh Insurance* (97 Southampton Row, WC1; ☎0171/436 4451) or *Columbus Travel Insurance* (17 Devonshire Square, London EC2; ☎0171/375 0011), who both offer similarly priced policies.

Before purchasing any insurance, **US and Canadian citizens** should check existing policies – you may find yourself already covered for medical expenses and loss or damage to vaulables while abroad. Bank or charge accounts often have certain levels of medical or other insurance included, as do home owners' or renters' insurance. Only after exhausting these possibilities might you want to contact a specialist travel insurance company, where you should be able to pick up a short-term combination policy covering medical expenses/baggage loss/flight cancellation for around $50–70 for 15 days. Some companies worth trying are *Travel Guard* (110 Centrepoint Drive, Steven Point, WI 54480; ☎715/

Pollution in Prague

Don't be fooled by the outward beauty of Prague's buildings. The city is sick, suffering some of the highest levels of sulphur dioxide of any European capital. And the worst place to be is the old town itself: every winter the pollution in the Staré Město exceeds the *WHO* safety limits. On at least ten days during each winter, pollution levels rise to nearly three times the *WHO* safety levels, forcing the municipal authorities to introduce a total ban on non-essential traffic within the city – domestic and foreign – unless fitted with catalytic converters.

Between October and March, Prague is plagued by a lethal cocktail of winter weather, the city's basin-like topography, and the brown coal which provides energy for industry and most of the city's heating. The heavy, cold air sits in the basin, trapped in by the warmer air above, and thus preventing the sulphur dioxide and carbon monoxide from dispersing. Car ownership looks set to rise dramatically over the next decade, and a year-round ban on cars in the city centre is a serious possibility.

345-0505 or 800/826-1300) and *Access America International* (600 Third Avenue, New York, NY 10163; ☎212/949-5960 or 800/284-8300).

One thing to bear in mind is that none of the policies currently available covers theft; they only cover loss or damage while in the custody of an identifiable, responsible third party – hotel porter, airline, luggage consignment, etc. If you are travelling via London, you may to take out a British policy, which routinely covers theft and is considerably cheaper.

In **Australia**, *CIC Insurance*, offered by *Cover-More Insurance Services* (Level 9, 32 Walker St, North Sydney; ☎02/202 8000; branches in Victoria and Queensland), has some of the widest cover available, costing from around A$140 for 31 days. Their policies can be arranged through most travel agents.

If you do have to pay for any medical treatment or drugs, when in Prague, keep the receipts for claiming on your insurance once you're home. If you have anything stolen (including money) register the loss immediately with the local police – without their report you won't be able to claim. For the address of the main police stations in Prague, see p.25.

Pharmacies, Doctors and Hospitals

If you should become ill, the easiest course of action is to go to a **pharmacy** (*lékárna*). Pharmacists are willing to give advice (though language may well be a problem), and able to dispense many drugs available only on prescription in other western countries. They usually keep normal shop hours, but several are open round the clock (there's a list below). If language proves an insurmountable barrier, and you wish to see an **English-speaking doctor**, you should go to the *Fakultní poliklinika* on the second floor at Karlovo náměstí 32, Nové Město.

If it's **first aid** you want, there are facilities on hand in every one of Prague's ten postal districts (the most central ones are listed below). If it's an **emergency**, dial ☎155 for an ambulance and you'll be taken to the nearest Czech hospital. This is no bad thing, though you can only guarantee English-speaking staff at the *Nemocnice na homolce*, Roentgenova 2, Motol (bus #167 from metro Anděl), a privately run hospital specifically geared towards foreigners. Take your passport and at least 1000kč to put down as a deposit.

24-hr pharmacies

Na příkopě 7, Nové Město; ☎24 21 02 30

Ječná 1, Nové Město; ☎29 29 40

Koněvova 210, Žižkov; ☎644 18 95

Pod Marjánkou 12, Střešovice; ☎35 26 41

Štefánikova 6, Břevnov; ☎24 51 11 12

First aid centres

Palackého 5, Nové Město; ☎24 22 25 20

Italská 3, Vinohrady; ☎25 97 86

Koněvova 205, Žižkov; ☎82 86 17

Kartouzská 6, Smíchov; ☎53 81 69

Anastázova 1120, Střešovice; ☎35 43 56

Hospitals

U nemocnice 2, Nové Město; ☎21 28 11 11

Vlašská, Malá Strana; ☎53 23 81

Na Františku, Staré Město; ☎231 33 24

Roentgenova 2, Motol; ☎52 92 21 46;
English-speaker available.

Emergency dentists

První pomoc zubní, Vladislavova 22, Nové Město ☎24 22 76 63

Information and Maps

With the demise of *ČEDOK* (the former state tourist board, now a private tour operator) and the break-up of the republic, a new Czech tourist board – otherwise known as the Czech Centre – has emerged. As an organization, it remains in its infancy and underfunded; it has few maps or pamphlets to give away, though staff should be able to answer any queries you have about the country (see right for addresses of Czech Centres abroad).

Maps

The best maps of Prague are produced by *Kartografie Praha*, whose 1:20,000 booklet (*plán města*) covering the whole city including suburbs is the most comprehensive. This, or something similar, should be available from the map suppliers listed below, though you'll get it more easily and cheaply in Prague itself at *PIS* offices, most bookstores (*knih-kupectví*) and some hotels. For more details on maps available in Prague, see p.35.

Czech Centres Abroad

Belgium
152 Avenue A. Buyl,
1050 Brussels   ☎02/647 5898

Germany
Leipzigerstrasse 60,
1080 Berlin   ☎030/208 2592

Slovakia
Hviezdoslavovo nám. 5,
814 99 Bratislava   ☎07/33 35 36

UK
30 Kensington Palace Gardens,
London W8 4QY   ☎0171/243 7981

USA
1109–1111 Madison Avenue,
New York, NY 10028   ☎212/535 8814

Map and Guide Outlets

Australia

Bowyangs, 372 Little Bourke St, Melbourne, VIC 3000; ☎03/670 4383

Hema, 239 George St, Brisbane, QLD 4000; ☎07/221 4330

The Map Shop, 16a Peel St, Adelaide, SA 5000; ☎08/231 2033

Perth Map Centre, 891 Hay St, Perth, WA 6000; ☎09/322 5733

Travel Bookshop, 20 Bridge St, Sydney, NSW 2000; ☎02/241 3554

Canada

Open Air Books and Maps, 25 Toronto St, Toronto M5R 2C1; ☎416/363-0719

Ulysses Travel Bookshop, 4176 St-Denis, Montreal; ☎514/289-0993

World Wide Books and Maps, 736A Granville St, Vancouver; ☎604/687 3320

UK

Daunt Books, 83 Marylebone High St, London W1 ☎0171/224 2295

National Map Centre, 22–24 Caxton St, London SW1 ☎0171/222 4945

Thomas Nelson and Sons, 51 York Place, Edinburgh EH1 ☎0131/557 3011

John Smith and Sons, 57–61 St Vincent St, Glasgow ☎0141/221 7472

Stanfords, 12–14 Long Acre, London WC2E 9LP ☎0171/836 1321

The Travellers' Bookshop, 25 Cecil Court, WC2 ☎0171/836 9132

US

British Travel Bookshop, 551 5th Ave, New York, NY 10176; ☎1-800/448-3039 or 212/490-6688

The Complete Traveler Bookstore, 199 Madison Ave, New York, NY 10016; ☎212/685-9007

The Complete Traveler Bookstore, 3207 Filmore St, San Francisco, CA 92123; ☎415/923-1511

Elliot Bay Book Company, 101 S Main St, Seattle, WA 98104; ☎206/624-6600

Pacific Traveler Supply, 529 State St, Santa Barbara 93101; ☎805/963-4438 (phone orders: ☎805/965-4402)

Rand McNally has 24 stores across the US; phone ☎800/33-0136 (ext 2111) for the address of your nearest store, or for direct mail maps.

Traveler's Bookstore, 22 W 52nd St, New York, NY 10019; ☎212/664-0995

Costs, Money and Banks

In general terms, Prague is still incredibly cheap for westerners. The one exception is accommodation, which is comparable with many EU countries. At the time of writing, inflation was pretty much under control, though before you get to thinking everything is rosy in the Czech Republic, it's worth bearing in mind that the average monthly wage for Czechs is currently between 5000 and 6000kč (£120–140/$190–220).

You'll find exact costs for accommodation, food and drink in the relevant sections of the book: see *Accommodation* (p.185) and *Eating and Drinking* (p.192). At the bottom end of the scale, if you stay in a hostel and stick to pubs and take-aways, you could get by on as little as £10/$16 a day. If you intend to stay in private accommodation or cheapish hotels, and eat in slightly fancier restaurants, then you could easily spend £25–30/$40–48 a day. The good thing about Prague, however, is that once you've accounted for your room, most restaurants, pubs, museums and galleries, beer and even night-clubs are far from expensive.

Currency

The **currency** in the Czech Republic is the Czech crown or *koruna česká* (abbreviated to kč), which is divided into one hundred heller or *halér* (abbreviated to h). Coins come in the denominations 10h, 20h, 50h, 1kč, 2kč, 5kč, 10kč, 20kč and 50kč; notes as 20kč, 50kč, 100kč, 200kč, 500kč, 1000kč, 2000kč and 5000kč. Since 1991, when the currency was drastically devalued, the

crown has been tied to the dollar and Deutschmark, with the **exchange rate** hovering around 40kč to the pound sterling, and 25kč to the US dollar. The Czech government plans to allow the crown to float more freely on the currency markets in the near future leading up to eventual full convertibility, so expect these rates to change. Until such time, it is still technically illegal to import or export more than 100 Czech crowns, though if you keep your exchange receipts, you can convert any surplus crowns back into western currency, for a small commission, of course.

Travellers' Cheques and Credit Cards

Probably the safest and easiest way to carry your funds is in **travellers' cheques** – sterling, US dollars or Deutschmarks are all equally acceptable; *American Express* and *Thomas Cook* are the most widely used – available for a small commission (usually one percent of the amount ordered) from any bank and some building societies, whether or not you have an account, and from branches of *American Express* and *Thomas Cook*.

Credit cards like *Visa, Master Card* (*Access*) and *Amex* are becoming more widely accepted: the majority of hotels, restaurants and shops, especially the more upmarket ones, should take plastic. You can also withdraw cash from the automatic teller/cashpoint machines which are now a feature of downtown Prague, though you'd be foolhardy to rely solely on this method. It's a good idea to keep at least some hard currency in **cash** for emergencies, as it will be accepted almost anywhere. If you lose your credit card, ring the Prague credit card hotline ☎ 236 66 88.

Changing Money

Most Czech **banks** should be prepared to change travellers' cheques, accept Eurocheques, and give cash advances on credit cards – look for the window marked *směnárna*. Commissions at banks are fairly reasonable (generally three percent or under) but the queues and the bureaucracy can mean a long wait. Quicker, but more of a ripoff in terms of commission are the exchange outlets (six percent commission is the norm) which can be found on just about every street corner in the centre of Prague.

Banking hours are usually Monday to Friday 8am to 5pm, often with a break at lunchtime. Outside of these times, you may find the odd bank open, but will otherwise have to rely on the exchange outlets and the international hotels. The 24-hour exchange desk at the airport run by the *Československá obchodní banka* is, somewhat surprisingly, an excellent place to change money, regularly charging a mere one or two percent commission.

Money-changing outlets

American Express, Václavské náměstí 56, Nové Město; ☎ 24 22 98 83

Česká spořitelna, Na příkopě 20, Nové Město; ☎ 26 36 96

Komerční banka, Na příkopě 20, Nové Město; ☎ 24 02 11 11

Thomas Cook, Opletalova 1, Nové Město; ☎ 26 31 06

Živnostenká banka, Na příkopě 20, Nové Město; ☎ 24 12 11 11

Disabled Travellers

In the past, very little attention has been paid to the needs of the disabled anywhere in the country. Attitudes are slowly changing, but there is still a long way to go, and the chronic shortage of funds for almost anything is not helping matters.

Transport is a major problem, since buses and trams are virtually impossible for wheelchairs. The following metro stations now have facilities for the disabled: Chodov, Florenc, Hlavní nádraží, Karlovo náměstí, Nádraží Holešovice, Roztyly and Skalka – though only the two railway stations (Hlavní nádraží and Nádraží Holešovice) actually have self-operating lifts.

At the time of writing, none of the **car rental** companies could offer vehicles with hand controls in Prague. If you're driving to Prague, most cross-Channel ferries now have adequate facilities, as does *British Airways* for those who are flying. A shortlist of **hotels** with wheelchair access to at least a handful of rooms appears in the box below; inevitably, most of these are fairly expensive.

Accessible Hotels

Atrium Pobřežní 1, Karlín	☎ 24 84 20 20
Diplomat Evropská 15, Dejvice	☎ 24 39 41 11
Forum Kongresová 1, Nusle	☎ 61 19 11 11
Grand Hotel Bohemia Praha Králodvorská 4, Staré Město	☎ 232 3417
Olympik Sokolovská 138, Karlín	☎ 66 18 11 11
Palace Panská 12, Nové Město	☎ 24 09 31 11
Paříž U obecního domu 1, Staré Město	☎ 24 22 21 51
Prague Renaissance V celnici 7, Nové Město	☎ 24 81 03 96
Savoy Keplerova 6, Hradčany	☎ 24 30 21 22

Contacts for Disabled Travellers

Australia

ACROD, PO Box 60, Curtain, ACT 2605; ☎06/682 4333

Barrier Free Travel, 36 Wheatley St, North Bellingen, NSW 2454; ☎066/551733

Canada

Jewish Rehabilitation Hospital, 3205 Place Alton Goldbloom, Montreal, PQ H7V 1R2; ☎514/688-9550, ext 226
Guidebooks and travel information.

Kéroul, 4545 ave. Pierre de Coubertin, CP 1000, Montreal, Quebec H1V 3R2; ☎512/252-3104
Travel for mobility-impaired people.

Czech Republic

Metatur, Štefaniková 48, Smíchov, Prague; ☎55 10 64
Only organization in Prague which campaigns for the disabled; English-speakers available.

New Zealand

Disabled Persons Assembly, PO Box 10–138, The Terrace, Wellington; ☎04/472 2626

UK

Holiday Care Service, 2 Old Bank Chambers, Station Road, Horley, Surrey RH6 9HW; ☎01293/774535
Information on all aspects of travel.

Mobility International, 228 Borough High St, London SE1 1JX ; ☎0171/403 5688
Information, access guides, tours and exchange programmes.

RADAR (The Royal Association for Disability and Rehabilitation), 25 Mortimer Street, London W1N 8AB; ☎0171/637 5400
Information on all aspects of travel.

USA

Directions Unlimited, 720 N Bedford Rd, Bedford Hills, NY 10507; ☎1-800/533-5343
Tour operator specializing in custom tours for people with disabilities.

Information Center for People with Disabilities, Fort Point Place, 27-43 Wormwood St, Boston, MA 02210; ☎617/727-5540 or 345-9743
Clearing house for information, including travel, primarily in Massachusetts.

Mobility International USA, PO Box 10767, Eugene, OR 97440; ☎ 503/343-1284
Information and referral services, access guides, tours and exchange programs.

Society for the Advancement of Travel for the Handicapped (SATH), 347 5th Ave, New York, NY 10016; ☎212/447-7284
Non-profit-making travel industry referral service that passes queries on to its members as appropriate; allow plenty of time for a response.

Travel Information Service, Moss Rehabilitation Hospital, 1200 West Tabor Rd, Philadelphia, PA 19141; ☎215/456-9600
Telephone information and referral service.

Twin Peaks Press, Box 129, Vancouver, WA 98666; ☎206/694-2462 or 1-800/637-2256
Publisher of the Directory of Travel Agencies for the Disabled ($19.95), listing more than 370 agencies worldwide; Travel for the Disabled ($14.95); the Directory of Accessible Van Rentals and Wheelchair Vagabond ($9.95), which is full of personal tips.

Post and Phones

Post

The **main post office** (*pošta*) in Prague is at Jindřišská 14 (☎24 22 88 56), just off Wenceslas Square. It is open 24 hours a day, although it operates a reduced service during the night. Make sure you queue at the right counter (there are 53 to choose from): *známky* (stamps) are currently sold from windows 8–15; the new phone cards (*telecarty*) are available from windows 20–22; *balky* (parcels) weighing under 2kg are dealt with at windows 6–7. Each postal district in Prague has several post offices, though these have far less comprehensive hours and services.

In Prague, **poste restante** (pronounced as five syllables in Czech) letters will arrive at the main post office mentioned above (the postcode is 110 00 PRAHA 1); go to window 28 (open Mon–

Fri 7am–8pm, Sat 7am–1pm). Alternatively, *American Express*, at Václavské náměstí 56 (Mon–Fri 9am–6pm, Sat 9am–noon), will hold mail for a month for card and/or cheque holders.

Outbound post is reasonably reliable, with letters or cards taking around five working days to Britain and Ireland, a week to ten days to North America or Australasia. You can buy **stamps** from newsagents, tobacconists and kiosks, as well as at the post offices. If you want to send a **parcel over 2kg**, (but below 15kg) you must go to the special parcel office at the junction of Plzeňská and Vrchlického in Prague 5 (tram #4, #6, #7 or #9 from metro Anděl). After filling in two separate forms for shipping and customs, you then have a choice of sending your parcel by ship, air or express. Alternatively, you can save a lot of hassle, and get the parcel there in no time at all by paying considerably more at a courier company like *DHL*, Na poříčí 4, Nové Město.

Phones

The Czech **telephone system** is antiquated, and you may have to dial the number you want at least three times before getting through. The majority of public phones in the centre of Prague take only **phone cards** (*telecarty*), currently available in 50 and 100 units from post offices, tobacconists and some shops (prices vary). You can make international calls from all card phones (calls currently cost over 30kč a minute to Britain and Ireland, over 60kč to the US, Canada and Australia, and a whopping 90kč to New Zealand. There are instructions in English, but if you have any problems, ring ☎0132 to get through to the international operator.

In the grey, **coin-operated phones**, you need to insert a minimum of 2kč to make a local call; in the old orange phones (only good for local calls), rest your coin in the slot and when someone answers the coin will automatically drop. The **dialling tone** is a short followed by a long pulse; the **ringing tone** is long and regular; **engaged** is short and rapid; the standard Czech response is *prosím*; the word for extension is *linka*.

You can also make phone calls from the **telephone exchange** situated in the main post

Some foreign countries in Czech
Australia – Austrálie
Austria – Rakousko
Canada – Kanada
Eire – Irsko
Germany – Německo
Great Britain – Velká Británie
Hungary – Maďarsko
Netherlands – Nizozemí
New Zealand – Nový Zéland
USA – Spojené státy americké

BASICS

Dialling Codes				
To Prague		**From Prague**		
From Britain & Ireland	☎ 00 42 2	UK		☎ 0044
From USA & Canada	☎ 011 42 2	Eire		☎ 00353
From Australia & New Zealand	☎ 0011 42 2	Australia		☎ 0061
Phoning from elsewhere in the Czech or Slovak Republic, the Prague city code is ☎ 02		New Zealand		☎ 0064
		USA and Canada		☎ 001

office (see above for address). Write down the town and number you want, leave a deposit of around 200kč and wait for your name to be called out. Avoid making any calls from hotels, where the surcharge is usually outrageous. To make a **collect call**, which will probably cost the recipient less than it costs you, you need to get through to the international operator in the country you're phoning: ring ☎ 00 42 00 44 01 for the UK; ring ☎ 00 42 00 01 01 for the US; ring ☎ 00 42 00 01 51 for Canada; these calls are not free.

Opening Hours, Holidays and Festivals

Shops in Prague are generally open Monday to Friday from 9am to 5pm, though most supermarkets and tourist shops stay open later. Smaller shops usually close for lunch for an hour sometime between noon and 2pm. Those shops that open on Saturday are generally shut by noon or 1pm; and very few open on Sunday. The majority of pubs and restaurants tend to close between 10 and 11pm, with food often unobtainable after 9pm.

Opening hours for **museums and galleries** are generally 9 or 10am to 5 or 6pm every day except Monday, all year round. Full opening hours are detailed in the text. Ticket prices are still negligible (rarely more than 40kč except for the most touristy sights like Prague Castle) – proof of student status will cut costs in half.

Getting into **churches** can present more of a problem. Most of the more central ones operate in much the same way as museums and occasionally even have an entry charge, particularly for their crypts or cloisters. Other churches – including the Týn Church – are usually kept locked, opening only for worship in the early morning (around 7 or 8am) and/or the evening (around 6 or 7pm). Synagogues in Josefov follow museum hours, except that they close on Saturdays rather than Mondays.

Outside Prague, in the high season, castles and monasteries open from 8 or 9am to noon or 1pm, and again from 2 to 4pm or later. On Mondays and from the end of October to the beginning of April, apart from a few notable exceptions, most places are closed. In April and

> ### Closed for technical reasons
>
> On any one day, anything up to a quarter of Prague's museums and galleries can be temporarily "closed for technical reasons", "closed due to illness", or, more permanently, "closed for reconstruction". Notices are rarely more specific than that, but the widespread shortage of staff and funds is often behind the closure. It's impossible to predict what will be closed when, but it's a good idea to make alternative plans when visiting galleries and museums, just in case.

October, opening hours are often restricted to weekends and public holidays only.

Whatever the time of year, if you want to see the interior of a building, nine times out of ten you'll be forced to go on a **guided tour** (nearly always in Czech, occasionally in German) that can last for an hour or more. Ask for an *anglický text*, an often unintentionally hilarious English resumé of the castle's history. Guided tours invariably set off on the hour, and the last one leaves an hour before the final closing time.

National Holidays

National holidays were always a potential source of contention with the old regime, and they remain controversial even today. **May Day**, once a nationwide compulsory march under dull Commie slogans, remains a public holiday, though only the skinheads and anarchists bother to slug it out on the streets. Of the other *slavné májové dny* (Glorious May Days), as they used to be known, **May 5**, the beginning of the 1945 Prague Uprising, has been binned, and VE Day is now celebrated along with the western Allies on **May 8** (not on May 9, as is the case in the former Soviet Union). To scupper any celebration of the founding of the First Republic on **October 28**, the Communists hijacked the date for their very own Nationalization Day. Some Czechs argue that whichever way you look at it, this Czechoslovak/Communist holiday – which the extreme right-wing Republican Party regularly disrupt – should be ditched in favour of September 28, the feast day of St Wenceslas.

National Holidays

January 1
Easter Monday
May 1
May 8 (VE Day)
July 5 (Introduction of Christianity)
July 6 (Death of Jan Hus)
October 28 (Foundation of the Republic)
December 24
December 25
December 26

Festivals

Prague's **annual festive calendar** is light compared to most European capitals, with just a couple of cultural events in addition to the usual religious festivities. To find out what's going on, check out one of the listings magazines mentioned on p.23.

The city's most famous festival is the *Pražské jaro* (Prague Spring), not to be confused with the political events of 1968. It begins every year on May 12, the anniversary of Smetana's death, with a procession from Smetana's grave in Vyšehrad to the Obecní dům, where the composer's *Má vlast* (My Country) is performed in the presence of the president. It ends three weeks later, on June 2, with Beethoven's Ninth Symphony, and generally attracts several top-class performers. Tickets can be extremely hard to come by, so book well in advance.

A new arrival on the cultural calendar is *Tanec Praha* (Dance Prague), an international festival of modern dance which takes place throughout the city in June. *Zlatý Golem*, Prague's new ten-day international film festival aims to usurp Karlovy Vary's more established festival as the country's foremost filmic forum. In October, Prague also puts on a modest **International Jazz Festival**, which attracts all the best names in Czech jazz as well as at least one big foreign artist.

The rest of Prague's stirrings are mostly of a religious nature. At **Easter** (*Velikonoce*), the age-old sexist ritual of whipping girls' calves with braided birch twigs tied together with ribbons (*pomlázky*) is still practised. To prevent such a fate, the girls are supposed to offer the boys a coloured easter egg and pour a bucket of cold water over them. What may once have been an innocent bucolic frolic has now become another excuse for Czech men to harass any woman who dares to venture onto the street during this period.

Halloween comes early to the Czech Republic, on April 30, when the **"Burning of the Witches"** takes place. Bonfires are lit across the country, old brooms thrown out and burned, as everyone celebrates the end of the long winter. As in the rest of Europe, **Christmas** (*Vánoce*) is a time for overconsumption and family gatherings and therefore a mostly private occasion. On December 4, the feast day of Saint Barbara, cherry tree branches are bought as decorations, the aim being to get them to blossom before Christmas.

On the evening of **December 5**, numerous trios, dressed up as *svatý Mikuláš* (Saint Nicholas), an angel and a devil, tour round the neighbourhoods, the angel handing out sweets and fruit to children who've been good, while the devil dishes out coal and potatoes to those who've been naughty. The Czech Saint Nicholas has white hair and a beard, and dresses not in red but in a white priest's outfit, with a bishop's mitre.

With a week or so to go, large barrels are set up in the streets from which huge quantities of live carp (*kapr*), the traditional Christmas dish, are sold. **Christmas Eve** (*štědrý večer*) is traditionally a day of fasting, broken only when the evening star appears, signalling the beginning of the Christmas feast of carp, potato salad, schnitzel and sweet breads. Only after the meal are the children allowed to open their presents, which miraculously appear beneath the tree, thanks not to Santa Claus, but to *Ježíšek* (Baby Jesus).

Birthdays are much less important for the Czechs than **saints' name days**, which fall on the same day each year. Thus popular names like Jan or Anna are practically national celebrations, and an excuse for everyone to get drunk since you're bound to know at least one person with those names.

The Media

It's a sign of the times that the most respected **Czech newspaper**, *Lidové noviny* (the best-known *samizdat* or underground publication under the Communists) is now owned by a Swiss company, Ringier. In fact over half the Czech press is now foreign-owned, including the country's most popular daily, *Blesk*, a sensationalist tabloid with lurid colour pictures, naked women and reactionary politics.

The next most popular paper is *Mlada Fronta Dnes*, former mouthpiece of the Communist youth movement, now a centre-right daily with solid coverage of local and international news. Third in the popularity stakes is *Rudé pravo*, once the official mouthpiece of the Communist Party, now a surprisingly successful "left-wing daily". The other positive independent political voice is the weekly *Respekt*, which prides itself on its investigative journalism.

The **English-language** weekly to look out for is *The Prague Post*, a quality paper with strong business coverage, and a useful pull-out **listings** section. If you speak just a little Czech, you'll be able to cope with the monthly listings magazine *Přehled*, and the much more comprehensive weekly listings broadsheet *Program*, both of which are easily decipherable. *Annonce* (now published three times a week) is the place to buy and sell anything, and to hunt down flats and jobs.

In the **magazine** market, western glossies now grab the attention of most of the nation more effectively than their domestic competitors. *Elle* and *Cosmopolitan* are now both available in Czech, though *Playboy* has had to fold after cut-price competition from the wide array of locally produced **porn** magazines and books.

The entire range of **foreign newspapers** is now available from the kiosks on Wenceslas Square and elsewhere. They're generally a day old, though one that you can buy on the day of issue is the European edition of *The Guardian*, printed in Frankfurt (it arrives on the streets of Prague around mid-morning).

TV and Radio

The state-owned *Česká televize* has two channels, *ČT1* and *ČT2*, both of which are pretty anodyne, with keep-fit classes and classical concerts still taking up much of peak-time viewing. Foreign films are occasionally screened with subtitles, but most serials are dubbed and everything shuts down well before midnight. *ČT2* shows news from the BBC on Monday to Friday at 7.25am. Given the competition, it's hardly surprising that the independent channel, *Nova*, only launched in 1994, is now the most popular TV station; in addition, it has exclusive rights to all Czech football. The other independent channel is *Premiéra*, broadcast only in the

Prague region, and yet to find its feet (or any real share of the audience).

As far as **radio** goes, the most popular station is still, as in Communist days, the state-run *Česká rozhlas* news-orientated station, (92.6/100.7FM), on which Havel broadcasts his presidential Sunday evening chat. The three top FM music channels are *Evropa 2* (88.2FM) and *Kiss 98 FM* which dish out bland Euro-pop, and *Country Radio* (89.5FM) which panders to the Czechs' strange obsession with American country & western music. More interesting are *Radio 1* (91.9FM), which plays a wide range of indie rock from east and west, and the state-run *Vltava* (102.5FM), with its mixture of news, classical and folk music. You can pick up the *BBC World Service* fairly easily now, on 101FM.

Trouble and the Police

Despite their change of name from *Veřejná bezpečnost* or *VB*, as the former Communist police were known, to *Policie*, the national police force are still extremely unpopular, certainly among the younger generation, and they know it. Their participation in the November 17 demo destroyed what little credibility they had left after forty years of Communist control.

Public confidence in their competence has also suffered a severe blow due to the dramatic rise in the level of **crime** since 1989. The murder rate has quadrupled, prostitution is widespread and corruption is rife in Prague. However, you shouldn't be unduly paranoid: the crime rate is still very low, especially when compared with most European or North American cities. Pickpockets are the biggest hassle, especially in summer around the most popular tourist sights and on the trams and metro.

There are just two main types of police nowadays: the aforementioned *Policie* and the municipal police. The *Policie*, in khaki-green uniforms (hence their nickname – *žáby* or "frogs") with red lapels and a red band on their caps are the national force, with the power of arrest, and are under the control of the Ministry of Interior. They often drive around in clapped-out green and white Škodas and Ladas. If you do need the police, though – and above all if you're reporting a serious crime – you should always go to the *Městská policie* (municipal police), run by the Prague city authorities, distinguishable by their all-black uniforms.

In addition, there are various private police forces, who also dress in black – hence their nickname, *Černé šerif* (Black Sheriffs) – employed mostly by hotels and banks. They are often very officious, incompetent and trigger-happy, though in reality they are little more than glorified security guards. They are allowed to carry guns, but have no powers of arrest, and you are not legally obliged to show them your ID.

Avoiding Trouble

Almost all the problems encountered by tourists in Prague are to do with **petty crime** – mostly theft from cars and hotel rooms – rather than more serious physical confrontations. Sensible precautions include making photocopies of your passport, leaving passport and tickets in the hotel safe and noting down travellers' cheque and credit card numbers. If you have a car, don't leave anything in view when you park it; take the cassette/radio with you if you can. Vehicles are rarely stolen, but

The following is a list of the main police stations for each of Prague's ten postal districts.

Prague 1 – Bartolomějská 6
Prague 2 – Legerova 2
Prague 3 – Lupáčova 11
Prague 4 – U plynárny 2
Prague 5 – Nádražní 16a
Prague 6 – V. P. čkalova 18
Prague 7 – Fr. Křížka 24
Prague 8 – Rosenbergových 1
Prague 9 – Jandova 1
Prague 10 – Přípotoční 300

luggage and valuables left in cars do make a tempting target and rental cars are easy to spot.

In theory, you're supposed to carry some form of **identification** at all times, and the police can stop you in the street and demand it. In practice, they're rarely bothered if you're clearly a foreigner (unless you're driving). In any case, the police are now so deferential that they tend to confine themselves to socially acceptable activities like traffic control and harassing Romanies.

What to do if you're robbed

If you are unlucky enough to have something stolen, you will need to **go to the police** to report it, not least because your insurance company will require a police report. It's unlikely that there'll be anyone there who speaks English, and even less likely that your belongings will be retrieved but, at the very least, you should get a statement detailing what you've lost for your insurance claim. Try the phrase *byl jsem oloupen* or (if you're a woman) *byla jsem oloupena* – "I have been robbed".

Emergencies	
Ambulance	☎ 155
Police	☎ 158
Fire	☎ 150

Sexual harassment

As far as **sexual harassment** is concerned, things are, if anything, marginally less intimidating than in western Europe, although without the familiar linguistic and cultural signs, it's easier to misinterpret situations. Specific places to avoid going after dark include Wenceslas Square, Uhelny trh, the train stations, Hlavní nádraží and nádraží Holešovice.

Finding Work

Unless you're fluent in Czech, have some particular skill and have applied for a job advertized in your home country, the only real chance of long-term work in Prague is teaching English, either privately or in one of the many language schools. With English having replaced Russian on most school syllabuses, there's a chronic shortage of English teachers, though you're more likely to strike lucky anywhere else in the country other than Prague.

Obviously it's best to have a TEFL (Teaching English as a Foreign Language) or ESL (English as a Second Language) certificate, but you may find that even without the qualification many language schools will still take you on. Finding a teaching job is mainly a question of perusing the

English-language weekly *Prague Post*, the thrice-weekly Czech advertizer *Annonce*, and scouring the notice boards in the American and British cultural centres (see "Directory", on p.230). Other options are to try advertizing private lessons (better paid, but harder to make a living at) on the university notice boards, or in *Annonce*. With unemployment creeping steadily upwards, finding temporary work of any kind is extremely unlikely.

If you have a legitimate job, getting a **work permit** should be easy, but getting a **residence permit** is a lengthy and bureaucratic process which, unless your employers are prepared to do it on your behalf, is not worth the hassle. If you want to be legitimate, however, you'll find details of how to obtain a residence permit on p.12.

The City

Introducing the City

With a population of just one and a quarter million, **Prague** is one of the smallest capital cities in Europe. It originally developed as four separate, self-governing towns and a Jewish ghetto, whose individual identities and medieval street plans have been preserved, more or less intact, to this day. Almost everything of any historical interest lies within these central districts, the majority of which are easy to master quickly on foot. Only in the last hundred years has Prague spread beyond its ancient perimeter, and its suburbs now stretch across the hills for miles on every side. There's a cheap and efficient transport system on which to explore them – a decent map is all you need to find your way around.

The castle district or **Hradčany** (Chapter 1) spreads across the hill on the left bank of the River Vltava where the first Slavs settled in the seventh or eighth century. At its eastern end is Prague Castle (known simply as the *Hrad* in Czech), which contains a whole series of important historical buildings, including the city's cathedral, the seat of the president, and the royal palace and gardens, as well as a host of museums and galleries. The rest of Hradčany lies to the west of the castle: a sleepy district ranging in scale from the miniature cottages of Nový Svět to the gargantuan facade of the Černín Palace. One art gallery you won't want to miss in Hradčany is the Šternberk Palace, housing the National Gallery's main European art collection.

Squeezed between the castle hill and the river are the Baroque palaces and houses of the "Little Quarter" or **Malá Strana** (Chapter 2) – around 150 acres of twisting cobbled streets and secret walled gardens – home to most of the city's embassies and dominated by one of the landmarks of the left bank, the green dome and tower of the church of sv Mikuláš. At the southern end of Malá Strana, a funicular railway carries you out of the cramped streets to the top of Petřín Hill, the city's most central leafy escape, with a wonderful view across the river.

The twisting matrix of streets is at its most confusing in the original medieval hub of the city, **Staré Město** (Chapter 3) – literally, the

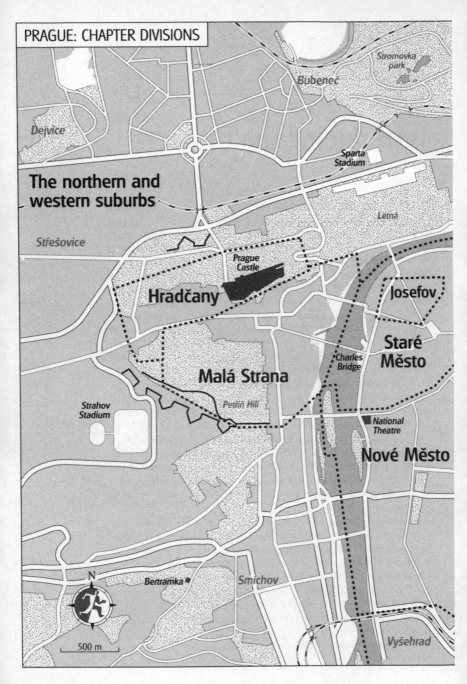

PRAGUE: CHAPTER DIVISIONS

Bubeneč

Stromovka park

Dejvice

Sparta Stadium

The northern and western suburbs

Letná

Střešovice

Prague Castle

Hradčany

Josefov

Staré Město

Charles Bridge

Malá Strana

Petřín Hill

Strahov Stadium

National Theatre

Nové Město

N

Bertramka

Smíchov

500 m

Vyšehrad

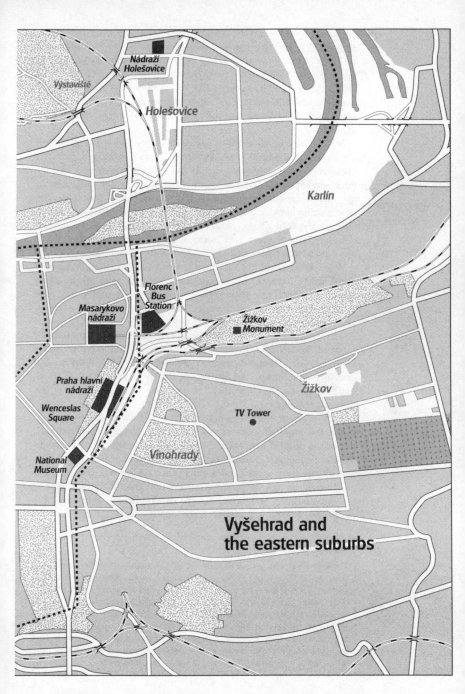

Vystaviště

Nádraží
Holešovice

Holešovice

Karlín

Florenc
Bus
Station

Masarykovo
nádraží

Žižkov
Monument

Praha hlavní
nádraží

Žižkov

Wenceslas
Square

TV Tower

National
Museum

Vinohrady

Vyšehrad and
the eastern suburbs

"Old Town" – on the right bank of the Vltava. The **Charles Bridge**, its main link with the opposite bank, is easily the city's most popular historical monument, bristling with Baroque statuary and one of the most beautiful places from which to view Prague Castle. Staré Město's other great showpiece is its main square, **Staroměstské náměstí**, where it's easy to sit for hours, soaking up the sights – the astronomical clock, the Hus monument and the spiky towers of the Týn church.

Nothing else in Staré Město can quite match these two spots, but it's worth spending at least an afternoon exploring the quarter's backstreets and alleyways, and in the process losing the crowds. Enclosed within the boundaries of Staré Město, to the northwest of the main square, is the Jewish quarter, or **Josefov** (Chapter 4). The ghetto walls have long since gone, and the whole area was remodelled at the turn of the century, but six synagogues, a medieval cemetery and a town hall survive as powerful reminders of a community which has existed here for over a millennium.

South and east of the old town is the large sprawling district of **Nové Město** (Chapter 5), whose main arteries make up the city's commercial and business centre. Despite its name – literally, "New Town" – Nové Město was founded back in the fourteenth century, and even its outer reaches are worth taking the trouble to explore. The nexus of Nové Město is **Wenceslas Square** (Václavské náměstí), focus of the political upheavals of the modern-day republic and a showcase of twentieth-century architecture. The district also contains numerous potent symbols of the Czech struggle for nationhood, such as the National Theatre, the Obecní dům and the National Museum.

Further afield lie various **suburbs**, most of which developed only in the last hundred years or so. The single exception is **Vyšehrad**, one of the original fortress settlements of the newly arrived Slavs in the last millennium. Nowadays, it's a peaceful escape from the city, and its cemetery is the final resting place for leading Czech artists of the modern age, including Smetana and Dvořák. To the east is the once wealthy residential suburb of **Vinohrady**, peppered with parks and squares; and **Žižkov**, traditionally a working-class district,

---

Addresses

The street name is always written before the number in **addresses**. The word for street (*ulice*) is either abbreviated to *ul.* or missed out altogether – Celetná ulice, for instance, is commonly known as Celetná. Other terms often abbreviated are *náměstí* (square), *třída* (avenue), and *nábřeží* (embankment), which become *nám.*, *tř.* and *nábř.* respectively. Prague is divided into numbered **postal districts** (see map) – these are too large to be very much help in orientation, so in this guide, we have generally opted for the names of the smaller districts as they appear on street signs, for example Hradčany, Nové Město, Smíchov etc.

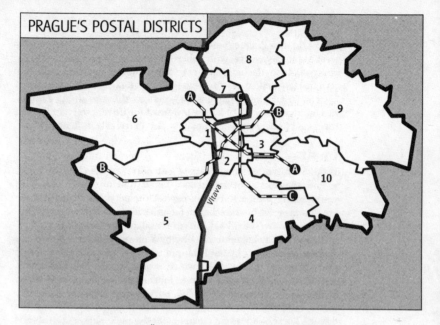

PRAGUE'S POSTAL DISTRICTS

whose two landmarks – the Žižkov monument and the futuristic television tower – are visible for miles around. All of these areas are
covered in Chapter 6.

Nineteenth-century suburbs also sprang up to the north of the
city centre in **Holešovice**, which boasts two huge swathes of greenery: the Letná plain, overlooking the city; and the Stromovka park,
beyond which lie the city chateau of **Troja** and the zoo. Further
west, leafy interwar suburbs like **Dejvice** and **Střešovice**, dotted
with modernist family villas, give an entirely different angle on
Prague. At the very edge of the city limits, the chateaux of **Hvězda**
and **Zbraslav** are easily visited in an afternoon, given their good
transport links. All these places are covered in Chapter 7.

If you're keen to head **out of the city** entirely, there's a wide
choice of destinations within an hour or so's journey from Prague.
The royal hideaway of **Karlštejn** is an obvious day trip, though the
surrounding woods, and those of nearby Křivoklát, are equally enticing. The medieval mining town of **Kutná Hora**, east of Prague,
boasts one of central Europe's most stunning pieces of ecclesiastical architecture, plus a host of other attractions. Last of all, the
legacy of the war hangs over two places to the northwest: **Lidice**,
which was razed to the ground by the Nazis; and the ghetto town of
Terezín (Theresienstadt), through which most of the country's Jews
passed, en route to the extermination camps. The above destinations are all covered in Chapter 8.

Arrival in Prague

If you fly into Prague, you'll find yourself more than 10km north-west of the city centre, with only a bus link to get you into town. By contrast, both the international train stations and the main bus terminal are linked to the centre by the fast and efficient metro system. Driving into Prague is easy enough, though the city authorities, quite rightly, make it very awkward for drivers to enter the old town, and finding a parking space is also extremely difficult.

By air

Despite a recent overhaul, Prague's **airport**, Ruzyně (☎334 11 11), is now thoroughly overstretched. You'll find few of the facilities you'd expect from a European capital's main point of entry; there are, however, 24-hour exchange facilities and a variety of accommodation agencies (see p.185) and car rental outlets (see p.39).

The airport is linked to the city by a cheap, regular **express bus service** (Mon–Fri 7.00am–11.45pm, Sat & Sun 7.30am–11.45pm; every 30min), run by *ČSA*, which stops first at Dejvická metro station, at the end of metro line A (journey time 15min) and ends up at the *ČSA* offices on Revoluční, on the edge of Staré and Nové Město (journey time 25min); to obtain a ticket simply pay the driver. There's an even cheaper (and much slower) **local bus** connection, too: bus #119 (4.30am–11.45pm; every 15min or so; journey time 25min) stops frequently and ends its journey outside the Dejvická metro station; you must buy your ticket from the orange machine just inside the airport exit, or from the newsagents at the far end of the airport. If you arrive after midnight, you can catch a **night bus** #510 to Divoká Šárka, the terminus for night tram #51, which will take you to Národní in the centre of town; you'll need to buy a ticket for both the bus and the tram from the orange machine at the airport.

Alternatively, **taxis** from the airport into the centre cost between 300kč and 400kč; make sure the driver turns on the meter, or, if in doubt, agree on a price before getting in.

By train and bus

International trains arrive either at the old Art-Nouveau **Praha hlavní nádraží**, on the edge of Nové Město and Vinohrady, or at **Praha-Holešovice**, which lies in an industrial suburb north of the city centre. At both stations you'll find exchange outlets (there's even a branch of the *PIS* tourist office at Hlavní nádraží), as well as a 24-hour left luggage office (see p.232) and accommodation agencies (see p.185). Both stations are on metro lines, and Hlavní nádraží is only a five-minute walk from Wenceslas Square. Some **domestic train** services wind up at the central **Masarykovo nádraží** on Hybernská, a couple of blocks east of náměstí Republiky.

If you're catching a **train out of Prague**, don't leave buying your ticket until the last minute, as the queues can be long and slow. You can buy international train tickets at either Praha hlavní nádraží (currently at windows 26, 28, 30 or 32 on the first floor) and Praha-Holešovice, or from *ČEDOK*, Na příkopě 22, Nové Město.

Prague's **main bus terminal** is **Praha-Florenc**, on the eastern edge of Nové Město, where virtually all long-distance international and domestic services terminate. It's a confusing (and ugly) place to end up, but its facilities include a 24-hour left luggage office (see p.232) and you can make a quick exit to the adjacent metro station.

Information and maps

Once in Prague, the main tourist office is the **Prague Information Service** or *PIS* (*Pražská informační služba*), whose main branch is at Na příkopě 20, Nové Město (Mon–Fri 8.30am–7pm, Sat & Sun 9am–5pm). The staff speak at least four languages between them, including English, and will be able to answer most enquiries; they offer private accommodation, sell maps and guides and act as a ticket agency, too. *PIS* also distributes some useful free publications, including *The Arts in Prague*, a monthly English-language booklet listing the major events, concerts and exhibitions. There are additional *PIS* offices in the main train station, Praha hlavní nádraží, on Valdštejnské náměstí in Malá Strana, and within the Staroměstská radnice (Old Town Hall) on Staroměstské náměstí. None of the above *PIS* offices will take enquiries over the phone, though there is an information line which you can ring (☎54 44 44).

The *PIS* should be able to furnish you with a quick reference **map** of central Prague, but to locate a specific street, or find your way round the suburbs, you'll need a detailed city map (*plán města*). *Kartografie Praha* produces the cheapest and most comprehensive ones: the 1:20,000 map covers the city centre as well as many of the suburbs and has a full street index, and the metro, tram and bus routes marked on – available in both booklet form (handier to carry about and leaf through) and the fold-out variety (better for the overall picture). You can get hold of either, and any other maps you may want, from *PIS* offices, street kiosks, most bookshops (*knihkupectví*) and some hotels.

Another good source of information is the weekly **English-language paper**, *Prague Post*, which carries invaluable **listings** on the latest exhibitions, shows, gigs and events around the capital.

Getting around

The centre of Prague, where most of the city's sights are concentrated, is reasonably small and best explored on foot. At some point, however, in order to cross the city quickly or reach some of the more widely dispersed attractions, you'll need to use the city's cheap and efficient public transport system, which comprises the metro and a network of trams and buses. To get a clearer picture, it's essential to invest in a **city map** (see above), which marks all the tram, bus and metro lines.

Tickets and passes

On all the city's public transport, a single **ticket** (*lístek*) currently costs 10kč for an adult and; 5kč for those aged 10–16; under-10s travel free. Tickets, which are standard for all forms of public transport, must be bought beforehand either from a tobacconist (*tabák*), street kiosk or newsagents, or from one of the orange ticket machines found at some bus and tram stops and inside all metro stations; if you don't have the right change in the metro, the person on duty in the office by the barriers will usually be able to give you change or sell you a ticket.

When you enter the metro, or board a tram or bus, you must validate your ticket by placing it in one of the electronic machines to hand. Your ticket is then valid for an hour, during which you may change trams, buses or metro lines as many times as you like. Buy as many tickets in advance as you think you'll need, to avoid the problem of trying to hoard change for the machines, or finding a machine that actually works. To save hassle, and money, most Praguers buy monthly or quarterly **passes** (which is why you see so few of them punching tickets). To do this, present ID and a passport-sized photo at the beginning of the month to the windows marked DP at major metro stations and ask for a *měsíční jízdenka*. After the first week of the month only I.P. Pavlova metro station will issue them. Monthly passes currently cost around 350kč.

Alternatively, if you're going to be using the transport system a lot (or just want to avoid a lot of hassle), it's worth getting hold of a one-day **tourist pass** (*turistická síťová jízdenka*) for 90kč; no photos or ID are needed. There's nothing to stop people from freeloading on the system, of course, since there are no barriers. However, plain-clothes inspectors make spot checks and will issue an on-the-spot fine of 200kč to anyone caught without a valid ticket or pass; ask for a receipt (*paragon*) if you suspect the controller is just going to pocket the money.

The metro

The vaguely futuristic Soviet-built **metro** is fast, smooth and ultra-clean, running daily from 5am to midnight with trains every two minutes during peak hours, slowing down to every six minutes by late in the evening. Its three lines (with a fourth planned) intersect at various points in the city centre and the route plans are easy to follow (see map opposite). The stations are fairly discreetly marked above ground with the logo as on the map opposite, in green (line

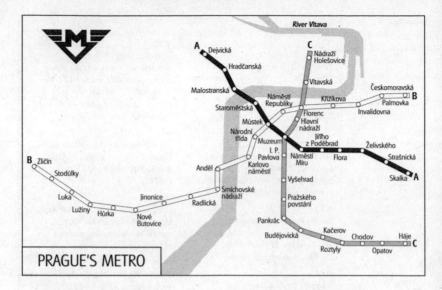

River Vltava

PRAGUE'S METRO

A), yellow (line B) or red (line C). The constant bleeping at metro
entrances is to enable blind people to locate the escalators. As with
the trams and buses, you don't have to use a fresh ticket each time
you change lines, though you must complete your journey within an
hour (it would be difficult not to). Few people are in a hurry,
though, and the escalators are a free-for-all, with no fast lane. Once
inside the metro, it's worth knowing that *výstup* means exit and
přestup will lead you to one of the connecting lines at an
interchange.

Trams and buses

The electric **tram system**, in operation since 1891, negogiates
Prague's hills and cobbles with remarkable dexterity. The majority
of Prague's red Škoda trams (many now plastered over with advertising) were designed in the 1950s, but are gradually being
replaced by more modern rolling stock. After the metro, trams are
the fastest and most efficient way of getting around, running every
ten to twenty minutes throughout the day – check the timetables
posted at every stop (*zastávka*), which list the departures times
from that specific stop, and bear in mind that Czech trams rival
Swiss trains in their punctuality.

Tram #22, which runs from Vinohrady to Hradčany via the centre
of town and Malá Strana, is a good way to get to grips with the lie of
the land, and a cheap way of sightseeing. In the summer, older trams
(#91), running less frequently, cater for tourists and charge twice
the normal fare for the privilege. Some lines operate only during rush
hour (Mon–Fri 6.30–8.30am & 3–6pm), others run seven days a

Night trams

#51
Nádraží Strašnice, metro Želivského, metro Flora, nám. Míru, nám. I. P. Pavlova, Lazarská, Národní, metro Staroměstská, nábř. kpt. Jaroše, metro Hradčanská, metro Dejvická, Evropská, **Divoká Šárka.**

#52
Hlubočepy, metro Anděl, Lazarská, Masarykovo nádraží, metro Florenc, metro Křižíkova, metro Palmovka, **Lehovec.**

#53
Metro Pankrác, Lazarská, Masarykovo nádraží, nábř. kpt Jaroše, nádraží Holešovice, Trojská, **Vozovna Kobylisy.**

#54
Nádraží Braník, Lazarská, Národní, metro Staroměstská, nábř. kpt Jaroše, nádraží Holešovice, metro Palmovka, **sídliště Jáblice.**

#55
Ústřední dílny DP, metro Strašnická, Vršovická, Karlovo nám., Lazarská, Václavské nám., Masarykovo nádraží, metro Florenc, metro Křižíkova, metro Palmovka, **Lehovec.**

#56
Spořilov, Nuselská, Bělehradská, Lazarská, Masarykovo nádraží, metro Florenc, metro Hradčanská, **Petřiny.**

#57
Nádraží Hostivař, Radošovická, nám. Míru, Lazarská, Národní, metro Malostranská, metro Hradčanská, **Bílá hora.**

#58
Spojovací, metro želivského, metro Flora, Olšanské nám., Lazarská, Národní, metro Anděl, **sídliště Řepy.**

week (5am–midnight) and the whole system slows down during July and August for the holidays. **Night trams** (see box below) run roughly every forty minutes from around midnight to 5am, and all pass by Lazarská Spálená in Nové Město.

You'll rarely need to use Prague's **buses**, which for the most part keep well out of the centre of town. If you're intent upon visiting or staying in some of the city's more obscure suburbs, though, you may need to use them: their hours of operation are similar to those of the trams (though generally less frequent), and route numbers are given in the text where appropriate. **Night buses** run just once an hour between midnight and 5am.

Taxis

Taxis come in all shapes and sizes, and, theoretically at least, are extremely cheap. There's a minimum charge of 10kč, and after that it's currently 12kč or more per kilometre, depending on the time of day and your location within the city. Tourists, however, are seen as easy prey by some taxi drivers; and stories of overcharging are too numerous to mention. A few tips to try and avoid such a situation are: hail a cab, rather than pick one up at the taxi ranks, many of which are controlled by the local mafia; if the meter isn't switched on, ask the driver to do so – *zapněte taxametr, prosím*; and, if you suspect you've been overcharged, asking for a receipt – *prosím, dejte mi potrzení* – should have the desired effect. The following cab companies have fairly good reputations: *Profitaxi* ☎61 04 55 55 or 692 13 32; *AAA taxi* ☎312 21 12 or 32 24 44.

Car rental

You really don't need a **car** in Prague, since much of the city centre is pedestrianized and the public transport system is so cheap and efficient. Should you want to drive out of Prague, however, **car rental** is easy to arrange but pricey. You'll need to be 21 and have been driving for at least a year, and, if you book from abroad, you're looking at a whopping £60/$96 per day for a small car (£250/$400 for a week, with special rates at the weekend). The big companies all have offices in Prague, and charge similar prices. You'll get a much cheaper deal if you go to a local agent like *Esocar* or *Lamia car*, though with very little of the back-up you'd get from an international firm should something go wrong.

Car rental firms in Prague

Avis		**Europcar**	
E. Krásnohorské 9,		Pařížská 12,	
Staré Město	☎231 55 15	Nové Město	☎24 81 05 15
Budget		**Hertz**	
Hotel Intercontinental,		Karlovo nám. 28,	
nám. Curieových,		Nové Město	☎29 18 51
Staré Město	☎231 95 95		
		Lamia Car	
Esocar		Na Míčánce 57,	
Husitská 58,		Dejvice	☎311 81 21
Žižkov	☎27 88 88		

Driving in Prague

Rules and regulations on Czech roads are pretty stringent – a legacy of the police state – though less strictly adhered to by Czechs nowadays. On-the-spot fines are still regularly handed out, up to a maximum of 500kč. The basic rules are driving on the right; compulsory wearing of seatbelts; and no alcohol at all in your blood when you're driving. Watch out for restricted streets, most notably Wenceslas Square, and don't overtake a tram when passengers are getting on and off if there's no safety island for them. Speed limits are 110kph on motorways, 90kph on other roads and 60kph in all cities. In addition, there's a special limit of 30kph for level crossings (you'll soon realize why if you try ignoring it). As in other continental countries, a yellow diamond means you have right of way; a black line through it means you don't. If you have **car trouble**, dial ☎154 at the nearest phone and wait for assistance.

Cycling

Cycling is only just beginning to catch on in Prague. The combination of cobbled streets, tram lines and sulphurous air is enough to put most people off. Facilities for **bike rental** are still not that widespread, though there's usually a few fly-by-night dealers around Staroměstské náměstí during the summer months. You can hire out mountain bikes all year round from *Rent-a-Bike*, (Školská 12, Nové Město; ☎22 10 63; metro Národní třída) or *Landa*, (Šumavská 33, Vinohrady; ☎253 99 82; metro náměstí Míru).

Petrol (*benzín*) comes in two types: *super* (96 octane) and *special* (90 octane); diesel (*nafta*) is also available but two-stroke fuel (*mix*), which powers the old East German Trabants and Wartburgs, is being phased out. **Lead-free** petrol (*natural* or *bezolovnatý*) is now available from most petrol stations in and around Prague. Remember that 24-hour petrol stations aren't as widespread as in western European capitals.

Vehicle crime is on the increase and western cars are a favourite target – never leave anything visible or valuable in the car. The other big nightmare is **parking**. Spaces in the centre are expensive and few and far between, and illegally parked cars are quickly towed away. If this happens, you'll find the **car pound** on Černokostelecká, way out in Prague 10 (tram #11). If you're staying in a private room outside the centre, you'll have no problems; if you're at a hotel in the centre, they'll probably have a few parking spaces reserved for guests in the neighbouring streets, though whether you'll find one vacant is another matter. Otherwise, your best option is to park near a metro station out of the centre.

Chapter 1

Hradčany

H RADČANY's *raison d'être* is its castle, or **Hrad**, built on the
site of one of the original hill settlements of the Slav tribes
who migrated here in the seventh or eighth century AD. The
Přemyslid prince, Bořivoj I, erected the first castle here sometime in
the late ninth century, and, since then, whoever has occupied the Hrad
has exercized authority over the Czech Lands. Consequently, unlike
the city's other districts, Hradčany has never had a real identity of its
own – it became a royal town only in 1598 – existing instead as a mere
appendage, its inhabitants serving and working for their masters in the
Hrad. The same is still true now. For although the odd café or *pivnice*
(pub) survives in amongst the palaces (and even in the Hrad itself),
there's very little real life here beyond the stream of tourists who trek
through the castle and the civil servants who work either for the president or in the multifarious ministries whose departmental tentacles
spread right across Hradčany and down into Malá Strana.

Stretched out along a high spur above the River Vltava, Hradčany
shows a suitable disdain for the public transport system. There's a
choice of **approaches** from Malá Strana, all of which involve at least
some walking. From Malostranská metro station, most people take the
steep short cut up the Staré zámecké schody, which brings you into the
castle from its rear end. A better approach is up the stately Zámecké
schody, where you can stop and admire the view, before entering the
castle via the main gates. The alternative to all this climbing is to take
tram #22 from Malostranská metro, which tackles the hairpin bends of
Chotkova with ease, and deposits you either outside the Royal Gardens
to the north of the Hrad, or, if you prefer, outside the gates of the
Strahov monastery, at the far western edge of Hradčany.

Prague Castle (Pražský hrad)

Viewed from the Charles Bridge, **Prague Castle** (popularly known
as the Hrad) stands aloof from the rest of the city, protected, not by
bastions and castellated towers, but by its palatial Neoclassical

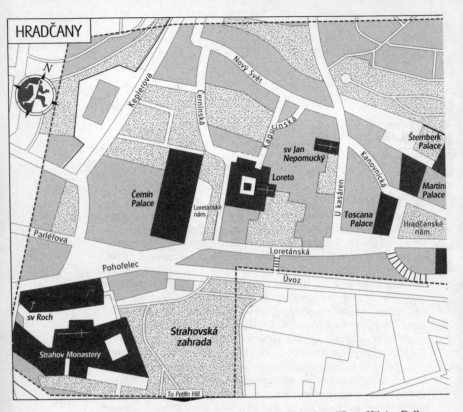

facade – an "immense unbroken sheer blank wall", as Hilaire Belloc described it – breached only by the great mass of St Vitus Cathedral. It's *the* picture-postcard image of Prague, though for the Czechs the castle has been an object of disdain as much as admiration, its alternating fortunes mirroring the shifts in the nation's history. The golden age and the dark ages, Masaryk's liberalism and Gottwald's terror – all emanated from the Hrad. When the first posters appeared in December 1989 demanding "*HAVEL NA HRAD*" (Havel to the Castle), they weren't asking for his reincarceration. Havel's occupancy of the Hrad was the sign that the reins of government had finally been wrested from the Communist regime.

The site has been successively built on since the first castle was erected here in the ninth century, but two **architects** in particular bear responsibility for the present outward appearance of the Hrad. The first is **Nicolo Pacassi**, court architect to Empress Maria Theresa, whose austere restorations went hand in hand with the deliberate run-down of the Hrad until it was little more than an administrative barracks. For the Czechs, his grey-green eighteenth-

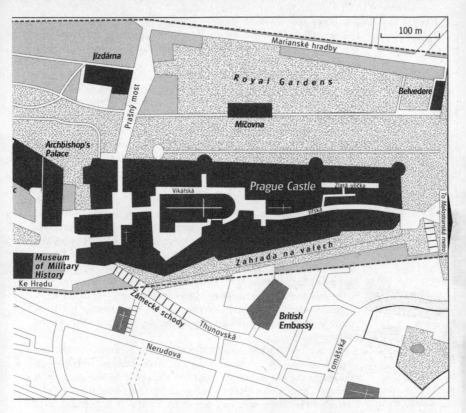

century cover-up, which hides a variety of much older buildings, is unforgivable. Less apparent, though no less controversial, is the hand of **Josip Plečnik**, the Slovene architect who was commissioned by T. G. Masaryk, president of the newly founded Czechoslovak Republic, to restore and modernize the castle in the 1920s (for more on Plečnik, see box on p.45).

The first and second courtyards

The **first courtyard** (první nádvoří), which opens on to Hradčanské náměstí, is guarded by Ignaz Platzer's *Battling Titans* – two gargantuan figures, one on each of the gate piers, wielding club and dagger and about to inflict fatal blows on their respective victims. Below them stand a couple of impassive presidential sentries, no longer kitted out in the paramilitary khaki of the last regime, but sporting new blue uniforms that deliberately recall those of the First Republic. They were designed by the Oscar-winning costume designer for Miloš Forman's film *Amadeus*, and chosen by Havel himself. The hourly changing of the guard is a fairly subdued affair, but every day at noon there's a much more elaborate parade, accompanied by a brass ensemble which appears at the first-floor windows to play local rock star Michal Kocáb's gentle, slightly comical, modern fanfare.

To reach the **second courtyard** (druhé nádvoří), you must pass through the early Baroque Matthias Gate (Matyášova brána) originally a freestanding triumphal arch in the middle of the long-since defunct moat, now set into one of Pacassi's blank walls. Grand stairways on either side lead to the presidential apartments in the south wing, and to the **Spanish Hall** (Španělský sál) and **Rudolf Gallery** (Rudofova galerie) in the north wing – two of the most stunning rooms in the entire complex. Sadly, both are generally out of bounds, though concerts are occasionally held in the Spanish Hall, which was decked out with gilded chandeliers and lined with mirrors for Emperor Franz Josef I's coronation, though in the end he never turned up. Once you've entered the rectangular courtyard, there's no escape from the monotonous onslaught of Pacassi's plastering and the smooth granite paving added in the 1960s. It's an unwelcoming and impersonal space, relieved only by Anselmo Lurago's **Chapel of the Holy Cross**, which cowers in one corner. Its richly painted interior used to house the treasury (klenotnice), a macabre selection of medieval reliquaries, but recently it's been rather brutally converted into a ticket office, with the chapel itself left empty.

In the north wing, the **Castle Gallery** (Obrazárna Pražského hradu) occupies what were once the royal stables and used to contain European paintings from the sixteenth to the eighteenth centuries, until it was closed some years ago following the theft of a Cranach. The collection was begun by Rudolf II, the Habsburgs' most avid art collector, but, sadly, the best of what he amassed was either taken as booty by the marauding Saxons and Swedes, or sold off by Rudolf's successors. The best of what's left includes *The Assembly of the Olympian Gods*, a vast, crowded canvas of portly naked figures by Rubens, a couple of fine paintings by Veronese, Titian's *Toilet of a Young Lady* and a *Flagellation* by Tintoretto. There's a bust of Rudolf by his court sculptor, Adriaen de Vries, and pictures by one of his court painters, Hans von Aachen, but sadly no works by the most unusual painter in Rudolf's employ, Giuseppe Arcimboldo, whose portrait of Rudolf – a surrealist collage of fruit, with his eyes as cherries, cheeks as apples and hair as grapes – now resides in Vienna.

The Castle Gallery is open Tues–Sun 10am–6pm; a separate entry ticket is necessary, available from the gallery box office.

Sights within Prague Castle *are open April–Oct daily 9am–5pm; Nov–March daily 9am–4pm; a single ticket, valid for three days and available from any ticket office in the Hrad, covers all sights, except the Old Bohemian Art Collection, the Toy Museum and the Lobkovic Palace. The castle courtyards and streets stay open until late.*

Prague
Castle

> **Josip Plečnik: post-modernist in the making**
>
> Born in Ljubljana, Josip Plečnik (1872–1957) studied under the great
> Viennese architect Otto Wagner at the turn of the century, and was
> appointed the chief architect to Prague Castle shortly after the foundation of
> the First Republic. Despite having the backing of the leading Czech architect
> Jan Kotěra, and President Masaryk himself, controversy surrounded him as
> soon as the appointment was announced; his non-Czech background and,
> moreover, his quirky, eclectic style placed him at odds with the architectural
> establishment of the day. He remained so until his rediscovery in the 1980s
> by the newly ascendant post-modernist movement. The darlings of post-
> modernism, Robert Venturi and Denise Scott-Brown, made special trips to
> Prague to see Plečnik's work, which, like their own, borrows elements from
> any number of genres from classical to Assyrian architecture.
>
> Plečnik's most conspicuous contributions to the castle – the fir-tree
> flag poles in the first courtyard and the granite obelisk in the third court-
> yard – are only a small sample of the work he carried out, which included
> the President's apartments, the South Gardens, and several halls in the
> west wing of the second courtyard. The gardens are now open to the
> public, and thanks partly to Havel (a keen Plečnik fan), there are plans to
> increase public access wherever possible, and to stage a special exhibition
> on Plečnik's work within the Hrad in the near future.

*Plečnik also
built one of
Prague's most
unusual
churches, in
Vinohrady (see
p.144).*

St Vitus Cathedral

St Vitus Cathedral (katedrála svatého Víta) takes up so much of the
third courtyard that it's difficult to get an overall impression of this
chaotic Gothic edifice. Its asymmetrical appearance is the product of
a long and chequered history, for although the foundation stone was
laid in 1344, the cathedral was not completed until 1929 – exactly
1000 years after the foundation of the first church within the Hrad.

The site of the present cathedral was originally a sacrificial altar
to the heathen fertility god **Svantovit**, which partly explains why the
first church, founded in 929 by Prince Václav, was dedicated to Saint
Vitus (*svatý Vít* in Czech), who allegedly exorcized the Emperor
Diocletian's son and was thereafter known as the patron saint of
epilepsy and of the convulsive disorder, Sydenham's chorea (hence
its popular name, St Vitus' Dance). The inspiration for the medieval
cathedral came from Charles IV, who, while still only heir to the
throne, not only wangled an independent archbishopric for Prague,
but also managed to gather together the relics of Saint Vitus.

Inspired by the cathedral at Narbonne, Charles commissioned
the Frenchman **Matthias of Arras** to start work on a similar structure. Matthias died eight years into the job in 1352, with the cathedral barely started, and Charles summoned **Peter Parler**, a
precocious 23-year-old from a family of great German masons, to
continue the work. For the next 46 years, Parler imprinted his
slightly flashier, more inventive *SonderGotik* ("Unusual Gothic")
style on the city, but the cathedral got no further than the construction of the choir and the south transept before his death in 1399.

*North of the
cathedral at
Vikářská 37,
there's an office
giving
information
about the castle;
opening hours
are the same as
for the castle.*

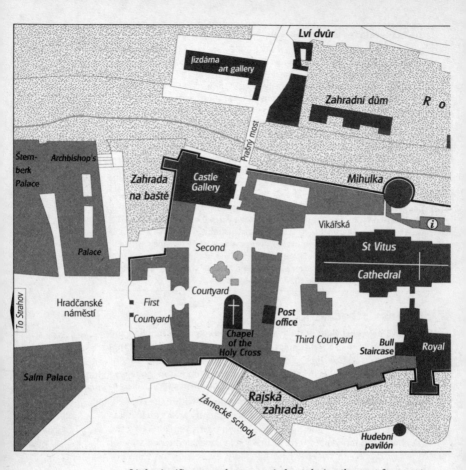

Little significant work was carried out during the next four centuries and the half-built cathedral became a symbol of the Czechs' frustrated aspirations to nationhood. Not until the Czech national revival or *národní obrození* of the nineteenth century did building begin again in earnest, with the foundation, in 1861, of the **Union for the Completion of the Cathedral**. A succession of architects, including Josef Mocker and Kamil Hilbert, oversaw the completion of the entire west end, and, with the help of countless other Czech artists and sculptors, the building was transformed into a treasure-house of Czech art. The cathedral was finally given an official opening ceremony in 1929, though work, in fact, continued right up to World War II.

The exterior

The sooty Prague air has made it hard now to differentiate between the two building periods. Close inspection, however, reveals that the

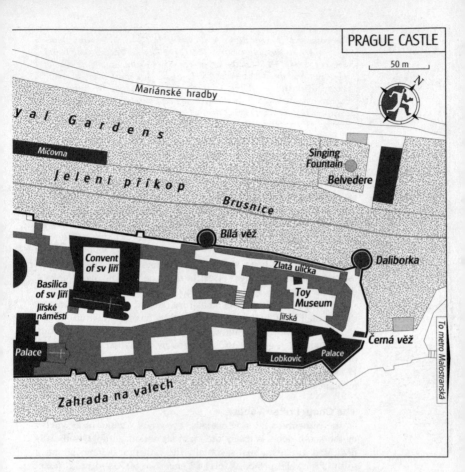

50 m

N

Mariánské hradby

val Gardens

Míčovna

Jelení příkop

Brusnice

Singing
Fountain

Belvedere

Bílá věž

Convent
of sv Jiří

Zlatá ulička

Daliborka

Basilica
of sv Jiří

Toy
Museum

Jiřské
náměstí

Jiřská

Palace

Černá věž

Lobkovic

Palace

To metro Malostranská

Zahrada na valech

western facade, including the twin spires, sports the rigorous if unimaginative work of the neo-Gothic restorers (their besuited portraits can be found below the rose window), while the **eastern section** – best viewed from the Belvedere – shows the building's authentic Gothic roots. The south door (see Zlatá brána, below) is also pure Parler. Oddly then, it's above the south door that the cathedral's tallest steeple reveals the most conspicuous stylistic join: Pacassi's Baroque topping resting absurdly on a Renaissance parapet of light stone, which is itself glued onto the blackened body of the original Gothic tower.

The nave

The cathedral is the country's largest, and once inside, it's difficult not to be impressed by the sheer height of the **nave**. This is the newest part of the building, and, consequently, is decorated with

Prague Castle

The cathedral is open daily April–Oct 9am–5pm; Nov–March 9am–4pm; entry to the main nave, the Chapel of sv Václav and to all services is free. To enter the crypt, chancel or ambulatory where the most interesting monuments are located, you must have a castle ticket, available from the box office in the south transept. The entrance to the South Tower, which you can climb (daily 10am–4pm, except in bad weather) is inside the cathedral.

modern furnishings. Of the later additions to the church, the most striking is František Bílek's **wooden crucifix**, in the north aisle, which breaks free of the neo-Gothic strictures that hamper other contemporary works inside. Also worth some attention are the cathedral's modern **stained-glass** windows, which on sunny days send shafts of rainbow light into the nave. Beautiful though the effect is, it's entirely out of keeping with Parler's original concept, which was to have almost exclusively clear glass windows. The most unusual windows are those by František Kysela, which look as though they have been shattered into hundreds of tiny pieces, a technique used to greatest effect in the rose window over the west door with its kaleidoscopic *Creation of the World* (1921).

In keeping with its secular nature, two of the works from the time of the First Republic were paid for by financial institutions: the *Cyril and Methodius* window, in the third chapel in the north wall, was commissioned from Alfons Mucha by the *Banka Slavie*; while on the opposite side of the nave, the window on the theme *Those Who Sow in Tears Shall Reap in Joy* was sponsored by a Prague insurance company.

The Chapel of sv Václav

Of the cathedral's 22 side chapels, the grand **Chapel of sv Václav** by the south door, is easily the main attraction. Although officially dedicated to Saint Vitus, spiritually the cathedral belongs as much to the Přemyslid prince, Václav (Wenceslas, of "Good King" fame, see box below), the country's patron saint, who was killed by his pagan brother, Boleslav the Cruel. Ten years later, in 939, Boleslav repented, converted, and apparently transferred his brother's remains to this very spot. Charles, who was keen to promote the cult of Wenceslas in order to cement his own Luxembourgeois dynasty's rather tenuous claim to the Bohemian throne, had Peter Parler build the present chapel on top of the original grave; the lion's head **door-ring** set into the north door is said to be the one to which Václav clung before being killed. The chapel's rich, almost Byzantine decoration is like the inside of a jewel casket: the gilded walls are inlaid with over 1372 semiprecious Bohemian stones (corresponding to the year of its creation), set around ethereal fourteenth-century frescoes of the *New Heavenly Jerusalem*, while the tragedy of Wenceslas unfolds above in the later paintings of the Litoměřice school.

Good King Wenceslas

As it turns out, there's very little substance to the story related in the nine-teenth-century Christmas carol, *Good King Wenceslas*, by J. M. Neale, itself a reworking of the medieval carol *Tempus adest floridum*. For a start, **Václav** was only a duke, and never a king (though he did become a saint); the St Agnes fountain, by which "yonder peasant dwelt" wasn't built until the thirteenth century; in fact, he wasn't even that "good", except in comparison with the rest of his family.

Born in 907, Václav inherited his title at the tender age of thirteen. His Christian grandmother, Ludmilla, was appointed regent in preference to Dragomíra, his pagan mother, who murdered Ludmilla in a fit of jealousy the following year. On coming of age in 925, Václav became duke in his own right, and took a vow of celibacy, intent on promoting Christianity throughout the dukedom. Even so, the local Christians didn't take to him, and when he began making conciliatory overtures to the neighbouring Germans, and invited German missionaries to Bohemia, they persuaded his pagan younger brother, Boleslav the Cruel, to do away with him. On September 20, 929, a good three months before the Feast of Stephen, Václav was stabbed to death by Boleslav at the entrance to a church just outside Prague.

Though a dazzling testament to the golden age of Charles IV's reign, it's not just the chapel's artistic merit which draws visitors. A door in the south wall gives access to a staircase leading to the coronation chamber (only rarely open to the public) which houses the **Bohemian crown jewels**, including the gold crown of Saint Wenceslas, studded with some of the largest sapphires in the world. Closed to the public since 1867, the door is secured by seven different locks, the keys kept by seven different people, starting with the president himself – like the seven seals of the holy scroll from *Revelations*. The tight security is partly to prevent any pretenders to the throne trying on the headgear, an allegedly fatal act: the Nazi *Reichsprotektor* Reinhard Heydrich tried it, only to suffer the inevitable consequences (see p.130). Replicas of the crown jewels are on display in the Lobkovic Palace (see p.56).

The chancel

Having sated yourself on Wenceslas Chapel, buy a ticket from the nearby box office, and head off to the north choir aisle – the only place where you can currently enter the **chancel**. Following the ambulatory round, make sure you check out the high-relief seventeenth-century wooden panelling between the arcading on the right, which glories in the flight of the "Winter King" (he's depicted crossing the Charles Bridge), following the disastrous Battle of Bílá hora. The remains of various early Czech rulers are scattered throughout the side chapels, most notably those of Přemysl Otakar I and II, in the Saxon Chapel (the fifth one along), whose limestone tombs are the work of Peter Parler and his workshop; you can also pay your respects to Rudolf II's internal organs buried in the chapel vault.

Slap bang in the middle of the ambulatory, close to the Saxon Chapel, is the perfect Baroque answer to the medieval chapel of sv Václav, the **Tomb of St John of Nepomuk**, plonked here in 1736. It's a work of grotesque excess, designed by Fischer von Erlach's son, and sculpted in solid silver with free-flying angels holding up the heavy drapery of the canopy. Where Charles sought to promote Wenceslas as the nation's preferred saint, the Jesuits, with Habsburg backing, replaced him with another Czech martyr, John of Nepomuk (Jan Nepomucký), who had been arrested, tortured, and then thrown – bound and gagged – off the Charles Bridge in 1383 on the orders of Václav IV, allegedly for refusing to divulge the secrets of the queen's confession. A cluster of stars was said to have appeared over the spot where he drowned, hence the halo of stars on every subsequent portrayal of the saint.

The Jesuits, in their efforts to get him canonized, exhumed his corpse and produced what they claimed to be his tongue – alive and licking, so to speak (it was in fact his very dead brain). In 1729, he duly became a saint, and, on the lid of the tomb, back-to-back with the martyr himself, a cherub points to his severed tongue, sadly no longer the "real" thing. The more prosaic reason for John of Nepomuk's death was simply that he was caught up in a dispute between the archbishop and the king over the appointment of the abbot of Kladruby, and backed the wrong side. Tortured along with several other priests, only John was physically unable to sign a document denying he had been tortured. The Vatican finally admitted this in 1961, some 232 years after his canonization.

Between the tomb of St John of Nepomuk and the chapel of sv Václav, Bohemia's one and only Polish ruler, Vladislav Jagiello, built a **Royal Oratory**, connected to his bedroom in the Royal Palace by a covered bridge. The balustrade sports heraldic shields from Bohemia's (at the time) quite considerable lands, while the hanging vault is smothered in an unusual branch-like decoration, courtesy of Benedikt Ried. To the left, the statue of a miner is a reminder of just how important Kutná Hora's silver mines were in funding such artistic ventures.

The Imperial Mausoleum and the Royal Crypt

At the centre of the choir, within a fine Renaissance grill, cherubs irreverently lark about on the sixteenth-century marble **Imperial Mausoleum**, commissioned by Rudolf II and containing his grandfather Ferdinand I, his Polish grandmother, and his father Maximilian II, the first Habsburgs to wear the Bohemian crown. Rudolf himself rests beneath them, in one of the two pewter coffins in the somewhat cramped **Royal Crypt** (the entrance is beside the Royal Oratory); his coffin features yet more cherubs, while the other one contains the remains of Maria Amelia, daughter of the Empress Maria Theresa. A good number of other Czech kings and queens are buried here, too, reinterred this century in incongruously modern

1930s sarcophagi, among them the Hussite King George of Poděbrady, Charles IV and, sharing a single sarcophagus, all four of his wives.

The third courtyard and Royal Palace

The rest of the **third courtyard** (třetí nádvoří) reveals yet more Pacassi plasterwork, the monotony broken by just a couple of distractions. A fourteenth-century **bronze statue**, executed by a couple of Transylvanian Saxon sculptors, depicts a rather diminutive Saint George astride a disturbingly large horse (actually two hundred years younger than the rest of the ensemble), slaying an extremely puny dragon; the original is in the Convent of sv Jiří (see below). Apart from Plečnik's polished granite **monolith**, an unfinished work celebrating the tenth anniversary of the foundation of Czechoslovakia, the only other reason for hanging about in the third courtyard is to admire Parler's **Zlatá brána** (Golden Gate), decorated with a multicoloured fourteenth-century mosaic of the *Last Judgement*, which was, at the time of writing, chronically overdue for its regular five-year cleanup operation.

There's a post office in the west wing of the third courtyard, open daily 8am–8pm

The Royal Palace

Across the courtyard from the Zlatá brána, the **Royal Palace** (Královský palác) was home to the princes and kings of Bohemia from the eleventh to the sixteenth centuries. It's a sandwich of royal apartments, built one on top of the other by successive generations, but left largely unfurnished and unused for the last three hundred years. The original Romanesque palace of Soběslav I now forms the cellars of the present building, above which Charles IV built his own Gothic chambers; these days you enter at the third and top floor, built at the end of the fifteenth century.

Immediately past the antechamber (which now serves as a ticket office) is the bare expanse of the massive **Vladislav Hall** (Vladislavský sál), the work of Benedikt Ried, the German mason appointed by Vladislav Jagiello as his court architect. It displays some remarkable, sweeping rib-vaulting which forms floral patterns on the ceiling, the petals reaching almost to the floor. It was here that the early Bohemian kings were elected, and since Masaryk in 1918 every president has been sworn into office in the hall – the last ceremony took place on December 29, 1989, when Václav Havel took office. In medieval times, the hall was also used for banquets and jousting tournaments, which explains the ramp-like **Riders' Staircase** in the north wing (now the exit).

From the southwest corner of the hall, you can gain access to the Ludvík Wing. The rooms themselves are pretty uninspiring but the furthest one, the **Bohemian Chancellery**, was the scene of Prague's **second defenestration**. After almost two centuries of uneasy coexistence between Catholics and Protestants, matters came to a head over the succession to the throne of the Habsburg archduke Ferdinand, a notoriously intolerant Catholic. On May 23, 1618, a posse of more than 100 Protestant nobles, led by Count Thurn, marched to the Chancellery for a showdown with Jaroslav Bořita z Martinic and Vilém Slavata, the two Catholic governors appointed by Ferdinand I. After a "stormy discussion", the two councillors (and their personal secretary, Filip Fabricius) were thrown out of the window. As a contemporary historian recounted: "No mercy was granted them and they were both thrown dressed in their cloaks with their rapiers and decoration head-first out of the western window into a moat beneath the palace. They loudly screamed *ach*, *ach*, *oweh!* and attempted to hold on to the narrow window-ledge, but Thurn beat their knuckles with the hilt of his sword until they were both obliged to let go." There's some controversy about the exact window from which they were ejected, although it's agreed that they survived to tell the tale, landing in a medieval dung heap below, and – so the story goes – precipitating the Thirty Years' War.

Details of the first defenestration are on p.130.

At the far end of the hall, to the right, there's a **viewing platform**, from which you can contemplate the councillors' trajectory, and enjoy a magnificent view of Prague (at its best in the late afternoon). On the opposite side of the hall, the second door along, to the right of the Riders' Staircase, leads to the **Diet**, laid out as if for a seventeenth-century session: the king on his throne, the archbishop to his right, the judiciary to his left, the nobility facing him – and one representative from the townsfolk (with just one vote), confined to the gallery by the window.

At the far end of the hall, you can look down onto **All Saints' Chapel** (Všech svatých), which Parler added to Charles IV's palace, but which had to be rebuilt after the 1541 fire, and has since been Baroquified. Its only point of interest is the remains of the Czech saint, Procopius, which are contained within an eighteenth-century wooden tomb along the north wall. A quick canter down the Riders' Staircase takes you to the **Gothic and Romanesque chambers** of the palace, equally bare, but containing a couple of interesting models showing the castle at various stages in its development, plus copies of busts by Peter Parler's workshop, including the architect's remarkable self-portrait; the originals are hidden from view in the triforium of the cathedral.

There are several other, equally atmospheric concert venues in Prague; see p.216 for a more comprehensive list.

The Basilica and Convent of sv Jiří

The only exit from the Royal Palace is via the Riders' Staircase, which deposits you in Jiřské náměstí. Don't be fooled by the uninspiring red Baroque facade of the **Basilica of sv Jiří** (St George) which dominates the square; inside is Prague's most beautiful Romanesque building, meticulously scrubbed clean and restored to recreate something like the honey-coloured stone basilica that replaced the original tenth-century church in 1173. The double

staircase to the chancel is a remarkably harmonious late Baroque
addition and now provides a perfect stage for chamber music
concerts. The choir vault contains a rare Romanesque painting of
the *New Heavenly Jerusalem*, while to the right of the chancel,
only partially visible, are thirteenth-century frescoes of the **burial
chapel of sv Ludmila** (St Ludmilla), grandmother of Saint
Wenceslas, who was strangled by her own daughter in 921 (see box
on p.49), thus becoming Bohemia's first Christian martyr and saint.
There's a replica of the recumbent Ludmilla, which you can inspect
at close quarters, in the south aisle.

The Old Bohemian Art Collection

Next door is Bohemia's first monastery, the **Convent of sv Jiří**,
founded in 973 by Mlada, sister of the Přemyslid prince Boleslav the
Pious, who became its first abbess. Like most of the country's religious institutions, it was closed down and turned into a barracks by
Joseph II in 1782, and now houses the National Gallery's **Old
Bohemian Art Collection**. The exhibition is arranged chronologi-
cally, starting in the crypt with a remarkable collection of Gothic
art, which first flourished here under the patronage of Charles IV.

The **earliest works** are almost exclusively symbolical depictions
of the Madonna and Child, the artists known only by their works
and locations, not by name. Here you'll find – among other things –
the monumental tympanum from the church of Panna Marie Sněžná
in Prague and nine panels from the altarpiece of the Cistercian
monastery at Vyšší Brod. The first named artist is **Master
Theodoric**, who painted over 100 panels for Charles IV's castle at
Karlštejn (see p.177); just six are on display here, their larger-than-
life portraits overflowing onto the edges of the panels.

On the next floor, are paintings by the **Master of Třeboň**,
whose work shows even greater variety of balance and depth,
moving ever closer to realistic portraiture. The following room
contains the stone-carved tympanum from the Týn church (see
p.92) – originally coloured and gilded – with high-relief figures by
Peter Parler's workshop, whose mastery of composition and depth
heralded a new stage in the development of Bohemian art. The last
room on this floor is devoted to a series of superb woodcuts by
Master I. P., including an incredibly detailed scene *Christ the
Redeemer before Death*, a skeleton whose entrails are in the
process of being devoured by a frog.

The transition from this to the next floor, where you are immediately thrown into the overtly sensual and erotic **Mannerist paintings** of Rudolf II's reign, is something of a shock. Few works survive
from Rudolf's superlative collection, but make sure you check out
Paulus Roy's clever optical illusion, *The Portrait of Three
Emperors*, and Josef Heintz's riotous orgy in his *Last Judgement*.
The rest of the gallery is given over to Czech **Baroque art**, as
pursued by the likes of Bohemia's Karel Skréta and Petr Brandl,

*The Old
Bohemian Art
Collection is
open Tues–Sun
10am–6pm.
Entry is not
covered by the
general castle
admission;
tickets are
available from
the ticket office
inside the
cloisters.*

whose paintings and sculptures fill chapels and churches across the Czech Lands. Michael Leopold Willmann's portrait of St Bartholomew being skinned alive is disturbingly gruesome, but aside from the works of Jan Kupecký and the statues of Matthias Bernhard Braun and Ferdinand Maximilian Brokof, this section is unlikely to hold your attention for long.

Zlatá ulička and the castle towers

Around the corner from the convent is the **Zlatá ulička** (Golden Lane), a seemingly blind alley of miniature sixteenth-century cottages in dolly-mixture colours, built for the 24 members of Rudolf II's castle guard, though the lane allegedly takes its name from the goldsmiths who followed (and modified the buildings) a century later. By the nineteenth century, it had become a kind of palace slum, attracting artists and craftsmen, its two most famous inhabitants being Jaroslav Seifert, the Czech Nobel prize-winning poet, and Franz Kafka. Kafka's youngest sister, Ottla, rented no. 22, and during a creative period in the winter of 1916 he came here in the evenings to write short stories. Finally, in 1951, the Communists kicked out the last residents and turned most of the houses into souvenir shops for tourists.

At no. 12, at the eastern end of Zlatá ulička, is a throughway to the **Černá věž**, (Black Tower), standing at the top of the Staré zamecké schody, which leads down to Malostranská metro. At the other end of the lane, at no. 24, you can climb a flight of stairs to the **Obranná chodba** (Defence corridor), which is lined with wooden shields, suits of armour and period costumes. The **Bílá věž** (white tower) at the western end of the corridor, was the city's main prison from Rudolf's reign onwards. Edward Kelley, the English alchemist, is alleged to have poisoned himself here, having been locked up by Rudolf for failing to turn base metal into gold, while the emperor's treasurer hanged himself by his chain of office, after being accused of embezzlement. There's a reconstructed torture chamber on the first floor, and in the shop on the floor above you can kit yourself out as a medieval knight with replica swords and maces, not to mention chastity belts and various torture instruments.

In the opposite direction, the corridor leads to **Daliborka** (April–Oct 9am–5pm), the castle tower dedicated to its first prisoner, the young Czech noble, Dalibor, accused of supporting a peasants' revolt at the beginning of the fifteenth century. According to Prague legend, he learnt to play the violin while imprisoned here, and his playing could be heard all over the castle – a tale that provided material for Smetana's opera, *Dalibor* – until his execution in 1498.

To get inside **Mihulka**, the **powder** tower which once served as the workshop of gunsmith and bell-founder Tomáš Jaroš, you'll have to backtrack to Vikářská, the street which runs along the north of

Rudolf II

In 1583 the Habsburg Emperor, **Rudolf II**, switched the imperial court
from Vienna to Prague. This was to be the first and last occasion in which
Prague would hold centre stage in the Habsburg Empire, and as such is
seen as something of a second golden age for the city (the first being
under Holy Roman Emperor Charles IV). Bad-tempered, paranoid and
probably insane, Rudolf had little interest in the affairs of state – instead,
he holed up in the Hrad and indulged his own personal passions of
alchemy, astrology and art. Thus, Rudolfine Prague played host to an
impressive array of international artists including the idiosyncratic
Giuseppe Arcimboldo, whose surrealist portraits were composed entirely
of fruit and vegetables. The astrologers, Johannes Kepler and Tycho de
Brahe, were summoned to Rudolf's court to chart the planetary movements and assuage Rudolf's superstitions. And the English alchemists,
Edward Kelley and John Dee, were employed in an attempt to transmute
base metal into gold, and discover the secret of the philosopher's stone.

Accompanied by his pet African lion, Otakar, Rudolf spent less and less
time in public, hiding out in the Hrad, where he "loved to paint, weave and
dabble in inlaying and watchmaking", according to modern novelist Angelo
Maria Ripellino. With the Turks rapidly approaching the gates of Vienna,
Rudolf spent his days amassing exotic curios for his strange and vast *Kunst-
und Wunderkammer*, which contained such items as "two nails from
Noah's Ark...a lump of clay out of which God formed Adam...and large
mandrake roots in the shape of little men reclining on soft velvet cushions in
small cases resembling doll beds". He refused to marry, though he sired
numerous bastards, since he had been warned in a horoscope that a legitimate heir would rob him of the throne. He was also especially wary of the
numerous religious orders who inhabited Prague at the time, having been
warned in another horoscope that he would be killed by a monk. In the end,
he was relieved of his throne by his younger brother, Matthias, in 1611, and
died the following year the day after the death of his beloved pet lion.

the cathedral. The powder tower's name comes from the lamprey
(*mihule*), an eel-like fish supposedly bred here for royal consumption, though it's actually more noteworthy as the place where
Rudolf's team of alchemists (including Kelley) were put to work
trying to discover the philosopher's stone. Despite its colourful
history, the exhibition currently on display within the tower is dull,
with just a pair of furry slippers and hat belonging to Ferdinand I to
get excited about.

The Toy Museum and Lobkovic Palace

If you continue east down Jiřská, which runs parallel with Zlatá
ulička, you'll come to a courtyard on the left which hides the newly
established **Toy Museum** (Muzeum hrašek). With brief, Czech-only
captions and unimaginative displays, this is a disappointing new
venture, which fails to live up to its potential. The succession of
glass cabinets contains everything from toy cars and motorbikes to
robots and even Barbie dolls, but there are only a few buttons for

*The Toy Museum
is open
Tues–Sun
9.30am–5.30pm;
admission
requires a
separate ticket,
available from
the ticket office
on the ground
floor.*

younger kids to press, and unless you're really lost for something to do, you could happily skip the whole enterprise.

The Lobkovic Palace

The hotchpotch historical collection in the **Lobkovic Palace**, on the opposite side of Jiřská, is marginally more rewarding, despite the ropey English text provided. The exhibition actually begins on the top floor, though by no means all the objects on display deserve attention; the following is a quick rundown of some of the more memorable exhibits. The first cabinet worth more than a passing nod is in the second room, and contains copies of the Bohemian crown jewels (the originals are hidden away above the Chapel of sv Václav in the cathedral). Next door, in the Hussite room, there's an interesting sixteenth-century carving of *The Last Supper*, originally an altarpiece from the Bethlehem Chapel, while, further on, Petr Vok's splendid funereal shield, constructed out of wood covered with cloth shot through with gold, hangs on the wall.

The Lobkovic Palace is open Tues–Sun 9am–5pm; admission requires a seperate ticket available from the ticket office on the ground floor.

All things post-1620 and pre-1848 are displayed in the six rooms downstairs, starting with the sword of the famous Prague executioner, Jan Mydlář, who could lop a man's head off with just one chop, a skill he demonstrated on 24 of the 27 Protestant leaders who were executed on Staroměstské náměstí in 1621; Mydlář's invoice covering labour and expenses is displayed beside the sword. Several rooms on are some more unusual exhibits – three contemporary scaled-down models of eighteenth-century altars, and further on still, three carved marionettes from later that century, among the oldest surviving in Bohemia.

The South Gardens

For recuperation and a superlative view over the rest of Prague – not to mention a chance to inspect some of Plečnik's quirky additions to the castle – head for the **South Gardens** (Jižní zahrady), accessible via Plečnik's copper-canopied Bull Staircase on the south side of the third courtyard. The spiral steps descend to the Garden on the Ramparts (Zahrada na valech), originally laid out in the sixteenth century, but thoroughly remodelled in the 1920s by Josip Plečnik; opposite the staircase he added an observation terrace and colonnaded pavilion, below which is an earlier eighteenth-century music pavilion (hudební pavilón). Two obelisks further east record the arrival of Slavata and Martinic after their defenestration from the royal palace above (see p.51); beyond them lies yet another of Plečnik's observation pavilions. In the opposite direction, beyond the Baroque fountain lies the smaller Paradise Garden (Rajská zahrada), on whose lawn Plečnik plonked a forty-ton granite basin suspended on two small blocks. At the far end of the garden, a quick slog up the monumental staircase will bring you out onto Hradčanské náměstí.

The South Gardens are open May–Oct Tues–Sun 10am–6pm.

Across the Prašný most

Before exploring the rest of Hradčany, though, it's worth making a
short detour beyond the official limits of the castle walls. From the
second courtyard, pass through the north gate and across the
Prašný most (Powder Bridge), first erected in the sixteenth century
to connect the newly established Royal Gardens with the Hrad (the
original wooden structure has long since been replaced). Below lies
the wooded **Jelení příkop** (Stag Ditch), once used by the Habsburgs
for growing figs and lemons, and storing game for the royal hunts,
but now populated only by bored castle guards.

Beyond the bridge, to the left, Jean-Baptiste Mathey's plain
French Baroque **Jízdárna** (Riding School) has been converted into
an open-plan art gallery, which currently serves as the city's main
exhibition space for twentieth-century Czech art. The temporary
installations are consistently impressive, but any hopes of a permanent collection will have to wait until the new museum in Holešovice
is up and running (see p.153).

*The Jízdárna is
open Tues–Sun
10am–6pm.*

The Royal Gardens and Belvedere

Opposite the Jízdárna is the entrance to the **Royal Gardens**
(Královská zahrada), founded by Emperor Ferdinand I in the 1530s
on the site of a former vineyard. Burned down by the Saxons and
Swedes, and blown up by the Prussians, the gardens were only
saved from French attack by the payment of thirty pineapples.
Today, this is one of the best-kept gardens in the capital, with fully
functioning fountains and immaculately cropped lawns.
Consequently, it's a very popular spot, though more a place for
admiring the azaleas and almond trees than lounging around on the
grass. It was here that tulips brought from Turkey were first accli-
matized to Europe, before being exported to the Netherlands, and
every spring there's an impressive, disciplined crop.

*The Royal
Gardens are
open May–Oct
Tues–Sun
10am–5.45pm.*

At the entrance to the gardens is the **Lví dvůr** (Lion's Court),
now a restaurant but originally built by Rudolf II to house his
private zoo, which included leopards, lynxes, bears, wolves and
lions, all of whom lived in heated cages to protect them from the
Prague winter. Rudolf was also responsible for the Renaissance ball-
game court, known as the **Míčovna** (open to the public for classical
music concerts only), built into the south terrace and tattooed with
sgraffito by his court architect Bonifaz Wolmut. If you look carefully
at the top row of figures on the facade, one of them is holding a
hammer and sickle, thoughtfully added by restorers in the 1950s.
Incidentally the guarded ochre building to the right of the Míčovna,
the **Zahradní dům**, is one of Havel's presidential pads, built as a
summer house by Dientzenhofer only to be destroyed during the
Prussian bombardment of 1757. It was later restored by Pavel Janák
who added the building's two modern wings on a post-war whim of
the ill-fated President Beneń.

*The Belvedere
is open
year-round
Tues–Sun
10am–6pm.*

*See p.150 for
details of the
Chotkovy sady,
beyond the
Belvedere.*

At the end of the gardens is Prague's most celebrated Renaissance legacy, the **Belvedere** or Queen Anne's Summer Palace (Belvedér or Letohrádek královny Anny), a delicately arcaded summerhouse topped by an inverted copper ship's hull, built by Ferdinand I for his wife, Anne. It was designed by the Genoese architect Paolo della Stella, one of a number of Italian masons who settled in Prague in the sixteenth century; to inspect it at close quarters, however, you must leave the Royal Gardens and head down Mariánské hradby. Unlike the gardens, the Belvedere is open all year and is now used for contemporary exhibitions, the artists chosen by the president himself. At the centre of the palace's miniature formal garden is the **Singing Fountain** (Zpívající fontána), built shortly after the palace and named for the musical sound of the drops of water falling in the metal bowls below – you have to stick your ears up close to get the full effect. From the garden terrace, you also have an unrivalled view of Prague Castle's finest treasure – the cathedral.

From Hradčanské náměstí to the Strahov Monastery

The monumental scale and appearance of the rest of Hradčany, outside the castle, is a direct result of the **great fire of 1541**, which swept up from Malá Strana and wiped out most of the old dwelling places belonging to the serfs, tradesmen, clergy and masons who had settled here in the Middle Ages. With the Turks at the gates of Vienna, the Habsburg nobility were more inclined to pursue their major building projects in Prague instead, and, following the Battle of Bílá hora in 1620, the palaces of the exiled (or executed) Protestant nobility were up for grabs too. The newly ensconced Catholic aristocrats were keen to spend some of their expropriated wealth, and over the next two centuries, they turned Hradčany into a grand architectural showpiece. As the Turkish threat subsided, the political focus of the empire gradually shifted back to Vienna and the building spree stopped. For the last two hundred years, Hradčany has been frozen in time, and, two world wars on, its buildings have survived better than those of any other central European capital.

Hradčanské náměstí

Hradčanské náměstí fans out from the castle gates, surrounded by the oversized palaces of the old Catholic nobility. For the most part, it's a tranquil space that's overlooked by the tour groups marching through, intent on the Hrad. The one spot everyone heads for is the ramparts in the southeastern corner, which allow an unrivalled view over the reddish-brown rooftops of Malá Strana, past the famous dome and tower of the church of sv Mikuláš and beyond, to the spires of Staré Město. Only the occasional bookish Praguer or tired traveller makes use of the square's central green patch, which is marked by a giant green wrought-iron lamppost decked with eight separate lamps – one of the few that have survived from the 1860s.

From Hradčanské náměstí to the Strahov Monastery

Until the great fire of 1541, the square was the hub of Hradčany, lined with medieval shops and stalls but with no real market as such. After the fire, the developers moved in; the **Martinic Palace** at no. 8 was one of the more modest newcomers, built in 1620 by one of the councillors who survived the second defenestration. Its rich sgraffito decoration, which continues in the inner courtyard, was only discovered during restoration work in the 1970s, and was part of the reason it was featured as Mozart's house in the film *Amadeus*. Mathey's rather cold, formal **Toscana Palace** (now in the hands of the Foreign Ministry) was built on a more ambitious scale, replacing the row of butchers' shops that once filled the west end of the square.

The powerful Lobkovic family replaced seven houses on the south side of the square with the over-the-top sgraffitoed pile at no. 2, known as the **Schwarzenberg Palace** after its last aristocratic owners (the present-day count, Karl, is one of Havel's closest advisers). For a brief period, it belonged to the Rožmberks, whose last in line, Petr Vok, held the infamous banquet at which the Danish astronomer Tycho de Brahe overdrank his fill, and staggered off with a burst bladder to his house in Nový Svět, where he died five days later. All of which makes the **Museum of Military History** (Vojenské muzeum), which now occupies the palace, seem considerably less gruesome. The Czechs have a long history of supplying top-class weaponry to world powers (most recently in the form of Semtex to the Libyans and tanks to the Syrians). It's no coincidence that one of the two Czech words to have made it into the English language is pistol (*pistole* in Czech). Among the endless uniforms and instruments of death – all of which are pre-1914 – you'll find an early Colt 45 and the world's largest mortar (courtesy of Škoda). Prague's more modern military collections are at the Military Museum on Žižkov Hill (see p.148).

The Museum of Military History is open May–Oct Tues–Sun 9.30am–4.30pm.

The adjacent **Salm Palace** (Salmovský palác), at no. 1, was another Schwarzenberg pile, which served as the Swedish Embassy until the 1970s when the dissident writer Pavel Kohout took refuge there. Frustrated in their attempts to force him out, the Communists closed the embassy down and left it to rot. It's currently under repair in order to transform it into a VIP hotel, literally on the castle's doorstep. On the opposite side of the square, just outside the castle gates, stands the sumptuous **Archbishop's Palace** (Archbiskupský palác), seat of the archbishop of Prague since the beginning of the Roman Catholic church's suzerainty over the Czechs, following the Battle of Bílá hora. The Rococo exterior only hints at the even more extravagant furnishings inside.

The Archbishop's Palace is open to the public only on Maundy Thursday – the Thursday before Easter.

Šternberk Palace – the European Art Collection

A passage down the side of the Archbishop's Palace leads to the early eighteenth-century **Šternberk Palace** (Šternberský palác), now the main building of the National Gallery, housing its **European Art Collection** (ie non-Czech) – which, though rich enough for most tastes, is relatively modest in comparison with those of other European capitals. The collection is divided into three sections: the first floor contains icons and Italian, German, Dutch and Flemish masters from the fourteenth to the sixteenth centuries; the second floor covers the rest of European art up to the twentieth century; and the final, most popular section is the "French Art" collection on the ground floor of the north wing, across the courtyard from the entrance.

The Šternberk Palace is open Tues–Sun 10am–6pm.

The **first floor** kicks off with Florentine religious art, most notably a series of exquisite miniature triptychs by Bernardo Daddi. Also worth checking out are the side rooms containing Orthodox icons from the Balkans to northern Russia. The section ends with a series of canvases by Breughel the Younger, and *Haymaking* by Breughel the Elder.

The **second floor** contains one of the most prized paintings in the whole collection, the *Feast of the Rosary* by Albrecht Dürer, depicting, among others, the Virgin Mary, the Pope, the Holy Roman Emperor, and even a self-portrait of Dürer himself (top right). This was one of Rudolf's most prized aquisitions (he was an avid Dürer fan), which was transported on foot across the Alps to Prague (he didn't trust wheeled transport with such a precious object). There are other outstanding works here, too: a Rembrandt, a Canaletto of the Thames, two richly-coloured Bronzino portraits, a whole series by the Saxon master, Lucas Cranach – including the striking, almost minimalist *Portrait of an Old Man* – and a mesmerizing *Head of Christ* by El Greco. Rubens' colossal *Murder of St Thomas* is difficult to miss, with its pink-buttocked cherubs hovering over the bloody scene. Nearby, there's a wonderful portrait of an arrogant "young gun" named Jasper by Frans Hals, followed by various Dutch masters from the eighteenth century.

At this point, you are suddenly propelled straight into the world of **twentieth-century art**, beginning with Klimt's mischievous *Virgins*, a mass of naked bodies and tangled limbs painted out in psychedelic colours. Although none of the artists here is Czech, many of them had close connections with Bohemia: Egon Schiele's mother came from Český Krumlov, the subject of a tiny autumnal canvas; and the handful of works by Oskar Kokoschka date from his brief stay here in the 1930s, when the political temperature got too hot in Vienna. Perhaps the most influential artist on show is Edvard Munch, whose one canvas, *Dance at the Seaside*, hardly does justice to the considerable effect he had on a generation of Czech artists after his celebrated exhibition in Prague in 1905.

By far the most popular section of the gallery is the "French" art section across the courtyard on the ground floor, featuring anyone of note who hovered around Paris in the fifty years from 1880 onwards. There are few of the artists' famous masterpieces here, but it's all high-quality stuff. Among those represented are Gauguin, Monet, Pissarro, Seurat, Van Gogh, Cézanne, Toulouse-Lautrec, Dufy and Matisse. Several works by Rodin are scattered around the room, particularly appropriate given his ecstatic reception by Czech sculptors at the beginning of this century, following his Prague exhibition in 1902. And there's a surprisingly good collection of Picassos, including several paintings and sculptures from his crucial early Cubist period (1907–08). Four of his works – worth an estimated thirty million dollars – were stolen in the summer of 1991 and only recently recovered, illustrating a problem common to all east European galleries since the opening up of the borders. Before you leave the gallery, check out the gardens, which harbour the odd sculpture and provide a great picnic spot in summer.

From Hradčanské náměstí to the Strahov Monastery

Nový Svět to the Loreto Chapel

At the other end of Hradčanské náměstí, Kanovnická heads off towards the northwest corner of Hradčany. Nestling in this shallow dip, Nový Svět (meaning "New World", though not Dvořák's) provides a glimpse of life on a totally different scale from Hradčanské náměstí. Similar in many ways to the Zlatá ulička in the Hrad, this cluster of brightly coloured cottages, which curls around the corner into Černínská, is all that's left of Hradčany's medieval slums, painted up and sanitized in the eighteenth and nineteenth centuries. Despite having all the same ingredients for mass tourist appeal as Zlatá ulička, it remains remarkably undisturbed, save for a few swish wine bars, and *Gambra*, a surrealist art gallery at Černínská 5 (Wed–Sun noon–6pm), which sells works by, among others, the renowned Czech animator, Jan Švankmajer, and his wife Eva, who live nearby.

Up the hill from Nový Svět, Loretánské náměstí is dominated by the phenomenal 135-metre-long facade of the Černín Palace (Černínský palác), decorated with thirty Palladian half-columns and supported by a swathe of diamond-pointed rustication. For all its grandeur – it's the largest palace in Prague, for the sake of which two whole streets were demolished – it's a pretty brutal building, commissioned in the 1660s by Count Humprecht Jan Černín, one-time imperial ambassador to Venice and a man of monumental self-importance. After quarrelling with the master of Italian Baroque, Giovanni Bernini, and disagreeing with Prague's own Carlo Lurago, Count Černín settled on Francesco Caratti as his architect, only to have the finished building panned by critics as a tasteless mass of stone. The grandiose plans, which were nowhere near completion when the count died, nearly bankrupted future generations of

The Černín Palace is not open to the public.

Černíns, who were eventually forced to sell the palace in 1851 to the Austrian state, which converted it into military barracks.

Since the First Republic, the palace has housed the Ministry of Foreign Affairs, and during the war it was, for a while, the Nazi *Reichsprotektor*'s residence. On March 10, 1948, it was the scene of Prague's third – and most widely mourned – defenestration. Only days after the Communist coup, **Jan Masaryk**, the only son of the founder of the Republic, and the last non-Communist in Gottwald's cabinet, plunged forty-five feet to his death from the top-floor bathroom window of the palace. Whether it was suicide (he had been suffering from bouts of depression, partly induced by the country's political path) or murder will probably never be satisfactorily resolved, but for most people Masaryk's death cast a dark shadow over the newly established regime.

The Loreto

The facade of the **Loreto** (Loreta), immediately opposite the Černín Palace, was built by the Dientzenhofers, a Bavarian family of architects, in the early part of the eighteenth century, and is the perfect antidote to Caratti's humourless monster. It's all hot flourishes and twirls, topped by a tower which lights up like a Chinese lantern at night – and by day clanks out the hymn *We Greet Thee a Thousand Times* on its 27 Dutch bells.

The Loreto is open Tues–Sun 9am–12.15pm & 1–4.30pm.

The facade and the cloisters, which were provided a century earlier to shelter pilgrims from the elements, are, in fact, just the outer casing for the focus of the complex, the **Santa Casa**, founded by Kateřina Lobkovic in 1626 and smothered in a mantle of stucco depicting the building's miraculous transportation from the Holy Land. Legend has it that the Santa Casa (Mary's home in Nazareth), under threat from the heathen Turks, was transported by a host of angels to a small village in Dalmatia and from there, via a number of brief stopoffs, to a small laurel grove (*lauretum* in Latin, hence *Loreto*) in northern Italy. News of the miracle spread across the Catholic lands, prompting a spate of copy-cat shrines, and during the Counter-Reformation, the cult was actively encouraged in an attempt to broaden the popular appeal of Catholicism. The Prague Loreto is one of fifty to be built in the Czech Lands, each of the shrines following an identical design, with pride of place given to a lime-wood statue of the *Black Madonna and Child*, encased in silver.

The Lobkovic family gave Prague its other famous pilgrimage shrine, the pražské Jezulátko, see p.76.

Behind the Santa Casa, the Dientzenhofers built the much larger **Church of the Nativity** (Kostel narození Páně), packed with some fairly gruesome Baroque kitsch. On either side of the main altar are glass cabinets containing the (fully clothed) skeletons of Saint Felicissimus and Saint Marcia, and next to them, paintings of Saint Apolena – who had her teeth smashed in during her martyrdom and is now invoked for toothache – and Saint Agatha, carrying her severed breasts on a dish. Last but not least of the weird and wonderful saints in Loreto is Saint Wilgefortis, a painting of whom is in the final chapel of the cloisters. Daughter of the King of Portugal, she was due to marry the King of Sicily, despite having taken a vow of virginity. God intervened and she grew a beard, whereupon the King of Sicily broke off the marriage and her father had her crucified. Wilgefortis thus became the patron saint of unhappily married women, and is traditionally depicted bearded on the cross.

You can get some idea of the Santa Casa's serious financial backing in the **treasury** (situated on the first floor of the west wing), much ransacked over the years but still stuffed full of gold. The padded ceilings and low lighting create a kind of giant jewellery box for the master exhibit, a tasteless Viennese silver monstrance studded with 6222 diamonds, standing over three feet high and weighing nearly two stone. It was constructed in 1699 to a design by Fischer von Erlach, on the posthumous orders of one of the Kolovrat family who had made the Loreto sole heir to her fortune.

From Hradčanské náměstí to the Strahov Monastery

The Strahov Monastery

Continuing westwards from Loretánské náměstí, Pohořelec, an arcaded street-cum-square, leads to the chunky remnants of the zigzag eighteenth-century fortifications that mark the edge of the old city, as defined by Charles IV back in the fourteenth century. Close by, to the left, is the **Strahov Monastery** (Strahovský klášter), founded in 1140 by the Premonstratensian order. Strahov was one of the lucky few to escape Joseph II's 1783 dissolution of the monasteries, a feat it managed by declaring itself a scholarly institution – the monks had, in fact, amassed one of the finest libraries in Bohemia. It continued to function until shortly after the Communists took power, when, along with all other religious establishments, it was closed down and most of its inmates thrown into prison; following the happy events of 1989, the monks have returned.

The Baroque entrance to the monastery is topped by a statue of Saint Norbert, founder of the Premonstratensian order, whose relics were brought here in 1627. Just inside the cobbled outer courtyard is a tiny deconsecrated church built by Rudolf II and dedicated to **sv Roch**, protector against plagues, one of which had very nearly rampaged through Prague in 1599; it's now a private art gallery. The other church in this peaceful little courtyard is the still functioning monastery church, first built back in the twelfth century, and given its last remodelling in Baroque times by Jean-Baptiste Mathey.

It's the monastery's two libraries that are the real reason for visiting Strahov, however; the entrance for both is to the right as you enter the outer courtyard. The first library you come to is the later of the two, the **Philosophical Hall** (Filosofický sál), built in some haste in the 1780s, in order to accommodate the books and bookcases from Louka, a Premonstratensian monastery in Moravia

The Philosophical and Theological halls are open Tues–Sun 9am–5pm.

that failed to escape Joseph's decree. The walnut bookcases are so tall they touch the library's lofty ceiling, which is busily decorated with frescoes by the Viennese painter Franz Maulpertsch on *The Struggle of Mankind to Know Real Wisdom*. Don't, whatever you do, miss the collection of curios exhibited in the glass cabinets outside the library, which features shells, turtles, crabs, lobsters, dried-up sea monsters, plastic fruit, moths and even a whale's penis. The other main room is the low-ceilinged **Theological Hall** (Teologický sál), studded with ancient globes, its wedding-cake stucco framing frescoes on a similar theme, executed by one of the monks seventy years earlier.

An archway on the far side of the church contains the ticket office for the **Museum of Czech Literature** (Památník národního písemnictví), housed in the nearby cloisters, across the main court-yard. Since the return of the monks, the museum has put on some superb temporary exhibitions, but most are of limited interest to non-Czech speakers. Of more general interest are the paintings displayed in the **Strahov Gallery** (Strahovská obrazárna), situated above the cloisters. The gallery's collection of religious art, church plate and reliquaries – a mere fraction of the monastery's total – may not be to everyone's taste, but it does contain the odd gem, including a portrait of Rudolf II by his court painter, Hans von Aachen, a portrait of Rembrandt's elderly mother by Gerard Dou and the odd Skréta and Brandl of note.

The Museum of Czech Literature and the Strahov Gallery are open Tues–Sun 9am–5pm.

If you leave the monastery through the narrow doorway in the eastern wall, you enter the gardens and orchards of the **Strahovská zahrada**, from where you can see the whole city in perspective. The gardens form part of Petřín Hill, and the path to the right contours round to the miniature Eiffel Tower (see p.78). Alternatively, you can catch tram #22 to Malostranská metro or the centre of town from outside the main entrance to Strahov.

Chapter 2

Malá Strana

More than anywhere else, **MALÁ STRANA**, the "Little Quarter", conforms to the image of Prague as the ultimate Baroque city. It was here that film director Miloš Forman chose to shoot many of the street scenes in *Amadeus*, judging that its picturesque alleyways resembled Mozart's Vienna more than Vienna itself. And it's true; the streets have changed very little since Mozart walked them, as he often did on his frequent visits to Prague between 1787 and 1791. Unlike Hradčany, its main square is filled with city life during the day; while around practically every corner, narrow cobbled streets lead to some quiet walled garden, the perfect inner-city escape.

Foolishly, many visitors never stray from the well-trodden paths that link the Charles Bridge with Hradčany, thus bypassing most of Malá Strana. This is easy to do, however, given that the whole town takes up a mere 600 square metres of land squeezed in between the river and the Hrad, but it means missing out on one of the greatest pleasures of Malá Strana – casually exploring its hilly eighteenth-century backstreets.

Long before the Přemyslid king, Otakar II, decided to establish a German community here in 1257, a mixture of Jews, merchants and monks had settled on the slopes below the castle. But, as with Hradčany, it was the fire of 1541 – which devastated the entire left bank of the Vltava – and the expulsion of the Protestants after 1620, that together had the greatest impact on the visual and social make-up of the quarter. In place of the old Gothic town, the newly ascendant Catholic nobility built numerous palaces here, though generally without quite the same destructive glee as up in Hradčany. In 1918, the majority of these buildings became home to the foreign embassies of the newly established First Republic, and after 1948 the rest of the real estate was turned into flats to alleviate the postwar housing shortage. The cycle has come full circle again since 1989, and property in Malá Strana – much of it in an extremely bad state of repair – is now among the most sought after in Prague. For the moment, though, the cash-strapped

Some of the city's best restaurants, jazz clubs and most exclusive vinárna are located within Malá Strana, see Chapters 10 and 11 for details.

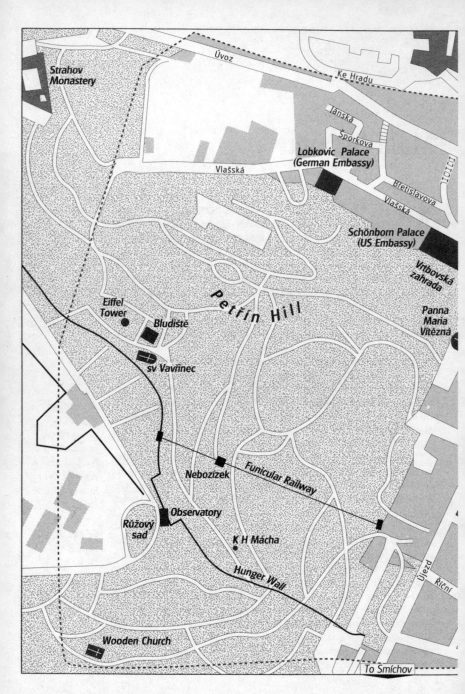

THE CITY: CHAPTER 2

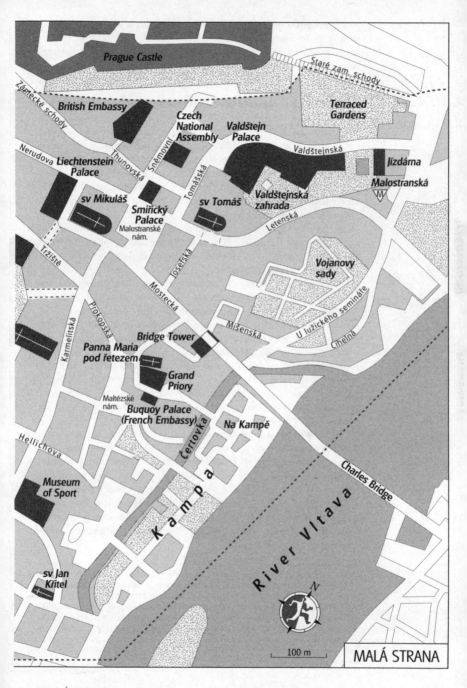

Prague Castle

Staré zam. schody

Zámecké schody

British Embassy

Czech National Assembly

Valdštejn Palace

Terraced Gardens

Valdštejnská

Jízdárna

Nerudova

Thunovská

Sněmovní

Liechtenstein Palace

Tomášská

Malostranská

sv Mikuláš

Smiřický Palace

sv Tomáš

Valdštejnská zahrada

Malostranské nám.

Letenská

Tržiště

Josefská

Vojanovy sady

Mostecká

U lužického semináře

Karmelitská

Prokopská

Mišeňská

Cihelná

Bridge Tower

Panna Maria pod řetezem

Grand Priory

Maltézské nám.

Buquoy Palace (French Embassy)

Čertovka

Na Kampě

Charles Bridge

Hellichova

Museum of Sport

K a m p a

River Vltava

sv Jan Křtel

Z

100 m

MALÁ STRANA

city authorities seem to be shying away from a wholesale sell-out to foreign investors, but the restitution law has brought back many former owners, and the face of Malá Strana is beginning to change once more.

Malostranské náměstí and around

The main focus of Malá Strana has always been the sloping, cobbled **Malostranské náměstí**, which is dominated and divided into two by the church of sv Mikuláš (see below). Trams and cars hurtle across it, regularly dodged by a procession of people – some heading up the hill to the Hrad, others pausing for coffee and cakes at the numerous bars and restaurants hidden in the square's arcades and Gothic vaults. At the time of writing, the most famous (and the most central) café, the **Malostranská kavárna** – established in 1874, and a regular haunt of Kafka, Brod, Werfel and friends in the 1920s – remained closed, due to an unresolved dispute over ownership.

On every side, musty Neoclassical facades line the square, few boasting the colour or grandeur of those of Hradčanské or Staroměstské náměstí. The largest of the developments that replaced the old town houses, the **Liechtenstein Palace** (currently housing a concert venue, art gallery and café), takes up the square's entire west side. Its pleasing frontage hides a history linked to repression: first as the home of Karl von Liechtenstein*, the man who pronounced the death sentence on the 27 Protestant leaders in 1621; then as headquarters for the Swedes during the 1648 siege; and later as home to the Austrian conservative Windischgrätz, scourge of the 1848 revolution.

On the north side, distinguished by its two little turrets, is the **Smiřický Palace** (no. 18), where the Protestant posse met up to decide how to get rid of Emperor Ferdinand's Catholic governors: whether to attack them with daggers, or, as they eventually attempted to do, kill them by chucking them out of the window (see p.51). Sněmovní, the sidestreet which runs alongside the palace's western facade, is the unlikely address of the **Czech National Council** (no. 4), the country's national parliament since Czechoslovakia split in 1993.

---

*Under the law of *restituce* (restitution), all property confiscated by the Communists from 1948 onwards can be claimed back by its former owners. This has dismayed the hundreds whose property was appropriated much earlier, either in 1945, 1938 or, as in the much publicized case of the Liechtensteins, 1918 (when all Habsburg property was nationalized). Prince Hans Adam II has officially requested compensation from the Czech government for the seizure of the Liechtensteins' former properties, which comprise something like 1600 square kilometres of land – ten times the area of present-day Liechtenstein. So far only this palace has been returned to the Grand Duchy and negotiations look likely to continue for some time.

The church of sv Mikuláš

Towering above the square, and the whole of Malá Strana, is the
church of sv Mikuláš (St Nicholas), easily the most magnificent
Baroque building in the city, and one of the last great structures to
be built on the left bank, begun in 1702. For Christoph
Dientzenhofer, a German immigrant from a dynasty of Bavarian
architects, this was his most prestigious commission and is, without doubt, his finest work. For the Jesuits, who were already
ensconced in the adjoining college, it was their most ambitious
project yet in Bohemia, the ultimate symbol of their stranglehold
on the country. When Christoph died in 1722, it was left to his son
Kilian Ignaz Dientzenhofer, along with Kilian's son-in-law,
Anselmo Lurago, to finish the project, which they did with a
masterful flourish, adding the giant green dome and tower – now
among the most characteristic landmarks on Prague's left bank.
Sadly for the Jesuits, they were able to enjoy the finished product
for just twenty years, before they were banished from the
Habsburg Empire in 1773.

Nothing about the relatively plain west facade prepares you
for the overwhelming High Baroque interior. The fresco in the
nave, by Johann Lukas Kracker, is one of the largest paintings in
Europe, covering an area of more than 1500 square metres and
portraying some of the more fanciful miraculous feats of Saint
Nicholas. Apart from his role as Santa Claus, he is depicted here
rescuing sailors in distress, saving women from prostitution by
throwing them bags of gold, and reprieving from death three
unjustly condemned men. Even given the overwhelming propor-

Mozart in Prague

As a young man, Mozart made the first of several visits to Prague in 1787,
staying with his friend and patron Count Thun in what is now the British
Embassy (Thunovská 14). A year earlier, his opera *The Marriage of
Figaro*, which had failed dismally to please the opera snobs in Vienna, had
been given a rapturous reception at Prague's *Nostitz Theater* (now the
Stavovské divadlo, see p.96); and on his arrival in 1787, Mozart was
already flavour of the month, as he wrote in his diary: "Here they talk about
nothing but Figaro. Nothing is played, sung or whistled but Figaro.
Nothing, nothing but Figaro. Certainly a great honour for me!".
Encouraged by this, he chose to premiere his next opera, *Don Giovanni*,
later that year, in Prague rather than Vienna. He arrived with an incomplete score in hand, and wrote the overture at the Dušeks' Bertramka Villa
in Smíchov (see p.159), dedicating it to the "good people of Prague". In
1791, the year of his death, *La Clemenza di Tito*, commissioned for the
coronation of Leopold II as King of Bohemia – and apparently written on
the coach from Vienna to Prague – was premiered here. Although Mozart
was buried in Vienna as a little-known pauper, in Prague 4000 people
turned out for his memorial service, held in Malá Strana's church of sv
Mikuláš to the strains of his *Requiem Mass*.

---

tions of the nave, the dome at the far end of the church, built by the younger Dientzenhofer, remains impressive, thanks, more than anything, to its sheer height. Leering over you as you gaze up at the dome are Ignaz Platzer's four terrifyingly oversized and stern Church Fathers, leaving no doubt as to the gravity of the Jesuit message.

Nerudova

Nerudova was once famous for its pubs, sadly only one of the originals – U kocoura – is left, though it has recently been joined by several new neighbours, see p.202 for details.

The most important of the various streets leading up to the Hrad from Malostranské náměstí is **Nerudova**, named after the Czech journalist and writer Jan Neruda (1834–91), who lived for a while at *U dvou slunců* (The Two Suns), a former inn at the top of the street. His tales of Malá Strana immortalized bohemian life on Prague's left bank, though he's perhaps best known in the West via the Chilean Nobel prize-winner, Pablo Neruda, who took his pen name from the lesser-known Czech. Historically, this is Prague's artists' quarter, and although few of the present inhabitants are names to conjure with, the various private galleries and craft shops that have sprouted up over the last few years continue the tradition.

The houses that line the steep climb up to the Hrad are typically restrained, many retaining their medieval barn doors, and most adorned with their own peculiar house signs (see box below). A short way up the hill, you'll pass two of the street's fancier build-

---

House Signs

As well as preserving their Gothic or Romanesque foundations, many houses throughout Prague retain their ancient **house signs**, which you'll see carved into the gables, on hanging wooden signs, or inscribed on the facade. The system originated in the fourteenth century, and still survives today, though it's now used predominantly by *pivnice* (pubs), restaurants and *vinárna*.

Some signs were deliberately chosen to draw custom to the business of the house, like *U zeleného hroznu* (The Green Bunch of Grapes), a wine shop in the Malá Strana; others, like *U železných dveří* (The Iron Door), simply referred to some distinguishing feature of the house, often long gone. The pervasive use of *zlatý* (gold) in the house names derives from the city's popular epithet, *Zlatá Praha* (Golden Prague), referring either to the halcyon days of Charles IV, when the new Gothic copper roofing shone like gold, or the period of alchemy under Rudolf II, depending on your viewpoint. Religious names, like *U černé Matky boží* (The Black Madonna), were popular, too, especially during the Counter-Reformation.

In the 1770s, the Habsburgs, in their rationalizing fashion, introduced a numerical system, with each house in the city entered onto a register according to a strict chronology; later, the conventional system of progressive street numbering was introduced. So, don't be surprised if seventeenth-century pubs like *U medvídků* (The Little Bears) have, in addition to a house sign, two numbers: in this case 7 and 345; the former, Habsburg number, written on a red background, the latter, modern number, on blue.

---

ings: at no. 5 is the **Morzin Palace,** now the Romanian Embassy, its
doorway designed by Giovanni Santini and supported by two Moors
(a pun on the owner's name) sculpted by Brokoff; diagonally opposite, at no. 20, two giant eagles by Braun, hold up the portal of the
Thun-Hohenstein Palace, now the Italian Embassy (also by
Santini). Further up the street, Casanova and Mozart are thought to
have met up at a ball given by the aristocrat owners of no. 33, the
Bretfeld Palace, in 1791, while the latter was in town for the
premiere of *La Clemenza di Tito* (see box on p.69).

Halfway up the hill, Nerudova halts at a crossroads where it
meets the cobbled hairpin of Ke Hradu which the royal coronation
procession used to ascend; continuing west along Úvoz (The
Cutting) takes you to the Strahov Monastery (see p.63). On the
south side of Úvoz, the houses come to an end, and a view opens
up over Malá Strana's red Baroque roofs, while to the north,
narrow stairways squeeze between the towering buildings of
Hradčany, emerging on the path to the Loreto chapel.

Tržiště and Vlašská

Running (very) roughly parallel to Nerudova – and linked to it by
several sidestreets and steps – is **Tržiště,** which sets off from the
south side of Malostranské náměstí. Halfway up on the left is the
Schönborn Palace, now the American Embassy. The entrance, and
the renowned gardens, are nowadays watched over by closed-circuit
TV and machine-gun-toting GIs – a far cry from the dilapidated
palace in which Kafka rented an apartment in March 1917, and
where he suffered his first bout of tuberculosis.

As Tržiště swings to the right, bear left up **Vlašská,** home to
yet another **Lobkovic Palace,** now the German Embassy. In the
summer of 1989, several thousand East Germans climbed over the
garden wall and entered the embassy compound to demand West
German citizenship, which had been every German's right since
partition. The neighbouring streets were soon jam-packed with
abandoned Trabants, as the beautiful palace gardens became a
muddy home to the refugees. Finally, the Czechoslovak government gave in and organized special trains to take the East
Germans over the federal border, cheered on their way by thousands of Praguers, and thus prompted the exodus that eventually
brought about *Die Wende*.

The palace itself is a particularly refined building, best
viewed from the rear – you'll have to approach it from Petřín Hill
(see p.77). The gardens, which were laid out in the early nineteenth century by Václav Skalník, who went on to landscape the
spa at Mariánské Lázně, are no longer open to the public but you
should be able to see David Černý's sculpture, *Quo Vadis?*, a
gold Trabant on legs, erected in memory of the fleeing East
Germans.

The Valdštejn Palace and gardens

To the north of Malostranské náměstí, up Tomášská, lies the **Valdštejn Palace**, which takes up the whole of the eastern side of Valdštejnské náměstí and Valdštejnská. As early as 1621, Albrecht von Waldstein started to build a palace which would reflect his status as commander of the Imperial Catholic armies of the Thirty Years' War. By buying, confiscating, and then destroying twenty-odd houses around the square, he succeeded in ripping apart a densely populated area of Malá Strana to make way for one of the first, largest and, quite frankly, most unappealing Baroque palaces in the city – at least from the outside.

The Comenius Museum is open Tues–Sun 10am–noon & 1–5pm.

The Ministry of Culture is now firmly ensconced in the palace, with just the former stables, housing the **Comenius Museum** (Pedagogické muzeum), accessible to the public. This is a small and none too exciting exhibition on Czech education and, in particular, the influential teachings of Jan Amos Komenský (1592–1670) – often anglicized to John Comenius – who was forced to leave his homeland after the victory of Waldstein's Catholic armies, eventually settling in Protestant England. To get to the exhibition, go through the main gateway and continue straight across the first courtyard; the museum is on your right. The only way to get to see the palace's magnificent main hall – used in the filming of *Amadeus* – is to go to one of the concerts occasionally held there.

Waldstein

Albrecht von Waldstein (known to the Czechs as Albrecht z Valdštejna, and to the English as Wallenstein – the name given to him by the German playwright Schiller in his tragic trilogy) was the most notorious warlord of the Thirty Years' War. If the imperial astrologer Johannes Kepler is to be believed, this is all because he was born at four in the afternoon on September 14, 1583. According to Kepler's horoscope Waldstein was destined to be greedy, deceitful, unloved and unloving. Sure enough at an early age he tried to kill a servant for which he was expelled from his Lutheran school. Recuperating in Italy, he converted to Catholicism (an astute career move) and married a wealthy widow who conveniently died shortly after the marriage. Waldstein used his new fortune to cultivate a friendship with Prince Ferdinand, heir to the Habsburg Empire, who in turn thought that a tame Bohemian noble could come in handy.

Within five years of the Battle of Bílá hora (1620; see p.159), Waldstein owned a quarter of Bohemia, either by compulsory purchase or in return for money or troops loaned to Ferdinand. It was a good time to go into property: Ferdinand's imperial armies, who were busy restoring Catholicism throughout Europe, provided a ready-made market for agricultural produce. And as a rising general, Waldstein could get away with a certain amount of insider trading, marching armies with as many as 125,000 men over enemy territory or land owned by rivals, laying fields waste and then selling his troops supplies from his own pristine Bohemian estates.

If you've no interest in pedagogical matters, the palace's formal gardens, the **Valdštejnská zahrada** – accessible only from a doorway in the palace walls along Letenská – are a good place to take a breather from the city streets. The focus of the gardens is the gigantic Italianate *sala terrena*, a monumental loggia decorated with frescoes of the Trojan Wars, which stands at the end of an avenue of sculptures by Adriaen de Vries. The originals, which were intended to form a fountain, were taken off as booty by the Swedes in 1648 and now adorn the royal gardens in Drottningholm. In addition, there's a café, a pseudo grotto along the south wall, with quasi-stalactites and a door which once led to Waldstein's observatory, and a small aviary, home to the gardens' peacock population.

On the opposite side of the gardens, the palace's former riding school, **Valdštejnská jízdárna**, has been converted into a gallery, which puts on temporary exhibitions of fine art and photography organized by the National Gallery. The riding school is accessible only from the courtyard of the nearby Malostranská metro station.

The Valdštejnská zahrada is open May–Sept daily 9am–7pm.

The Valdštejnská jízdárna is open Tues–Sun 10am–6pm.

Letenská and sv Tomáš

Walking southwest along Letenská from the gardens back towards Malostranské náměstí, takes you past U **svatého Tomáše**, the oldest *pivnice* in Prague, established in 1352 by Augustinian monks who brewed their own lethal dark beer on the premises. Unfortunately, the Communists succeeded in kicking out the monks and closing down the

---

As Waldstein ranged further afield in Germany, conquering Jutland, Pomerania, Alsace and most of Brandenburg on Ferdinand's behalf, his demands for reward grew ever more outrageous. Already Duke of Friedland and Governor of Prague, Waldstein was appointed Duke of Mecklenburg in 1628. This upset not only the existing duke, who had backed Ferdinand's opponents, but even the Emperor's loyalist supporters. If Ferdinand thought fit to hand one of the greatest German titles to this Czech upstart, what family's inheritance could be secure? By 1630, Waldstein had earned himself the right to keep his hat on in the imperial presence as well as the dubious honour of handing the Emperor a napkin after he had used his fingerbowl. However, at this point Waldstein's services became too expensive for Ferdinand, so the duke was relieved of his command.

The following year, the Saxons occupied Prague, and the Emperor was forced to reinstate Waldstein. Ferdinand couldn't afford to do without the supplies from Waldstein's estates, but knew he was mortgaging large chunks of the Empire to pay for his services. More alarmingly, there were persistent rumours that Waldstein was about to declare himself King of Bohemia and defect to the French enemy. In 1634, Waldstein openly rebelled against Ferdinand, who immediately hatched a plot to murder Waldstein, sending a motley posse including English, Irish and Scottish mercenaries to the border town of Cheb, where they cut the general down in his nightshirt as he tried to rise from his sickbed. Some see him as the first man to unify Germany since Charlemagne, others see him as a wily Czech hero. In reality he was probably just an ambitious, violent man, as his stars had predicted.

The Valdštejn Palace and gardens

brewery – the surviving pub is now shamelessly touristy and over-priced. Better preserved are the cloisters and priory church of **sv Tomáš** (St Thomas), which bears few traces of its Gothic origins since its rebuilding by Kilian Ignaz Dientzenhofer in the 1720s. The rich burghers of Malá Strana spared no expense, buying a couple of Rubens for the altarpiece and two dead saints (St Just and St Boniface) to give the church extra kudos. The Rubens now hangs in the National Gallery, but the saints' fully dressed skeletons survive, as do Václav Vavřinec Reiner's frescoes and Dientzenhofer's glorious dome.

Malá Strana's terraced gardens

One of the chief joys of Malá Strana is its **terraced gardens**, hidden away behind the Baroque palaces on Valdštejnská, on the slopes below the castle, where the royal vineyards used to be, and commanding superb views over Prague. All the gardens are theoretically open to the public except the Polish Embassy's Fürstenberská zahrada. At the time of writing, however, they were all, without exception, closed to the public, supposedly undergoing restoration, though with no fixed date for completion.

The best-loved of the three adjoining gardens is the **Kolowrat** or **Černín Garden**, which makes the most of its cramped site with a jumble of balustrades and terraces which culminate in a small *sala terrena* by Giovanni Alliprandi, as does the **Ledeburg Garden** to the west. The largest of the gardens is the central **Pállfy Garden**, made up of two older plots, joined together and renovated in Rococo style in 1751. If all the above are closed, try instead the **Vojanovy sady**, securely concealed behind a ring of high walls off U lužického semináře. Originally a monastic garden belonging to the Carmelites, it's now an informal public park, with sleeping babies, weeping willows, and lots of grass on which to lounge about; outdoor art exhibitions and occasional concerts also take place here.

Southern Malá Strana

Karmelitská is the busy cobbled street that runs south from Malostranské náměstí along the base of Petřín Hill towards the industrial suburb of Smíchov, becoming Újezd at roughly its halfway point. Between here and the River Vltava are some of Malá Strana's most picturesque and secluded streets. Although there are no major sights around here, the island of **Kampa**, in particular, makes up one of the most peaceful stretches of riverfront in Prague.

Maltézské náměstí and around

From the trams and traffic fumes of Karmelitská, it's a relief to cut across to the calm restraint of **Maltézské náměstí**, one of a number of delightful little squares between here and the river. It takes its

name from the Order of the Knights of St John of Jerusalem (better
known by their later title, the Maltese Knights), who founded the
nearby church of **Panna Maria pod řetězem** (Saint Mary below-the-
chain) in 1160. The original Romanesque church was pulled down
by the Knights themselves in the fourteenth century, but only the
chancel and towers were successfully rebuilt by the time of the
Hussite Wars. The two severe Gothic towers are still standing and
the apse is now thoroughly Baroque, but the nave remains unfinished, an open, grassy, ivy-strewn space.

The Knights have recently returned to reclaim (and restore) the
church and the adjacent Grand Priory, which backs onto
Velkopřevorské náměstí, another pretty little square to the south,
which echoes to the sound of music from the nearby Prague
Conservatoire. Following the violent death of John Lennon in 1980,
Prague's youth established an ad hoc shrine smothered in graffiti
tributes to the ex-Beatle along the Grand Priory's garden wall. The
running battle between police and graffiti artists continued well into
the Nineties, and there are now moves afoot to preserve the central
mural of Lennon's head, whilst making the rest of the wall graffiti-
proof. On the opposite side of the square from the wall, sitting
pretty in pink behind a row of chestnut trees, is the Rococo **Buquoy
Palace**, built for a French family and appropriately enough now the
French Embassy.

Kampa

The two or three streets that make up **Kampa**, the largest of the
central islands, contain no notable palaces or museums; just a
couple of old mills, an exquisite main square, and a serene riverside
park – in other words, plenty enough diversion for a lazy summer
afternoon. The island is separated from the left bank by Prague's
"Little Venice", a thin strip of water called **Čertovka** (Devil's
Stream), which used to power several mill-wheels until the last one
ceased to function in 1936. In contrast to the rest of the left bank,
the fire of 1541 had a positive effect on Kampa, since the flotsam
from the blaze effectively stabilized the island's shifting shoreline.
Nevertheless, Kampa was still subject to frequent flooding right up
until the Vltava was dammed in the 1950s.

For much of its history, the island was the city's main wash
house, a fact commemorated by the church of sv Jan Na Prádle (St
John at the Wash House) on Říční, near the southernmost tip of the
island. It wasn't until the sixteenth and seventeenth centuries that the
Nostitz family, who owned Kampa, began to develop the northern
half of the island; the southern half was left untouched, and today is
laid out as a public park, with riverside views across to Staré Město.
To the north, the oval main square, **Na Kampě**, once a pottery
market, is studded with slender acacia trees and cut through by the
Charles Bridge, to which it is connected by a double flight of steps.

Karmelitská and Újezd

On the corner of Karmelitská and Tržiště, at no. 25, is the entrance to one of the most elusive of Malá Strana's many Baroque gardens, the **Vrtbovská zahrada**, founded on the site of the former vineyards of the Vrtba Palace. Laid out on Tuscan-style terraces, dotted with ornamental urns and statues of the gods by Matthias Bernhard Braun, the gardens twist their way up the lower slopes of Petřín Hill to an observation terrace, from where there's a spectacular rooftop perspective on the city. Predictably enough, these gardens, like those off Valdštejnská, are currently closed for repair.

Further down, on the same side of the street, is the rather plain church of **Panna Maria Vítězná**, which was begun in early Baroque style by German Lutherans in 1611, and later handed over to the Carmelites after the Battle of Bílá hora. The main reason for coming here is to see the *pražské Jezulátko* or *Bambino di Praga*, a high-kitsch wax effigy of the infant Jesus enthroned in a glass case illuminated with strip-lights, donated by one of the Lobkovic family's Spanish brides in 1628. Attributed with miraculous powers, the *pražské Jezulátko* became an object of international pilgrimage equal in stature to the Santa Casa in Loreto, similarly inspiring a whole series of replicas. It continues to attract visitors (as the multilingual prayer cards attest) and boasts a vast personal wardrobe of expensive swaddling clothes, regularly changed by the sisters.

A block or so further south, Karmelitská becomes Újezd, the site of another former nunnery, this time Dominican, at no. 40. The Kinský family later built a Renaissance palace here, but from 1787 it fell into disrepair and remained so until the *Sokol* nationalist sports movement bought it in 1921. The sports faculty of the Charles University and the **Museum of Physical Culture and Sport** (Muzeum tělesné výchovy a sportu) are now housed here. Sport played an important part in the Czech national revival (*národní obrození*) through *Sokol*, the extremely popular nationalist organization set up in 1862, in direct response to the German *Turnverband* physical education movement. The Communists outlawed *Sokol* (as the Nazis had also done) and, in its place, established a tradition of *Spartakiáda*, extravaganzas of synchronized gymnastics held every five years in the Strahov stadium, behind Petřín Hill. Even the *Spartakiáda* were popular, but, indelibly tainted by their political past. The last one, due to have been held in 1990, was cancelled and there are now moves afoot to re-establish *Sokol* gatherings instead. The museum fails to mention the *Spartakiáda*, and instead traces the history of *Sokol*, focusing on the postwar Olympic successes of the likes of the Czech long-distance runner (and Party stooge), Emil Zátopek.

The Museum of Physical Culture and Sport is open Tues–Sun 9am–5pm.

Petřín Hill

The scaled-down version of the Eiffel Tower is the most obvious landmark on **Petřín Hill**, the largest green space in the city centre. The tower is just one of the exhibits built for the 1891 Prague Exhibition, whose modest legacy includes the **funicular railway** (lanová dráha) which climbs up from a station just off Újezd. The original funicular was powered by a simple but ingenious system whereby two carriages, one at either end of the steep track, were fitted with large watertanks that were alternately filled at the top and emptied at the bottom; it was replaced in the 1960s by the current electric system. As the carriages pass each other at the half-way station of Nebozízek, you can get out and soak in the view from the restaurant of the same name.

The funicular runs every ten to fifteen minutes from 9.15am to 8.45pm – tickets are the same as for the rest of the public transport system.

Along the Hunger Wall

At the top of the hill, it's possible to trace the southernmost perimeter wall of the old city – popularly known as the **Hunger Wall** (Hladová zeď) – as it creeps eastwards back down to Újezd, and northwestwards to the Strahov Monastery. Instigated in the 1460s by Charles IV, it was much lauded at the time (and later by the Communists) as a great public work which provided employment for the burgeoning ranks of the city's destitute (hence its name); in fact, much of the wall's construction was paid for by the expropriation of Jewish property.

Follow the wall southeast and you come to the aromatic **Růžový sad** (rose garden), laid out in front of Petřín's **observatory** (Hvězdárna), which offers a range of telescopes for use by the city's amateur astronomers. A little further down the hill, on the other side of the wall from the observatory, stands a bust of the leading Czech Romantic poet **Karel Hynek Mácha**, who penned the poem *Maj*, on the subject of unrequited love. In spring, and in particular on the first of May, the statue remains a popular place of pilgrimage for courting couples.

The observatory is open Tues–Sun; hours vary month by month.

Another curiosity, hidden in the trees on the southern side of the Hunger Wall, is a **wooden church** that was brought here, log by log, from an Orthodox village in Ruthenia (now part of Ukraine) in 1929. Churches like this are still common in eastern Slovakia, and this is a particularly ornate example from the eighteenth century, with multiple domes like piles of giant acorns.

Back at the Růžový sad, follow the wall northwest and you'll come to Palliardi's twin-towered church of **sv Vavřinec** (St Lawrence), from which derives the German name for Petřín Hill – Laurenziberg. Dotted along the nearby paths are the Stations of the Cross, culminating in the graffitied Calvary Chapel, just beyond the church. Opposite the church are a series of buildings from the 1891 Exhibition, starting with the diminutive **Eiffel**

Petřín Hill

The Eiffel Tower is open April–Oct daily 9.30am–11pm; Nov–March Sat & Sun 9.30am–6pm.

The Mirror Maze is open April–Oct daily 9.30am–6.30pm; Nov–March Sat & Sun 9am–4pm.

Tower (Rozhledna), an octagonal interpretation – though a mere fifth of the size – of the tower which shocked Paris in 1889, and a tribute to the city's strong cultural and political links with Paris at the time; naturally, the view from the public gallery is terrific in fine weather.

The next building along is a mini neo-Gothic castle complete with mock drawbridge, its interior converted into a **Mirror Maze** (Bludiště), a stroke of infantile genius by the exhibition organizers. The humour of the convex and concave mirrors inside is so simple, it has both adults and kids giggling away. The maze also contains an action-packed, life-sized diorama of the Prague students' and Jews' victory over the Swedes on the Charles Bridge in 1648. From the tower and maze, the path contours round to the northwest, giving great views over Petřín's palatial orchards and a sea of red tiles until it ducks under the perimeter wall of the Strahov Monastery (see p.63).

Staré Město

S TARÉ MĚSTO, literally the "Old Town", is Prague's most
central, vital ingredient. People still live, work and sleep here
in contrast to many European city centres; many of the capital's best markets, shops, restaurants and pubs are located in the
area; and during the day a gaggle of shoppers and tourists fills its
complex web of narrow streets. The district is bounded on one side
by the river, on the other by the arc of Národní, Na příkopě and
Revoluční, and at its heart is **Staroměstské náměstí**, Prague's showpiece main square, easily the most magnificent in central Europe.

Merchants and craftsmen began settling in what is now Staré
Město as early as the tenth century, and in the mid-thirteenth century
it was granted town status, with jurisdiction over its own affairs. The
fire of 1541, which ripped through the quarters on the other side of
the river, never reached Staré Město, though the 1689 conflagration
made up for it. Nevertheless, the victorious Catholic nobles built
fewer large palaces here than on the left bank, leaving the medieval
street plan intact with the exception of the Klementinum (the Jesuits'
powerhouse) and the largely reconstructed Jewish Quarter that sits
within the old town (see *Josefov*, p.102). But like so much of Prague,
Staré Město is still, on the surface, overwhelmingly Baroque, built
literally on top of its Gothic predecessor to guard against the floods
which plagued the town.

From the Charles Bridge to Celetná

In their explorations of Staré Město, most people unknowingly
retrace the **králová cesta**, the traditional route of the coronation
procession from the medieval gateway, the Prašná brána (see
p.124), to the Hrad. Established by the Přemyslids, the route was
followed, with a few minor variations, by every king until the
Emperor Ferdinand IV in 1836, the last of the Habsburgs to bother
having himself crowned in Prague. It's also the most direct route

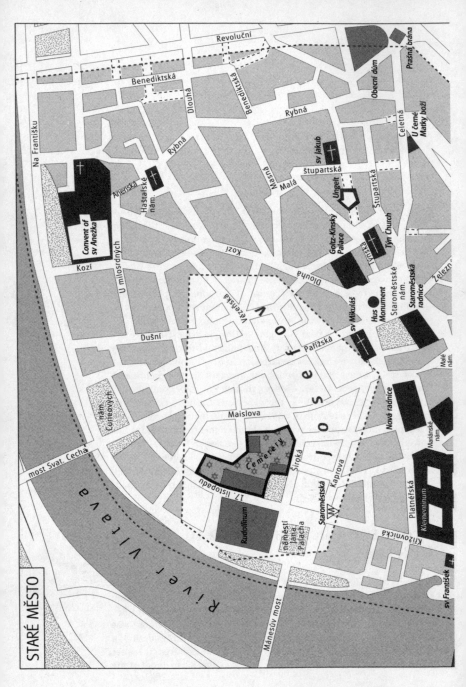

STARÉ MĚSTO

River Vltava

Josefov

Revoluční

Benediktská

Na Františku

Dlouhá

Rybná

Benediktská

Rybná

Anenská

Haštalské nám.

Convent of sv Anežka

Kozí

Kozí

U milosrdných

Vězeňská

Dušní

nám. Curieových

most Svat. Čecha

Maislova

Pařížská

Široká

Cemetery

17. listopadu

Rudolfinum

náměstí Jana Palacha

Mánesův most

Masná

Malá

štupartská

sv Jakub

Štupartská

Ungelt

Týn Church

Goltz-Kinský Palace

Týnská

Staroměstská radnice

Dlouhá

Staroměstské nám.

Hus Monument

sv Mikuláš

Nová radnice

Kaprova

Staroměstská

Platnéřská

Křížovnická

Klementinum

Obecní dům

Prašná brána

Celetná

U černé Matky boží

Železn

Malé nám.

Mariánské nám.

sv František

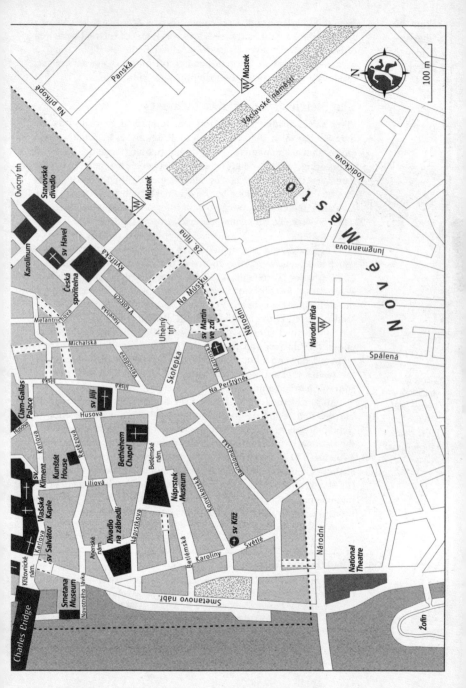

from the Charles Bridge to the main square, Staroměstské náměstí, and therefore a natural choice. However, many of the real treasures of Staré Město lie away from the *králová cesta*, so if you want to escape the crowds, it's worth heading off into the quarter's silent, twisted matrix of streets, then simply follow your nose.

The Charles Bridge (Karlův most)

The Charles Bridge – which for over four hundred years was the only link between the two halves of Prague – is by far the city's most familiar monument. It's an impressive piece of medieval engineering, aligned slightly askew between two mighty Gothic gateways, but its fame is due almost entirely to the magnificent Baroque statues, additions to the original structure, that punctuate its length. Individually, only a few of the works are outstanding, but taken collectively, set against the backdrop of the Hrad, the effect is breathtaking.

The bridge was begun in 1357 to replace an earlier structure which had been swept away by one of the Vltava's frequent floods in 1342. Charles IV commissioned his young German court architect, Peter Parler, to carry out the work, which was finally completed in the early fifteenth century. For four hundred years thereafter it was known simply as the Prague or Stone Bridge – only in 1870 was it officially named after its patron. Since 1950, the bridge has been closed to vehicles, and is now one of the most popular places to hang out, day and night; apart from the steady stream of sightseers, the niches created by the bridge-piers are keenly fought over by souvenir hawkers and buskers.

You can climb the taller Malá Strana bridge tower daily June–Sept 10am–6pm and Oct–May 10am–5pm.

A bronze crucifix has stood on the bridge since its construction, but the first sculpture wasn't added until 1683, when St John of Nepomuk appeared. His statue was such a propaganda success with the Catholic church authorities that another 21 were added between 1706 and 1714. These included works by Prague's leading Baroque sculptors, led by Matthias Bernhard Braun and Maximilian Brokoff; the Max brothers unimaginatively filled in the remaining piers in the mid-nineteenth century. The original sculptures, mostly crafted in sandstone, have weathered badly over the years and are gradually being replaced by copies.

Building the bridge

There are countless legends regarding the bridge's initial construction: the most persistent is that the builders mixed eggs (and, in some versions, wine) with the mortar to strengthen it. Having quickly depleted the city's egg supply, orders were sent out for contributions from the surrounding villages: the villagers of Velvary, who were worried that raw eggs wouldn't have quite the right consistency, hard-boiled theirs, and from Unhošt curd, cheese and whey were sent to bond the bricks even harder.

The Malá Strana bridge towers

The following account of the statuary starts from the Malá Strana side, where two unequal bridge towers, connected by a castellated arch, form the entrance to the bridge. The smaller, stumpy tower was once part of the original Judith Bridge (named after the wife of Vladislav I, who built the twelfth-century original); the taller of the two, crowned by one of the pinnacled wedge-spires more commonly associated with Prague's right bank, can be climbed for a bird's-eye view.

The statues

In the first statue group on the left, paid for by the university medical faculty, Jesus is flanked by **Saint Cosmas and Saint Damian (1)**, both dressed in medieval doctors' garb – they were renowned for offering their medical services free of charge to the poor. Opposite stands **Saint Wenceslas (2)**, added by Czech nationalists in the nineteenth century. On the next pier, Brokoff's **Saint Vitus (3)** is depicted as a Roman legionary, his foot being gently nibbled by one of the lions that went on to devour him in a Roman amphitheatre. Facing him is one of the most striking sculptural groups, the founders of the **Trinitarian Order (4)**, again by Brokoff: Saints John of Matha, Felix of Valois and his pet stag (plus, for some unknown reason, Saint Ivan), whose good works included ransoming persecuted Christians – three petrified souls can be seen through the prison bars below – from the infidels, represented by a bored Turkish jailor and his rabid dog.

Amid all the blackened sandstone, the lightly coloured figure of the (at the time) only recently canonized Servite friar, **Saint Philip Benizi (5)**, stands out as the only marble statue on the bridge. At his feet sits the papal crown, which he refused to accept when it was offered to him in 1268. Opposite stands Prague's second bishop, the youthful **Saint Adalbert (6)**, who was hounded out of the city on more than one occasion by the blissfully pagan citizens of Prague. Another (at the time) recently canonized saint is **Cajetan (7)**, founder of the Theatine Order (and of a whole chain of non-profit-making pawnshops in Naples), who stands in front of a column of cherubs sporting a sacred heart.

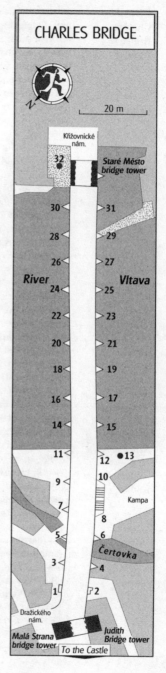

CHARLES BRIDGE

20 m

Křížovnické nám.

32

Staré Město bridge tower

30 31

28 29

26 27

River Vltava

24 25

22 23

20 21

18 19

16 17

14 15

11 12 13

9 10

7 Kampa

8

5 6

Čertovka

3 4

1 2

Dražického nám.

Malá Strana bridge tower

Judith Bridge tower

To the Castle

One of the most successful statues is that of the blind Cistercian nun, **Saint Lutgard (8)**, sculpted by Braun when he was just twenty-six years old. She is depicted here in the middle of her celebrated vision, in which Christ appeared to show off his wounds. The Augustinians sponsored the next duo, on the other side of the steps leading down to Kampa Island: **Saint Augustine (9)**, and one of his later followers, **Saint Nicholas of Tolentino (10)**, who is depicted dishing out bread to the poor. On the top-floor balcony of the house immediately behind Saint Nicholas of Tolentino is a strange collection of objects – a Madonna, a mangle and a lantern. The story goes that the Madonna was retrieved from the river during a particularly bad flood, and saved the house from further inundation. She then went on to save a washerwoman whose sleeves got caught in the mangle; as for the lantern, if it goes out while you're passing by, it means you'll die within the year.

Next pier along, the apostle **Saint Jude Thaddaeus (11)**, patron saint of those in dire straits, holds the club with which the pagans beat him to death. On the opposite side, the Dominican friar **Saint Vincent Ferrer (12)** stands over one of his converts to self-flagellation, while the inscription below lists his final conversion total – 8000 Muslims and 25,000 Jews, not to mention countless demons. He is joined on his pedestal, somewhat inexplicably, by Bohemia's best-loved hermit, **Saint Procopius**. If you look over the side of the bridge at this point, you'll see a nineteenth-century sculpture of **Roland (13)** – known as *Bruncvík* in Czech – brandishing his miraculous golden sword.

The Franciscan pier – **Saint Anthony of Padua (14)**, and a lifeless nineteenth-century figure of **Saint Francis of Assisi**, accompanied by two angels **(15)** – is worth passing over to reach the bridge's earliest and most popular sculpture, **Saint John of Nepomuk (16)**. The only bronze statue on the bridge, it's now green with age, the gold-leaf halo of stars and palm branch gently blowing in the breeze. Saint John's appearance in 1683, on the bridge from which he was thrown to his death, was part of the Jesuits' persistent campaign to have him canonized; the statue later inspired hundreds of copies, which adorn bridges throughout central Europe. On the base, there's a bronze relief depicting his martyrdom, the figure of John now extremely worn through years of being touched for good luck. Facing Saint John is Bohemia's first martyr, a rather androgenous version of **Saint Ludmilla (17)**, holding the veil with which she was strangled and standing alongside her grandson, Saint Wenceslas, here depicted as a young child; his future martyrdom is recounted in the base relief (for more on Wenceslas and co, see p.49).

For the story of Saint John of Nepomuk's martyrdom, see p.50.

With the exception of the Jesuit general **Saint Francis Borgia (19)**, the next two piers are glum nineteenth-century space-fillers: a trio of Bohemian saints – **Norbert**, **Sigismund** and, for the third time, **Wenceslas (18)** – followed by **John the Baptist (20)** and

Saint Christopher (21). Between the piers, on the left, a small bronze cross is set into the wall marking the spot where John of Nepomuk was dumped in the river (see above). In 1890, the two Jesuit statues on the next pier were swept away by a flood: the statue of the founder of the order, Saint Ignatius Loyola, was replaced with the most recent additions to the bridge (completed in 1938), saints Cyril and Methodius (22), the ninth-century missionaries who first introduced Christianity to the Slavs; the other, the Jesuit missionary Saint Francis Xavier (23), survived the order's unpopularity and was replaced by a copy. This is one of the more unusual sculptural groups on the bridge: the saint, who worked in India and the Far East, is held aloft by three Moorish and two "Oriental" converts; Brokoff placed himself on the saint's left side.

From the Charles Bridge to Celetná

Next in line are Jesus, Mary, and Mary's mother, Saint Anne (24) and, facing them, with a slightly older Jesus at his feet, Joseph (25), a nineteenth-century replacement for another Brokoff, this time destroyed by gunfire during the 1848 revolution. The Crucifixion scene (26) is where the original fourteenth-century crucifix stood alone on the bridge for two hundred years. The gold-leaf, Hebrew inscription, "Holy, Holy, Holy" was added in 1696, paid for by a Prague Jew who was ordered to do so by the city court, having been found guilty of blasphemy before the cross. Apart from Christ himself, all the figures, and the Pietà opposite (27), were added by the Max brothers.

On the penultimate pier, the Dominicans placed their founder, Saint Dominic, and their other leading light, Saint Thomas Aquinas, beside the Madonna (28); in amongst the cherubs is the order's emblem, a dog with a burning torch in his mouth. Opposite, Saint Barbara, the patron saint of miners, whose beautifully sculpted hands so impressed Kafka, is accompanied by Saint Margaret and Saint Elizabeth (29). There's one final Madonna (30), this time presiding over the kneeling figure of Saint Bernard, and a bubbling mass of cherubs mucking about with the instruments of the Passion – the cock, the dice and the centurion's gauntlet. Lastly, Saint Ivo (31), patron saint of lawyers, flanked by Justice and a prospective client, stands with an outstretched hand, into which Prague law students traditionally place a glass of beer after their finals.

The Staré Město bridge tower

On the Staré Město side is arguably the finest bridge tower of the lot, its eastern facade still encrusted in Gothic cake-like decorations from Peter Parler's workshop, plus a series of mini-sculptures. The central figures are Saint Vitus, flanked by Charles IV on the right and his son, Václav IV, on the left; above stand two of Bohemia's patron saints, Adalbert and Sigismund. The severed heads of twelve of the Protestant leaders were suspended from the tower in iron baskets following their execution on Staroměstské náměstí in 1621, and all but one remained there until the Saxons passed through the

The bridge tower viewing gallery is open daily June–Sept 10am–6pm; Oct–May 10am–5pm.

capital ten years later. In 1648, it was the site of the last battle of
the Thirty Years' War, fought between the besieging Swedes and an
ad hoc army of Prague's students and Jews, which trashed the western facade of the bridge tower.

Křižovnické náměstí to Malé náměstí

Pass under the Staré Město bridge tower and you're in Křižovnické
náměstí, an awkward space hemmed in by its constituent buildings,
and – with traffic hurtling across the square – a dangerous spot for
unwary pedestrians. Hard by the bridge tower is a nineteenth-
century cast-iron statue of Charles IV (32), erected on the 500th
anniversary of his founding of the university, and designed by a
German, Ernst Julius Hähnel, in the days before the reawakening of
Czech sculpture. To his left is an unusual plaque commemorating a
Czech who was shot by mistake by the Red Army during the battles
of May 1945.

The two churches facing onto the square are both quite striking.
The half-brick church of sv František (St Francis) was built by
Jean-Baptiste Mathey for the Order of Knights of the Cross with a
Red Star, the original gatekeepers of the old Judith Bridge, who
were at the zenith of their power in the seventeenth century, when
they supplied most of the archbishops of Prague. The single dome
plan and rich marble furnishings inside are both untypical in
Prague. Over the road is the church of sv Salvátor, its facade prick-
ling with blackened saints which are lit up enticingly at night. Built
between 1578 and 1602, sv Salvátor marks the beginning of the
Jesuits' rise to power and, like many of their churches, is designed
along the lines of the Gesù church in Rome. It's worth a quick look,
if only for the frothy stucco work and delicate ironwork in its triple-
naved interior.

Along Karlova

Running from Křižovnické náměstí all the way to Malé náměstí is
the narrow street of Karlova, packed with people winding their
way towards Staroměstské náměstí, their attention divided
between checking out the waffle stalls and souvenir shops, and not
losing their way. At the first wiggle in Karlova, you come to the
Vlašská kaple (Italian Chapel), a tiny oval chapel which served the
community of Italian masons, sculptors and painters who settled in
Prague during the Renaissance period, and is still, strictly speaking, the property of the Italian state. The Vlašská kaple is rarely
open, though you may have more luck with the adjacent church of
sv Kliment, accessible from the same portal. It's a minor gem of
Prague Baroque by Dientzenhofer with statues by Braun, a spectacular set of frescoes depicting the life of Saint Clement (whose
fate was to be lashed to an anchor and hurled into the Black Sea),
and an unusual modern screen added by its new owners, the

Uniate Church, who observe Orthodox rites but, confusingly, belong to the Roman Catholic church. On the opposite side of Karlova, at the junction with Liliová, is U zlatého hada (The Golden Serpent), where the Armenian Deomatus Damajan opened the city's first coffee house in 1708. According to legend, the café was always full, not least because Damajan had a red-wine fountain inside. It's still a café now, though sadly minus the fountain and its original furnishings.

The Klementinum

As they stroll down Karlova, few people notice the **Klementinum**, the former Jesuit College on the north side of the street, which covers an area second in size only to the Hrad. In 1556, Ferdinand I summoned the Jesuits to Prague to help bolster the Catholic cause in Bohemia, giving them the church of sv Kliment (see above), which Dientzenhofer later rebuilt for them. Initially, the Jesuits proceeded with caution, but once the Counter-Reformation set in, they were put in control of the whole university and provincial education system. From their secure base at sv Kliment, they began to establish space for a great Catholic seat of learning in the city by buying up the surrounding land, demolishing more than thirty old town houses, and, over the next two hundred years, gradually building themselves a palatial headquarters. In 1773, soon after the Klementinum was completed, the Jesuits were turfed out of the country and the building handed over to the university authorities.

Nowadays the Klementinum houses the National Library's collection of over five million volumes, but much of the original building has been left intact. The **entrance**, inconspicuously placed just past the church of sv Kliment, lets you into a series of rather plain courtyards. The entrance to the **Zrcadlová kaple** (Mirrored Chapel) is immediately to the left after passing through the archway on the far side of the first courtyard; its interior of fake marble, gilded stucco and mirror panels, boasts fine acoustics and is regularly used for concerts.

The Mirrored Chapel is open only for concerts and special exhibitions.

The Klementinum hides several other attractions inside, but the authorities are none too keen to let the public inside. One sight that is sporadically open is the Rococo **Music Library** (Hudební oddělení) on the first floor to the west of the chapel, a stunning reading room filled with leather tomes, ancient globes and lovely Baroque frescoes. In the same wing there are temporary exhibitions of some of the library's prize possessions, which include the world's largest collection of works by the early English reformer, Yorkshireman John Wycliffe, whose writings had an enormous impact on the fourteenth-century Czech religious community, inspiring preachers like Hus to speak out against the social conditions of the time.

The library is open Mon, Wed & Thurs noon–6pm, Tues & Fri 9am–3pm, Sat 9am–noon.

At roughly the centre of the Klementinum complex is the **observatory tower** from where seventeenth-century Prague's most illus-

trious visiting scientist, Johannes Kepler, did his planet-gazing. A
religious exile from his native Germany, Kepler succeeded Tycho de
Brahe as court astronomer to Rudolf II, and lived at no. 4 Karlova
for a number of years, during which time he drew up the first laws
on the movement of the planets.

Mariánské náměstí and around

Where the Klementinum ends, the corner house U zlaté studné
(The Golden Well), now a flashy wine bar, stands out like a wedge
of cheese; its thick stucco reliefs of assorted saints were commissioned by the owner in gratitude for having been spared the plague.

A short diversion here, down Seminářská, brings you out onto
Mariánské náměstí, generally fairly deserted compared to Karlova.
It's hard to believe that the rather severe Nová radnice (New Town
Hall), on the east side of the square, was built by Osvald Polívka,
architect of the exuberant Art-Nouveau Obecní dům (see p.125). Its
most striking features are the two gargantuan figures which stand
guard at either corner, by the sculptor of the Hus Monument,
Ladislav Šaloun. The one on the left, looking like Darth Vader, is the
"Iron Knight", mascot of the armourers' guild; to the right is the
somewhat grotesquely caricatured sixteenth-century Jewish sage
and scholar, Rabbi Löw, who was visited by Death on several occasions, but allowed to live to the ripe old age of ninety-six, provided
he did not stray from his religious studies – here, a naked woman
tries unsuccessfully to attract his attentions.

*For the full
story of Rabbi
Löw, see p.107.*

To get back to Karlova, head down Husova, past the Baroque
Clam-Gallas Palace (Clam-Gallasův palác; not open to the public),
which, despite its size – it takes up a good five or six old houses – is
easy to overlook in this narrow space. It's a typically lavish affair by
the Viennese architect Fischer von Erlach, with big and burly
Atlantes supporting the portals. Also on Husova, at no. 23 near the
Karlova end of the street, is the excellent Pražský dům fotografie
(Prague's House of Photography) which puts on some of the best
photo exhibitions in Prague and sells prints of the works on show –
if you've a couple of thousand crowns to spare.

*The Pražský
dům fotografie
is open daily
11am–6pm.*

Malé náměstí

After a couple more shops, boutiques, hole-in-the-wall bars and a
final twist in Karlova, you emerge onto Malé náměstí, a square originally settled by French merchants in the twelfth century. The square
was also home to the first pharmacy in Prague, opened by a
Florentine in 1353, and the tradition is continued today by the
lékárna at no. 13, which boasts chandeliers and a restored Baroque
interior. The square's best-known building, though, is the russet-red,
neo-Renaissance Rott Haus, an ironmongers' shop founded by V. J.
Rott in 1840, whose facade is smothered in agricultural scenes and
motifs inspired by the Czech artist Mikuláš Aleš. The original house
sign of three white roses has been preserved on the central gable.

Staroměstské náměstí

East of Malé náměstí is **Staroměstské náměstí** (Old Town Square),
easily the most spectacular square in Prague, and the traditional
heart of the city. Most of the brightly coloured houses look solidly
eighteenth-century, but their Baroque facades hide considerably
older buildings. From the eleventh century onwards, this was the
city's main marketplace, known simply as Velké náměstí (Great
Square), to which all roads in Bohemia led, and where merchants
from all over Europe gathered. When the five towns that made up
Prague were united in 1784, it was the Old Town Square's town hall
that was made the seat of the new city council, and for the next two
hundred years the square was the scene of the country's most
violent demonstrations and battles. For a long time now, the whole
place has been closed to traffic: the cafés spread out their tables in
summer, and the tourists pour in to watch the town hall clock
chime, to sit on the steps of the Hus Monument, and to drink in this
historic showpiece.

The Hus Monument

The most recent arrival in the square is the colossal **Jan Hus
Monument**, a turbulent sea of blackened bodies – the oppressed to
his right, the defiant to his left – out of which rises the majestic
moral authority of Hus himself, gazing into the horizon. For the
sculptor Ladislav Šaloun, a maverick who received no formal training, the monument was his life's work, commissioned in 1900 when
the Viennese Secession was at its peak, but strangely old-fashioned
by the time it was completed in 1915. It would be difficult to claim
that it blends in with its Baroque surroundings, yet this has never
mattered to the Czechs, for whom its significance goes far beyond
aesthetic merit.

*For a brief
biography of
Jan Hus, see
p.99.*

The Austrians refused to hold an official unveiling; in protest,
on July 6, 1915, the 500th anniversary of the death of Hus,
Praguers smothered the monument in flowers. Since then it has
been a powerful symbol of Czech nationalism: in March 1939, it was
draped in swastikas by the invading Nazis, and in August 1968, it
was shrouded in funereal black by Praguers, protesting at the Soviet
invasion. The inscription along the base is a quote from *The Will of
Comenius*, one of Hus' later followers, and includes Hus' most
famous dictum, *Pravda vítězí* (Truth Prevails), which has been the
motto of just about every Czech revolution since then.

The Staroměstská radnice

It wasn't until the reign of King John of Luxembourg (1310–46)
that Staré Město was allowed to build its own town hall, the
Staroměstská radnice. Short of funds, the citizens decided against
an entirely new structure, buying a corner house on the square
instead and simply adding an extra floor; later on, they added the

east wing, with its graceful Gothic oriel and obligatory wedge-tower.
Gradually, over the centuries, the neighbouring merchants' houses
to the west were incorporated into the building, so that now it
stretches all the way across to the richly sgraffitoed Dům U minuty,
which juts out into the square.

On May 8, 1945, on the final day of the Prague Uprising, the
Nazis still held on to Staroměstské náměstí, and in a last desperate
act set fire to the town hall – one of the few buildings to be irrevoca-
bly damaged in the last war. The tower and oriel chapel were rebuilt
immediately, but of the neo-Gothic **east wing**, which stretched
almost to the church of sv Mikuláš, only a crumbling fragment
remains; the rest of it is marked by a small stretch of grass.
Embedded in the wall of the tower is a plaque marked "Dukla", and
a case containing a handful of earth from the Slovak pass where
some 80,000 Soviet and Czechoslovak soldiers lost their lives in the
first battle to liberate the country in October 1944.

Below, set into the paving, are 27 **white crosses** commemorating the Protestant leaders who were condemned to death on the
orders of the Emperor Ferdinand II, following the Battle of Bílá
hora. They were publicly executed in the square on June 21, 1621
by the Prague executioner, Jan Mlydář: twenty-four enjoyed the
nobleman's privilege and had their heads lopped off; the three
remaining commoners were hung, drawn and quartered. Mlydář also
chopped off the right hand of three of the nobles, and hacked off
the tongue of the rector of Prague University, Johannes Jessenius,
which he then nailed to their respective severed heads for public
display on the Charles Bridge.

Today, the town hall's most popular feature is its *orloj* or
Astronomical Clock – every hour, a crowd of tourists and Praguers
gather in front of the tower to watch a mechanical dumbshow by the
clock's assorted figures. The Apostles shuffle past the top two
windows, bowing to the audience, while perched on pinnacles below
are the four threats to the city as perceived by the medieval mind:
Death carrying his hourglass and tolling his bell, the Jew with his
moneybags (but minus his stereotypical beard since 1945), Vanity
admiring his reflection, and a turbaned Turk shaking his head.
Beneath the moving figures, four characters representing virtues
stand motionless throughout the performance. Finally, a cockerel
pops out and flaps its wings to signal that the show's over; the clock
then chimes the hour.

The clock itself has been here since the beginning of the
fifteenth century; the working figures were added in 1490 by a
Master Hanuš who, legend has it, was then blinded with a red-hot
poker by the town councillors, to make sure he couldn't repeat the
job for anyone else. In retaliation, he groped his way around the
clock, succeeded in stopping it, and then promptly died of a heart
attack – the clock stayed broken for over eighty years. The complex
clock face tells not only the current time, but also Old Bohemian

time and Babylonian time, as well as charting – as the medieval astrologer saw it – the movements of the sun and planets around the earth, and of course, the movement of the sun and moon through the signs of the zodiac. The revolving dial below the clock face is decorated with bucolic paintings of the "cycle of twelve idylls from the life of the Bohemian peasant" by Josef Mánes, a leading light in the Czech national revival.

The powder-pink facade on the south side of the town hall now forms the **entrance** to the whole complex. A twenty-minute guided tour of the four rooms that survived the last war sets off every hour, when the clock has finished striking (more frequently in summer). It was in these rooms that the Bohemian kings were elected until the Habsburgs established hereditary rule, and in 1422 Jan Želivský, the fiery Hussite preacher and inspiration behind Prague's first defenestration (see p.130), was executed here. Despite being steeped in history, there's not much of interest here, apart from a few decorated ceilings, striped with chunky beams, and a couple of Renaissance portals. You'll probably get more enjoyment from climbing the tower – with access for the disabled – for the panoramic sweep across Prague's spires.

*The
Staroměstská
radnice is open
to the public
Mon
11am–5pm
and Tues–Sun
9am–5pm.*

The church of sv Mikuláš

The destruction of the east wing of the town hall in 1945 rudely exposed Kilian Ignaz Dientzenhofer's church of **sv Mikuláš**, built in just three years between 1732 and 1735. The original church was founded by German merchants in the thirteenth century, and served as Staré Město's parish church until the Týn Church (see below) was completed. Later, it was handed over to the Benedictines, who commissioned Dientzenhofer to replace it with the present building. His hand is obvious: the south front is decidedly luscious – painted in pale white, with Braun's blackened statuary popping up at every cornice – promising an interior to surpass even its sister church of sv Mikuláš in Malá Strana, which Dientzenhofer built with his father immediately afterwards (see p.69).

*The church of
sv Mikuláš is
open to the
public on Tues,
Wed & Fri
10am–1pm,
Thurs 2–5pm.*

Inside, however, it's a curious mixture. Although caked in the usual mixture of stucco and fresco and boasting an impressive dome, the church has been stripped over the years of much of its ornament and lacks the sumptuousness of its namesake on the left bank. This is partly due to the fact that Joseph II closed down the monastery and turned the church into a storehouse, and partly because it's now owned by the very "low", modern, Czech Hussite Church.

The rest of the square

The largest secular building on the square is the Rococo **Goltz-Kinský Palace** (palác Golz-Kinských), designed by Kilian Ignaz Dientzenhofer and built by his son-in-law Anselmo Lurago. In the nineteenth century it became a German *Gymnasium*, which was

*The palace is
open Tues–Sun
10am–6pm.*

*Gottwald's
appearance
forms the
opening to
Milan
Kundera's
novel* The Book
of Laughter and
Forgetting; *see
Books, p.264.*

*Dům U
kamenného
zvonu is open
Tues–Sun
10am–6pm.*

attended by Kafka (whose father ran a haberdashery shop on the ground floor). The palace is perhaps most notorious, however, as the venue for the fateful speech by the Communist prime minister, Klement Gottwald, who walked out on to the grey stone balcony one snowy February morning in 1948, flanked by his Party henchmen, to address the thousands of enthusiastic supporters who packed the square below. It was the beginning of *Vítězná února* (Victorious February), the bloodless coup which brought the Communists to power and sealed the fate of the country for the next forty-one years. The top floor now hosts top-flight exhibitions of graphic art put on by the National Gallery, but the entire palace was recently purchased by the Kafka Society who plan to turn it eventually into a vast museum and library dedicated to Kafka.

Until recently, the adjacent **Dům U kamenného zvonu** (House at the Stone Bell) was much like any other of the merchant houses that line Staroměstské náměstí – covered in a thick icing of Baroque plasterwork and topped by an undistinguished roof gable. In the process of restoration in the 1970s, however, it was stripped down to its Gothic core, uncovering the original honey-coloured stonework and simple wedge roof, and it now serves as a central venue for cutting-edge modern art exhibitions, lectures and concerts.

The south side of the square boasts a fine array of facades, mostly Baroque, with the notable exception of the neo-Renaissance **Štorch House**, adorned with a sgraffito painting of Saint Wenceslas by Mikuláš Aleš. Next door, **U bílého jednorožce** (The White Unicorn) – the sixteenth-century house sign actually depicts a one-horned ram – was Prague's one and only *salon*, run by Berta Fanta. An illustrious membership, including Kafka, Max Brod and Franz Werfel, came here to attend talks given by, among others, Albert Einstein and Rudolf Steiner.

The Týn Church and Ungelt

Staré Město's most impressive Gothic structure, the mighty **Týn Church** (Matka boží před Týnem), whose two irregular towers, bristling with baubles, spires and pinnacles, rise like giant antennae above the arcaded houses which otherwise obscure its facade, is a building of far more confidence than sv Mikuláš. Like the nearby Hus monument, the Týn Church, begun in the fourteenth century, is a source of Czech national pride. In an act of defiance, George of Poděbrady, the last Czech and the only Hussite King of Bohemia, adorned the high stone gable with a statue of himself and a giant gilded *kalich* (chalice), the mascot of all Hussite sects. The church remained a hotbed of Hussitism until the Protestants' crushing defeat at the Battle of Bílá hora, after which the chalice was melted down to provide the newly ensconced statue of the Virgin Mary with a golden halo, sceptre and crown.

Despite being one of the main landmarks of Staré Město, it's well-nigh impossible to appreciate the church from anything but a considerable distance, since it's boxed in by the houses around it, some of which are actually built right against the walls. To reach the entrance, take the third arch on the left, which passes under the Venetian gables of the former Týn School. Given the church's significance, it's sad that the **interior** is mostly dingy, unwelcoming and in need of repair, with little of the feel of the original Gothic structure surviving the church's ferocious Catholicization. One exception is the fine north portal and canopy, which bears the hallmark of Peter Parler's workshop; the fifteenth-century pulpit also stands out from the dark morass of black and gold Baroque altarpieces, its panels enhanced by some sensitive nineteenth-century icons.

The pillar on the right of the chancel steps contains the red marble **tomb of Tycho de Brahe**, the famous Danish astronomer who arrived in Prague wearing a silver and gold false nose, having lost his own in a duel over a woman in Rostock. Court astronomer to Rudolf II for just two years, Brahe laid much of the groundwork for Johannes Kepler's later discoveries – Kepler getting his chance of employment when Brahe died of a burst bladder after one of Petr Vok's notorious binges in 1601 – hence the Czech expression *nechci umřít jako Tycho de Brahe* ("I don't want to die like Tycho de Brahe", in other words I need to go to the toilet).

*The Týn Church
is open Tues,
Wed & Sun
12.30–5pm,
Thurs & Fri
12.30–3pm, Sat
2–6pm.*

Behind the Týn Church lies the Týn Court or **Ungelt** (meaning "No Money", a pseudonym used to deter marauding invaders), which, as the trading base of German merchants, was one of the first settlements on the Vltava. A hospice, church and hostel were built for the use of the merchants, and by the fourteenth century the area had become an extremely successful international marketplace; soon afterwards the traders moved up to the Hrad, and the court was transformed into a palace. Part of the complex now serves as a luxury hotel, the Dominicans have reclaimed another section, while the rest is undergoing restoration, thanks in part to money pledged by Prince Charles. To get a sneek preview, you can enter the courtyard from the Malá Štupartská to the east.

Celetná and around

Celetná, whose name comes from the bakers who used to bake a particular type of small loaf (*calty*) here in the Middle Ages, leads east from Staroměstské náměstí direct to the Prašná brána, one of the original gateways of the old town. It's one of the oldest streets in Prague, lying along the former trade route from the old town market square, as well as on the *králová cesta*. Its buildings were smartly refaced in the Baroque period, and their pastel shades are now crisply maintained. Most of Celetná's shops veer towards the chic end of the Czech market, making it a popular place for a bit of window-shopping, but the spruced-up surroundings are only skin-

deep. Dive down one of the covered passages to the left and you're
soon in Staré Město's more usual, dilapidated backstreets.

Dům U černé Matky boží

Two-thirds of the way along Celetná, at the junction with Ovocný
trh, is the Dům U černé Matky boží (House at the Black Madonna),
built as a department store in 1911–12 by Josef Gočár and one of
the best examples of Czech Cubist architecture in Prague. It was a
short-lived style, whose most surprising attribute, in this instance, is
its ability to adapt existing Baroque motifs: Gočár's house sits much
more happily amongst its eighteenth-century neighbours than, for
example, the functionalist Baťa shoe-shop opposite – one of Gočár's
later designs from the 1930s.

Happily, the building has recently been renovated and now
houses, among other things, the Czech Museum of Fine Arts
(České muzeum výtvarných umění). The top two floors contain a
small, permanent exhibition of Czech Cubist art: everything from
sofas and sideboards by Gočár himself, to porcelain and
paintings, plus some wonderful sculptures by Otto Gutfreund. To
whet your appetite further, there are photographs of the Cubist
villas in Vyšehrad (covered on p.143) and plans to restore the
Cubist café which originally graced the first floor. In the
meantime, the first, second and third floors are currently given
over to temporary exhibitions of twentieth-century Czech art,
while the basement has been converted into a cheap
café/restaurant.

*The Museum of
Fine Arts is
open Tues–Sun
10am–6pm.*

The church of sv Jakub

Celetná ends at the fourteenth-century Prašná brána (see p.124),
beyond which is náměstí Republiky, at which point, strictly speaking, you've left Staré Město behind. Back in the old town, head
north from Celetná into the backstreets which conceal the bubbling,
stucco facade of the Franciscan church of sv Jakub, on Malá
Štupartská. Its massive Gothic proportions – it has the longest nave
in Prague after the cathedral – make it a favourite venue for organ
recitals, Mozart masses and other concerts. After the great fire of
1689, Prague's Baroque artists remodelled the entire interior,
adding huge pillasters, a series of colourful frescoes and over
twenty side altars. The most famous of these is the tomb of the
Count of Mitrovice, in the northern aisle, designed by Fischer von
Erlach and Prague's own Maximilian Brokoff.

The church has close historical links with the butchers of
Prague, who were given a chapel in gratitude for their defence of
the city in 1611 and 1648. Hanging from the west wall, on the right
as you enter, is a thoroughly decomposed human forearm. It has
been there for over four hundred years now, ever since a thief tried
to steal the jewels of the Madonna from the high altar. As the thief

reached out, the Virgin supposedly grabbed his arm and refused to let go. The next day the congregation of butchers had no option but to lop it off, and it has hung there as a warning ever since.

From the Charles Bridge to Celetná

The Convent of sv Anežka

Further north through the backstreets, the Convent of sv Anežka (Klášter svatého Anežky české), Prague's oldest surviving Gothic building, stands within a stone's throw of the river as it loops around to the east. It was founded in 1233 as a convent for the Order of the Poor Clares, and named after Agnes (Anežka), youngest sister of King Václav I, who left her life of regal privilege to become the convent's first abbess. Agnes herself was beatified in 1874 to try and combat the spread of Hussitism amongst the Czechs, and there was much speculation about the wonders that would occur when she was officially canonized, an event which finally took place on November 12, 1989, when Czech Catholics were invited to a special mass at St Peter's in Rome. Four days later the Velvet Revolution began: a happy coincidence, even for agnostic Czechs.

The convent itself was closed down in 1782, and fell into rack and ruin. It was squatted for most of the next century, and though saved from demolition by the Czech nationalist lobby, its restoration only took place in the 1980s. The convent now houses the National Gallery's nineteenth-century Czech art collection, and if the art inside is not always of the highest quality, it is at least interesting in terms of the Czech national revival, while the building itself is also worth inspecting.

The art collection inside the convent is open to the public Tues–Sun 10am–6pm.

The well-preserved cloisters are filled with unremarkable Bohemian glass, porcelain and pewter dating from the nineteenth century; the fine art is housed in the three remaining chapels and continues on the first floor. The predominant trend in Czech painting at this time was the depiction of events of national significance: favourite themes – on display in several works here – ranged from legendary figures such as Břetislav and Jitka to the real-life tragedy of the Battle of Bílá hora. Far superior to these in technique is the work of Josef Václav Myslbek, the grand master of Czech sculpture, whose simple statue of Saint Agnes from his *Monument to St Wenceslas* (see p.118) is the gallery's outstanding exhibit.

There's a much more impressive collection of nineteenth- and twentieth-century sculpture in the Museum of Modern Art, see p.153.

Upstairs, the rooms are dominated by the romanticized landscapes of Antonín Mánes, Josef Navrátil and Antonín Chittussi, which lovingly portray the rolling hills of Bohemia. In the same vein, though they were to be more influential on later generations of Czech artists, are the portraits and landscapes of Josef Mánes, who took an active part in the 1848 disturbances in Prague and consistently espoused the nationalist cause in his paintings. The final room is given over to the graphics of Mikuláš Aleš, whose designs can be seen in the sgraffito on many of the city's nineteenth-century buildings.

Southern Staré Město

The southern half of Staré Město is bounded by the *králová cesta* (the coronation route; see p.79) to the north, and the curve of Národní and Na příkopě, which follow the course of the old fortifications, to the south. There are no showpiece squares like Staroměstské náměstí here, but the complex web of narrow lanes and hidden passageways, many of which have changed little since medieval times, make this an intriguing quarter to explore.

From Ovocný trh to Uhelný trh

*For more on
Mozart's time
in Prague, see
p.69.*

Heading southwest from the Dům U černé Matky boží (see above), you enter **Ovocný trh**, site of the old fruit market, its cobbles recently restored along with the lime-green and white **Stavovské divadlo** (Estates Theatre), which lies at the end of the marketplace. Built in the early 1780s by Count Nostitz (after whom the theatre was originally named) for the entertainment of Prague's large and powerful German community, the theatre is one of the finest Neoclassical buildings in Prague, reflecting the enormous self-confidence of its patrons. The theatre also has a place in Czech history too, for it was here that the Czech national anthem, *Kde domov můj* (Where is My Home), was first performed, as part of the comic opera *Fidlovačka*, by J. K. Tyl (after whom the theatre was later renamed). It is also something of a mecca for Mozart fans, since it was here rather than in the hostile climate of Vienna that the composer chose to premiere both *Don Giovanni* and *La Clemenza di Tito*. This is, in fact, one of the few opera houses in Europe which remains intact from Mozart's time, a major factor in Miloš Forman's decision to film the concert scenes for his Oscar-laden *Amadeus* here.

On the north side of the Stavovské divadlo is the home base of the **Karolinum** or Charles University, named after its founder Charles IV, who established it in 1348 as the first university in this part of Europe. Although it was open to all nationalities, with instruction in Latin, it wasn't long before differences arose between the German-speaking students, who were in the majority, and the Czechs, who, with Jan Hus as their rector, successfully persuaded Václav IV to curtail the privileges of the Germans. In protest, the Germans upped and left for Leipzig, the first of many ethnic problems which continued to bubble away throughout the university's six-hundred-year history until the forced expulsion of Germans after World War II.

To begin with, the university had no fixed abode; it wasn't until 1383 that Václav IV bought the present site. All that's left of the original fourteenth-century building is the Gothic oriel window which emerges from the south wall; the rest was trashed by the Nazis in 1945. The new main entrance is a peculiarly ugly red-brick curtain wall by Jaroslav Fragner, set back from the street and

The former Gottwald Museum

One block west of the Stavovské divadlo, at no. 29 Rytířská, is the former **Prague Savings Bank**, a large, pompous neo-Renaissance building designed in the 1890s by Osvald Polívka, before he went on to erect some of Prague's most flamboyant Art-Nouveau structures.

For over thirty years it housed the museum all Praguers loved to hate – dedicated to **Klement Gottwald**, the country's first Communist president. A joiner by trade, a notorious drunkard and womanizer by repute, he led the Party with unswerving faith from the beginnings of Stalinism in 1929 right through to the show trials of the early 1950s. He died shortly after attending Stalin's funeral in 1953 – either from grief or, more plausibly, from drink.

Remarkably, his reputation survived longer than that of any other East European leader. While those whom he had wrongfully sent to their deaths were posthumously rehabilitated, and the figure of Stalin denigrated, Gottwald remained sacred, his statue gracing every town in the country for the last forty-odd years. As late as October 1989, the Communists were happily issuing brand new 100kčs notes emblazoned with his bloated face, only to have them withdrawn from circulation a month later, when the regime toppled.

Not surprisingly, the museum has closed and the building is once again a savings bank, this time the Česká spořitelna. It's worth a peek inside; go upstairs to the left and check out the main hall.

inscribed with the original Latin name *Universitas Karolina*. Only a couple of small departments and the chancellor's office and administration are now housed here, with the rest spread over the length and breadth of the city. The heavily restored Gothic vaults, on the ground floor of the south wing, are now used as a public **art gallery** for contemporary Czech art.

The gallery is open daily April–Oct 10.30am–8pm; Nov–March 10.30am–7pm.

Around sv Havel

The junction of Melantrichova and Rytířská is always teeming with people pouring out of Staroměstské náměstí and heading for Wenceslas Square. Clearly visible from Melantrichova is Santini's undulating Baroque facade of the church of **sv Havel**, sadly no relation to the playwright-president but named after the Irish monk, Saint Gall. It was built in the thirteenth century to serve the local German community who had been invited to Prague partly to replace the Jewish traders killed in the city's 1096 pogrom. After the expulsion of the Protestants, the church was handed over to the Carmelites who redesigned the interior, now only visible through an iron grille.

Straight ahead of you as you leave sv Havel is Prague's last surviving **open-air market** – a poor relation of its Germanic predecessor, which stretched all the way from Ovocný trh to Uhelný trh. Traditionally a flower and vegetable market, it runs the full length of the arcaded Havelská, and sells everything from celery to CDs. The stalls on V kotcích, the narrow street parallel to Havelská, sell mainly clothes.

Uhelný trh, sv Martin and Bartolomějská

Both markets run west into Uhelný trh, which gets its name from the *uhlí* (coal) that was sold here in medieval times. Nowadays however it's Prague red-light district – you'll see little evidence during the day, but at night it can get busy (there are plans afoot, however, to establish a legitimate red-light area around Florenc bus station). South of Uhelný trh, down Martinská, the street miraculously opens out to make room for the twelfth-century church of **sv Martin ve zdi** (St Martin-in-the-Walls), originally built to serve the Czech community of the village of sv Martin, until it found itself the wrong side of the Gothic fortifications when they were erected in the fourteenth century. It's still essentially a Romanesque structure, adapted to suit Gothic tastes a century later, and thoroughly restored at the beginning of this century by its present owners, the Czech Brethren, who added the creamy neo-Renaissance tower. For them, it has a special significance as the place where communion "in both kinds" (ie bread and wine), one of the fundamental demands of the Hussites, was first administered to the whole congregation, in 1414.

Around the corner from sv Martin ve zdi is the gloomy lifeless street of **Bartolomějská**, dominated by a tall, grim-looking building on its south side, which served as the main interrogation centre of the universally detested secret police, the *Státní bezpečnost*, or *StB*. Although now officially disbanded, the *StB* continues to be one of the most controversial issues of the post-revolutionary period. As in the rest of Eastern Europe, the accusations (often unproven) and revelations of who exactly collaborated with the *StB* have caused the downfall of a number of leading politicians right across the political spectrum. The building is now back in the hands of the Franciscan nuns who occupied the place prior to 1948, and now run a small *pension*.

It's possible to stay the night in Havel's old cell, see p.188 for details.

Betlémské náměstí

After leaving the dark shadows of Bartolomějská, the brighter aspect of **Betlémské náměstí** comes as a welcome relief. The square is named after the **Bethlehem Chapel** (Betlémská kaple), whose high wooden gables face on to the square. This was founded in 1391 by the leading Czech reformists of the day, who were denied the right to build a church, so proceeded instead to build the largest chapel in Bohemia, with a total capacity of 3000. Sermons were delivered not in the customary Latin, but in the language of the masses – Czech. From 1402 to 1413, **Jan Hus** preached here (see below), regularly pulling in more than enough commoners to fill the chapel. Hus was eventually excommunicated for his outspokenness, found guilty of heresy and burnt at the stake at the Council of Constance in 1415.

The Bethlehem Chapel is open daily 9am–6pm.

The chapel continued to attract reformists from all over Europe for another two centuries – the leader of the German Peasants'

Revolt, **Thomas Müntzer**, preached here in the sixteenth century –
until the advent of the Counter-Reformation in Bohemia. Inevitably,
the chapel was handed over to the Jesuits, who completely altered
the original building, only for it to be demolished after they were
expelled by the Habsburgs in 1773. Of the original building, only
the three outer walls remain, with patches of their original decoration – biblical scenes which were used to get the message across to
the illiterate congregation. The rest is a scrupulous reconstruction
of the fourteenth-century building by Jaroslav Fragner, using the
original plans and a fair amount of imaginative guesswork. The
initial reconstruction work was carried out after the war by the
Communists, who were keen to portray Hus as a Czech nationalist
and social critic as much as a religious reformer, and, of course, to
dwell on the revolutionary Müntzer's later appearances here.

At the western end of the square stands the **Náprstek Museum**
(Náprstkovo muzeum), whose founder, Czech nationalist Vojta
Náprstek, was inspired by the great Victorian museums of London
while in exile following the 1848 revolution. On his return, he
turned the family brewery into a museum, initially intending it to
concentrate on the virtues of industrial progress. Náprstek's interests gradually shifted towards anthropology, however, and the
museum now displays just his fantastic American, Australasian and
Oceanic ethnographic collections; the original technological exhibits are now housed in Prague's National Technical Museum (see
p.153), while Náprstek's Asian and Oriental collections are housed
in the chateau at Liběchov (see p.165).

*The Náprstek
Museum is
open Tues–Sun
9am–noon &
1–5.30pm.*

Jan Hus

The legendary preacher – and Czech national hero – **Jan Hus** (often anglicized to John Huss) was born in a small village in South Bohemia around
1369. From a childhood of poverty, he enjoyed a meteoric rise through
the education system to become rector of Charles University in 1403. He
was a controversial choice of candidate, since his radical sermons criticiz-
ing the social conditions of the time had already caused a scandal in
Prague the previous year.

Hus was not the first to draw attention to the plight of the city's poor,
nor did he ever actually advocate many of the more famous tenets of the
heretical religious movement that took his name – Hussitism. For example, he never advocated giving communion "in both kinds" – bread and
wine – to the general congregation, nor did he ever denounce his
Catholicism. In fact, it was his outspokenness against the sale of indulgences to fund papal wars that prompted his unofficial trial at the Council
of Constance in 1415. He refused to renounce his beliefs and was burnt at
the stake as a heretic, despite having been guaranteed safe conduct by
Emperor Sigismund himself. The Czechs were outraged, and Hus became
a national hero overnight, inspiring thousands to rebel against the authorities of the day. In 1965, the Vatican finally overturned the sentence, and
the anniversary of his death is now a national holiday.

Husova and around

Between Betlémské náměstí and Karlova lies a confusing maze of streets, passageways and backyards, containing few sights as such, but nevertheless a joy to explore. One building that might catch your eye is the church of sv Jiljí (St Giles), on Husova, whose outward appearance suggests another Gothic masterpiece, but whose interior is decked out in the familiar white and gold excess of the eighteenth century. The frescoes by Václav Vavřinec Reiner (who's buried in the church) are full of praise for his patrons, the Dominicans, who took over the church after the Protestant defeat of 1620. They were expelled, in turn, after the Communists took power, only to return following the events of 1989.

Reiner's paintings also depict the unhappy story of Giles himself, a ninth-century hermit who is thought to have lived somewhere in Provence. Out one day with his pet deer, Giles and his companion were chased by the hounds of King Wanda of the Visigoths. The hounds were rooted to the spot by an invisible power, while the arrow from the hunters struck Giles in the foot as he defended his pet – the hermit was later looked upon as the patron saint of cripples.

The house is open May–Sept Tues–Sun 10am–noon & 1–6pm.

A short step away, just off Husova on Řetězová, is the **House of the Lords of Kunštát and Poděbrady** (Dům pánů z Kunštátu a Poděbrad), the home of George of Poděbrady before he became the Czechs' first and last Hussite king in 1458. It's not exactly gripping, but it does give you a clear impression of the antiquity of the houses in this area, and illustrates the way in which the new Gothic town was built on top of the old Romanesque one. Thus the floor on which you enter was originally the first floor of a twelfth-century palace, whose ground floor has been excavated in the cellars.

To the waterfront

Continuing west along Řetězová and Anenská brings you eventually to the waterfront. On Anenské náměstí, just before you reach the river, is the **Divadlo na zábradlí** (Theatre on the Balustrade). This was at the centre of Prague's absurdist theatre scene in the 1960s, with Havel himself working first as a stagehand and later as resident playwright, and is currently enjoying something of a renaissance.

The gaily decorated neo-Renaissance building at the very end of Novotného lávka, on the riverfront itself, was once the city's waterworks but now houses a pleasant riverside café (*Lávka*; see p.200) and theatre on the ground floor and, on the first floor, the **Smetana Museum**, currently closed and facing an uncertain future. Smetana, despite being a German-speaker, was without doubt the most nationalist of all the great Czech composers, taking an active part in the 1848 revolution and the later national revival movement. Towards the end of his life he went deaf, and eventually died of

syphilis in a mental asylum. Outside, beneath the large weeping
willow that droops over the embankment, the statue of the seated
Smetana is rather unfortunately placed, with his back towards one
of his most famous sources of inspiration, the River Vltava (Moldau
in German).

Chapter 4

Josefov

It is crowded with horses; traversed by narrow streets not remarkable for cleanliness, and has altogether an uninviting aspect. Your sanitary reformer would here find a strong case of overcrowding.

Walter White,
"A July Holiday in Saxony, Bohemia and Silesia" (1857)

L ess than half a century after Walter White's comments, all that was left of the former ghetto of **JOSEFOV** were six synagogues, the town hall and the medieval cemetery. At the end of the nineteenth century, a period of great economic growth for the Empire, it was decided that Prague should be turned into a beautiful bourgeois city, modelled on Paris. The key to this transformation was the "sanitization" of the ghetto, a process, begun in 1893, which reduced the notorious malodorous backstreets and alleyways of Josefov to rubble and replaced them with block after block of luxurious five-storey mansions. The Jews, gypsies and prostitutes were cleared out and the area became a desirable residential quarter, rich in Art-Nouveau buildings festooned with decorative murals, doorways and sculpturing – the beginning of the end for a community which had existed in Prague for almost a millennium.

In any other European city occupied by the Nazis in World War II, what little was left of the old ghetto would have been demolished. But although Prague's Jews were transported to the new ghetto in Terezín, by a grotesque twist of fate Hitler chose to preserve the ghetto itself as the site for his planned "Exotic Museum of an Extinct Race". With this in mind, Jewish artefacts from all over central Europe were gathered here, and now make up one of the richest collections of Judaica in Europe – and one of the most fascinating sights in Prague.

A history of Jewish settlement in Prague
Jews probably settled in Prague as early as the tenth century in what is now Malá Strana. From the outset they were subjected to

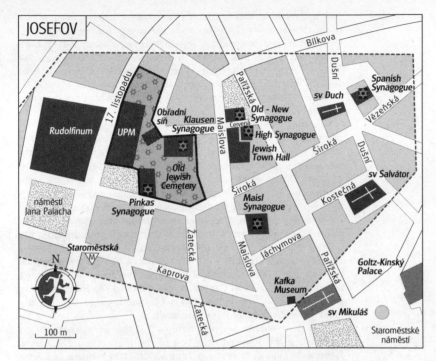

JOSEFOV

Bílkova · Dušní · Spanish Synagogue · sv Duch · 17. listopadu · Pařížská · Vězeňská · Obřadní síň · Klausen Synagogue · Old - New Synagogue · UPM · Maislova · Červená · High Synagogue · Široká · Rudolfinum · Old Jewish Cemetery · Jewish Town Hall · Dušní · sv Salvátor · náměstí Jana Palacha · Pinkas Synagogue · Široká · Maisl Synagogue · Kostečná · Staroměstská · Žatecká · Maislova · Jáchymova · Pařížská · Goltz-Kinský Palace · N · Kaprova · Kafka Museum · sv Mikuláš · Žatecká · 100 m · Staroměstské náměstí

violent pogroms, and harsh, often arbitrary persecution, through laws restricting their choice of profession, their movements and dress. The first dress codes were introduced under Vratislav II (1061–92) and required Jews to wear a yellow cloak; later, it was enough to wear a yellow circle, but some form of visible identification remained a constant feature of ghetto life.

In 1096, at the time of the first crusade, the first recorded pogrom took place, though it wasn't until the thirteenth century (300 years before the word "ghetto" was coined in Venice) that Jews were actually herded into a **walled ghetto** within Staré Město, cut off from the rest of the town and subject to a curfew. Prague's Jews effectively became the personal property of the king, protected by him when the moment suited, used as scapegoats when times were hard. During one of the worst pogroms, in 1389, 3000 Jews were massacred over Easter, some while sheltering in the Old-New Synagogue – an event which is still commemorated there every year on Yom Kippur. In 1541, following a wave of expulsions right across central Europe, Emperor Ferdinand I ordered Prague's Jews to leave. In the end he relented, and a small number of families were allowed to remain.

By contrast, the reign of Rudolf II (1576–1612) was a time of economic and cultural prosperity for the community. The Jewish mayor, **Mordecai Maisl**, Rudolf's minister of finance, became one of the richest men in Bohemia and the success symbol of a generation; his money bought the Jewish quarter a town hall, a bath house, pavements and several synagogues. This was the golden age of the ghetto: the time of **Rabbi Löw**, who, according to Jewish legend, created the famous "golem" (see box on p.107), and David Gans, the Jewish chronicler, both of whom are buried in the old cemetery.

In 1648, the Jews, along with the city's students, repelled the marauding Swedes on the Charles Bridge, for which they won the lasting respect of Ferdinand III (1637–57). At this time the ghetto was considerably enlarged, and the population grew to around 11,500. Things went into reverse again during the eighteenth century, until in 1745, Empress Maria Theresa used the community as a scapegoat for her disastrous war against the Prussians, and ordered the expulsion of all Jews from Prague. She allowed them to return three years later, though only after much pressure from the guilds, who were missing Jewish custom. It was the enlightened **Emperor Joseph II** (1780–90) who did most to lift the restrictions on Jews. His 1781 Toleration Edict ended the dress codes, opened up education to all non-Catholics, and removed the gates from the ghetto. In 1850, the community paid him homage by officially naming the ghetto Josefov, or Josefstadt.

The down side to Joseph's reforms was that he was hellbent on assimilating the Jews into the rest of the population. The use of Hebrew or Yiddish in business transactions was banned, and Jews were ordered to Germanize their names (the list of permitted names comprised 109 male ones and 35 female). It wasn't until the social upheavals of 1848 that Jews were given equal status within the Empire and allowed officially to settle outside the confines of the ghetto – concessions which were accompanied by a number of violent anti-Semitic protests on the part of the Czechs.

From 1848 to the present day

From 1848, the ghetto went into terminal decline. The more prosperous Jewish families began to move to other districts of Prague, leaving behind only the poorest Jews and strictly Orthodox families, who were rapidly joined by the underprivileged ranks of Prague society: gypsies, beggars, prostitutes and alcoholics. By 1890, only twenty percent of Josefov's population was Jewish, yet it was still the most densely populated area in Prague. The ghetto had become a carbuncle in the centre of bourgeois Prague, a source of disease and vice: in the words of Gustav Meyrink, a "demonic underworld, a place of anguish, a beggarly and phantasmagorical quarter whose eeriness seemed to have spread and led to paralysis".

The ending of restrictions, and the destruction of most of the old ghetto, increased the pressure on Jews to assimilate, a process which brought with it its own set of problems. Prague's Jews were predominantly German- or Yiddish-speaking, and therefore seen by the Czech nationalists as a Germanizing influence. By 1900 two-thirds of Prague's German population were Jewish. Tensions between the country's German-speaking minority and the Czechs grew steadily worse in the run-up to World War I, and the Jewish community found itself caught in the firing line – "like powerless stowaways attempting to steer a course through the storms of embattled nationalities", as one Prague Jew put it.

Despite several anti-Semitic riots in the first few years following the war, the foundation of the new republic in 1918, and, in particular, its founder and first president, T. G. Masaryk, whose liberal credentials were impeccable, were welcomed by most Jews. For the first time in their history, Jews were given equal rights as a recognized ethnic minority, though only a small number opted to be registered as Jewish. The interwar period was probably the nearest Prague's Jewish community came to a second golden age, a time most clearly expressed in the now famous flowering of its *Deutsche Prager Literatur*, led by writers such as Franz Werfel, Franz Kafka, Max Brod and Egon Erwin Kisch.

After Hitler occupied Prague on March 15, 1939, the city's Jews were subject to an increasingly harsh set of regulations, which saw them barred from most professions, placed under curfew, and compelled once more to wear a yellow Star of David. In November 1941, the first transport of Prague Jews set off for the new ghetto in Terezín, 60km northwest of Prague. Of the estimated 55,000 Jews in Prague at the time of the Nazi invasion, over 36,000 died in the camps. Many survivors emigrated to Israel and the USA. Of the 8000 who registered as Jewish in the Prague census of 1947, a significant number joined the Communist Party, only to find themselves victims of Stalinist anti-Semitic wrath during the 1950s.

It's difficult to calculate how many Jews now live in Prague – around 1000 were officially registered as such prior to 1989 – though their numbers (and funds) have undoubtedly been bolstered by the new influx of Jewish Americans and Israelis. The controversy over Jewish property – most of which was seized by the Nazis, and therefore not covered by the original restitution law – has finally been resolved, allowing the community to reclaim at least some of its buildings, most importantly the six synagogues, town hall and cemetery of Josefov itself.

The former ghetto

Geographically, Josefov lies to the northwest of Staroměstské náměstí, between the main square and the Vltava river. Through the heart of the old ghetto runs the ultimate bourgeois avenue, Pařížská, a riot of turn-of-the-century sculpturing, spikes and

The former ghetto

> All the "sights" of Josefov, bar the Old-New Synagogue, are covered by just one ticket, available from any of the quarter's ticket offices. Opening hours vary but are basically daily except Sat April–Oct 9.30am–6pm; Nov–March 9.30am–5pm; sometimes with a short break around noon for lunch.

turrets. If Josefov can still be said to have a main street, this is it, a glitzy rash of international airline offices and boutiques; once you leave it, however, you're immediately in the former ghetto, now one of the most restful parts of the old town.

The Old-New Synagogue and the Jewish Town Hall

Halfway down Pařížská, on the left, are the steep, jagged brick gables of the **Old-New Synagogue** (Staronová synagóga or Altneuschul), the oldest functioning synagogue in Europe. Begun in the second half of the thirteenth century, it's one of the earliest Gothic buildings in Prague and still the religious centre for Prague's Orthodox Jews. Since Jews were prevented by law from becoming architects, the synagogue was most probably constructed by the Franciscan builders working on the convent of sv Anežka. Its five-ribbed vaulting is unique for Bohemia; the extra, purely decorative rib was added to avoid any hint of a cross.

Prague's other working synagogue is in Nové Město, see p.126.

To enter the synagogue, you must buy a separate ticket from the ticket office opposite the synagogue's entrance on Červená. Men are asked to cover their heads out of respect – paper *yarmulkas* are on sale at the ticket office. To get to the **main hall**, you must pass through one of the two low vestibules from which women are allowed to watch the proceedings. Above the entrance is an elaborate tympanum covered in the twisting branches of a vine tree, its twelve bunches of grapes representing the tribes of Israel. The low glow from the chandeliers is the only light in the hall, which is mostly taken up with the elaborate wrought-iron cage enclosing the *bimah* in the centre. In 1357, Charles IV allowed the Jews to fly their own municipal standard, a moth-eaten remnant of which is still on show. The other flag – a tattered red banner – was a gift to the community from Emperor Ferdinand III for helping fend off the Swedes in 1648. On the west wall a glass cabinet, shaped like Moses' two tablets of stone, is filled with tiny personalized light bulbs, which are paid for by grieving relatives and light up on the anniversary of the person's death (there's even one for Kafka).

Just south of the synagogue is the **Jewish Town Hall** (Židovnická radnice), one of the few such buildings to survive the Holocaust. Founded and funded by Maisl in the sixteenth century, it was later rebuilt as the creamy-pink Baroque house you now see, housing a pricey kosher restaurant. The belfry, permission for which was granted by Ferdinand III, has a clock on each of its four sides, plus a Hebrew one stuck on the north gable which, like the Hebrew script, goes "backwards". On the other side of the synagogue is one of the many statues in Prague that were hidden from the Nazis for the duration of the war: an anguished statue of Moses by František Bílek, himself a committed Protestant.

The former ghetto

The Old Jewish Cemetery

The main reason most people visit Josefov is to see the **Old Jewish Cemetery** (Starý židovský hřbitov), called *Beth Chaim* in Hebrew, meaning "House of Life". Established in the fifteenth century, it was in use until 1787, by which time there were an estimated 100,000 buried here, one on top of the other, as many as twelve layers deep. The oldest grave, dating from 1439, belongs to the poet Avigdor Karo, who lived to tell the tale of the 1389 pogrom. Get there before the crowds – a difficult task at the height of summer – and the cemetery can be a poignant reminder of the ghetto, its inhabitants subjected to inhuman overcrowding even in death. The rest of

There are two entrances to the cemetery, the main one is beside the Klausen Synagogue, the second is via the Pinkas Synagogue on Široká.

The Golem

Legends concerning the animation of unformed matter (which is what the Hebrew word *golem* means), using the mystical texts of the *Kabbala*, were around long before Frankenstein started playing around with corpses. Two hungry fifth-century rabbis may have made the most practical golem when they sculpted a clay calf, brought it to life and then ate it; but the most famous is undoubtedly **Rabbi Löw**'s giant servant made from the mud of the Vltava, who was brought to life when the rabbi placed a *shem* in its mouth, a tablet with a magic Hebrew inscription.

There are numerous versions of the tale: in some, Yossel, the golem, is a figure of fun, flooding the rabbi's kitchen rather in the manner of Disney's *Sorcerer's Apprentice*; others portray him as the guardian of the ghetto, helping Rabbi Löw in his struggle with the anti-Semites at Rudolf II's court. In almost all, however, the golem finally runs amok. One particularly appealing tale is that the golem's rebellion was because Löw forgot to allow his creature to rest on the sabbath. He was conducting the service when news of its frenzy arrived, and he immediately ran out to deal with it. The congregation, reluctant to continue without him, merely repeated the verse in the psalm the rabbi had been reciting until Löw returned. This explains the peculiarity at the Old-New Synagogue where a line in the sabbath service is repeated even today. In all the stories, the end finally comes when Löw removes the *shem* once and for all, and carries the remains of his creature to the attic of the Old-New Synagogue, where they have supposedly resided ever since (a fact disputed by the pedantic journalist Egon Erwin Kisch, who climbed in to check).

The legends are amended at each telling, and have proved an enduringly popular theme for generations of artists and writers. Paul Wegener's German expressionist film version and the dark psychological novel of Gustav Meyrink are probably two of the most powerful treatments. Meyrink's golem lives in a room which has no windows and no doors, emerging to haunt the streets of Prague every 33 years. By which reckoning, it should be back some time in the mid-1990s.

**The former
ghetto**

*The New Jewish
Cemetery, where
Kafka, among
others, is buried,
is in Žižkov, see
p.147.*

*For a full
account of
Terezín
(Theresienstadt),
see p.167.*

Prague recedes beyond the sombre lime trees and cramped
perimeter walls, the haphazard headstones and Hebrew inscriptions
casting a powerful spell.

Each headstone bears a symbol denoting the profession or tribe
of the deceased: a pair of hands for the Cohens; a jug for the Levis;
scissors for a tailor; a violin for a musician; etc. On many graves
you'll see pebbles, some holding down small messages, as a mark of
remembrance. The greatest number of pebbles sits on the grave of
Rabbi Löw, creator of the "golem", who is buried by the wall directly
opposite the entrance; followed closely by the rich Renaissance
tomb of Mordecai Maisl, some ten metres to the southeast.

Immediately on your left as you leave the cemetery is the
Obřadní síň, a grim neo-Renaissance house built in 1906 as a ceremonial hall by the Jewish Burial Society. It's now devoted to an exhibition of harrowing drawings from the Jewish ghetto in Terezín; the
most disturbing section contains naive drawings by children, most of
whom later perished in the camps.

On Kafka's Trail

*Prague never lets go of you . . . this dear little mother has
sharp claws*

Franz Kafka was born on July 3, 1883, above the *Batalion* schnapps bar
on the corner of Maislova and Kaprova (the original building has long
since been torn down, but a gaunt-looking modern bust now commemorates the site). He spent most of his life in and around Josefov. His father
was an upwardly mobile small businessman from a Czech-Jewish family of
kosher butchers (Kafka himself was a vegetarian), his mother from a
wealthy German-Jewish family of merchants. The family owned a haberdashery shop, located at various premises on or near Staroměstské
náměstí. In 1889, they moved out of Josefov and lived for the next seven
years in the beautiful Renaissance Dům U minuty, next door to the
Staroměstská radnice, during which time Kafka attended the *Volksschule*
on Masná (now a Czech primary school), followed by a spell at an exceptionally strict German *Gymnasium*, located on the third floor of the
Goltz-Kinský Palace.

At eighteen, he began a law degree at the German half of Charles
University, which was where he met his lifelong friend and posthumous
biographer and editor, Max Brod. Kafka spent most of his working life
as an insurance clerk, until he was forced to retire through ill health in
1922. Illness plagued him throughout his life and he spent many months
as a patient at the innumerable spas in *Mitteleuropa*. He was engaged
three times, twice to the same woman, but never married, finally leaving
home at the age of thirty-one for bachelor digs on the corner of Dlouhá
and Masná, where he wrote the bulk of his most famous work, *The
Trial*. He died of tuberculosis in a Viennese sanatorium on June 3,
1924, at the age of forty, and is buried in the New Jewish Cemetery in
Žižkov (see p.147).

As a German among Czechs, a Jew among Germans, and an agnostic
among believers, Kafka had good reason to live in a constant state of fear,

The other synagogues

Close to the entrance to the cemetery is the **Klausen Synagogue**
(Klausová synagóga), a late seventeenth-century building, founded
in the 1690s by Mordecai Maisl on the site of several medieval
prayer halls (*klausen*), in what was then a notorious red-light
district of Josefov. The ornate Baroque interior contains a display of
Jewish prints and manuscripts (the world's first Jewish printing
house was founded in Prague in 1512).

The neo-Gothic **Maisl Synagogue** (Maislova synagóga), set back
from the neighbouring houses on Maislova, has recently reopened
after a lengthy restoration. Founded and paid for entirely by Mordecai
Maisl, in its day it was without doubt one of the most ornate synagogues in Josefov. Nowadays, it is almost entirely bare apart from the
rich offerings of its glass cabinets, which contain gold and silverwork,
hanuka candlesticks, *torah* scrolls and other religious paraphernalia.

Jutting out at an angle on the south side of the cemetery, with its
entrance on Široká, the **Pinkas Synagogue** (Pinkasova synagóga)

---

or *Angst*. Life was precarious for Prague's Jews, and the destruction of
the Jewish quarter throughout his childhood – the so-called "sanitization"
– had a profound effect on his psyche, as he himself admitted. It comes as
a surprise to many Kafka readers that anyone immersed in so beautiful a
city could write such claustrophobic and paranoid texts; and that as a
member of the café society of the time, he could write in a style so
completely at odds with his verbose, artistic friends. It's also hard to
accept that Kafka could find no publisher for *The Castle* or *The Trial*
during his lifetime.

After his death, Kafka's works were published in Czech and German
and enjoyed brief critical acclaim, before the Nazis banned them, first
within Germany, then across Nazi-occupied Europe. Even after the war,
Kafka, along with most German-Czech authors, was deliberately overlooked in his native country, since he belonged to a community and a
culture which had been exiled. In addition, his account of the terrifying
brutality and power of bureaucracy over the individual, though not in fact
directed at totalitarian systems as such, was too close to the bone for the
Communists. The 1962 Writers' Union conference at Liblice finally broke
the official silence on Kafka, and, for many people, marked the beginning
of the Prague Spring. In the immediate aftermath of the 1968 Soviet invasion, the Kafka bust was removed from Josefov, and his books remained
unpublished in Czechoslovakia until 1990.

Nowadays, thanks to his popularity with western tourists, Kafka has
become an extremely marketable commodity: his image is plastered
across T-shirts, mugs and postcards all over the city centre. A small **Kafka
Museum**, next door to the church of sv Mikuláš, retells Kafka's life simply
but effectively with pictures and quotes (in Czech, German and English).
It's run by the Kafka Society, as is the Franz Kafka bookshop and Café
Milena, situated opposite the town hall on Staroměstské náměstí. The
society also plans to open a much bigger museum and cultural centre in
the Goltz-Kinský Palace (see p.91).

*The Kafka
Museum is
open Tues–Fri
10am–6pm, Sat
10am–5pm.*

was built for the powerful Pinkas family, and has undergone countless restorations over the centuries. In 1958, the synagogue was
transformed into a chilling memorial to the 77,297 Czech and Slovak
Jews killed during the Holocaust – every bit of wall space being taken
up with the carved stone list of victims, stating simply their name,
date of birth and date of transportation to the camps. The memorial
was destroyed in the 1970s – by damp, according to the Communists
– and remained closed, allegedly due to problems with the masonry,
until very recently. It is now open to the public once more and is in
the process of being fully restored.

Adjacent to the town hall it was once part of is the **High
Synagogue** (Vysoká synagóga), whose rich interior stands in
complete contrast to its dour, grey facade. The huge vaulted hall
was, until recently, used to display a selection of the hundreds of
Jewish textiles, dating from the sixteenth to the early twentieth
century, which were gathered here by the Nazis for their infamous
museum. The building has now been restored as a working, non-
Orthodox synagogue, and is closed to the general public. East of
Pařížská, up Široká, is the **Spanish Synagogue** (Španělská
synagóga), which has been closed "for electrical rewiring" since
1980 and used for storage in the meantime. This is a great shame,
since it is one of the most ornate synagogues in Josefov, rebuilt at
the turn of the century in a Moorish style recalling its fifteenth-
century roots, when it was founded by Sephardic Jews fleeing the
Spanish Inquisition.

Around náměstí Jana Palacha

As Kaprova and Široká emerge from Josefov, they meet at the newly
christened **náměstí Jana Palacha**, previously called náměstí
Krasnoarmejců (Red Army Square) and embellished with a
flowerbed in the shape of a red star, in memory of the Soviet dead
who were temporarily buried here in May 1945. It was probably
*Palach is also
honoured at the
memorial to
victims of
Communism on
Wenceslas
Square, see
p.118.*
this, as much as the fact that the building on the east side of the
square is the Faculty of Philosophy, where Palach was a student,
that prompted the new authorities to make the first of the street
name changes here in 1989 (there's a bust of Palach on the corner
of the building). By a happy coincidence, the road which intersects
the square from the north is called 17 listopadu (17 November),
originally commemorating the students' anti-Nazi demonstration of
1939, but now equally good for 1989 march (see p.121).

The north side of the square is taken up by the **Rudolfinum** or
Dům umělců (House of Artists), designed by Josef Zítek and Josef
Schulz. One of the proud civic buildings of the nineteenth-century
Czech national revival, it was originally built to house an art gallery,
museum and concert hall for the Czech-speaking community. In
1918, however, it became the seat of the new Czechoslovak parlia-

ment, until 1938 when it was closed down by the Nazis. According to Jiří Weil, the Germans were keen to rid the building's balustrade of its statue of the Jewish composer Mendelssohn. However, since none of the statues was actually named, they decided to remove the one with the largest nose; unfortunately for the Nazis, this turned out to be Wagner, Hitler's favourite composer. In 1946, the building returned to its original artistic purpose and in the last couple of years it's been sandblasted back to its original woody-brown hue. It's now one of the capital's main exhibition and concert venues (it's home to the Czech Philharmonic), with a wonderfully grand café (see p.200), open to the general public on the first floor.

Around náměstí Jana Palacha

UPM – the Decorative Arts Museum

A short way down 17 listopadu from the square is the UPM (Umělecko-průmyslové muzeum), installed in another of Schulz's worthy nineteenth-century creations, richly decorated in mosaics, stained glass and sculptures. Literally translated, this is a "Museum of Decorative Arts", though the translation hardly does justice to what is one of the most fascinating museums in the capital. From its foundation in 1885 through to the end of the First Republic, the UPM received the best that the Czech modern movement had to offer – from Art Nouveau to the avant-garde – and judging from previous catalogues and the various short-term exhibitions mounted in the past, its collection is unrivalled.

The UPM is open Tues–Sun 10am–6pm.

Unfortunately, the permanent exhibition consists of just a sample from each of the main artistic periods from the Renaissance to the 1930s, giving only the vaguest hints at the wealth of exhibits stored away in the museum's vaults. Worse still, the top floor, which covers the period from the 1880s to the 1930s, has been closed for a number of years at the time of writing. As a consolation, the museum's ground and first floors (and occasionally the nearby Rudolfinum) are used for some of the best temporary exhibitions in Prague, mostly taken from its twentieth-century collections. There's also a public library in the building , specializing in catalogues and material from previous exhibitions, and an excellent café on the ground floor (see p.200).

The public library is open Mon noon–6pm, Tues–Fri 10am–6pm; closed July & Aug.

Chapter 5

Nové Město

A lthough it comes over as a sprawling late nineteenth-century bourgeois quarter, **NOVÉ MĚSTO** was actually founded in 1348 by Charles IV, as an entirely new town – three times as big as Staré Město – intended to link the southern fortress of Vyšehrad with Staré Město to the north. Large market squares, wide streets, and a level of town-planning far ahead of its time were employed to transform Prague into the new capital city of the Holy Roman Empire. Instead, however, Nové Město quickly became the city's poorest quarter after Josefov, renowned as a hotbed of Hussitism and radicalism throughout the centuries. In the second half of the nineteenth century, the authorities set about a campaign of slum clearance similar to that inflicted on the Jewish quarter; only the churches and a few important historical buildings were left standing, but Charles' street layout survived pretty much intact. The leading architects of the day began to line the wide boulevards with ostentatious examples of their work, which were eagerly snapped up by the new class of status-conscious businessman – a process that has continued into this century, making Nové Město the most architecturally varied part of Prague.

Today, Nové Město remains the city's main commercial and business district, housing most of the hotels, nightclubs, cafés, fast-food outlets and department stores. The obvious starting point, and

---

An Art-Nouveau hit list

Prague's Art Nouveau (the term is *secesní* in Czech) ranges from the vivacious floral motifs of the Paris metro to the more restrained style of the Viennese Secession. The following are some of the more striking examples covered in this chapter.

Grand Hotel Evropa	p.118	Pojišťovna Praha	p.122
Hlahol	p.133	Praha hlavní nádraží	p.120
Hotel Central	p.125	Topičův dům	p.122
Obecní dům	p.125	U Dorflerů	p.124
Peterkův dům	p.117	U Nováků	p.128

probably the only place in Prague most visitors can put a name to, is **Wenceslas Square**, hub of the modern city, and somewhere you're bound to find yourself passing through again and again. The two principal streets which lead off it are **Národní** and **Na příkopě**, the latter pedestrianized and sporting benches, buskers, and a handful of convenient café terraces from which to view the streetlife. Together, these streets also contain some of Prague's finest late nineteenth-century and Art-Nouveau architecture. Along with Wenceslas Square, Národní and Na příkopě form the *zlatý kříž* or golden cross, Prague's commercial centre and probably the most expensive slice of real estate in the capital.

The rest of Nové Město, which spreads out northeast and southwest of the square, is much less explored, and for the most part solidly residential; unusually for Prague, using the tram and metro systems to get around here will save some unnecessary legwork. A few specific sights are worth singling out for attention – the **Dvořák Museum** on Ke Karlovu and the **Mánes Gallery** on the waterfront, for example – but the rest is decidedly less exciting than all that's gone before. However, if your ultimate destination is Vyšehrad (see p.137), you can easily take in some of the more enjoyable bits of southern Nové Město en route.

Wenceslas Square and around

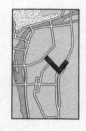

The natural pivot around which modern Prague revolves, and the focus of the events of November 1989, is **Wenceslas Square** (Václavské náměstí), more of a wide, gently sloping boulevard than a square as such. It's scarcely a conventional – or even convenient – space in which to hold mass demonstrations, yet night after night following the November 17 *masakr* (see p.121), more than 250,000 people crammed into the square, often enduring subzero temperatures to call for the resignation of the Party leaders and demand free elections. On November 27, the whole of Prague came to a standstill, a bigger crowd than ever converging on the square to show their support for the two-hour nationwide general strike called by the opposition umbrella group, Občanské fórum (Civic Forum), who led the revolution. It was this last mass mobilization that proved decisive – by noon the next day, the Communist old guard had thrown in the towel.

The square's **history of protest** goes back to the revolutionary events of 1848, which began with a large outdoor mass held here. On the crest of the nationalist disturbances, the square – which had been known as Koňský trh (Horse Market) since its foundation as such by Charles IV – was given its present name. It was appropriate, then, that the First Republic was declared here in 1918. In 1948, the square was filled to capacity once more, this time with Communist demonstrators in support of the February coup. In

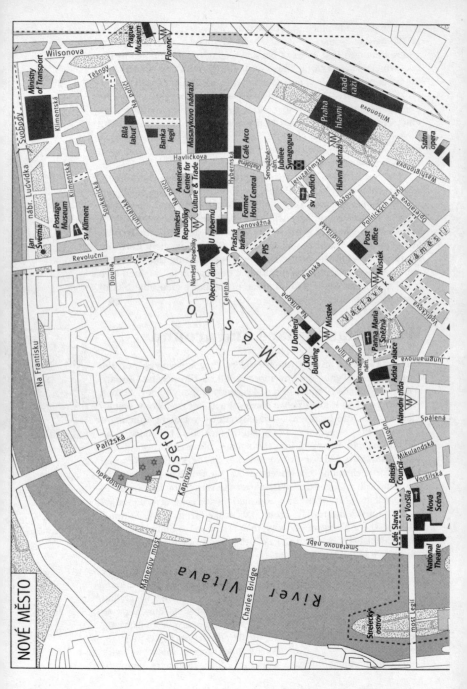

NOVÉ MĚSTO

Wilsonova
Ministry of Transport
Svobody
nábř. Ludvíka
Klimentská
Těšnov
Na poříčí
Prague Museum
Florenc
Jan Švermy
nábř. Ludvíka
Klimentská
Klimentská
Soukenická
Bílá labuť
Banka legií
Masarykovo nádraží
Praha hlavní nádraží
Wilsonova
Státní opera
Postage Museum
sv Kliment
Na poříčí
Havlíčkova
Hybernská
Café Arco
Senovážné nám.
Jubilee Synagogue
Jeruzalémská
Hlavní nádraží
Washingtonova
Opletalova
Revoluční
Náměstí Republiky
American Center for Culture & Trade
Former Hotel Central
Diažďená
sv Jindřich
Růžová
Politických věznu
Opletalova
Dlouhá
Náměstí Republiky
Obecní dům
Celetná
U hybernů
Prašná brána
Senovážná
PIS
Panská
Jindřišská
Post office
Václavské náměstí
Můstek
Na Františku
s t
a
r
é
M ě s t o
Na příkopě
U Donňerů
Můstek
28 října
Můstek
Panna Maria Sněžná
Jungmannovo nám.
Jungmannova
Pařížská
Josefov
Kaprova
17
CKD Building
Adria Palace
Národní třída
Vodičkova
Maiselova
Mánesův most
Charles Bridge
River Vltava
Smetanovo nábř.
Národní
British Council
Café Slavia
sv Voršila
Mikulandská
Voršilská
Nová Scéna
Spálená
National Theatre
Střelecký ostrov
most Legií

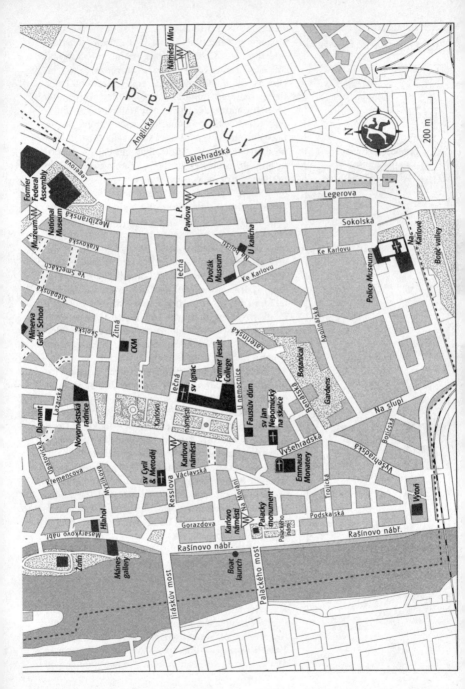

Náměstí Míru

Vinohrady

Anglická

Bělehradská

N

200 m

Legerova

Former Federal Assembly

Legerova

National Museum

Muzeum

Mezibranská

I. P. Pavlova

Sokolská

Na Karlově

Krakovská

Ke Karlovu

Bořič valley

Ve Smečkách

Na bojišti

U kalicha

Štěpánská

Ječná

Dvořák Museum

Police Museum

Ke Karlovu

Minerva Girls' School

Školská

Žitná

Apolinářská

Katerinská

CKM

Former Jesuit College

Ječná

Lazarská

sv Ignác

U nemocnice

Botanical Gardens

Benátská

Diamant

Opatovická

Novoměstská radnice

Karlovo

Karlovo náměstí

Faustův dům

sv Jan Nepomucký na skalce

Na slupi

Kremencova

Myslíkova

Resslova

Vyšehradská

Vyšehradská

Botičská

sv Cyril & Metoděj

Karlovo náměstí

Václavská

Emmaus Monastery

Trojická

Vyton

Hlahol

Gorazdova

Na Moráni

Karlovo náměstí

Palacký monument

Podskalská

Masarykovo nábř.

Palackého most

Rašínovo nábř.

Rašínovo nábř.

Žofín

Mánes gallery

Jiráskův most

Boat launch

Palackého most

NOVÉ MĚSTO

115

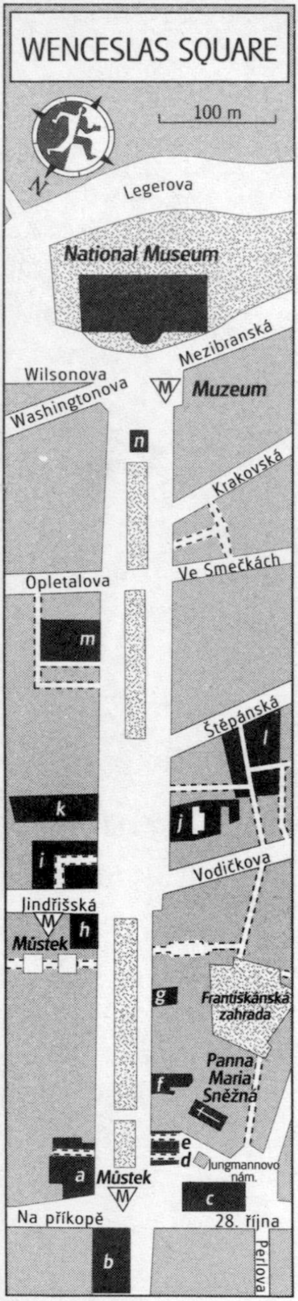
WENCESLAS SQUARE
100 m
N
Legerova
National Museum
Mezibranská
Wilsonova
Washingtonova
Muzeum
n
Krakovská
Ve Smečkách
Opletalova
m
Štěpánská
l
k
j
i
Vodičkova
Jindřišská
Můstek
h
g
Františkánská zahrada
Panna Maria Sněžná
f
e
d
Jungmannovo nám.
a
Můstek
c
Na příkopě
28. října
b
Perlova

August 1968, it was the scene of some of the most violent confrontations between the Soviet invaders and the local Czechs, during which the National Museum came under fire – according to the Czechs, the Soviet officer in charge mistook it for the Parliament building, though they were most probably aiming for the nearby Radio Prague building, which was transmitting news of the Soviet invasion out to the West. And, of course, it was here on January 19, 1969, that Jan Palach set fire to himself in protest at the continuing occupation of the country by Russian troops.

Despite the square's medieval origins, its oldest building dates from the eighteenth century, and the vast majority are much younger. As the city's money moved south of Staré Město during the industrial revolution, so the square became the architectural showpiece of the nation, and is now lined with self-important six- or seven-storey buildings, representing every artistic trend of the last hundred years, from neo-Renaissance to Socialist Realism. Even if you've no interest in modern architecture, there's plenty to keep you occupied in the shops, arcades, cinemas, theatres and general hubbub of the square.

Wenceslas Square has always been the place to be seen, and above all to parade the latest four-wheeled frivolity, from luxury coach to Lamborghini. Gone are the times when unfamiliarity with western vehicles meant that even a Vespa was looked on as if it were a recently landed intergalactic spaceship; these days, more than a little post-revolutionary cynicism accompanies the stares. This is also the one place in Prague where life goes on after midnight – the hotels and nightclubs buzzing, and the police playing cat-and-mouse with the pimps and prostitutes, while turning a blind eye to most of the nation's new-found vices.

The bottom of the square

The busiest part of Wenceslas Square and a popular place to meet up before hitting town is around Můstek, the city's most central metro station, at the northern end of the square. It's dominated by a hulking wedge of sculptured concrete and gold, the **Palác Koruna (a)**, built for an insurance company in 1914 by one of Jan Kotěra's many pupils and employing a rare mixture of heavy constructivism and gilded Secession-style ornamentation. The rather half-hearted neo-modernism of the ČKD dům (b), directly above the main entrance/exit to Můstek, is no architectural match for it, though its rooftop café does boast an unbeatable view straight up Wenceslas Square. For a street-level lookout, try the café terrace on the ground floor of the former **Civic Forum headquarters (c)**, which is, strictly speaking, on 28 října, the short street connecting Wenceslas Square with Národní.

From Baťa to Kafka

On the opposite side of the square from Palác Koruna are two functionalist buildings designed by Ludvík Kysela in the late 1920s, billed at the time as the first glass curtain-wall buildings. Along with the Hotel Juliš (see below), they represent the perfect expression of the optimistic mood of progress and modernism that permeated the interwar republic. The building on the right as you face them (d) was the first to be erected by the chocolate firm, Lindt; the **Baťa store (e)**, on the left, followed a few years later. The latter was built for the Czech shoe magnate, Tomáš Baťa, one of the greatest patrons of avant-garde Czech art, who fled the country in 1948, when the Communists nationalized the shoe industry; the store was returned to the family, along with a number of their shoe factories, after 1989 and has now reopened as a shoe shop. Even if you've no intention of buying a pair of Baťa boots, it's worth taking the lift to the top floor, which hosts the occasional Baťa exhibition and has a bird's-eye view onto the square.

Twenty-five years earlier, Czech architecture was in the throes of its own version of Art Nouveau, one of whose earliest practitioners was Jan Kotěra. The **Peterkův dům (f)**, a slender essay in the new style, was his first work, undertaken at the tender age of 28. Kotěra, a pupil of the great Otto Wagner, came from the restrained Viennese school of the Secession, and very soon moved on to a much more brutal constructivism. Another supreme example of Czech functionalism, a few doors further up at no. 22, is the **Hotel Juliš (g)**, designed by Pavel Janák, who had already made his name as one of the leading lights of the short-lived Czech Cubist (and later Rondo-Cubist) movement (see p.143). Another point of interest, on the corner of Jindřišská, is the neo-Baroque **Assicurazione Generali (h)** – now home to the Polish Cultural Institute. It was designed by Osvald Polívka and Bedřich Ohmann, and was where the young Kafka worked for a couple of years as an insurance clerk.

Družba to Jalta

One of the Communists' most miserable attempts to continue the square's tradition of grand architecture was the **Družba** department store (i), which stands like a 1970s reject on the other side of Jindřišská. Diagonally opposite is the **Melantrich** publishing house (j), whose first floor is occupied by the offices of the Socialist Party newspaper, *Svobodné slovo* (The Free Word). For forty years, the Socialist Party was a loyal puppet of the Communist government, but on the second night of the November 1989 demonstrations, the newspaper handed over its well-placed balcony to the opposition speakers of Občanské fórum (Civic Forum), and later witnessed the historic appearance of Havel and Dubček.

Melantrich House faces probably the most famous and the two most ornate buildings on the entire square, the Art-Nouveau **Grand Hotel Evropa (k)**, and its slim neighbour, the Hotel Meran, both built in 1903–05 by two of Ohmann's disciples, Bendelmayer and Dryák. They represent everything the Czech modern movement stood against: chiefly, ornament for ornament's sake, not that this has in any way dented the *Evropa*'s popularity. The café terrace has always had a reputation for low-key cruising and a great deal of posing, but it's worth forgoing the sunlight for the sumptuous interior, with its symbolist art and elaborate brass fittings and light fixtures, unchanged since the hotel first opened.

Opposite the hotel is the vast **Lucerna Palace (l)**, one of the more appealing of the square's numerous dimly lit shopping arcades, designed in the early part of this century in Moorish style by, among others, Havel's own grandfather. The main entrance is just up Štěpánská, and gives access to the palace's lavishly decorated cinema and vast concert hall. Apart from a brief glance at the **Hotel Jalta (m)**, built in the Stalinist aesthetic of the 1950s, there's nothing more to stop for, architecturally speaking, until you get to the Wenceslas Monument.

The Wenceslas Monument

A statue of Saint Wenceslas (sv Václav) has stood at the top of the square since 1680 but the present **Wenceslas Monument (n)**, by the father of Czech sculpture, Josef Václav Myslbek, was not finally unveiled until 1912, after thirty years on the drawing board. The Czech patron saint sits astride his mighty steed, surrounded by smaller-scale representations of four other Bohemian saints – his mother Ludmilla, Procopius, Adalbert and Agnes – added in the 1920s. It was at the foot of this monument that the new republic of Czechoslovakia was declared in 1918, while World War I was still raging on the western front. In 1968, and again in 1989, the monument was used as a national political noticeboard, constantly festooned in posters, flags and slogans; even now, it remains the city's favourite soapbox venue.

*For a brief
biography of
Wenceslas, see
p.49.*

A few metres below the statue, on January 19, 1969, the 21-year-old student Jan Palach set himself alight in protest against the continuing occupation of his country by the Soviets. His example was emulated four days later by another four people around the country, and, on the same spot, on February 25 – the anniversary of the Communist coup – by a fifth, Jan Zajíc. An impromptu martyrs' shrine, set up in the aftermath of the 1989 revolution, has now been formalized as a simple memorial to *obětem komunismu* (the victims of Communism), adorned with flowers and photos of Palach and Zajíc.

The National Museum

At the top, southern, end of Wenceslas Square sits the broad, brooding hulk of the **National Museum**, built by Josef Schulz. Deliberately modelled on the great European museums of Paris and Vienna, it dominates the view up the square like a giant golden eagle with outstretched wings. Along with the National Theatre (see below), this is one of the great landmarks of the nineteenth-century Czech *národní obrození*, sporting a monumental gilt-framed glass cupola, worthy clumps of sculptural decoration and narrative frescoes from Czech history.

The National Museum is open Mon & Fri 9am–4pm, Wed, Thurs, Sat & Sun 9am–5pm.

Unless you're a geologist or a zoologist, you're unlikely to be excited by most of the exhibits – room after room of stuffed animals and skeletons, plus endless display cases full of rocks – but it's worth taking at least a quick look at the ornate marble entrance hall, and the **Pantheon** of Czech notables at the top of the main staircase. Arranged under the glass-domed hall are some forty-eight busts and statues of distinguished Czech men (plus a couple of token women and Slovaks), including the universally adored T. G. Masaryk, the country's founding president, whose statue was removed by the Communists from every other public place. Since the revolution, the appeal of the museum's temporary exhibitions (on themes ranging from Masaryk to dinosaurs) has increased dramatically, so it's always worth checking to see what's on.

Wilsonova

At the southern end of Wenceslas Square is some of the worst blight that Communist planners inflicted on Prague; above all, the six-lane highway that now separates Nové Město from the residential suburb of Vinohrady to the east and south, and effectively cuts off the National Museum from Wenceslas Square. Previously known as Vitězného února (Victorious February) after the 1948 Communist coup, the road was renamed **Wilsonova** in honour of US President Woodrow Wilson (a personal friend of the Masaryk family), who effectively gave the country its independence from Austria-Hungary in 1918.

The Prague Stock Exchange building alongside the National Museum, only completed in the 1930s but rendered entirely redundant by the 1948 coup, was another victim of postwar "reconstruction". The architect Karel Prager was given the task of designing a new "socialist" **Federal Assembly** building on the same site, without destroying the old bourse: he opted for a supremely unappealing bronze-tinted plate-glass structure, supported by concrete stilts and sitting uncomfortably on top of its diminutive predecessor. Since the break-up of the country, the building has lost its *raison d'être* and now provides a home for, among other things, *Radio Free Europe*.

Next to the Parliament building, the grandiose **Státní opera** (State Opera), built by the Viennese duo Helmer and Fellner, looks stunted and deeply affronted by the traffic which now tears past its front entrance. It was opened in 1888 as the *Neues Deutsches Theater*, shortly after the Czechs had built their own National Theatre on the waterfront. Always second fiddle to the Stavovské divadlo, though equally ornate inside, it was one of the last great building projects of Prague's once all-powerful German minority. The velvet and gold interior is still as fresh as it was when the Bohemian-born composer Gustav Mahler brought the traffic to a standstill, conducting the premiere of his Seventh Symphony.

The last building on this deafening freeway is **Praha hlavní nádraží**, Prague's main railway station, and one of the final glories of the dying Empire, designed by Josef Fanta and officially opened in 1909 as the *Franz Josefs Bahnhof*. Trapped in the overpolished subterranean modern section, it's easy to miss the station's surviving Art-Nouveau parts. The original entrance on Wilsonova still exudes imperial confidence, with its wrought-iron canopy and naked figurines clinging to the sides of the towers; on the other side of the road, two great glass protrusions signal the new entrance in the Vrchlického sady.

Národní and Na příkopě

Národní and Na příkopě trace the course of the old moat, which was finally filled in in 1760. Their boomerang curve marks the border between Staré Město and Nové Město (strictly speaking, the dividing line runs down the middle of the street). Ranged along both streets are a variety of stylish edifices and some of the city's most flamboyant Art-Nouveau buildings.

Jungmannovo náměstí

Before you hit Národní proper, the short street of 28 října (October 28 – the foundation of the First Republic) connects the northern end of Wenceslas Square with **Jungmannovo náměstí**. The square takes its name from Josef Jungmann (1772–1847), a prolific writer, translator and leading light of the Czech national revival, whose pensive, seated statue was erected here in 1878. This small, ill-proportioned square boasts an unrivalled panoply of Czech architectural curiosities, including Emil Králíček and Matěj Blecha's unique **Cubist streetlamp** (and seat) from 1912, hidden away beyond the Jungmann statue in the far eastern corner of the square and the gleaming, functionalist facade of the ARA department store (now the Investiční banka), built on the corner of Perlova and 28 října.

The Adria Palace

Národní and
Na příkopě

Diagonally opposite the ARA department store is the square's most
imposing building, the chunky charcoal-coloured, vigorously-
sculptured **Adria Palace**, on the south side of the square. It was
designed in the early 1920s by Pavel Janák and Josef Zasche, with
sculptural extras by Otto Gutfreund and a central *Seafaring* group
by Jan Štursa. Janák was a pioneering figure in the short-lived,
prewar Czech Cubist movement; after the war, he and Josef Gočár
attempted to create a national style of architecture appropriate for
the newly founded republic. The style was dubbed "Rondo-Cubism"
– semi-circular motifs are a recurrent theme – though the Adria
Palace owes as much to the Italian Renaissance as it does to the new
national style.

*There's an
earlier, purer
example of
Rondo-Cubism
at no. 4
Jungmannovo
náměstí,
decorated in
the Czech
national
colours of red
and white, and
you'll find
another
example of the
style on p.127.*

Originally built for the Italian insurance company *Reunione
Adriatica di Sicurità* – hence its current name – the basement of
the Adria Palace was until very recently a studio theatre for the multimedia **Laterna magika** (Magic Lantern) company. In 1989, it
became the underground nerve centre of the Velvet Revolution, when
Civic Forum found temporary shelter here shortly after their inaugu-
ral meeting on the Sunday following the November 17 demonstration. Against a stage backdrop for Dürenmatt's *Minotaurus*, the
Forum thrashed out tactics in the dressing rooms and gave daily
press conferences in the auditorium during the crucial fortnight
before the Communists relinquished power. Since then, *Laterna
magika* have moved to much bigger venues, and the *Divadlo za
branou III* is now based here instead. Upstairs, there's a good café-
terrace (see p.200) from which to observe life on the square below.

The Church of Panna Maria Sněžná

Right beside the Cubist streetlamp is the medieval gateway of the
church of **Panna Maria Sněžná** (St Mary-of-the-Snows), once one of
the great landmarks of Wenceslas Square, when it towered over the

---

The masakr – November 17, 1989

On the night of Friday, November 17, 1989, a 50,000-strong, officially
sanctioned student demonstration, organized by the students' union, *SSM*
(League of Young Socialists), worked its way down Národní with the
intention of reaching Wenceslas Square. Halfway down the street they
were confronted by the *bílé přílby* (white helmets) and *červené barety*
(red berets) of the hated riot-police. For what must have seemed like
hours, there was a stalemate as the students sat down and refused to
disperse, some of them handing flowers out to the police. Suddenly, without any warning, the police attacked and what became known as the
masakr (massacre) began – no one was actually killed, though it wasn't
for want of trying by the police. Under the arches of Kaňka's house
(Národní 16), there's a small symbolic bronze relief of eight hands reaching out for help, a permanent shrine in memory of the hundreds who were
hospitalized in the violence.

---

backs of the old two-storey houses that lined the square, but now
barely visible from any of the surrounding streets. If the gates are
shut, try going through the unpromising courtyard back near the
Jungmann statue.

Like most of Nové Město's churches, the Panna Maria Sněžná
was founded by Charles IV, who envisaged a vast coronation church
on a scale comparable with the St Vitus Cathedral, on which work
had just begun. Unfortunately, the money ran out shortly after
completion of the chancel; the result is curious – a church which is
short in length, but equal to the cathedral in height. The hundred-
foot-high vaulting – which collapsed on the Franciscans who inherited the half-built building in the seventeenth century – does little to
stave off claustrophobia, further compounded by an overbearing
Baroque altar which touches the ceiling. To get an idea of the
intended scale of the finished structure, take a stroll through the
Františkánská zahrada, to the south of the church; these gardens
make a lovely hide-away from Nové Mesto's bustle, marred only by
the intrusive modern garden furniture.

Národní

The eastern end of **Národní** is taken up with shops, galleries and
clubs, all of which begin to peter out as you near the river. At the
last crossroads before the waterfront is the new **British Council**
building, which formerly belonged to the old GDR. On the outside,
the original constructivist facade, designed in the 1930s by Osvald
Polívka, has been kept intact, while the light interior has been thoroughly and imaginatively modernized in an interesting synthesis of
central European and British architectural styles, using ample helpings of the country's surplus glass. There's a window gallery on the
ground floor overlooking Národní, which is run by the British
Council, and you're free to walk in an take a peek at the lobby – the
entrance is up Voršilská – where you can pick up information on the
latest cultural offerings sponsored by the BC.

Further down Národní, on the right-hand side, is an eye-catching
duo of much earlier Art-Nouveau buildings, designed by Polívka in
1907–08. The first, at no. 7, was built for the **pojišťovna Praha** (Prague
Savings Bank), hence the beautiful mosaic lettering above the windows
advertising *život* (life insurance) and *kapital* (loans), as well as help
with your *důchod* (pension) and *věno* (dowry). Next door, the slightly
more ostentatious **Topičův dům**, headquarters of *Československý
spisovatel*, the official state publishers, provides the perfect
accompaniment, with a similarly ornate wrought-iron and glass canopy.

Opposite, the convent and church of **sv Voršila** (St Ursula) are
distinguished by the rare sight (in this part of town) of a tree sticking out of its white facade. When it was completed in 1678, this was
one of the first truly flamboyant Baroque buildings in Prague, and
its white stucco and frescoed interior have recently been restored to

their original state. The Ursuline nuns were booted out by the Communists, but have returned post-1989 to found one of the first ecclesiastical schools in the country.

Národní and Na příkopě

The National Theatre and around

At the western end of Národní, overlooking the Vltava, is the gold-crested **National Theatre** (Národní divadlo), proud symbol of the Czech nation. Refused money by the Austrian state, Czechs of all classes dug deep into their pockets to raise funds for the venture themselves. The foundation stones, gathered from various histori-cally significant sites in Bohemia and Moravia, were laid in 1868 by the historian and politician, František Palacký, and the composer, Bedřich Smetana; the architect, Josef Zítek, spent the next thirteen years on the project. In August 1881, just days before the official opening night, fire ripped through the building, destroying every-thing except the outer walls. Within two years the whole thing was rebuilt – even the emperor contributed this time – under the supervi-sion of Josef Schulz (who went on to design the National Museum), and it opened once more to the strains of Smetana's opera *Libuše*. The grand portal on the north side of the theatre is embellished with suitably triumphant allegorical figures, and, inside, every square inch is taken up with paintings and sculptures by leading artists of the Czech national revival. Tickets are relatively cheap but most produc-tions are in Czech, so unless there's an opera or ballet on, content yourself with a quick peek at the decor prior to a performance.

See p.215 for details of Prague's theatres and box offices.

Standing behind the National Theatre, and in dramatic contrast with it, is the theatre's state-of-the-art extension, the ultra-modern glass box of the **Nová scéna**, designed by Karel Prager, the leading architect of the Communist era, and completed in 1983. It's one of those buildings most Praguers love to hate – it was described by one Czech as looking like "frozen piss" – though compared to much of Prague's Communist-era architecture, it's not that bad. Just for the record, the lump of molten rock in the courtyard is a symbolic evocation of *My Socialist Country*, by Malejovský.

The famous **Café Slavia**, opposite the theatre, has been a favourite haunt of the city's writers, dissidents and artists (and, inevitably, actors) since the days of the First Republic. The Czech avant-garde movement, *Devětsil*, led by Karel Teige, used to hold its meetings here in the 1920s, recorded for posterity by another of its members, the Nobel prize-winner Jaroslav Seifert, in his *Slavia Poems*. It's been carelessly modernized since those arcadian days, and for the last few years has been closed. The lease is currently in the hands of an American company, who have been widely criticized for taking so long in refurbishing what is a very popular Prague institution. Legal battles, and a brief and unofficial opening by disgruntled Czechs, have created bad feeling on both sides of the Atlantic; despite all this, the café will hopefully open again some-time in the near future.

For more on Jaroslav Seifert, see p.146.

Na příkopě

Heading northeastwards from Můstek at the bottom end of Wenceslas Square, you can join the crush of bodies ambling down **Na příkopě** (literally "On the moat"). The street was once lined on both sides with grandiose buildings, like the former *Haas* department store at no. 4, built in 1869–71 by Theophil von Hansen, the architect responsible for much of the redevelopment of the Ring in Vienna. Many of the finest buildings, though – like the *Café Corso* and the *Café Français*, once the favourite haunts of Prague's German-Jewish literary set – were torn down and replaced during the enthusiastic construction boom of the interwar republic. The Art-Nouveau U **Dorflerů**, at no. 7, from 1905, is one of the few survivors along this stretch, its gilded floral curlicues gleaming in the midday sun.

The PIS tourist office is at no. 22.

Further along, there are another couple of interesting buildings at no. 18 and 20, originally designed by Polívka for the *Zemská banka* and connected by a kind of Bridge of Sighs suspended over Panská. It's worth nipping inside the **Živnostenka banka**, on the left, built in the 1890s in no-expense-spared neo-Renaissance style, to appreciate the financial might of Czech capital in the last decades of the Austro-Hungarian Empire. On the right is the **Státní banka**, built some twenty years later, an arresting blend of the competing styles of the day – Art Nouveau and nineteenth-century historicism. Yet more financial institutions, this time from the dour 1930s, line the far end of Na příkopě, as it opens up into náměstí Republiky.

Northern Nové Město

Náměstí Republiky is worth pausing at, if only to admire the Obecní dům – Prague's most alluring Art-Nouveau structure – but this apart, there's nothing in the northern or eastern part of Nové Město that merits a special trip. Nevertheless, you may find yourself in this part of town by dint of its shops, restaurants and hotels, or perhaps en route to Prague's main domestic train station, Masarykovo nádraží. Tourists rarely venture this far east, and for that reason alone, it makes an interesting diversion, revealing a side to Prague that few visitors see.

Náměstí Republiky

Náměstí Republiky is an unruly space, made more so since the construction of its metro station and the ugly brown *Kotva* department store, built by Swedish architects in the 1970s. The oldest structure on the square is the **Prašná brána** (Powder Tower), one of the eight medieval gate-towers that once guarded Staré Město. The present tower was begun by King Vladislav Jagiello in 1475, shortly after he'd moved into the royal court, which was situated next door

The Powder Tower is open daily 10am–5pm.

at the time. Work stopped when he retreated to the Hrad to avoid the wrath of his subjects; later on, it was used to store gunpowder – hence the name and the reason for the damage incurred in 1757. The small historical exhibition inside traces the tower's architectural metamorphosis over the centuries, up to its present remodelling courtesy of the nineteenth-century restorer, Josef Mocker. Most people, though, ignore the displays, and climb straight up for the modest view from the top.

The Obecní dům

Attached to the tower, and built on the ruins of the old royal court, the **Obecní dům** (Municipal House) is by far the most exciting Art-Nouveau building in Prague, one of the few places that still manages to conjure up the atmosphere of Prague's turn-of-the-century café society. Conceived as a cultural centre for the Czech community, it's probably the finest architectural achievement of the Czech national revival, designed by Osvald Polívka and Antonín Balšánek, and extravagantly decorated inside and out with the help of almost every artist connected with the Czech Secession. From the lifts to the cloakrooms, just about all the furnishings remain as they were when the building was completed in 1911, and the simplest way of soaking up the cavernous interior – peppered with mosaics and pendulous brass chandeliers – is to have a beer and a bite to eat in the *restaurace*, or sit around the fountain at the far end of the equally spacious *kavárna*, though both are likely to remain closed for some time whilst the building is restored (see p.201 & p.209).

It's worth wandering upstairs, too, if you can, for a peek at the central **Smetanova síň**, the city's largest concert hall, where the opening salvo of the Prague Spring Festival – traditionally a rendition of Smetana's *Má vlast* (My Country) – takes place in the presence of the president. Recently, there have been **guided tours** of the building, showing off its abundant treasures (which include paintings by Alfons Mucha, Jan Preisler and Max Švabinský, among others); check at the *PIS* for the current state of affairs. Otherwise, there's a chance you may be able to just stroll around much of the building unsupervised.

Hybernská and Senovážné náměstí

Large exhibitions – occasionally worth a look – are held in **U hybernů** (The Hibernians), a haughty Neoclassical building situated opposite the Obecní dům, built as a customs office in the Napoleonic period, on the site of a Baroque church which belonged to the order of Irish Franciscans who fled Tudor England in the seventeenth century (hence its name). If you walk down **Hybernská** from here, you'll pass the Art-Nouveau **Hotel Central** (now housing a theatre – the Komorní divadlo) on the right. Designed by Dryák and Bendelmayer (who built the Grand Hotel Evropa) and dating from 1900, this is one of the few restored buildings in the area, its gilded decoration all the more startling for it.

Opposite the hotel is the former headquarters of the Social Democratic Party, which was forcibly amalgamated with the Communist Party shortly after the 1948 coup. The party regained its independence in 1989, but, unable to shake off the stigma of its past collaboration, failed to win any significant support in the polls; the building is now the American Center for Culture and Trade. In January 1912, a small backroom was given over to a congress of the Russian Social Democratic Labour Party. The party was deeply divided, and the meeting poorly attended, with only fourteen voting delegates present (all but two of them were Bolsheviks), and Lenin himself in the chair. It was this meeting which pushed through the formal takeover of the party by the Bolsheviks, to the exclusion of the Mensheviks and others, and gave the Czech Communists the perfect excuse for turning the whole place into a vast museum dedicated to Lenin, of which there is now, not surprisingly, absolutely no trace.

Around Masarykovo nádraží and Senovážné náměstí

A little further down, a wrought-iron canopy marks the entrance to Prague's first railway station, **Masarykovo nádraží**, opened in 1845 – a modest, almost provincial affair compared to the Art-Nouveau Praha hlavní nádraží. On the opposite side of Hybernská is the **Café Arco**, once a favourite of Kafka (who worked nearby), and the circle of writers known as the *Arconauts*. The current incumbents make nothing of its literary associations, and have filled the place with slot machines and pool tables.

South of Masarykovo nádraží, down Dlážděná, is the old hay market, **Senovážné náměstí** (still occasionally referred to as Gorkého náměstí), packed out with parked cars and a couple of market stalls. Its most distinguished feature is the freestanding fifteenth-century belfry of the church of **sv Jindřich** (St Henry); both have undergone several facelifts, most recently by the ubiquitous Gothic restorer, Josef Mocker.

Prague's other synagogues are covered in Chapter 4.

A short way up Jeruzalémská, you'll find the **Jubilee Synagogue** (Jubilejní synagóga), built in the early part of this century, in a colourful Moorish style similar to that of the Spanish Synagogue in Josefov. This and the Old-New Synagogue are the only synagogues in Prague that still hold regular sabbath services; at all other times, it's usually closed.

North of Masarykovo nádraží

Running roughly parallel with Hybernská, to the north of Masarykovo nádraží, is the much busier street of **Na poříčí**, an area that, like sv Havel in Staré Město, was originally settled by German merchants. Kafka spent most of his working life as a frustrated and unhappy clerk for the *Arbeiter-Unfall-Versicherungs-Anstalt*

(Workers' Accident Insurance Company), in the grand nineteenth-century building at no. 7. Further along on the right is a much more unusual piece of corporate architecture, the **Banka legií**, one of Pavel Janák's rare Rondo-Cubist efforts from the early 1920s. Set into the bold smoky-red moulding is a striking white marble frieze by Otto Gutfreund, depicting the epic march across Siberia undertaken by the Czechoslovak Legion and their embroilment in the Russian Revolution. The glass curtain-walled **Bílá labuť** (White Swan) department store, opposite, is a good example of the functionalist style which Janák and others went on to embrace in late 1920s and 1930s.

For more on Janák and the Cubists, see p.143.

As a lively shopping street, Na poříčí seems very much out on a limb, as do the cluster of hotels at the end of the street, and around the corner in **Těšnov**. The reason behind this is the now defunct Těšnov train station, which was demolished in the 1960s to make way for the monstrous Wilsonova flyover. The neo-Renaissance mansion housing the **Prague Museum** (Muzeum hlavní města Prahy), on the other side of the flyover to the south, is the lone survivor of this redevelopment. Inside, there's an ad hoc collection of the city's art, a number of antique bicycles, and usually an intriguing temporary exhibition on some aspect of the city. The museum's prize possession, though, is Antonín Langweil's paper model of Prague which he completed after eleven years in 1834. It's a fascinating insight into early nineteenth-century Prague – predominantly Baroque, with the cathedral incomplete and the Jewish quarter "unsanitized" – and, consequently, has served as one of the most useful records for the city's restorers. The most surprising thing, of course, is that so little has changed.

The Prague Museum is open Tues–Sun 10am–6pm.

Nábřeží Ludvika Svobody and around

North of Na poříčí, close to the riverbank, nábřeží Ludvika Svobody, there's another museum which might appeal to some: the **Postage Museum** (Poštovní muzeum), housed in the Vávra mill on Nové mlýny, near one of Prague's many water towers. The first floor contains a series of jolly nineteenth-century wall paintings of Romantic Austrian landscapes, and a collection of drawings on postman themes. The real philately is on the ground floor – a vast international collection of stamps arranged in vertical pull-out drawers. The Czechoslovak issues are historically and artistically interesting, as well as of appeal to collectors. Stamps became a useful tool in the propaganda wars of this century; even such short-lived ventures as the Hungarian-backed Slovak Socialist Republic of 1918–19 and the Slovak National Uprising of autumn 1944 managed to print special issues. Under the First Republic, the country's leading artists, notably Alfons Mucha and Max Švabinský, were commissioned to design stamps, some of which are exceptionally beautiful.

The Postage Museum is open Tues–Sun 9am–5pm.

As you leave the Postage Museum, look across to your left towards Revoluční – if the statue of **Jan Šverma** is still standing, it will be one of the few Communist-era monuments to have survived the post-1989 iconoclasm that brought countless statues tumbling down. Šverma, who joined the Communist Party shortly after it was formed in 1921 and died fighting against the Nazis in 1944, is currently being targeted by the Prague branch of the Confederation of Political Prisoners who want him removed from his pedestal, and the nearby bridge (currently Švermův most) renamed. Further east along the embankment is another monument of the Communist era, the former headquarters of the Party's Central Committee, now the **Ministry of Tranport**, where Dubček and his fellow reformers were arrested in August 1968, before being spirited away to Moscow for frank and fraternal discussions.

Southern Nové Město

The streets south of Národní and Wenceslas Square still run along the medieval lines of Charles IV's town plan, though they're now lined with grand, nineteenth-century buildings. Such is their scale, however, that some of these broad boulevards – like Žitná and Ječná – have become the main arteries for Prague's steadily increasing traffic. Together with the large distances involved, this makes southern Nové Město one part of the city where trams can come in useful.

South to Karlovo náměstí

Of the many roads which head down towards Karlovo náměstí, **Vodičkova** is probably the most impressive, running southwest for half a kilometre from Wenceslas Square. You can catch several trams (#3, #14, #24) along this route, though there are a handful of buildings worth checking out on the way, so you may choose to walk. The first, **U Nováků**, is impossible to miss, thanks to Jan Preisler's mosaic of bucolic frolicking (its actual subject, *Trade and Industry*, is confined to edges of the picture), and Polívka's curvilinear window frames and delicate, ivy-like ironwork. Originally built for the *Novák* department store in the early 1900s, for the last sixty years it has been a cabaret hall, restaurant and café all rolled into one; however, the original fittings have long since been destroyed.

Halfway down the street, at no. 15, the *McDonald's* "restaurant" – the first to open in the Czech Republic in March 1992 – must qualify as a landmark of sorts. It occupies the site of the dining halls which once belonged to the imposing neo-Renaissance school on the opposite side of the road. Covered in bright-red sgraffito patterning, the **Minerva girls' school** was founded in 1866 and was the first such institution in Prague. At the beginning of this century, the school became notorious for the antics of its pupils, the "Minervans", who shocked bourgeois Czech society with their experimentations with fashion, drugs and sexual freedom (see box above). As Vodičkova curves left towards Karlovo náměstí,

Milena Jesenská

The most famous "Minervan" was **Milena Jesenská**, born in 1896 into a
Czech family whose ancestry stretched back to the sixteenth century.
Shortly after leaving school, she was confined to a mental asylum by her
father when he discovered that she was having an affair with a Jew. On her
release, she married the Jew and moved to Vienna, where she took a job as
a railway porter to support the two of them. While living in Vienna, she
sent a Czech translation of one of Kafka's short stories to his publisher;
Kafka wrote back himself, and so began their platonic, mostly epistolary,
relationship. Kafka described her later as "the only woman who ever under-
stood me", and with his encouragement she took up writing professionally.
Tragically, by the time Milena had extricated herself from her disastrous
marriage, Kafka, still smarting from three failed engagements with other
women, had decided never to commit himself to anyone else; his letters
alone survived the war, as a moving testament to their love.

Milena returned to Prague in 1925, and moved on from writing exclusively fashion articles to critiques of avant-garde architecture, becoming
one of the leading journalists on the main centrist newspaper of the day.
She married again, this time to the prominent functionalist architect
Jaromír Krejcar, but later, a difficult pregnancy and childbirth left her
addicted to morphine. She overcame her dependency only after joining the
Communist Party, but was to quit after the first of Stalin's show trials in
1936. She continued to work as a journalist in the late 1930s, and wrote a
series of articles condemning the rise of fascism in the Sudetenland.

When the Nazis rolled into Prague in 1939, Milena's Vinohrady flat had
already become a centre for resistance. For a while, she managed to hang
on to her job, but her independent intellectual stance and provocative
gestures – like wearing a yellow star – soon attracted the attention of the
Gestapo, and after a brief spell in the notorious Pankrác prison, she was
sent to Ravensbrück, the women's concentration camp near Berlin, where
she died of nephritis (inflammation of the kidneys) in May 1944.

Lazarská, meeting point of the city's night trams, leads off to the
right. At the bottom of this street is **Diamant**, another of Prague's
Cubist buildings, completed in 1912 by Emil Králíček. It's grubby
with pollution now, but the geometric sculptural reliefs on the
facade, the main portal and the frame enclosing a Baroque statue of
St John of Nepomuk on Spálená, remain worth viewing nonetheless.

Karlovo náměstí

Once Prague's biggest square, **Karlovo náměstí**'s impressive
proportions are no longer so easy to appreciate, obscured by a tree-
planted public garden and cut in two by the busy thoroughfare of
Ječná. It was created by Charles IV as Nové Město's cattle market
(Dobytčí trh) and used by him for the grisly annual public display of
saintly relics, though now it actually signals the southern limit of the
city's commercial district.

The **Novoměstská radnice** (New Town Hall), at the northeastern corner of the square, sports three impressive triangular gables
embellished with intricate tracery. It was built, like the one on

For details of
Prague's second
defenestration,
see p.51.

Staroměstské náměstí, during the reign of King John of Luxembourg, though it has survived rather better, and thanks to its recent facelift, is now one of the finest Gothic buildings in the city. After the amalgamation of Prague's separate towns in 1784, however, it was used solely as a criminal court and prison, and even today there's still no public access. It was here that Prague's **first** **defenestration** took place on July 30, 1419, when the radical Hussite preacher Jan Želivský and his penniless religious followers stormed the building, mobbed the Catholic councillors and burghers and threw several of them out of the town hall windows onto the pikes of the Hussite mob below. Václav IV, on hearing the news, suffered a stroke and died just two weeks later. So began the long and bloody Hussite Wars.

Following the defeat of Protestantism two centuries later, the Jesuits were allowed to demolish 23 houses on the east side of the square to make way for their college (now one of the city's main hospitals) and the accompanying church of **sv Ignác** (St Ignatius), begun in 1665 by Carlo Lurago and Paul Ignaz Bayer. The latter is modelled, like so many Jesuit churches, on the Gesù in Rome, but it's worth looking in if only for the wedding-cake stucco on the ceiling.

The Assassination of Reinhard Heydrich

The assassination of Reinhard Heydrich in 1942 was the only attempt the Allies ever made on the life of a leading Nazi. It's an incident which the Allies have always billed as a great success in the otherwise rather dismal seven-year history of the Czech resistance. But, as with all acts of brave resistance during the war, there was a price to be paid. Given that the reprisals meted out to the Czech population were entirely predictable, it remains a controversial, if not suicidal, decision to have made.

The target, **Reinhard Tristan Eugen Heydrich**, was a talented and upwardly mobile anti-Semite (despite rumours that he was partly Jewish himself), a great organizer and a skilful concert violinist. He was a late recruit to the Nazi Party, signing up in 1931, after having been dismissed from the German Navy for dishonourable conduct towards a woman. However, he swiftly rose through the ranks of the SS to become second in command after Himmler, and in the autumn of 1941, he was appointed *Reichsprotektor* of the puppet state of *Böhmen und Mähren* – effectively, the most powerful man in the Czech Lands. Although his rule began with brutality, it soon settled into the tried and tested policy which Heydrich liked to call *Peitsche und Zucker* (literally, "whip and sugar").

On the morning of May 27, 1942, as Heydrich was being driven by his personal bodyguard, *Oberscharführer* Klein, in his open-top Mercedes from his manor house north of Prague to his office in Hradčany, three Czechoslovak agents (parachuted in from England) were taking up positions in the northeastern suburb of Libeň. As the car pulled into Kirchmayer Boulevard (now V Holešovičkách), one of them, a Slovak called Gabčík, pulled out a sten gun and tried to shoot. The gun jammed, at

No. 40–41, at the southern end of the square, is the so-called **Faustův dům** (Faust House), a late Baroque building with a long and diabolical history of alchemy. An occult priest from Opava owned the house in the fourteenth century, and, two hundred years later, the English alchemist and international con-man Edward Kelley was summoned here by the eccentric Emperor Rudolf II to turn base metal into gold. The building is also the traditional setting for the Czech version of the Faust legend, with the arrival one rainy night of a penniless and homeless student, Jan Šťastný (meaning lucky, or *Faustus* in German). Finding money in the house, he decided to keep it – only to discover that it was put there by the Devil, who then claimed his soul in return. Seemingly unperturbed by the historical fate of the site, a new pharmacy now plies its trade on the ground floor.

Southern Nové Město

The Orthodox Cathedral of sv Cyril and Metoděj

West off Karlovo náměstí, down Resslova, the noisy extension of Ječná, is the eighteenth-century church of **sv Cyril and Metoděj**, originally constructed for the Roman Catholics by Bayer and Dientzenhofer, but since the 1930s, the main base of the Orthodox church in the Czech Republic. Amid all the traffic, it's extremely

---

which Heydrich, rather than driving out of the situation, ordered Klein to stop the car and attempted to shoot back. At this point, another agent, Kubiš, threw a bomb at the car. The blast injured Kubiš and Heydrich, and stopped the car, but failed to harm Klein, who immediately leapt out and began firing at Kubiš who, with blood pouring down his face, jumped on his bicycle and fled downhill. Gabčík meanwhile pulled out a second gun and exchanged shots with Heydrich, until the latter collapsed from his wounds. Gabčík immediately fled into a butcher's, shot Klein in the legs and escaped down the backstreets.

Meanwhile back at the Mercedes, a baker's van was flagged down by a passer-by, but refused to get involved. Eventually, a small truck carrying floor polish was commandeered and Heydrich taken to the Bulovka hospital. Heydrich died eight days later from shrapnel wounds and was given full Nazi honours at his Prague funeral; the cortège passed down Wenceslas Square, in front of a crowd of thousands. As the home resistance had forewarned, revenge was quick to follow. The day after Heydrich's funeral, the village of **Lidice** (see p.179) was burnt to the ground and its male inhabitants murdered; two weeks later the village of Ležáky suffered a similar fate.

The plan to assassinate Heydrich had been formulated in the early months of 1942 by the Czechoslovak government-in-exile in London, without consultation with the Czech Communist leadership in Moscow, and despite fierce opposition from the resistance within Czechoslovakia. Since it was clear that the reprisals would be horrific – thousands were executed in the aftermath – the only logical explanation for the plan is that this was precisely the aim of the government-in-exile's operation – to forge a solid wedge of resentment between the Germans and Czechs. In this respect, if in no other, the operation was ultimately successful.

Southern Nové Město

The church crypt is open Mon–Sat 9–11am.

difficult to imagine the scene here on June 18, 1942, when seven of the Czechoslovak secret agents involved in the most dramatic assassination of World War II (see box above) were besieged in the church by over 700 members of the Waffen SS. Acting on the basis of a tip-off by one of the Czech resistance who turned himself in, the Nazis surrounded the church just after 4am and fought a pitched battle for over six hours, trying explosives, flooding and any other method they could think of to drive the men out of their stronghold in the crypt. Eventually, all seven agents committed suicide rather than give themselves up. There's a plaque at street level on the south wall commemorating those who died, but, if you can, it's worth timing your visit with the brief opening hours of the exhibition and memorial situated in the crypt itself, which has been left pretty much as it was.

Along the embankment

Magnificent turn-of-the-century mansions line the Vltava's right bank, almost without interruption, for some two kilometres from the Charles Bridge south to the rocky outcrop of Vyšehrad. It's a long walk, even just along the length of **Masarykovo** and **Rašínovo nábřeží**, though there's no need to do the whole lot in one go: you can hop on a tram (#17 or #21) at various points, drop down from the embankments to the waterfront itself, or escape to one of the two islands connected to them, Střelecký or Slovanský ostrov.

Access to either of the two islands in the central section of the Vltava is from close to the National Theatre. The first, **Střelecký ostrov**, or Shooters' Island, is where the army held their shooting practice, on and off, from the fifteenth until the nineteenth century. Closer to the other bank, and accessible via most Legií (Legion's Bridge) it became a favourite spot for a Sunday promenade and it's still popular, especially in summer. The first *Sokol* festival took place here in 1882 (see p.76); the first May Day demonstrations in 1890, and, one hundred years on, having been used and abused by the Communists for propaganda purposes, the traditional low-key *Májales* celebrations have returned.

The second island, Slovanský ostrov, more commonly known as **Žofín** (after the island's concert hall, itself named for Sophie, the mother of the Emperor Franz Josef I), came about as a result of the natural silting of the river in the eighteenth century. By the late nineteenth century it had become one of the city's foremost pleasure gardens, where, as the composer Berlioz remarked, "bad musicians shamelessly make abominable music in the open air and immodest young males and females indulge in brazen dancing, while idlers and wasters . . . lounge about smoking foul tobacco and drinking beer". On a good day, things seem pretty much unchanged from those heady times. Concerts, balls, and other social gatherings take place here in the newly renovated and very yellow cultural centre, built in 1835, and there are rowing boats for hire from May to October.

Southern
Nové Město

At the southern tip of Slovanský ostrov stands the onion-domed Šítek water tower, which provided a convenient look-out post for the Czech secret police, whose job it was to watch over Havel's Prague flat (see below). Close by, spanning the narrow channel between the island and the river bank, is the striking white functionalist box of the **Mánes Gallery**. Designed in open-plan style by Otakar Novotný in 1930, the gallery is named after Josef Mánes, a traditional nineteenth-century landscape painter and Czech nationalist, and puts on some of the more unusual exhibitions in Prague; in addition there's a café and an upstairs restaurant (see p.200), suspended above the channel. Most of the ornate apartment buildings along the waterfront itself are private, and therefore inaccessible. One exception is the Art-Nouveau concert hall, **Hlahol**, at Masarykovo nábřeží 16, built for the Hlahol men's choir in 1903–06, and designed by the architect of the main railway station, Josef Fanta, with a pediment mural by Mucha and statues by Šaloun – check with the *PIS* (or the posters outside the hall) for details of forthcoming concerts.

The Mánes Gallery is open Tues–Sun 10am–6pm.

For details of fish restaurants near the embankment, see p.209.

Fred and Ginger, Havel and Palackého náměstí

If the Mánes Gallery seems at odds with the turn-of-the-century architecture along the embankment, it is as nothing to what is being built on the bombsite at the beginning of **Rašínovo nábřeží** (named after the interwar Minister of Finance, Alois Rašín, who was assassinated by a non-Party communist in the 1920s). The building in question, designed by the Canadian-born Frank O. Gehry and the Yugoslav-born Vlado Milunić, has been nicknamed **"Fred and Ginger"**, after the shape of one of the building's towers, which look vaguely like a couple ballroom dancing. Clearly the building is not meant to meld with its surroundings, but just how quickly it will win over sceptical Praguers remains to be seen. The site is all the more controversial as it stands next door to an apartment block built at the turn of the century by Havel's grandfather, where, until recently, Havel, his wife Olga and his brother Ivan lived in the top-floor flat.

Further along the embankment, at **Palackého náměstí**, the buildings retreat for a moment to reveal an Art-Nouveau sculpture to rival Šaloun's monument in Staroměstské náměstí (see p.89): the **Monument to František Palacký**, the great nineteenth-century Czech historian, politician and nationalist, by Stanislav Sucharda. Like the Hus Monument, which was unveiled three years later, this mammoth project – fifteen years in the making – had missed its moment by the time it was finally completed in 1912, and found universal disfavour. The critics have mellowed over the years, and nowadays it's appreciated for what it is – an energetic and inspirational piece of work. Ethereal bronze bodies, representing the world of the imagination, shoot out at all angles, contrasting sharply with the plain stone mass of the plinth, and below, the giant seated figure of Palacký himself, representing the real world.

Vyšehradská and Ke Karlovu

Behind Palackého náměstí, on **Vyšehradská**, the twisted concrete spires of the **Emmaus monastery** (Emauzy or Klášter na Slovanech) are an unusual modern addition to the Prague skyline. The monastery was one of the few important historical buildings to be damaged in the last war, in this case by a stray Anglo-American bomb. Charles IV founded the monastery for Croatian Benedictines, who used the Old Slavonic liturgy (hence its Czech name, na Slovanech, or "at the Slavs"), but after the Battle of Bílá hora it was handed over to the more mainstream Spanish Benedictines. The cloisters contain some extremely valuable Gothic frescoes, but since the return of the monks from their forty-year exile, access has become unpredictable.

The Botanical Gardens are open daily April–Aug 10am–6pm; Sept, Oct & Jan–March 10am–5pm; Nov & Dec 10am–4pm.

Rising up behind Emmaus, is one of Kilian Ignaz Dientzenhofer's little gems, the church of **sv Jan Nepomucký na skalce** (St John of Nepomuk on the rock), perched high above Vyšehradská, with a facade that displays the plasticity of the Bavarian's Baroque style in all its glory. Heading south, Vyšehradská descends to a junction, where you'll find the entrance to the university's **Botanical Gardens** (Botanická zahrada), laid out in 1897 on a series of terraces up the other side of the hill. Though far from spectacular – the 1930s' greenhouses are a bit sad – they're one of the few patches of green in this part of town.

On the far side of the gardens, Apolinářská runs along the south wall and past a grimly Gothic red-brick maternity hospital, with steeply-sided stepped gables, before joining up with **Ke Karlovu**. Head left up here and the first street off to the right is Na bojišti, which is usually packed with tour coaches. The reason for this is the **U kalicha** pub, on the right, which was immortalized in the opening passages of the consistently popular comic novel *The Good Soldier Švejk*, by Jaroslav Hašek. In the story, on the eve of the Great War, Švejk (*Schweik* to the Germans) walks into *U kalicha*, where a plain-clothes officer of the Austrian constabulary is sitting drinking and, after a brief conversation, finds himself arrested in connection with the assassination of Archduke Ferdinand. Whatever the pub may have been like in Hašek's day (and even then, it wasn't his local), it's now unashamedly oriented towards reaping in the Deutschmarks, and about the only authentic thing you'll find inside – albeit at a price – is the beer.

The Dvořak Museum

Further north along Ke Karlovu, set back from the road behind wrought-iron gates, is a more rewarding place of pilgrimage, the russet-coloured **Vila Amerika** (named after the local pub), now a museum devoted to Czech composer, **Antonín Dvořák**, who lived for a time on nearby Žitná. Even if you've no interest in Dvořák, the house itself is a delight, built as a Baroque summer palace around 1720 and one of Kilian Ignaz Dientzenhofer's most successful secular works. Dvořák, easily the most famous of all Czech composers, for many years had to play second fiddle to Smetana in the orchestra at the National Theatre, where Smetana was the conductor. In his forties, Dvořák received an honorary degree from Cambridge before leaving for the "New World", and his gown is one of the very few items of memorabilia to have found its way into the museum, along with the programme of a concert given at London's Guildhall in 1891. But the tasteful period rooms with the composer's music wafting in and out, and the tiny garden dotted with Baroque sculptures compensate for what the display cabinets may lack.

*Southern
Nové Město*

*The Dvořák
Museum is
open Tues–Sun
10am–5pm.*

The Police Museum and Na Karlově church

There's a metro station (I. P. Pavlova) not far from Vila Amerika, but if you've got a few hundred more metres left in you, head south down Ke Karlovu. At the end of the street, the former Augustinian monastery of Karlov is now the **Police Museum** (Muzeum Policie), formerly the Museum of the Security Forces – and, in the heyday of "normalization" in the 1970s, one of the most fascinating museums in the city. Works by Trotsky, photos of Bob Dylan, plays by Havel and contraband goods were all displayed in the grand room of dissidence; closed-circuit TV watched over your every move; and the first thing you saw on entry were two hundred pistols confiscated from western secret agents pointing at you from the wall. But the most famous exhibit was undoubtedly a stuffed German shepherd dog called Brek, who saw twelve years' service on border patrols, intercepted sixty "lawbreakers", was twice shot in action and eventually retired to an old dogs' home.

*The Police
Museum is
open Tues–Sun
10am–5pm.*

With the barbed wire and border patrols all but disappeared, and the police at the nadir of their popularity, the new exhibition concentrates on road and traffic offences, and the force's latest challenges: forgery, drugs and murder. It's not what it used to be, but it's still mildly diverting, with several participatory displays, including a quiz on the Highway Code (in Czech) and a particularly gruesome section on forensic science.

Attached to the museum is **Na Karlově** church, founded by Charles IV (of course), designed in imitation of Charlemagne's tomb in Aachen, and quite unlike any other church in Prague. If it's open, you should take a look at the dark interior, which was remodelled in the sixteenth century by Bonifaz Wohlmut. The stellar vault has no central supporting pillars – a remarkable feat of engineering for its time, and one which gave rise to numerous legends about the architect being in league with the devil.

*Na Karlově is
open Sun
2–5.15pm.*

Southern Nové Město

From outside the church, there's a great view south across the Botič valley, to the twin delights of the skyscraper *Hotel Forum* and the low-lying **Palác kultury** (Palace of Culture), originally used for party congresses and now the country's biggest concert venue ; to the right of the Palác kultury is Vyšehrad (see p.137). The nearest metro (Vyšehrad) is across Nuselské most; alternatively, you can walk down to the the bottom of the valley and catch a tram (#7, #18 or #24).

Chapter 6

Vyšehrad and the eastern suburbs

B y the end of his reign in 1378, Charles IV had laid out his city on such a grand scale that it wasn't until the industrial revolution hit Bohemia in the mid-nineteenth century that Prague began to spread beyond the boundaries of the medieval town. The first of the suburbs, Karlín, was rigidly planned, with public parks and grid street plans strictly laid out to the east of thé old town; twentieth-century suburbs have tended to grow with less grace, trailing their tenements across the hills, and swallowing up existing villages on the way. **Vinohrady** and **Žižkov**, which are covered in this chapter, still retain their individual nineteenth-century identities, which makes them worth checking out on even a short visit to the city; they also contain one or two specific sights to guide your wandering. **Vyšehrad**, which was actually one of the earliest points of settlement in Prague, is something of an exception to all the above, and is by far the most enticing of the outlying areas. Its cemetery contains the remains of Bohemia's artistic elite; the ramparts afford superb views over the river; and below its fortress, there are several examples of Czech Cubist architecture.

Vyšehrad

At the southern tip of Nové Město, around 3km south of the city centre, the rocky red-brick fortress of **VYŠEHRAD** (literally "High Castle") has more myths attached to it per square inch than any other place in Bohemia. According to Czech legend, this is the place where the Slav tribes first settled in Prague, where the "wise and tireless chieftain" Krok built a castle, and whence his youngest daughter Libuše went on to found *Praha* itself. Alas, the archeological evidence doesn't bear this claim out, but it's clear that Vratislav II (1061–92), the first Bohemian ruler to bear the title "king", built

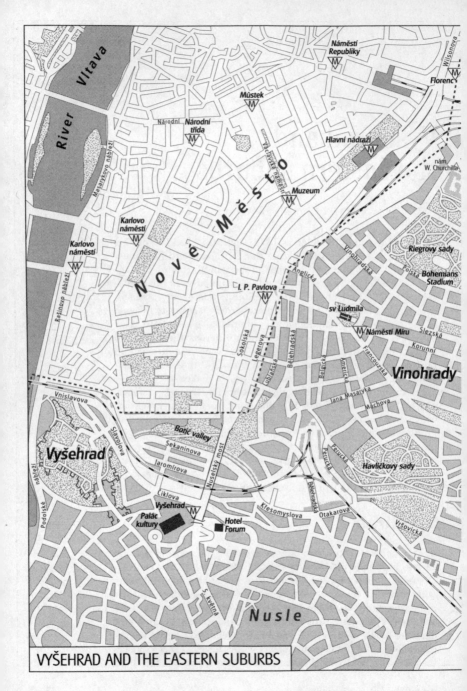

VYŠEHRAD AND THE EASTERN SUBURBS

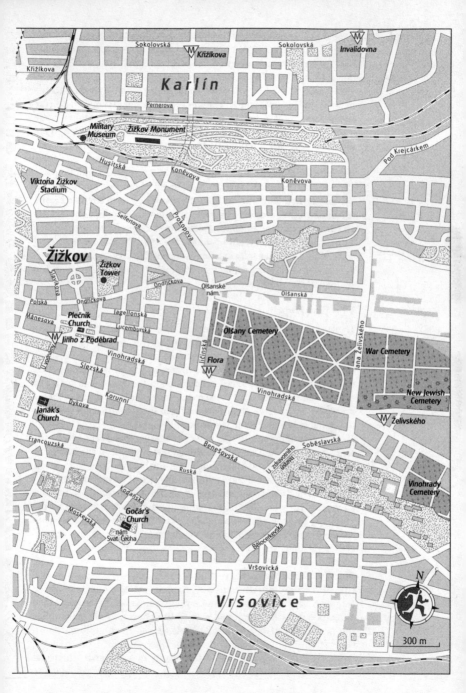

a royal palace here, to get away from his younger brother who was lording it in the Hrad. Within half a century the royals had moved back to Hradčany, into a new palace, and from then on Vyšehrad began to lose its political significance.

Charles IV had a system of walls built to link Vyšehrad to the newly founded Nové Město, and decreed that the *králová cesta* (the coronation route) begin from here; these fortifications were destroyed by the Hussites in 1420, but the hill was settled again over the next two hundred years. In the mid-seventeenth century, the Habsburgs turfed everyone out and rebuilt the place as a fortified barracks, only to tear it down in 1866 to create a public park. The Czech national revival movement became interested in Vyšehrad when only the red-brick fortifications were left as a reminder of its former strategic importance; they rediscovered its history and its legends, and gradually transformed it into a symbol of Czech nationhood. Today, Vyšehrad makes for one of the most rewarding trips away from the human congestion of the city, a perfect afternoon escape and a great place from which to watch the evening sun set behind the Hrad.

The fortress

The nearest metro is Vyšehrad.

There are several approaches to the **fortress** (see map on pp.138–39), depending on where you arrive in Vyšehrad. From Vyšehrad metro station, walk west past the modern Palác kultury, and enter through the Leopoldova brána (**a**); if you've come by tram #3, #7, #17 or #21, which trundle along the waterfront, you can either wind your way up Vratislavova and enter through the Cihelná brána (**b**), or take the steep stairway that leads up through the trees to a small side entrance in the west wall.

The last approach brings you out right in front of the blackened sandstone church of **sv Petr and Pavel** (**c**), rebuilt in the 1880s by Josef Mocker in neo-Gothic style (with further, even more ruthless, additions completed in the 1900s) on the site of an eleventh-century basilica. The twin openwork spires are the fortress's most familiar landmark; the church's polychrome interior is often closed to the public to protect against vandalism and to allow archeologists to search for the remains of the eleventh-century royal palace, discovered here some time ago.

The Vyšehrad Cemetery

One of the first initiatives of the national revival movement was to establish the **Vyšehrad Cemetery** (Vyšehradský hřbitov), which spreads out to the north and east of the church. It's a measure of the part that artists and intellectuals played in the foundation of the nation, and the regard in which they are still held, that the most prestigious graveyard in the city is given over to them: no soldiers, no politicians, not even the Communists managed to

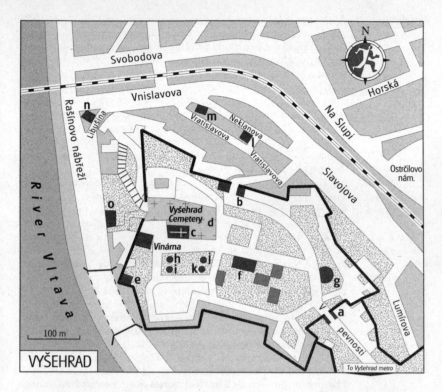

Svobodova
Vnislavova
Rašínovo nábřeží
Libušina **n**
m Vratislavova
Neklanova
Vratislavova
Na Slupi
Horská
Slavojova
Ostrčilovo nám.
o
Vyšehrad Cemetery
b
d
c
Vinárna
h **i**
i **k**
e
f
g
a
V pevnosti
Lumírova
River Vltava
100 m
VYŠEHRAD
To Vyšehrad metro

muscle their way in here. Sheltered from the wind by its high walls, lined on two sides by arcades, it's a small cemetery, filled with well-kept graves, many of them designed by the country's leading sculptors.

To the uninitiated only a handful of figures are well known, but for the Czechs the place is alive with great names (there's a useful plan of the most notable graves at the entrance nearest the church). **Dvořák**'s grave, under the arches, is one of the more showy ones, with a mosaic inscription, studded with gold stones, glistening behind wrought-iron railings. **Smetana**, who died twenty years earlier, is buried in comparatively modest surroundings near the Slavín monument (see below). The Spring Music Festival begins with a procession from his grave to the Obecní dům, on the anniversary of his death (May 12).

Other graves that attract (mostly Czech) pilgrims are those of the nineteenth-century writer Božena Němcová, by the east end of the church; and Karel Čapek – his grave faces the arcades – who coined one of the two Czech words to have entered the English language – "robot" (the other was "pistol"). Several graves of lesser-known individuals stand out artistically, too: in particular,

The cemetery is open daily May–Sept 8am–7pm; March, April & Oct 8am–6pm; Nov–Feb 9am–4pm.

Vyšehrad

Bílek's towering statue of *Sorrow* on the grave of V. B. Třebizský, which aroused a storm of protest when it was first unveiled; Bohumil Kafka's headstone for Dr J. Kaizl, with a woman's face peeping out from the grave; and Karel Hladík's modern *Cathedral* sculpture, which sits above his own grave.

The focus of the cemetery, though, is the **Slavín monument (d)**, a big bulky stele designed by Antonín Wiehl, covered in commemorative plaques and topped by a sarcophagus and a statue representing Genius. It's the communal resting place of more than fifty Czech artists, including the painter Alfons Mucha, the sculptors Josef Václav Myslbek and Ladislav Šaloun, the architect Josef Gočár, and the opera singer Ema Destinová.

Mácha's remains were brought here from a cemetery in Litoměřice in 1938, when the Nazis took over the Sudetenland.

The grave of the Romantic poet **Karel Hynek Mácha** was the assembly point for the demonstration on November 17, 1989, which triggered the Velvet Revolution. This was organized to commemorate the fiftieth anniversary of the funeral of **Jan Opletal**, a student at the university who was killed during the student protests against the Nazi occupation. His funeral took place on November 17, 1939, and provoked more violent disturbances: the Nazis responded by executing various student leaders, packing thousands off to the camps and shutting down all Czech higher education institutes. In 1989, a 50,000-strong crowd gathered at the cemetery, and attempted to march to Wenceslas Square, only to be stopped short in Národní, where the infamous *masakr* took place (see box, p.121).

The rest of the fortress

The rest of the deserted fortress makes for a pleasant afternoon stroll; you can walk almost the entire length of the ramparts, which give some superb views out across the city. The small museum of historical drawings in one of the bastions (e) and the exhibition in the neo-Gothic New Deanery (f) are both pretty dull, though you might want to head for the latter to buy some postcards. The rotunda of sv Martin (g) – one of a number of Romanesque rotundas scattered across Prague – is the sole survivor of the medieval fortress, originally built by Vratislav II in the eleventh century but heavily restored by nineteenth-century nationalists.

Time is better spent lounging on the patch of grass to the south of the church, where you'll come across the gargantuan statues by Myslbek that used to grace the city's Palackého most. Four couples are dotted across the green, all taken from Prague legends: *Přemysl and Libuše* (h), the husband and wife team who founded Prague and started Bohemia's first royal dynasty, the Přemyslids; *Lumír and Píseň* (i), the legendary Czech singer and his muse, Song; *Záboj and Slavoj* (j), two mythical Czech warriors; and *Ctirad and Šárka* (k), for whose story, see p.157.

Food and drink can be found at *Na Vyšehradě* (open daily 10am–10pm), a reasonably priced *vinárna* (wine bar) opposite the

church of sv Petr and Pavel. There are also several good pubs and
restaurants in the streets below the fortress (see p.204 & p.209).

Czech Cubism in Vyšehrad

Even if you harbour only a passing interest in modern architecture, it's worth seeking out the cluster of **Cubist villas** below the
fortress in Vyšehrad. Whereas Czech Art Nouveau was heavily
influenced by the Viennese Secession, it was Paris rather than the
imperial capital that provided the stimulus for the short-lived but
extremely productive Czech Cubist movement. In 1911, the
Skupina výtvarných umělců or *SVU* (Group of Fine Artists)
was founded in Prague, and quickly became the movement's
organizing force. **Pavel Janák** was the *SVU*'s chief theorist, **Josef
Gočár** its most illustrious exponent, but **Josef Chochol** was the
most successful practitioner of the style in Prague.

Cubism is associated mostly with painting, and the unique contribution of its Czech offshoot was to apply the theory to furniture
(some of which is now on permanent display at the Dům U černé
Matky boží, see p.94) and **architecture**. In Vyšehrad alone, Chochol
completed three buildings, close to one another below the fortress,
using prismatic shapes and angular lines to produce the sharp
geometric contrasts of light and dark shadows characteristic of
Cubist painting. Outside the Czech Republic, only the preparatory
drawings by the French architect Duchamp-Villon for his *Maison
Cubiste* (never realized), can be considered remotely similar.

The *SVU*'s plans were cut short by World War I, after which
Janák and Gočár attempted to establish a specifically Czechoslovak
style of architecture incorporating prewar Cubism. The style was
dubbed **Rondo-Cubism** since the prismatic moulding had been
replaced by semicircles, but only a few projects got off the ground
before Czech architects turned to the functionalist ideals of the
international modernist movement.

The buildings

The most impressive example of Czech Cubist architecture, brilliantly
exploiting its angular location, is Chochol's apartment block (l), at
Neklanova 30, begun in 1913 for František Hodek and now housing a
restaurant on its ground floor. Further along Neklanova at no. 2,
there's Antonín Belada's Cubist street facade (m), and around the
corner is the most ambitious project of the lot – Chochol's
Kovařovicova vila (n), which backs onto Libušina. The front, on
Rašínovo nábřeží, is presently concealed behind some overenthusias-
tic shrubs, but it's still possible to appreciate the clever, slightly askew
layout of the garden, designed right down to its zigzag garden railings.
Further along the embankment is Chochol's largest commission, the
triple house (o), a large building complex with a heavy mansard roof,
a central "Baroque" gable and room enough for three families.

Vyšehrad

Cubist and Rondo-Cubist buildings in Prague

Prague's unique Cubist and Rondo-Cubist buildings, most of which are covered in the text, are scattered right across the city. Here is a checklist of where to find the best examples of the style.

Staré Město		Vyšehrad	
Gočár's Dům U černé Matky boží	p.94	Chochol's apartment block	p.143
		Belada's street facade	p.143
Nové Město		Chochol's Kovařovicova vila	p.143
Janák & Zasche's Adria Palace	p.121	Chochol's triple house	p.143
Blecha & Králíček's lamppost	p.120	**The suburbs**	
Gočár's Banka legií	p.127	Gočár's double house	p.150
Králíček's Diamant	p.129		

Vinohrady

Southeast of Nové Město is the well-to-do nineteenth-century suburb of **VINOHRADY**, home over the years to many of the country's most notable personages. Although these days it has a run-down air about it, it's still a desirable part of town to live in, boasting two spacious parks – the **Riegrovy sady**, to the north, and the **Havlíčkovy sady**, to the south – and a fabulous array of turn-of-the-century apartment buildings. In terms of conventional sightseeing, Vinohrady is definitely low priority, but there are a few places here (and in neighbouring Žižkov) worth a visit, most of them quick and easy to reach by metro.

If Vinohrady has a centre, it's **náměstí Míru**, a leafy square centred on the neo-Gothic church of sv Ludmila. The church has recently been joined by a statue commemorating the Čapek brothers, writer Karel and painter Josef, who together symbolized the golden era of the interwar republic. Karel died in 1938, shortly after the Nazi invasion, while Josef perished in Belsen seven years later; their influence was deliberately underplayed by the Communists, hence the delay in erecting an appropriate memorial. From náměstí Míru, block after block of decaying tenements, each clothed in its own individual garment of sculptural decoration, form a grid-plan of grand bourgeois avenues stretching eastwards to the city's great cemeteries (see below).

Plečník's church

The nearest metro is náměstí Míru.

Vinohrady's other main square, **náměstí Jiřího z Poděbrad**, halfway between náměstí Míru and the cemeteries, contains Prague's most celebrated modern church, **Nejsvětější Srdce Páně** (Most Sacred Heart of Our Lord), built in 1928 by Josip Plečník, the Slovene architect responsible for much of the remodelling of the Hrad (see box on p.45). It's a marvellously eclectic and individualistic work, employing a sophisticated potpourri of architectural styles: a Neoclassical pediment and a great slab of a clock tower with a giant transparent face in imitation of a Gothic rose window, as well as the bricks and mortar of contemporary constructivism. Plečník also had a sharp eye for detail; look out for the little gold crosses inset into the brickwork like stars, inside and out, and the celestial orbs of light suspended above the heads of the congregation. If you can collar the priest, it may be possible to climb the clock tower. And before you leave the area, you might like to pay a visit to the excellent café/bookstore, *U knihomola* (The Bookworm), west of the square, at Mánesova 79 (see p.228).

Vinohrady

The nearest metro is Jiřího z Poděbrad.

Janák and Gočár's functionalist churches
Further afield are two more uncompromisingly modernist churches. The first is the **Husův sbor** (Hussite Church), three blocks south of Plečník's church down U vodárny, on the corner of Dykova. Built in the early 1930s by Pavel Janák, the church's most salient feature is its freestanding hollow tower, which encloses a corkscrew spiral staircase and is topped by a giant copper chalice, symbol of the Hussite faith. A memorial on the wall commemorates the church's pioneering role in the Prague Uprising against the Nazis in May 1945, when it served as the base for the resistance's clandestine radio.

Josef Gočár's equally severe, functionalist church of **sv Václav**, built around the same time, lies a kilometre or so southeast on náměstí Svatopluka Čecha. Here it forms the centrepiece of a sloping green square, with a distinctive stepped roof rising up from a slender, smoothly rendered 80m-high tower.

Gočár's Church can be reached by tram #4 or #22.

Žižkov

Unlike Vinohrady, **ŽIŽKOV** is a traditionally working-class area – and was a Communist Party stronghold even before the war, earning it the nickname "Red Žižkov". Nowadays it's home to a large proportion of Prague's Romany community and other less privileged sections of Czech society. The main reason for venturing into Žižkov is to visit its two landmarks – ancient (Žižkov hill) and modern (the television tower) – and the city's main cemeteries, at the eastern end of Vinohradská.

The Žižkov television tower
At over 100m, the Žižkov television tower (Televizní vysílač), is the tallest (and the most unpopular) building in Prague. Close up, though, it's difficult not to be impressed by this truly intimidating piece of futuristic architecture, its smooth grey exterior giving no hint of humanity. Begun in the 1970s in a desperate bid to jam West

German television transmission, the tower has only become fully operational within the last few years. In the course of its construction, however, the Communists saw fit to demolish part of a nearby Jewish cemetery, that had served the community between 1787 and 1891; a small section survives to the northwest of the tower. You used to be able to take a lift to the viewing platform on the eighth floor to enjoy a spectacular view across Prague, but the place never took off as a commercial venture and is currently closed to the public. To get to the tower, take the metro to Jiřího z Poděbrad and walk northeast a couple of blocks.

The cemeteries

The cemeteries are open daily dawn to dusk: the nearest metro to the Olšany cemeteries is Flora; the nearest metro to the War cemetary is Želivského.

Approaching from the west, the first and the largest of Prague's vast cemeteries – each of which is bigger than the entire Jewish quarter – are the **Olšany cemeteries** (Olšanské hřbitovy), originally created for the victims of the great plague epidemic of 1680. The perimeter walls are lined with glass cabinets, stacked like shoe-boxes, containing funereal urns and mementoes, while the graves themselves are a mixed bag of artistic achievements, reflecting the funereal fashions of the day as much as the character of the deceased. The cemeteries are divided into districts and crisscrossed with cobbled streets; at each gate there's a map, and an aged janitor ready to point you in the right direction.

There's a memorial to Palach and other victims of the Communist era on Wenceslas Square, see p.118, and a box on Gottwald on p.97.

The cemeteries' two most famous incumbents are an ill-fitting couple: Klement Gottwald, the country's first Communist president, whose ashes were removed from the mausoleum on Žižkov Hill after 1989 and reinterred here, and Jan Palach, the philosophy student who set light to himself in January 1969 in protest at the Soviet occupation. More than 750,000 people attended Palach's funeral in January 1969, and in an attempt to put a stop to the annual vigils at his graveside, the secret police removed his body in 1973 and reburied him in his home town, 60km outside Prague. His place was taken by an unknown woman, Maria Jedličková, who for the next seventeen years had her grave covered in flowers instead. Finally, in

---

Jaroslav Seifert of Žižkov

The Czech Nobel prize-winning poet, **Jaroslav Seifert** (1901–86) was born and bred in the Žižkov district. He was one of the founding members of the Czechoslovak Communist Party, and in 1920 helped found *Devětsil*, the most daring and provocative avant-garde movement of the interwar republic. Always accused of harbouring bourgeois sentiments, Seifert and eight other Communist writers were expelled from the Party when Gottwald and the Stalinists hijacked the Party at the Fifth Congress in 1929. After the 1948 coup, he became *persona non grata*, though he rose to prominence briefly during the 1956 Writers' Union congress, when he attempted to lead a rebellion against the Stalinists. Later on, he became involved in Charter 77, and in 1984, amidst much controversy, he became the one and only Czech to win the Nobel Prize for Literature.

1990, Palach's body was returned to Olšany; you'll find it just to the east of the main entrance on Vinohradská.

To the east of Olšany cemeteries, and usually totally deserted, is the **War Cemetery** (Vojenský hřbitov); the entrance is 200m up Jana Želivského, on the right. Its centrepiece is the monument to the 436 Soviet soldiers who lost their lives on May 9, 1945 in the liberation of Prague, surrounded by a small, tufty meadow dotted with simple white crosses. Nearby, the graves of Czechs who died fighting for the Habsburgs on the Italian front in World War I are laid out in a semicircle.

The New Jewish Cemetery

Immediately south of the war cemetery is the **New Jewish Cemetery** (Nový židovský hřbitov), founded in the 1890s, when the one by the Žižkov television tower was full (see p.146). It's a melancholy spot, particularly so in the east of the cemetery, where large empty allotments wait in vain to be filled by the generation who perished in the Holocaust. In fact, the community is now so small that it's unlikely the graveyard will ever be full. Most people come here to visit **Franz Kafka**'s grave, 400m east along the south wall and signposted from the entrance. He is buried, along with his mother and father (both of whom outlived him), beneath a plain headstone; the plaque below commemorates his three sisters who died in the camps.

The New Jewish Cemetery is open daily except Fri & Sat April–Aug 8am–5pm; Sept–March 8am–4pm. For more on Kafka's associations with Prague, see p.108.

Žižkov hill

Žižkov hill (also known as Vítkov) is the thin green wedge of land that separates Žižkov from Karlín, a grid-plan industrial district to the north. From its westernmost point, which juts out almost to the edge of Nové Město, is the definitive panoramic view over the city centre. It was here, on July 14, 1420, that the Hussites enjoyed their first and finest victory at the **Battle of Vítkov**, under the inspired leadership of the one-eyed general, Jan Žižka (hence the name of the district). Ludicrously outnumbered by something like ten to one, Žižka and his fanatically-motivated troops thoroughly trounced Emperor Sigismund and his papal forces.

Despite its overblown totalitarian aesthetics, the giant concrete **Žižkov monument** which graces the crest of the hill, was actually built between the wars as a memorial to the Czech nation – the gargantuan equestrian statue of the mace-wielding Žižka, which fronts the monument, is reputedly the world's largest. The building was later used by the Nazis as an arsenal, and eventually became a Communist mausoleum: presidents Gottwald, Zápotocký and Svoboda were all buried here, along with the Unknown Soldier and various other Party hacks. Žižkov was an ideal resting place, lying as it does in the heart of "Red Žižkov", from where the Communists drew so much of their working-class support.

Žižkov

The Military Museum is open Tues–Sun April–Oct 8.30am–5pm; Nov–March 9.30am–4.30pm; see p.59 for the pre-1914 military museum.

Gottwald himself was originally pickled and embalmed (à la Lenin) but a fire damaged his corpse so much, the leader had to be cremated in 1963. In 1990, the bodies were quietly reinterred in Olšany, and at present there's an ongoing legal battle over what should happen next with the monument.

To get to the monument, take the metro to Florenc, walk under the railway lines, and then up the steep lane U památníku. On the right as you climb the hill is the post-1914 section of the **Military Museum** (Vojenské muzeum), guarded by a handful of unmanned tanks, howitzers and armoured vehicles. Before 1989, this place was a glorification of the Warsaw Pact, pure and simple; its recent overhaul has produced a much more evenly balanced account of both world wars, particularly in its treatment of the previously controversial subjects of the Czechoslovak Legion, the Heydrich assassination (see p.130) and the Prague Uprising.

Chapter 7

The northern and western suburbs

T he **northern and western suburbs**, on the left bank of the
Vltava, cover a larger area than those to the east of the river.
They are also far more varied: some, like Holešovice and parts
of Smíchov, date from the time of the industrial revolution, whereas the
much posher areas of Dejvice and Střešovice were laid out as garden
suburbs and built between the wars. The left bank also boasts plenty of
greenery, including the city's largest public park, Stromovka. All this
goes to make up a fascinating patchwork of communities, which few

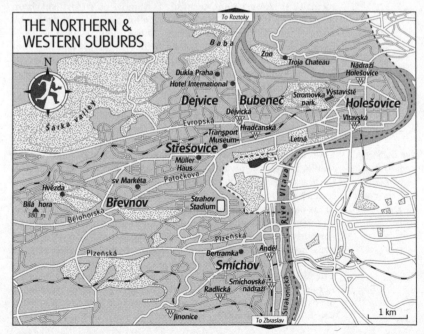

tourists bother to see. It's worth the effort, though, if only to remind yourself that Prague doesn't begin and end at the Charles Bridge.

There are several specific sights in each suburb that can lend structure to your meanderings. A few, like the Mozart Museum in **Smíchov** and the Technical Museum in **Holešovice**, are included in most people's tours of the city. Others – like the functionalist villa quarters in **Dejvice** and **Střešovice** – are of more specialized interest; and some are simply unknown to most visitors, like the Renaissance chateau of **Hvězda**.

Holešovice and Bubeneč

The districts of HOLEŠOVICE and BUBENEČ, tucked into a huge U-bend in the Vltava, have little in the way of magnificent architecture, but they make up for it with two huge splodges of green: to the south **Letná**, where Prague's greatest gatherings generally occur, and to the north the **Stromovka park**, bordering the Výstaviště funfair and international trade fair grounds.

The Chotkovy sady and Bílkova vila

These first two sights are strictly speaking part of the Hradčany that lies to the northeast of the castle, but for convenience sake, they begin this chapter. The easiest way to this part of town is to take the metro to Hradčanská and head up Tychonova, a street flanked on one side by a military barracks and training ground, on the other by a series of semi-detached houses. These include **Josef Gočár's** rodinný dvojdům at no. 4 & 6, built with a traditional mansard roof in a restrained Cubist style, similar to that employed on the Dům U černé Matky boží in Staré Město (see p.94).

The Chotkovy sady

At the top of Tychonova, the leafy avenue of Marianské hradby slopes down to the left, past the Belvedere, to the **Chotkovy sady**, Prague's first public park, founded in 1833 by the ecologically minded city governor, Count Chotek. The atmosphere here is a lot more relaxed than in the nearby Royal Gardens, and you can happily stretch out on the grass and soak up the sun, or head for the south wall, which enjoys an unrivalled view of the bridges and islands of the Vltava. At the centre of the park there's a bizarre, melodramatic grotto-like memorial to the nineteenth-century Romantic poet Julius Zeyer, an elaborate monument from which life-sized characters from Zeyer's works, carved in white marble, emerge from the blackened rocks amid much drapery.

The Belvedere and the Royal Gardens are both covered in Chapter 1, see p.57.

The Bílkova vila

Across the road from the park, hidden behind its overgrown garden at Mieckiewiczova 1, the **Bílkova vila** honours one of the most unusual Czech sculptors, František Bílek. Born in 1872 in a part of South

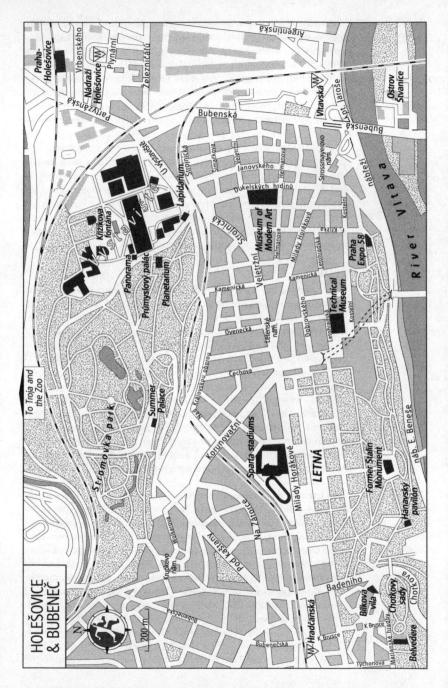

HOLEŠOVICE & BUBENEČ

N

200 m

To Troja and the Zoo

Praha-Holešovice

Nádraží Holešovice

Vrbenského

Pivňární

Partyzánská

Železničářů

Argentinská

Bubenská

Vltavská

Ostrov Štvanice

Bubenská

Smäčkova

Veletržní

Janovského

Šternberkova

Strossmayerovo nám.

Dukelských hrdinů

Kostelní

náběží

U Výstaviště

Lapidárium

Šupichová

Hermanova

Milady Horákové

Veletržní Museum of Modern Art

Křížíková fontána

Výstaviště

Panorama

Průmyslový palác

Planetárium

Kamenická

Leitnerova

Dobrovského

Kamenická

Letenská

Praha Expo 58

Technical Museum

River Vltava

Ovenecká

Tetřenské nám.

Leitnerova

Kostelní

Stromovka park

Summer Palace

Nad Královskou oborou

Čechova

Korunovační

Sparta stadiums

Milady Horákové

Former Stalin Monument

Hanavský pavilón

LETNÁ

náb. E. Beneše

Walterova

Krupkovo nám.

Pod kaštany

Na Zátorce

Hradčanská

Badeniho

Bilkova vila

Chotkovy sady

Chotkova

Bubenečská

Bubenečská

K Brusce

K Brusce

Belvedere

Mariánské hradby

Tychonova

Bohemia steeped in the Hussite tradition, Bílek lived a monkish life, spending years in spiritual contemplation, reading the works of Hus and other Czech reformers. The villa was built in 1911 to Bílek's own design, intended as both a "cathedral of art" and the family home. Even so, at first sight, it's a strangely mute red-brick building, out of keeping with the extravagant Symbolist style of Bílek's sculptures: from the outside, only the front porch, supported by giant sheaves of corn, and the sculptured figures in the garden – the fleeing Comenius and followers – give a clue as to what lies within.

*The Bílkova
vila is open
mid-May to
Sept Tues–Sun
9am–5pm.*

Inside, the brickwork gives way to bare stone walls lined with Bílek's religious sculptures – giving the impression that you've walked into a chapel rather than an artist's studio. In addition to his sculptural and relief work in wood and stone, often wildly expressive, there are also ceramics, graphics and a few mementoes of Bílek's life. His work is little known outside his native country, but his contemporary admirers included Franz Kafka, Julius Zeyer, and Otakar Březina, whose poems and novels provided the inspiration for much of Bílek's art.

Letná

A high plateau hovering above the city, the flat green expanse of the **Letná** plain has been the traditional assembly point for invading and besieging armies. It was laid out as a public park in the mid-nineteenth century, but its main post-1948 function was as the site of the May Day parades. For these, thousands of citizens were dragooned into marching past the south side of the city's main football ground, the Sparta stadium, where the old Communist cronies would take the salute from a giant red podium.

On November 26, 1989, the park was the scene of a more genuine expression of popular sentiment, when over 750,000 people gathered here to join in the call for a general strike against the Communist regime. Unprecedented scenes followed in April 1990, when a million Catholics came to hear Pope John Paul II speak on his first visit to an Eastern Bloc country other than his native Poland.

The former Stalin monument

Letná's – indeed Prague's – most famous monument is one which no longer exists. The **Stalin monument**, the largest in the world, was once visible from almost every part of the city: a thirty-metre-high granite sculpture portraying a procession of Czechs and Russians being led to Communism by the Pied Piper figure of Stalin, but popularly dubbed *tlačenice* (the crush) because of its resemblance to a Communist-era bread queue. Designed by Jiří Štursa and Otakar Švec, it took 600 workers 500 days to erect the 14,200-tonne monster. Švec, the sculptor, committed suicide shortly before it was unveiled, as his wife had done three years previously, leaving all his money to a school for blind children, since they at least would not have to see his creation. It was eventually revealed to the cheering masses on May 1, 1955 – the first and last popular celebration to take place at the monument. Within a year, Khrushchev had denounced his predecessor and, after pressure from Moscow, the monument was blown to smithereens by a series of explosions spread over a fortnight in 1962.

Holešovice and Bubeneč

All that remains above ground is the statue's vast concrete platform, on the southern edge of the Letná plain, now graced with David Černý's symbolic giant metronome; it's also a favourite spot for skateboarders and another good viewpoint, with the central stretch of the Vltava glistening in the afternoon sun. Built into the hillside below is Prague's one and only nuclear bunker, intended to preserve the Party elite, post-armageddon. For years, it was actually used to store the city's slowly rotting potato mountain; more recently it has been sporadically squatted and used as a nightclub venue.

If you're in need of some refreshment, head for the pricey café and restaurant (see p.211) housed in the nearby **Hanavský pavilón**, originally built for the 1891 Prague Exhibition and looking rather like a Russian Orthodox church. It was devised as a showpiece of wrought-ironwork by Count Hanavský in a flamboyant style which anticipated the arrival of Art Nouveau a few years later.

East of Letná: the National Technical Museum and the Museum of Modern Art

At present Holešovice boasts just one fully functioning museum, the **National Technical Museum** (Národní technické muzeum) on Kostelní, which was begun by Vojta Náprstek in the nineteenth-century, and now contains a host of old planes, trains and automobiles, and an impressive gallery of motorbikes. The showpiece is the hangar-like main hall, packed with machines from Czechoslovakia's industrial heyday between the wars, when the country's Škoda cars and Tatra limos were really something to brag about. Upstairs, there are interactive displays (a rarity in a Czech museum) tracing the development of early photography, and a collection of some of Kepler's and Tycho de Brahe's astrological instruments. Below ground, a mock-up of a coal mine offers guided tours every other hour, kicking off at 11am.

The National Technical Museum is open Tues–Sun 9am–5pm.

The National Gallery's **Museum of Modern Art** (Galerie moderního umění) – ten minutes' walk northeast of the Museum of Technology, at the corner of Dukelských hrdinů and Veletržní – is, at the time of writing, still undergoing refurbishment, despite constant rumours of its imminent opening. The building being restored for the purpose is the 1928 Prague Trade Fairs Building, a magnificent seven-storey glass curtain-wall design by Oldřich Tyl and Josef Fuchs, that in many ways is Prague's ultimate functionalist masterpiece. It certainly blew Le Corbusier's mind, as he himself admitted in 1930: "When I first saw the Trade Fair building in Prague I felt totally depressed, I realised that the large and conver-

A permanent Cubist exhibition is housed in Dům U černé Matky boží (see p.94); temporary exhibitions are currently staged at the Jízdárna in Prague Castle (see p.57).

gent structures I had been dreaming of really existed somewhere, while at the time I had just built a few small villas". If the museum is still closed, you can drown your sorrows in *The Globe*, an English-language bookshop and café, one block east of Dukelských hrdinů on Janovského, around which much of the American ex-pat scene revolves (see p.201).

Výstaviště

Five minutes' walk north up Dukelských hrdinů takes you right to the front gates of the **Výstaviště**, a motley assortment of buildings, originally created for the 1891 Prague Exhibition, which have served as the city's main trade fair arena and funfair ever since. The Communist Party held its rubber-stamp congresses here from 1948 until the late 1970s, and more recently several brand new permanent structures were built for the 1991 Prague Exhibition, including a circular theatre. The canopy over the main entrance, off U výstaviště, is another such addition – a modern echo of the flamboyant glass and iron **Průmyslový palác** at the centre of the complex.

Výstaviště is open Tues–Fri 2–10pm and Sat & Sun 10am–10pm; to get there take trams #5, #12 or #17 from Nádraží Holešovice.

The park is at its busiest on summer weekends, when hordes of Prague families descend on the place to down hot dogs, drink beer and listen to traditional brass band music. Apart from the annual fairs and lavish special exhibitions, there are a few permanent attractions, such as the city's **planetarium**, the **Maroldovo panorama**, a giant diorama of the 1434 Battle of Lipany (see *Contexts* for the significance of this battle); and the **Dětský svět**, a funfair and playground for kids. In the long summer evenings, there's also an open-air cinema (*letní kino*), and regular performances by the **Křižíkova fontána**, dancing fountains devised by the Czech inventor František Křižík, which perform a music and light show to packed audiences.

The Lapidarium is open Tues–Fri noon–6pm, Sat & Sun 10am–6pm.

Lastly, Výstaviště also contains the National Museum's **Lapidarium**, official depository for the city's sculptures, which are under threat either from demolition or from the weather. It's actually a much overlooked art collection, that includes works such as the plague column from Staroměstské náměstí, rescued from marauding Czech nationalists in 1918, and many of the original Charles Bridge sculptures.

Stromovka park

To the west of Výstaviště lies the *královská obora* or royal enclosure, more commonly known as **Stromovka park**, originally laid out as hunting grounds for the noble occupants of the Hrad, and – again thanks to Count Chodek – now Prague's largest and leafiest public park. If you're heading for Troja and the city zoo (see below), to the north, a stroll through the park is by far the most pleasant approach. If you want to explore a little more of the park, head west sticking to the park's southern border and you'll come to a water tunnel, built by the surrealist court painter, Giuseppe Arcimboldo as

part of Rudolf II's ambitious horticultural scheme to carry water
from the Vltava to the lakes he created a little to the north.

Further west still is Stromovka's main sight, the **summer palace**
(Místodržitelský letohrádek), one of the earliest neo-Gothic structures in the city, begun way back in 1805. Originally conceived as a
royal hunting chateau, it served as the seat of the Governor of
Bohemia until 1918, and now houses the National Museum's period-
icals collection and is closed to the public. To continue on to Troja
and the zoo, head north under the railway, over the canal, and on to
the Císařský ostrov (Emperor's Island) – and from there to the right
bank of the Vltava.

Troja

Though still well within the municipal boundaries, the suburb of
TROJA, across the river to the north of Holešovice and Bubeneč, still
has a distinctly country feel to it. Its most celebrated sight is
Prague's only genuine **chateau**, perfectly situated against a hilly
backdrop of vines. Troja's other attraction is the city's slightly dilapidated, but still enormously popular **zoo**.

*The chateau is
open
April–Sept
Tues–Sun
10am–5pm;
take bus #112
from metro
Nádraží
Holešovice;
from
April–Sept you
can reach Troja
by boat from
the boat launch
between
Jiráskův and
Palackého most;
see Nové Město
map
(pp.114–15).*

The chateau

The **Troja Chateau** (Trojský zámek) was designed by Jean-Baptiste
Mathey for the powerful Šternberk family towards the end of the
seventeenth century. Despite a recent renovation and rusty red
repaint, its plain early Baroque facade is no match for the action-
packed, blackened figures of giants and titans who battle it out on
the chateau's monumental balustrades. To visit the **interior**, you'll
have to join one of the guided tours. The star exhibits are the gush-
ing frescoes depicting the victories of the Habsburg Emperor
Leopold I (1657–1705) over the Turks, which cover every inch of
the walls and ceilings of the grand hall. Alternatively, you can
simply take a wander through the chateau's pristine French-style
formal **gardens** (open all year), the first of their kind in Bohemia.

The zoo

On the other side of U trojského zámku, which runs along the west wall
of the chateau, is the city's capacious **zoo** (zoologická zahrada),
founded in 1931 on the site of one of Troja's numerous hillside vineyards. Despite its rather weary appearance, all the usual animals are
on show here, and kids, at least, have few problems enjoying themselves. Thankfully, a programme of modernization is currently under
way, though only the new lion and tiger building, to the south, has so
far been completed. In the summer, you can take a "ski-lift" (lanová
dráha) from the duck pond to the top of the hill, where the prize exhibits – a rare breed of miniature horse known as Przewalski – hang out.

*The zoo is open
daily April
9am–5pm; May
9am–6pm;
June–Sept
9am–7pm;
Oct–March
9am–4pm.*

Dejvice, Střešovice and beyond

Spread across the hills to the northwest of the city centre are the leafy, garden suburbs of **Dejvice** and **Střešovice**, peppered with once-swanky villas, built between the wars for the upwardly mobile Prague bourgeoisie and commanding magnificent views across the north of the city. Both districts are short on conventional sights, but interesting to explore all the same. Some distance further west, the **Šárka valley** is about as far as you can get from an urban environment without leaving the city. To the south of Šárka is the battlefield of **Bílá hora**, and the **Hvězda** park, which contains a pretty star-shaped chateau that's well worth the effort to see.

Dejvice

DEJVICE was planned and built in the early 1920s for the First Republic's burgeoning community of civil servants and government and military officials. Its unappealing main square, **Vítězné náměstí** (metro Dejvická), is practically unavoidable if you're planning to explore any of the western suburbs, since it's a major public transport interchange. There's nothing much of note in this central part of Dejvice, though you can't help but notice the **Hotel International** at the end of Jugoslávských partyzánů, a Stalinist skyscraper that is disturbingly similar to the universally loathed Palace of Culture in Warsaw. For followers of Socialist Realist chic, its workerist motifs merit closer inspection – somewhat incredibly it's recently been bought up by the Holiday Inn hotel chain (see p.189).

To get to the Hotel International take tram #20 or #25 from metro Dejvická.

Baba

Dejvice's most intriguing villas are located to the north in **Baba**, a model neighbourhood of 33 functionalist houses, each individually commissioned and built under the guidance of one-time Cubist and born-again functionalist, Pavel Janák. A group of leading architects affiliated to the Czech Workers' Alliance, inspired by a similar project in Stuttgart, initiated what was, at the time, a radical housing project to provide simple, single-family villas. The idea was to use space and open-plan techniques rather than expensive materials to create a luxurious living space.

To get to Baba, take bus #131 from metro Hradčanská.

Despite the plans of the builders, the houses were mostly bought up by Prague's artistic and intellectual community. Nevertheless, they have stood the test of time better than most utopian architecture, not least because of the fantastic site – facing south and overlooking the city. Some of them remain exactly as they were when first built, others have been thoughtlessly altered, but as none of them is open to the public you'll have to be content with surreptitious peeping from the following streets: Na ostrohu, Na Babě, Nad Paťankou and Průhledová.

Střešovice

STŘEŠOVICE, southwest of Dejvice, has no central square and is dominated rather by its wealthy villa quarter, **Ořechovka**, to which Havel has recently moved. The most famous of the villas is the **Müller Haus** (Loosova vila) at Nad hradním vodojemem 14, designed by the Brno-born architect, Adolf Loos. Completed in 1930 (after planning permission had been refused ten times), it was one of Loos' few commissions, a typically uncompromising white box, wiped smooth with concrete rendering. Now grey with pollution, it's not exactly a wonder to behold, but then Loos believed that "a building should be dumb on the outside and reveal its wealth only on the inside". However, since you can't get inside, there's no way to appreciate the careful choice of rich materials and minimal furnishings that were Loos' hallmark. There are plans to turn the house into a museum to Loos – regarded by many as one of the founders of modern architecture – but for the moment, surrounded by hundreds of similarly boxy houses, you may well wonder what all the fuss is about.

The Šárka valley

If you've had your fill of postcards and crowds, take tram #20 or #26 from metro Dejvice to the last stop and walk north down into the **Šárka valley**, a peaceful limestone gorge that twists eastwards back towards Dejvice. The first section (Divoká Šárka) is particularly dramatic, with grey-white crags rising up on both sides – it was here that Šárka plunged to her death (see below). Gradually the valley opens up, with a grassy meadow to picnic on, and a swimming pool

Dejvice, Střešovice and beyond

To reach the Müller Haus, take tram #1 or #18 from metro Hradčanská.

Střešovice is also home of the city's Transport Museum (Museum MHD), on Patočka, for more on which see p.222.

Šárka and Ctirad

The Šárka valley takes its name from the Amazonian **Šárka**, who, according to Czech legend, committed suicide here sometime back in the last millennium. The story begins with the death of Libuše, the founder and first ruler of Prague. The women closest to her, who had enjoyed enormous freedom and privilege in her court, refused to submit to the new patriarchy of her husband, Přemysl. Under the leadership of a woman called Vlasta, they left Vyšehrad and set up their own proto-feminist, separatist colony on the opposite bank of the river.

They scored numerous military victories over the men of Vyšehrad, but never managed to finish off the men's leader, a young warrior called **Ctirad**. In the end they decided to ensnare him and tied one of their own warriors naked to a tree, sure in the knowledge that Ctirad would take her to be a maiden in distress and come to her aid. Šárka offered to act as the decoy, and everything went according to plan. However, in her brief meeting with Ctirad, Šárka fell madly in love with him and, overcome with grief at what she had done, threw herself off the aforementioned cliff. And just in case you thought the legend had a feminist ending, it doesn't. Roused by the cruel death of Ctirad, Přemysl and the lads had a final set-to with Vlasta and co, and butchered the lot of them.

nearby, both fairly popular on summer weekends. There are various
points further east from which you can pick up a city bus back into
town, depending on how far you want to walk. The full walk to where
the Šárka stream flows into the Vltava, just north of Baba, is about 6
or 7km all told, though none of it is particularly tough going.

Hvězda, Bílá hora and Břevnov

A couple of kilometres southwest of Dejvice, trams #1, #2 and #18
terminate close to the main entrance to the hunting park of **Hvězda**
(obora Hvězda), one of Prague's most beautiful and peaceful parks.
The park's wide, soft, green avenues of trees radiate from a bizarre
star-shaped building (Hvězda means "Star") that was designed by
the Archduke Ferdinand of Tyrol for his wife in 1555. Fully restored
in the 1950s, it now houses a worthy but dull **museum** (devoted to
the reactionary writer Alois Jirásek (1851–1930), who popularized
old Czech legends during the national revival, and the artist Mikuláš
Aleš (1852–1913), whose drawings were likewise inspired by Czech
history. There's also a small exhibition on the Battle of Bílá hora

*The museum is
open Tues–Sat
9am–4pm, Sun
10am–5pm.*

The Battle of Bílá hora

The **Battle of Bílá hora** (White Mountain) may have been a skirmish of
minor importance in the Thirty Years' War, but, for the Czechs, it was to
have devastating consequences. The victory of the Catholic forces of
Habsburg emperor Ferdinand II in 1620 set the seal on German-speaking
domination of the Czech Lands for the next three hundred years. It
prompted an emigration of religious and intellectual figures that relegated
the country to a cultural backwater for most of modern history. The
defeat also unleashed a decimation of the Czech aristocracy, which meant
that, unlike their immediate neighbours, the Poles and Hungarians, the
Czechs had to build their national revival around writers and composers,
rather than counts and warriors.

Vastly outnumbered by the Catholic forces – despite verbal support
from the Germans, Dutch and English, only the rebel Prince of
Transylvania actually sent troops to aid the Czechs – the Protestants
assumed the chalky hill to the west of Prague, hoping it would provide a
secure base from which to defend the city. Shortly after noon, the imperial troops (under the nominal command of the Virgin Mary) attacked the
Czechs' left flank, which, in under two hours, prompted a full-scale flight.
The Czech commander, Christian von Anhalt, went hot-foot back to the
Hrad, where he met the Czech king, Frederick of Palatinate, who was late
for the battle, having been delayed during lunch with the English ambassador. Frederick, dubbed the "Winter King" for his brief reign, had once
tossed silver coins to the crowd, and entertained them by swimming
naked in the Vltava. Now, abandoned by his allies, he gathered up his
crown jewels and left Prague in such a hurry he almost forgot his youngest son, who was playing in the nursery. The city had no choice but to
surrender to the Catholics, who spent a week looting the place, before
executing twenty-seven of the rebellion's leaders on Staroměstské náměstí
(see p.90).

(see below) on the top floor. It's the building itself, though – decorated with delicate stucco work and frescoes – that's the real reason for venturing inside; it makes a perfect setting for the chamber music concerts occasionally staged here.

A short distance southwest of Hvězda is the once entirely barren limestone summit of **Bílá hora** (White Mountain), accessible from Hvězda through one of the many holes in the park's southern perimeter wall. It was here, on November 8, 1620, that the first battle of the Thirty Years' War took place, sealing the fate of the Czech nation for the following three hundred years. In little more than an hour, the Protestant forces under Count Thurn and the "Winter King" Frederick of Palatinate were roundly beaten by the Catholic troops of the Habsburg Emperor Ferdinand. As a more or less direct consequence, the Czechs lost their aristocracy, their religion, their scholars and, most importantly, the remnants of their sovereignty. There's nothing much to see now, apart from the small monument (*mohyla*), and a pilgrims' church, just off Nad višňovkou. This was erected by the Catholics to commemorate the victory, which they ascribed to the timely intercession of the Virgin Mary – hence its name, **Panna Maria Vítězná** (St Mary the Victorious).

Rather than heading straight back into town, if you've time to spare, the idyllic Baroque monastery of **sv Markéta** in Břevnov is just five minutes' walk east of the park, down Zeyerova alej. Founded as a Benedictine abbey by Saint Adalbert, tenth-century bishop of Prague, it was worked over in the eighteenth century by both Christoph and Kilian Ignaz Dientzenhofer, and bears their characteristic interconnecting ovals, inside and out. The monks have recently returned, which has made it easier to gain access to the church. To get back into town, take tram #8 or #22 from just below the monastery.

To get to Bílá hora, take tram #8 from metro Hradčanská or #22 from metro Malostranská to the western terminus, then walk up Nad višňovkou and across the field.

There are guided tours of the monastery Sat at 9 & 10.30am, 2 & 4pm, Sun 10.30am, 2 & 4pm; at other times it's possible to peek inside.

Smíchov

SMÍCHOV is for the most part an old nineteenth-century working-class suburb, home to the city's largest brewery, and a large community of Romanies, its skyline peppered with satanic mills and chimneys dutifully belching out smoke. To the west, as it gains height, the run-down tenements give way to another of Prague's sought-after villa quarters. To the north, it borders with Malá Strana, and, officially at least, takes in a considerable part of the woods of Petřín, south of the Hunger Wall (see p.77).

Bertramka (Mozart Museum)

Mozart stayed with the Dušeks at their **Bertramka** Villa on several occasions – it was here in 1787 that he put the finishing touches to his *Don Giovanni* overture, the night before the premiere at the Stavovské divadlo (see p.96). As long ago as 1838, the villa was turned into a shrine to Mozart, though very little survives of the house he knew, thanks to a fire on New Year's Day 1871 – not that this has deterred generations of Mozart lovers from flocking here. These days, what the museum lacks in memorabilia, it makes up for in Rococo ambience and the odd Mozart recital. To get to Bertramka, take the metro to Anděl, walk a couple of blocks west up Plzeňská, then left up Mozartova.

Bertramka is open Tues–Sun 9.30am–6pm; for more on Mozart's links with Prague, see box on p.69.

The Pink Tank

Smíchov's greatest claim to fame is the episode of the **pink tank**. Until 1991, Tank 23 sat proudly on its plinth in náměstí Sovětských tankistů (Soviet tank drivers' square), one of a number of obsolete tanks generously donated by the Soviets after World War II to serve as monuments to the 1945 liberation. Tank 23 was special, however, as it was supposedly the first tank to arrive to liberate Prague, on May 9, hotfoot from Berlin.

According to many Czechs, however, the real story of the liberation of Prague was rather different. When the Prague uprising began on May 5, the first offer of assistance actually came from two divisions of the anti-Communist Russian Liberation Army (KONR), under the renegade general, **Andrei Vlasov**. Vlasov was a high-ranking Red Army officer, who was instrumental in pushing the Germans back from the gates of Moscow, but switched sides after being captured by the Nazis in 1942. In the closing stages of the war the KONR switched sides once more to fight alongside the Czech resistance against the small pockets of SS who were still at large in Prague. The deal was that the Czechs would guarantee Vlasov's men asylum from the advancing Soviets in return for military assistance. In reality, the Czechs were unable to honour their side of the bargain when the Red Army finally arrived in Prague, and many of Vlasov's troops were simply gunned down by the Soviets. Even those KONR who gave themselves up to the Americans were eventually handed over to the Russians and shared the fate of their leader Vlasov who was tried *in camera* in Moscow and executed by the Soviets.

The unsolicited reappearance of Soviet tanks on the streets of Prague in 1968 left most Czechs feeling somewhat ambivalent towards the old monument. And in the summer of 1991, situationist artist David Černý painted the tank bubble-gum pink, and placed a large phallic finger on top of it, while another mischievous Czech daubed "Vlasov" on the podium. Since the country was at the time engaged in delicate negotiations to end the Soviet military presence in Czechoslovakia, the new regime, despite its mostly dissident leanings, roundly condemned the act as unlawful. Havel, in his characteristically even-handed way, made it clear that he didn't like tanks anywhere, whether on the battlefield or as monuments.

In the end, the tank was hastily repainted khaki green and Černý was arrested under the familiar "crimes against the state" clause of the penal code, which had been used by the Communists with gay abandon on several members of the present government. In protest at the arrest of Černý, twelve members of the federal parliament turned up the following day in their overalls and, taking advantage of their legal immunity, repainted the tank pink. Finally, the government gave in, released Černý and removed the tank from public view. There's now no trace of tank, podium or plaque, and even the square has been renamed náměstí Kinských.

Out from the City

F ew capital cities can boast such extensive unspoilt tracts of
woodland so near at hand as Prague. Once you leave the
half-built high-rise estates of the outer suburbs behind, the
traditional provincial feel of **Bohemia** (Čechy) immediately makes
itself felt. Many towns and villages still huddle below the grand
residences of their former lords, their street layout little changed
since medieval times.

To the north, several such chateaux grace the banks of the
Vltava, including the wine-producing town of **Mělník**, on the Labe
(Elbe) plain. Beyond Mělník lie the wooded gorges of the
Kokořínsko region, too far for a day trip unless you've your own
transport, but perfect for a weekend in the country. Further away,

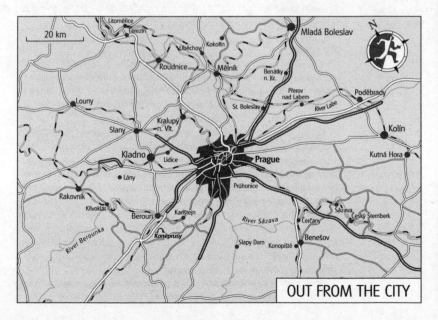

OUT FROM THE CITY

but better served by public transport, is **Terezín**, the wartime Jewish ghetto that is a living testament to the Holocaust. One of the most obvious day-trip destinations is to the east of Prague: **Kutná Hora**, a medieval silver-mining town with one of the most beautiful Gothic churches in the country, and a macabre gallery of bones in the suburb of Sedlec.

Further south, there's a couple of sights worth visiting along the **Sázava valley**; while nearby, two chateaux, **Průhonice** and **Konopiště**, are set in exceptionally beautiful and expansive grounds – with a car, you could take in all four in a day. Southwest of Prague, a similar mix of woods and rolling hills surrounds the popular castle of **Karlštejn**, a gem of Gothic architecture, dramatically situated above the River Berounka. There are numerous possibilities for walking in the region around Karlštejn, and further upstream, in the forests of **Křivoklátsko**. West of Prague, there are two places of pilgrimage: **Lány** is the resting place of the founder of modern Czechoslovakia, and summer residence of the president; and **Lidice**, razed to the ground by the SS, is another town which recalls the horror of Nazi occupation.

Getting around

For details of car rental firms, see p.39; for bike rental, see p.40.

Transport throughout Bohemia is fairly straightforward, thanks to a comprehensive network of railway lines and regional bus services, though connections can be less than smooth, and journeys slow. If you're planning to try and see more than one or two places outside Prague, however, or one of the more difficult destinations to reach, it might be worth considering hiring a car.

By train

The most relaxing way to day-trip from Prague is by **train**. The antiquated rolling stock is a pleasure to travel in. However, the system, which has changed little since it was bequeathed to the country by the Habsburgs in 1918, is often a lot slower than the buses – though still extremely cheap compared with western Europe.

Czech Railways, *České dráhy* (*ČD*), run two main **types of train**: *rychlík* trains are the faster ones which stop only at major towns, while *osobní* trains stop at just about every station, averaging as little as 30kph. To buy a ticket, simply state your destination – it will be assumed that you want a ticket for an *osobní* train. If you want a return ticket (*zpáteční*), you must say so. First-class carriages (*první třída*) exist only on fast trains. There are half-price **discount fares** for children under twelve, and you can take two children under five for free (providing they don't take up more than one seat). There are even some "crèche carriages" on the slower trains, for the exclusive use of mothers with children under five.

With very few English-speakers employed on the railways, it can be difficult getting **train information**. The larger stations have a simple airport-style flip-over arrivals and departures board, which includes information on delays under the heading *zpoždění*. Many stations have poster-style displays of arrivals and departures, the former on white paper, the latter on yellow, with fast trains printed in red. If you're going to be travelling by train a lot, it's a good idea to invest in a *ČD* timetable (*jízdní řád*), which comes out every May (and often sells out soon afterwards).

In addition to the above, all but the smallest stations have a comprehensive display of timings and route information on rollers. These timetables may seem daunting at first, but with a little practice they should become increasingly decipherable. First find the route you need to take on the diagrammatic map and make a note of the number printed beside it; then follow the timetable rollers through until you come to the appropriate number. The only problem now is language since everything will be written in Czech. Arrivals are *příjezd* (*příj.* in short form) and departures are *odjezd* (*odj.* in short form). A platform or *nástupiště* is usually divided into two *kolej* on either side. Some of the more common notes at the side of the timetable are *jezdí jen v* (only running on), or *nejezdí v* or *nechodí v* (not running on), followed by a date or a symbol: a cross or an "N" for a Sunday; a big "S" for a Saturday; two crossed hammers for a workday; "A" for a Friday and so on. Small stations may simply have a board with a list of departures under the title *směr* (direction) followed by a town.

By bus

Since the reduction of state subsidies on the railways, travelling by bus (*autobus*) has become an even more attractive alternative to the trains. Most routes are still run by the state bus company, *ČSAD*. With just a few exceptions, *ČSAD* buses are nearly always faster (and cheaper) than the train. Bear in mind, though, that in rural areas timetables are often designed with the working and/or school day in mind. That means up and out at 6am and back at around 3pm during the week, and completely different services at weekends.

In places outside Prague, the bus station is often adjacent to the train station, though you may be able to pick up the bus from the centre of town, too. The bigger terminals in Prague, like Praha-Florenc, are run with train-like efficiency, though finding the right departure stand can be a daunting task. For most minor routes, simply buy your ticket from the driver.

Bus timetables are even more difficult to figure out than train ones, as there are no maps at any of the stations. Each service is listed separately, so you may have to scour several timetables before you discover when the next bus is. Make sure you check on which day the service runs, since many run only on Mondays, Fridays or at the weekend (see the above section on trains for the key phrases).

Minor bus stops are marked with a rusty metal sign saying *zastávka*. If you want to get off, ask *já chci vystoupit?*; "the next stop" is *příští zastávka*. If you're feeling really keen, you could try and get hold of volume 1 of the *ČSAD* regional bus timetables, (*jízdní řád*), which covers the area around Prague.

Mělník and around

Occupying a spectacular, commanding site at the confluence of the Vltava and Labe rivers, MĚLNÍK, 33km north of Prague, lies at the heart of Bohemia's tiny wine-growing region. The town's history goes back to the ninth century, when it was handed over to the Přemyslids as part of Ludmilla's dowry when she married Prince Bořivoj. And it was here, too, that she introduced her heathen grandson Václav (later to become Saint Wenceslas, aka "Good King") to the joys of Christianity. Viticulture became the town's economic mainstay only after Charles IV, aching for a little of the French wine of his youth, introduced grapes from Burgundy (where he was also king).

The old town

The chateau is open daily March, April & Oct–Dec 10am–4pm; May–Sept 10am–6pm.

Mělník's greatest monument is its Renaissance **chateau**, perched high above the flat plains and visible for miles around. The present building, covered in familiar sgraffito patterns, has recently been returned to its last aristocratic owners, the Lobkovic family, who are in the process of restoring the chateau's magnificently proportioned rooms, which also provide great views out over the plain. Visits are by guided tour only, and you've a choice between exploring seven rooms of the castle interior, filled with artefacts and Old Masters returned to the family since 1989, or taking the shorter tour round the wine museum in the cellars, finishing up with a glass of plonk (you get six glasses of better-quality tipple if you take the "fine wines" tour).

The ossuary is open daily 10am–4pm.

Below the chateau, vines cling to the south-facing terraces, as the land plunges into the river below. From beneath the great tower of Mělník's onion-domed church of **sv Petr and Pavel**, next door to the chateau, there's an even better view of the rivers' confluence, and the subsidiary canal, once so congested with vessels that traffic lights had to be introduced to avoid accidents. The church itself contains a compellingly macabre ossuary or charnel house, filled with bones of medieval plague victims, fashioned into weird and wonderful skeletal shapes by students in the early part of this century.

The rest of the old town is pleasant enough for some casual strolling, though pretty small. One half of the main square, náměstí Míru, is arcaded Baroque and typical of the region, and there's an old medieval gateway nearby, which has been converted into an art gallery, but apart from the rare sight of a Soviet tank on U tanku, there's little else to detain you.

Practicalities

There's no direct train service to Mělník from Prague, as the main line veers northwest, beyond Nelahozeves. There is, however, a regular **bus service** which leaves from metro Holešovice and stand 18 at Florenc, and takes under an hour. On arrival at Mělník bus station, to reach the older part of town, simply head up Krombholcova in the direction of the big church tower. If your next destination is Liběchov or Terezín, you have the choice of either the bus or the train; the **train station** is still further from the old town, a couple of blocks northeast of the bus station, down Jiřího z Poděbrad.

As for **food and drink**, the chateau restaurant is as good (and cheap) a place as any to sample some of the local wine (and enjoy the view): the red *Ludmila* is the most famous of Mělník's wines, and there's even a rare Czech rosé produced by the castle vineyards, but if you prefer white, try a bottle of *Tramín*. Equally good views can be had from *Stará škola* restaurant, behind the church; otherwise, you could try *U sv Václava* at Svatováclavská 22, a *vinárna* beside the main entrance to the chateau, or tuck into basic food and *Krušovice* beer served at the *Zlatý beránek* on náměstí Míru.

Liběchov

Seven kilometres north and ten minutes by train from Mělník – just out of sight of the giant coal-fired power station that provides most of Prague's electricity – is the rhubarb-and-custard coloured chateau at LIBĚCHOV (Liboch). Even without the sickly colour scheme, it's a bizarre place: formal and two-dimensional when viewed from the French gardens at the front, but bulging like an amphitheatre around the back by the entrance. Inside is another surprise, a **museum of Asian and Oriental cultures**, based around the collections of Czech explorer, Vojta Náprstek, and featuring endless Buddhas, Mongolian printing equipment, Balinese monster gear and Javanese puppets – all of which make for a fascinating half-hour tour. The main dining hall, now full of Asian musical instruments, is curious, too, smothered in its original barley-sugar decor with little sculpted jesters crouching mischievously in the corners of the ceiling.

The museum is open Tues–Sun 9am–noon & 1–3.30pm; Náprstek's American and Australasian collections are housed in Prague's Náprstek Museum, see p.99.

For all the chateau's excesses, the **village** itself is little more than a *hostinec* (pub) and a bend in the road, but straggling up the valley are the remains of what was once an attractive spa resort for ailing Praguers. Many of the old *Gasthäuser* are still standing, including the *Pension Stüdl* where Kafka spent the winter of 1918. It was here that he met and became engaged to Julie Wohryzek, daughter of a

OUT FROM THE CITY

> **The Levý heads: A Walk from Liběchov**
>
> For a brief and not too strenuous walk from Liběchov, take the blue-marked path opposite the chateau, which follows the Liběchovka stream and then heads east towards some thickly wooded hills. The first hill contains some unremarkable sandstone caves, but the second is covered in sandstone rocks, two of which have been sculpted into giant grimacing faces, one with a goatish beard, the other baring its teeth. Known as the Čertovy hlavy (Devil's heads), these are the work of the nineteenth-century sculptor Václav Levý, who was the cook for a while at Liběchov chateau, until his boss, Count Veith, encouraged him to take up sculpture and became one of his leading patrons.

Jewish shoemaker from Prague – a match vigorously opposed by his father. Kafka was prompted to write his vitriolic *Letter to His Father*, which he passed on to his mother, who wisely made sure it never got any further.

Kokořínsko

Northeast of Mělník, you leave the low plains of the Labe for a plateau region known as **Kokořínsko**, a hidden pocket of wooded hills which takes its name from the Gothic castle rising through the tree tops at its centre. The sandstone plateau has weathered over the millennia to form sunken valleys and bizarre rocky outcrops, which means there's a lot of scope for some gentle hiking here. With picturesque valleys such as the Kokořínský důl, dotted with well-preserved, half-timbered villages and riddled with marked paths, it comes as a surprise that the whole area isn't buzzing all summer.

At the centre of the region is the village of KOKOŘÍN, whose dramatic setting and spectacular medieval **castle** greatly inspired the Czech nineteenth-century Romantics. The castle is a perfect hideaway, ideal for the robbers who used it as a base after it fell into disrepair in the sixteenth century. Not until the end of the nineteenth century did it get a new lease of life, from a jumped-up local landowner, Václav Špaček, who bought himself a title and refurbished the place as a family memorial. There's precious little inside and no incentive to endure the half-hour tour, as you can explore the ramparts and climb the tallest tower on your own.

Practicalities

If you've got your own transport, Kokořínsko makes a pleasant day trip from Prague. For those on public transport there's one direct bus a week from the Praha-Holešovice bus station in summer (leaving at around 7.45am); otherwise, take the regular buses to Mělník and change there. Alternatively, you could catch the local train from Mělník to **Mšeno**, from where it's a three-kilometre walk west to Kokořín on the green-marked path.

Terezín

The road from Prague to Berlin passes right through the fortress
town of TEREZÍN (Theresienstadt), just over 60km northwest of
the capital. Purpose-built in the 1780s by the Habsburgs to defend
the northern border against Prussia, it was capable of accommodating 14,500 soldiers and hundreds of prisoners. In 1941, the
population were ejected and the whole town turned into a **Jewish
ghetto**, and used as a transit camp for Jews whose final destination was Auschwitz.

Although the **Main Fortress** (Hlavní pevnost) has never been
put to the test in battle, Terezín remains a garrison town. Today, it's
an eerie, soulless place, built to a dour eighteenth-century grid plan,
its bare streets still ringing with the sounds of soldiers and military
police. As you enter, the red-brick fortifications are still an awesome
sight, though the huge moat has been put out of action by local
gardening enthusiasts.

A brief history of the ghetto

In October 1941, Reinhard Heydrich and the Nazi high command
decided to turn the whole of Terezín into a Jewish ghetto. It was an
obvious choice: fully fortified, close to the main Prague–Dresden
railway line, and with an SS prison already established in the Small
Fortress nearby. The original inhabitants of the town – less than
3500 people – were moved out, and transports began arriving at
Terezín from many parts of central Europe. Within a year, nearly
60,000 Jews were interned here in appallingly overcrowded conditions; the monthly death rate rose to 4000. In October 1942, the
first transport left for Auschwitz. By the end of the war, 140,000
Jews had been deported to Terezín; fewer than 17,500 remained
when the ghetto was finally liberated on May 8, 1945.

One of the perverse ironies of Terezín is that it was used by the
Nazis as a cover for the real purpose of the *Endlösung* or "final solution", devised at the Wannsee conference in January 1942 (at which
Heydrich was present). The ghetto was made to appear self-governing,
with its own council or *Freizeitgestaltung*, its own bank printing
ghetto money, its own shops selling goods confiscated from the intern-
ees on arrival, and even a café on the main square. For a while, a
special "Terezín family camp" was even set up in Auschwitz, to continue
the deception. The deportees were kept in mixed barracks, allowed to
wear civilian clothes and – the main purpose of the whole thing – send
letters back to their loved ones in Terezín telling them they were OK.
After six months "quarantine", they were sent to the gas chambers.

Despite the fact that Terezín was being used by the Nazis as
cynical propaganda, the ghetto population turned their unprecedented freedom to their own advantage. Since the entire population
of the Protectorate (and Jews from many other parts of Europe)

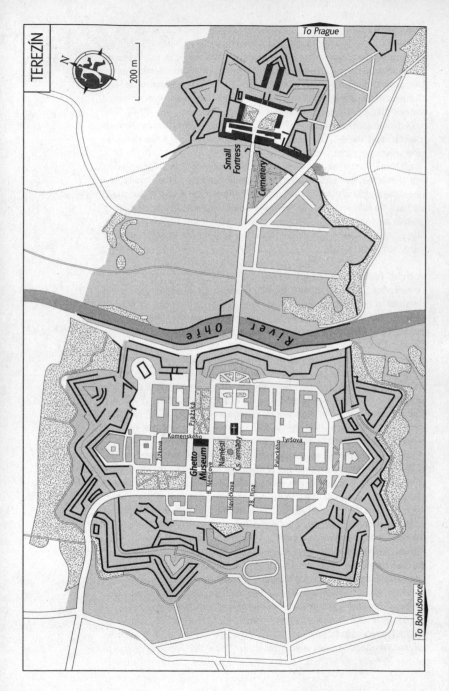

TEREZÍN

N

200 m

To Prague

Small Fortress

Cemetery

River Ohře

Pražská

Komenského

Jiřkova

Ghetto Museum

B. Němcove

Havlíčkova

Náměstí

Čs. armády

28. října

Palackého

Tyršova

To Bohušovice

passed through Terezín, the ghetto had an enormous number of outstanding Jewish artists, musicians, scholars and writers (many of whom perished in the camps). Thus, in addition to the officially sponsored activities, countless clandestine cultural events were organized in the cellars and attics of the barracks: teachers gave lessons to children, puppet theatre productions were held, and literary evenings were put on.

Towards the end of 1943, the so-called *Verschönerung* or "beautification" of the ghetto was implemented, in preparation for the arrival of the International Red Cross inspectors. Streets were given names instead of numbers, and the whole place was decked out as if it were a spa town. When the International Red Cross asked to inspect one of the Nazi camps, they were brought here and treated to a week of Jewish cultural events. A circus tent was set up in the main square; a children's pavilion erected in the park; numerous performances of Hans Krása's children's opera, *Brundibár* (Bumble Bee), staged; and a jazz band, called the *Ghetto Swingers*, performed in the bandstand on the main square. The Red Cross visited Terezín twice, once in June 1944, and again in April 1945; both times the delegates filed positive reports.

The Ghetto Museum

The unnerving feel of the place apart, there's just one thing to see here, the **Ghetto Museum** (Muzeum Ghetta), which was finally opened in 1991, on the fiftieth anniversary of the arrival of the first transports in Terezín. After the war, the Communists had followed the consistent Soviet line by deliberately underplaying the Jewish perspective on Terezín. Instead, the emphasis in the museum set up in the Small Fortress (see below) was on the war as an anti-fascist struggle, in which good (Communism and the Soviet Union) had triumphed over evil (Fascism and Nazi Germany). It wasn't until the Prague Spring of 1968 that the idea of a museum dedicated specifically to the history of the Jewish ghetto first emerged. In the 1970s, however, the intended building was turned into a Museum of the Ministry of the Interior instead.

The museum is open daily May–Sept 9am–6.30pm; Oct–April 9am–4.30pm.

Now that it's finally open, this extremely informative and well laid-out exhibition at last attempts to do some justice to the extraordinary and tragic events which took place here between 1941 and 1945, including background displays on the measures which led up to the *Endlösung*. There's also a fascinating video (with English subtitles) showing clips of the Nazi propaganda film shot in Terezín – *Hitler gives the Jews a Town* – intercut with harrowing interviews with survivors.

The Small Fortress

On the other side of the River Ohře, east down Pražská, lies the **Small Fortress** (Malá pevnost), built as a military prison in the

The Small Fortress opens at 8am; otherwise same hours as Ghetto Museum.

1780s, at the same time as the main fortress. The young Bosnian, Gavrilo Princip, who succeeded in shooting Archduke Ferdinand in 1914, was interned and died here during World War I. In 1940 it was turned into an SS prison by Heydrich and, after the war, it became the official memorial and museum of Terezín. The vast cemetery laid out by the entrance to the fortress is now dominated by a large Christian cross, an insensitive recent addition given that the vast majority of Terezín's victims were Jewish.

There are guides available (often survivors from Terezín), or else you can simply buy the brief broadsheet guide to the prison in English, and walk around yourself. The infamous Nazi refrain *Arbeit Macht Frei* (Work Brings Freedom) is daubed across the entrance on the left, which leads to the exemplary washrooms, still as they were when built for the Red Cross tour of inspection. The rest of the camp has been left empty but intact, and graphically evokes the cramped conditions under which the prisoners were kept half-starved and badly clothed, subject to indiscriminate cruelty and execution. The main **exhibition** is housed in the smart eighteenth-century mansion set in the prison gardens, which was home to the camp *Kommandant*, his family and fellow SS officers. A short documentary, intelligible in any language, is regularly shown in the cinema that was set up in 1942 to entertain the prison officers.

Practicalities

Terezín is about an hour's **bus** ride from Prague's Florenc terminal (buses leave from stands 17, 19 & 20) and therefore easy to visit on a day trip. The nearest train station to Terezín is at BOHUŠOVICE, 2km south of the fortress. Foodwise, you're best off either bringing a picnic, or heading for either of the following **restaurants**: *Teresian*, on the main square, which serves simple but good Czech food, or *U hojtašů*, on Komenského.

Kutná Hora

For two hundred and fifty years or so, KUTNÁ HORA (Kuttenberg) was one of the most important towns in Bohemia, second only to Prague. At the end of the fourteenth century its population was equal to that of London, its shantytown suburbs straggled across what are now green fields, and its ambitious building projects set out to rival those of the capital itself. Today, Kutná Hora is a small provincial town with a population of just over 20,000, but the monuments dotted around it, the superb Gothic cathedral, and the remarkable monastery and ossuary in the suburb of **Sedlec**, make it one of the most enjoyable of all possible day trips from Prague.

Kutná Hora's road to prosperity began in the late thirteenth century with the discovery of **silver deposits** in the surrounding area. German miners were invited to settle and work the seams, and around 1300 Václav II founded the royal mint here and sent for Italian craftsmen to run it. Much of the town's wealth was used to fund the beautification of Prague, but it also allowed for the construction of one of the most magnificent churches in central Europe and a number of other prestigious Gothic monuments in Kutná Hora itself.

At the time of the Hussite Wars, the town was mostly German, and therefore staunchly Catholic; local miners used to throw captured Hussites into the deep mine shafts and leave them to die of starvation. Word got out, and the town was besieged and eventually taken by Žižka's fanatical Táborites in 1421, only to be recaptured by Sigismund and his papal forces shortly afterwards, and again by Žižka, the following year.

While the silver stocks remained high the town was able to recover its former prosperity, but at the end of the sixteenth century the mines dried up and Kutná Hora's wealth and importance came to an abrupt end – when the Swedes marched on the town during the Thirty Years' War, they had to be bought off with beer rather than silver. The town has never fully recovered, shrivelling to less than a third of its former size, its fate emphatically sealed by a devastating fire in 1770.

The Town

The small, unassuming houses that line the town's main square, Palackého náměstí, and medieval lanes give little idea of Kutná Hora's former glories. A narrow alleyway on the south side of the square, however, leads to the more appealing, leafy Havlíčkovo náměstí, on which stands the **Vlašský dvůr** (Italian Court), originally conceived as a palace by Václav II, and for three centuries the town's bottomless purse. It was here that Florentine minters produced the Prague Groschen (*pražské groše*), a silver coin widely used throughout central Europe until the nineteenth century. The building itself has been mucked about with over the years, most recently – and most brutally – by nineteenth-century restorers, who left only the chestnut trees, a fourteenth-century oriel window (capped by an unlikely looking wooden onion dome) and the statue of a miner unmolested. The original workshops of the minters have been bricked in, but the outlines of their little doors and windows are still visible in the courtyard. The short **guided tour** of the old chapel, treasury and royal palace gives you a fair idea of the building's former importance.

The Vlašský dvůr is open daily 10am–6pm.

Outside the court is a statue of the country's founder and first president, T. G. Masaryk, twice removed – once by the Nazis and

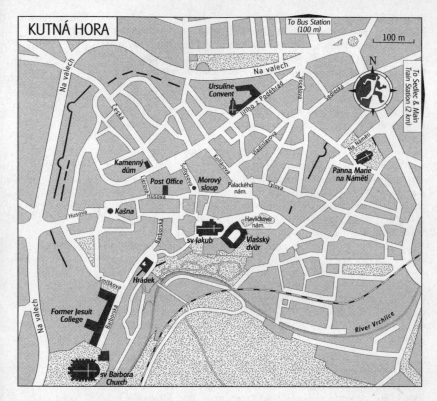

once by the Communists – but now returned to its pride of place. Before you leave, take a quick turn in the court gardens, which climb down in steps to the Vrchlice valley below. This is undoubtedly Kutná Hora's best profile, with a splendid view over to the cathedral of sv Barbora (see opposite).

Behind the Vlašský dvůr is **sv Jakub** (St James), the town's oldest church, begun a generation or so after the discovery of the silver deposits. Its grand scale is a clear indication of the town's quite considerable wealth by the fourteenth century, though in terms of artistry it pales in comparison with Kutná Hora's other ecclesiastical buildings. The leaning tower is a reminder of the precarious position of the town, the church's foundations being prone to subsidence from the disused mines below. If you want to see some of these, head for the **Hrádek**, an old fort which was used as a second mint and now serves as a **Mining Museum** (Muzeum a středověké důlní dílo). Here you can pick up a white coat, miner's helmet and torch, and visit some of the medieval mines that were discovered beneath the fort in the 1960s.

The museum is open April–Oct Tues–Sun 9am–noon & 1–5pm.

The Cathedral of sv Barbora

Kutná Hora's cathedral of **sv Barbora** is arguably the most beautiful church in central Europe. Not to be outdone by the great monastery at Sedlec (see overleaf) or the St Vitus Cathedral in Prague, the miners of Kutná Hora began financing the construction of a great Gothic cathedral of their own, dedicated to Saint Barbara, the patron saint of miners and gunners. The foundations were probably laid by Parler in the 1380s, but work was interrupted by the Hussite wars, and the church remains unfinished, despite a flurry of building activity at the beginning of the sixteenth century by, among others, Benedikt Reith.

The cathedral is open summer Tues–Sun 8am–noon & 1–5pm; winter 9am–noon & 1–4pm.

The approach road to the cathedral, Barborská, is lined with a parade of gesticulating Baroque saints and cherubs that rival the sculptures on the Charles Bridge; on the right-hand side is the palatial former Jesuit College. The church itself bristles with pinnacles, finials and flying buttresses which support its most striking feature, a roof of three tent-like towers, culminating in unequal needle-sharp spires. Inside, cold light streams through the plain glass windows, illuminating a playful vaulted nave whose ribs form branches and petals stamped with coats of arms belonging to Václav II and the local miners' guilds. The wide spread of the five-aisled nave is remarkably uncluttered: a Gothic pulpit – half wood, half stone – creeps tastefully up a central pillar, and black and gold Renaissance confessionals hide discreetly in the north aisle. On the south wall is the Minters' Chapel, decorated with fifteenth-century wall frescoes showing the Florentines at work, while in the ambulatory chapels some fascinating paintings – unique for their period – depict local miners at work.

The rest of the town

There are a few minor sights worth seeking out in the rest of the town. On Rejskovo náměstí, the squat, many-sided **Kašna** (fountain) by Matouš Rejsek strikes an odd pose – anything less like a fountain would be hard to imagine. At the bottom of the sloping Šultysova is a particularly fine **Morový sloup** (Plague Column), giving thanks for the end of the plague of 1713; while just around the corner, at the top of Lierova, is one of the few Gothic buildings to survive the 1770 fire, the **Kamenný dům** built around 1480 and covered in an ornate sculptural icing. This used to contain an unexceptional local museum, which has now been moved a couple of blocks down Jiřího z Poděbrad, to Kilian Ignaz Dientzenhofer's unfinished **Ursuline convent**. Only three sides of the convent's ambitious pentagonal plan were completed, its neo-Baroque church added in the late nineteenth century while sv Barbora was being restored.

Sedlec

Buses #1 and #4 run 3km northeast to SEDLEC, once a separate village but now a suburb of Kutná Hora. Adjoining Sedlec's defunct eighteenth-century Cistercian monastery (now the largest tobacco

Kutná Hora

factory in Europe, owned by Phillip Morris) is the fourteenth-century church of **Panna Maria** (St Mary), imaginatively redesigned in the eighteenth century by Giovanni Santini, who specialized in melding Gothic with Baroque. Here, given a plain French Gothic church gutted during the Hussite wars, Santini set to work on the vaulting, adding his characteristic sweeping stucco rib patterns, relieved only by the occasional Baroque splash of colour above the chancel steps. For all its attractions, however, the church seems to be permanently covered in scaffolding, and closed except for the occasional service.

The ossuary is open Tues–Sun summer 8am–noon & 1–5pm; winter 9am–noon & 1–4pm.

Cross the main road, following the signs, and you come to the monks' graveyard, where an ancient Gothic chapel leans heavily over the entrance to the macabre subterranean **kostnice** or ossuary, full to overflowing with human bones. When holy earth from Golgotha was scattered over the graveyard in the twelfth century, all of Bohemia's nobility wanted to be buried here and the bones mounted up until there were more than 40,000 complete sets. In 1870, worried about the ever-growing piles, the authorities commissioned František Rint to do something creative with them. He rose to the challenge and moulded out of bones four giant bells, one in each corner of the crypt, designed wall-to-ceiling skeletal decorations, including the Schwarzenberg coat of arms, and, as the centrepiece, put together a chandelier made out of every bone in the human body. Rint's signature (in bones) is at the bottom of the steps.

Practicalities

The simplest way to get to Kutná Hora is to take a **bus** from stand 56 at Praha-Florenc or from metro Želivského (1hr 15min). Fast **trains** from Prague's Masarykovo nádraží take around an hour (there's only one in the morning); slow ones take two hours; trains from Praha hlavní nádraží involve a change at Kolín. The main **train station** (Kutná Hora hlavní nádraží) is a long way out of town, near Sedlec; bus #2 or #4 will take you into town, or there's an occasional shuttle train service to Kutná Hora město train station, near the centre of town.

The town has a highly efficient system of orientation signs, and at almost every street corner a pictorial list of the chief places of interest keeps you on the right track. Having said that, the train station signposted is not the main one. As for **eating and drinking**, *U Hrnčíře*, Barborská 24, is the best place in terms of food, though there are plenty of good pubs, too, where you can get more simple fare. Try *U kamenného domu*, on Lierova, for a sampling of the local *Dačický* beer, *U anděla*, at the beginning of Jiřího z Poděbrad, which serves *Bernard* beer, or *U havířů on* Šultysova, which offers a variety of brews including *Gambrinus*.

Průhonice and the Sázava valley

A short train ride **southeast** of Prague is enough to transport you from the urban sprawl of the capital into one of the prettiest regions of central Bohemia, starting with the park at **Průhonice**. Until the motorway to Brno and Bratislava ripped through the area in the 1970s, the roads and railways linking the three big cities took the longer, flatter option, further north along the Labe valley. As a result, commerce and tourism passed the **Sázava Valley** by, and, with the notable exception of **Konopiště**, it remains undeveloped, unspoilt and out of the way.

Průhonice

Barely outside the city limits, and just off the country's one and only motorway, PRŮHONICE throngs with Czech weekenders during the summer season. For the great majority, it's the 625-acre **park** they come to see and not the **chateau**, a motley parade of neo-Renaissance buildings, most of them closed to the public anyway. The park is a botanical and horticultural research centre, so the array of flora is unusually good here. Though few do, it's worth paying a passing visit to the chateau's **art gallery**, which features a permanent collection of twentieth-century Czech paintings and sculpture, including a hefty series of canvases by the Czech Cubists.

The park is open daily April–Oct.

There's a regular **bus** service to Průhonice from metro Opatov, or else you can walk the 4km along the red-marked route, via the artificial Hostivař lake, starting at the penultimate tram stop on trams #22 or #26. For something to **eat** in Průhonice, look no further than *U zámku*, the local *hostinec* by the chateau entrance.

Sázava and Český Šternberk

Rising majestically above the slow-moving waters of the river Sázava, the **Sázava monastery** was founded by the eleventh-century Prince Oldřich, on the instigation of a passing hermit called **Prokop** (St Procopius), whom he met by chance in the forest. The Slavonic liturgy was used at the monastery and, for a while, Sázava became an important centre for the dissemination of Slavonic texts. Later, a large Gothic church was planned, and this now bares its red sandstone nave to the world, incomplete but intact. The chancel was converted into a Baroque church and, later still, the Tieg family bought the place and started to build themselves a modest chateau. Of this architectural hotchpotch, only the surviving Gothic frescoes – in the popular "Beautiful Style", but of a sophistication unmatched in Bohemian art at the time – are truly memorable. The village itself thrived on the glass trade, and the rest of the monastery's overlong guided tour concentrates on the local glassware.

The monastery is open April & Oct Sat & Sun 9am–4pm; May–Sept Tues–Sun 8am–noon & 1–5pm.

Without your own transport, it'll take a good hour and a half by bus or train to cover the 55km from Prague to Sázava. Of the two, the **train** ride (change at Čerčany) is the more visually absorbing, especially along the branch line that meanders down the Sázava valley.

Český Šternberk

*The castle is
open April,
Sept & Oct
Tues–Sun
9am–noon &
1–4pm;
May–Aug
Tues–Sun
8am–noon &
1–5pm.*

Several bends in the Sázava river later, the great mass of the **castle** at ČESKÝ ŠTERNBERK is strung out along a knife's edge above the river – a breathtaking sight. Unfortunately, that's all it is, since apart from its fiercely defensive position, little remains of the original Gothic castle. Add to that the dull guided tour, the castle's popularity with coach parties, and the full two-hour journey by train or bus from Prague (again, change trains at Čerčany), and you may decide to skip it altogether.

Konopiště

Other than for its proximity to Prague, the popularity of **Konopiště** remains something of a mystery. Coach parties from all over the world home in on this unexceptional Gothic castle, stuffed with dead animals and dull weaponry. The only interesting thing about the place is its historical associations: King Václav IV was imprisoned for a while by his own nobles in the castle's distinctive round tower, and Archduke Franz Ferdinand lived here until his assassination in Sarajevo in 1914. The archduke's prime interest seems to have been the elimination of any living creature foolish enough to venture into the castle grounds: between 1880 and 1906, he killed no fewer than 171,537 birds and animals, the details of which are recorded in his *Schuss Liste* displayed inside.

There's a choice of two equally tedious **guided tours**: the shorter forty-minute tour of the *Zámecké sbírky* takes you past the stuffed bears, deer teeth and assorted lethal weapons; the tour of the *Zámecké salony* takes you round the period interiors and is less gruesome but ten minutes longer. There are occasionally tours in English, French and German, too, so ask at the box office before you sign up. Alternatively, simply head off into the 225-acre **park**, which boasts several lakes, a rose garden and a deer park. As Konopiště is only 45km from Prague the castle is a fifteen-minute walk or short bus ride west from the railway station at **Benešov**.

Karlštejn and Křivoklát

The green belt area to the **west of Prague** has its fair share of rolling hills, but spend more time here and you'll find it's easily the most varied of the regions around the city, and consequently one of

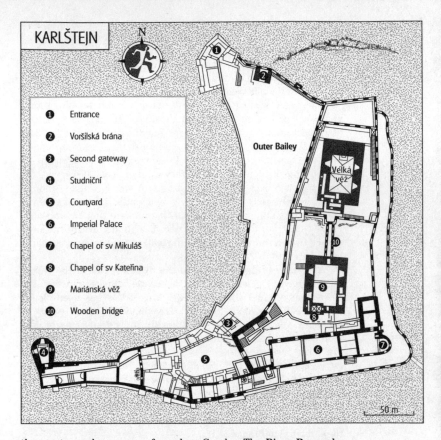

KARLŠTEJN

1 Entrance

2 Voršilská brána

3 Second gateway

4 Studniční

5 Courtyard

6 Imperial Palace

7 Chapel of sv Mikuláš

8 Chapel of sv Kateřina

9 Mariánská věž

10 Wooden bridge

Outer Bailey

Velká věž

50 m

the most popular escapes for urban Czechs. The **River Berounka** carves itself an enticingly craggy valley up to Charles IV's magnificent country castle at **Karlštejn**, the busiest destination of all, and continues further upstream to the castle of **Křivoklát**.

Karlštejn

Trains for KARLŠTEJN leave Prague's Smíchovské nádraží roughly every hour, and take about thirty minutes to cover the 28km from Prague. Over the river from the station is a small T-shaped village (now part of Karlštejn village but originally the separate hamlet of Budňany), strung out along one of the tributaries of the Berounka – pretty, but not enough to warrant a coach park the size of a football pitch. It's the **castle**, occupying a defiantly unassailable position above the village, which draws in the mass of tourists (well over quarter of a million a year). Designed in the fourteenth century by Matthias of Arras for Emperor Charles IV, as a giant safe-box for

The castle is open Tues–Sun March, April & Oct–Dec 9am–noon & 1–4pm; May–Sept 8am–noon & 1–6pm; tours last for half an hour and start from the main inner courtyard.

the imperial crown jewels and his large personal collection of precious relics, it quickly became Charles' favourite retreat from the vast city he himself had masterminded. Women were strictly forbidden to enter the castle, and the story of his third wife Anna's successful break-in (in drag) became one of the most popular Czech comedies of the nineteenth century.

The castle was ruthlessly restored in the nineteenth century and now looks much better from a distance. Inside, the centuries of neglect and generations of over-zealous restorers have taken their toll. Most of the rooms visited on the guided tour contain only the barest of furnishings, the empty spaces taken up by uninspiring displays on the history of the castle. However, the top two chambers make the whole trip worth while – though unfortunately, only the emperor's residential **Mariánská věž** is open to the public at the moment. It was here that Charles shut himself off from the rest of the world, with any urgent business passed to him through a hole in the wall of the tiny ornate chapel of **sv Kateřina**.

A wooden bridge leads on to the highest point of the castle, the **Velká věž**, which contains the castle's finest treasure, the **Holy Rood Chapel** (Kaple svatého kříže); this has been closed now since 1980 and it's looking increasingly like it will remain so for many years to come. Traditionally, only the Emperor, the archbishop and the electoral princes could enter this gilded treasure house, whose six-metre-thick walls contain 2200 semiprecious stones and 128 painted panels, the work of Master Theodoric, Bohemia's greatest fourteenth-century painter. The imperial crown jewels, once secured here behind nineteen separate locks, were removed to Hungary after an abortive attack by the Hussites, while the Bohemian jewels are now stashed away in the cathedral in Prague.

A small selection of Master Theodoric's panels are exhibited in Prague's Convent of sv Jiří, see p.53.

Křivoklátsko

The beautiful mixed woodland that makes up the UNESCO nature reserve of **Křivoklátsko**, further up the Berounka, is just out of reach of most day-trippers, making it an altogether sleepier place than the area around Karlštejn. The agonized twists (*křivky*) of the Berounka cast up the highest crags of the region, which cluster around the castle of **Křivoklát** – somehow elevated above everything around it. The one-hour guided tour of the castle takes in most of its good points, including the Great Hall and the chapel, both of which date back to the thirteenth century and have an austere beauty quite at odds with the castle's reputation as a venue for bacchanalian goings-on.

The castle is open Tues–Sun March, April, Oct–Dec 9am–4pm; May & Sept 9am–5pm; June–Aug 9am–6pm.

With such a perfect location in the heart of the best hunting ground in Bohemia, Křivoklát naturally enjoyed the royal patronage of the Přemyslids, whose hunting parties were legendary. From the outside it's a scruffy but impressive stronghold, dominated by the round tower where the English alchemist Edward Kelley was incarcerated for two and a half years. Kelley was, by all accounts, a slippery character, a swindler and a seducer, with a hooked nose and no ears (they were cut off by the Lancastrians as a punishment for forgery). He was imprisoned for failing to reveal the secret of the philosopher's stone to Rudolf II, and, in an attempt to escape, jumped out of the window only to break his leg so badly it had to be amputated.

Karlštejn and Křivoklàt

Practicalities

Apart from a direct Saturday morning service, all journeys by **train** from Prague to Křivoklát require a change at Beroun. **Buses** from metro Dejvice run frequently only at weekends, and take around an hour and a half. Křivoklát castle is the region's only real sight, though you could happily spend a day exploring the surrounding countryside on the network of well-marked footpaths.

Lidice and Lány

The small mining village of LIDICE, 18km northwest of Prague, hit world headlines on June 10, 1942, at the moment when it ceased to exist. On the flimsiest pretext, it was chosen as scapegoat for the assassination of the Nazi leader Reinhard Heydrich. All 173 men from the village were rounded up and shot by the SS, the 198 women were sent to Ravensbrück concentration camp, and the 89 children either went to the camps, or, if they were Aryan enough, were packed off to "good" German homes, while the village itself was burnt to the ground.

For a detailed account of Heydrich's assassination, see p.130.

Knowing all this as you approach Lidice makes the modern village seem almost perversely unexceptional. At the end of the straight tree-lined main street, 10 června 1942 (June 10, 1942), there's a dour concrete memorial with a small but horrific **museum** where you can watch a short film about Lidice, including footage shot by the SS themselves as the village was burning. The spot where the old village used to lie is just south of the memorial, now merely smooth green pasture punctuated with a few simple reminders and a new bronze memorial to the 82 local children who were gassed in the camps.

The museum is open daily April–Sept 8am–4pm; Oct–March 8am–5pm.

After the massacre, the "Lidice shall live" campaign was launched and villages all over the world began to change their name to Lidice. The first was Stern Park Gardens, Illinois, soon followed by villages in Mexico and other Latin American countries. From Coventry to Montevideo, towns twinned themselves with Lidice, so that rather than "wiping a Czech village off the face of the earth" as Hitler had hoped, the Nazis created an international symbol of anti-fascist resistance.

There are regular buses from Florenc bus station, which pass by Lidice en route to Kladno; the journey takes 45 minutes.

TGM

Tomáš Garrigue Masaryk – known affectionately as TGM – was born in 1850 in Hodonín, a town in a part of Moravia where Slovaks and Czechs lived harmoniously together. His father was an illiterate Slovak peasant who worked for the local bigwig, his mother a German, while Tomáš himself trained as a blacksmith. From such humble beginnings, he rose to become professor of philosophy at the Charles University, a Social Democrat MP in the Viennese Reichskrat, and finally the country's first, and longest-serving, president. A liberal humanist through and through, Masaryk created what was, at the time, probably the most progressive democracy in central Europe, featuring universal suffrage, an enviable social security system and a strong social democratic thrust. At the time of his death in 1937, Czechoslovakia was one of the few democracies left in Central Europe, "a lighthouse high on a cliff with the waves crashing on it on all sides", as Masaryk's less fortunate successor, Edvard Beneš, put it. The whole country went into mourning – a year later the Nazis marched into Sudetenland.

After the 1948 coup, the Communists began to dismantle the myth of Masaryk, whose name was synonymous with the "bourgeois" First Republic. All mention of him was removed from textbooks, street names were changed and his statue was taken down from almost every town and village in the country. However, during liberalization in 1968, his bespectacled face and goatee beard popped up again in shop windows, and his image returned again in 1989 to haunt the beleagered Communists.

Lány

On summer weekends, Škoda-loads of Czech families, pensioners and assorted pilgrims make their way to LÁNY, a plain, grey village by the edge of the Křivoklát forest, 12km beyond Kladno. They congregate in the pristine cemetery to pay their respects to one of the country's most important historical figures, Tomáš Garrigue Masaryk, the founding father and president of Czechoslovakia from 1918 to 1935.

The Masaryk plot is separated from the rest of the cemetery (*hřbitov*) by a little wooden fence and flanked by two bushy trees.

For details of the controversy surrounding Jan Masaryk's death, see p.62.

Tomáš is buried alongside his American wife, Charlotte Garrigue Masaryková, who died some fifteen years earlier, and their son Jan, who became Foreign Minister in the post-1945 government, only to die in mysterious circumstances shortly after the Communist coup. The Masaryks have recently been joined by their daughter, Alice, who founded the Czechoslovak Red Cross, and died in exile in 1966.

After laying their wreaths, the crowds generally wander over to the presidential summer chateau, with its blue-liveried guards, on the other side of the village. Its rooms are strictly out of bounds, as Havel is often in residence, but the large English gardens, orangerie and deer park, which were landscaped by Josip Plečnik, are open to the public at weekends and on public holidays. To get to Lány, you must either change buses at Kladno, or take the slow train from Prague's Masarykovo nádraží to Chomutov, getting out at Stochov, which lies 3km northeast of Lány.

Part 3

Prague: Listings

Chapter 9

Accommodation

Except in July and August, finding a place to stay in Prague is no longer a real problem. Although the city still suffers from a shortage of cheap hotels, the number of private rooms now available has relieved most of the difficulties visitors used to encounter. That said, accommodation is still likely to be by far the largest chunk of your daily expenditure, with most private rooms starting at around 400kč per person. At the extreme ends of the spectrum, you could spend around 150–

Accommodation Agencies in Prague

AVE

☎ 24 22 35 21; daily summer 7am–midnight, reduced hours in winter.
AVE are the largest agency in Prague, with offices at the airport and both international train stations, Praha hlavní nádraží and nádraží Holešovice, plus a booking desk at the PIS offices at Na příkopě 20 and inside the Staroměstská radnice. They can book hotels from 900kč per person, hostels from 350kč and private rooms from 400kč.

City of Prague Accommodation Service

Haštalské náměstí 3, Staré Město; metro náměstí Republiky; ☎ 231 02 02; daily 9am–noon, 2–5pm, 6–8pm.
More upmarket outfit with centrally located private rooms from 500kč per person.

CKM

Žitná 12, Nové Město; metro Karlovo náměstí; ☎ 24 91 57 67; Mon–Fri 9am–noon & 1–6pm.
Hostels only from 250kč per person.

Hello

Senovážné náměstí 3, Nové Město; metro Hlavní nádraží; ☎ 24 21 27 41; daily 9am–10pm.
A short walk from the main train station. Hostels for 250kč per person; private rooms from 400kč; private apartments from 600kč per person.

Pragotour

Staroměstské náměstí 22, Staré Město; metro Můstek; ☎ 231 12 35; Mon–Fri 8am–6pm, Sat & Sun 8.30am–4pm.
Private rooms from 500kč per person; hotels from 800kč a night.

Prague Suites

Melantrichova 8, Staré Město; metro Můstek; ☎ 24 22 99 61; Mon–Fri 9am–6pm, Sat 9am–2pm.
Private rooms from 600kč per person; private apartments from 1250kč per person; better deals for long-term stays.

Toptour

Rybná 3, Staré Město; metro náměstí Republiky; ☎ 232 10 77; Mon–Fri 9am–8pm, Sat & Sun 10am–7pm.
Private rooms from 500kč per person, and self-contained apartments from 1000kč a night.

Accommodation

200kč per person for the cheapest youth hostel bed or 2000kč and upwards in the various hotels with three or more stars – some of which are firmly in the super-luxury class. If you're going to Prague during high season (from Easter to September, and over the Christmas holidays), it's sensible to arrange accommodation before you arrive through one of the specialist agencies listed on p.4 and p.10. As for camping, the main sites are a fair trek from the centre of town, and have only minimal facilites; but cheapness is their virtue: for two people and a tent pitch prices start at around 200kč.

Private rooms

Renting a **private room** remains by far the most popular way to stay in Prague. Most Czechs keep their places very tidy and clean, but before agreeing to part

---

If you're thinking of taking a private room or hotel somewhere in Prague, it's as well to know a little about the merits, or otherwise, of the various **postal districts** in the city (see map on p.33.

Prague 1
Prague 1 covers all of the old city on both sides of the river, and half of Nové Město, and consequently is the most expensive part of the capital in which to stay. Anything in this area will be within easy walking distance of the main sights, and will save you a lot of hassle, though it's as well to know that, strictly speaking, it's illegal to rent out private accommodation to tourists in this part of town.

Prague 2
Prague 2 is another prime central area, taking in the southern half of Nové Město and western half of Vinohrady, a nineteenth-century des. res. with good metro connections.

Prague 3
The less salubrious, eastern half of Vinohrady in Prague 3 is nevertheless well served by the metro; Žižkov, on the other hand, is a crumbling, working-class district, connected to the centre only by trams.

Prague 4
Covers a wide area in the southeast of the city, stretching from predominantly nineteenth-century suburbs such as Nusle, Podolí and Braník to the grim high-rise *panelák* buildings of Chodov and Háje. If you find yourself in either of the latter two areas, you can at least be sure of quick metro connections to the city centre.

Prague 5
Vast area in the hilly southwest of the city, with clean air and attractive family villas predominating and a metro line running through much of it. The area closest to the city, however, is Smíchov, a polluted, working-class district, with correspondingly cheap rooms to rent.

Prague 6
The perfect, hilly villa district to the north of the centre, a favourite with foreign embassies and their staff (not to mention Havel himself). The metro only goes as far as Dejvická, however, which means that only Dejvice and Bubeneč enjoy really fast connections with the centre.

Prague 7
The nineteenth-century suburb of Holešovice in the northeast is served by the metro and has become something of an ex-pat haunt. Troja, home to numerous ad hoc campsites, is almost bucolic and correspondingly difficult to get to.

Prague 8
The grid-plan streets of nineteenth-century Karlín are close to the centre and well served by the metro, which extends as far as Libeň; the rest of the area is neither aesthetically pleasing, nor easy to reach.

Prague 9
This is a real last resort area in the northeast of the city – dominated by factories, and difficult to get to (Vysočany is the only district with metro connections) – avoid if at all possible.

Prague 10
Prague 10 extends right into the countryside, though areas like Strašnice and Vršovice in the southeast of the city are closer to the centre of things and served, in part, by the metro.

with any money, be sure you know exactly where you're staying and check about transport to the centre – some places can be a long way out of town. It's also worth asking whether or not you'll be sharing bathroom, cooking facilities etc with the family – Czech hospitality can be somewhat overwhelming, although meals other than breakfast are not generally included in the price. It's quite possible to rent a self-contained flat, if you wish, though it will cost a lot more.

The enormous supply of private accommodation in Prague means it's not really necessary to book in advance – although it can be worth doing to save time, and for some peace of mind, especially if you're arriving in July or August (see "Getting There" in *Basics* for lists of relevant travel agencies). If you arrive without a room reservation, the easiest thing to do is head for one of the many **accommodation agencies** at the airport or main train stations. If the queues are horrendous, as they can be in peak season, and you've not arrived too late in the day, then try one of the other agencies in town (see box on p.185). Alternatively, you're almost certain to be approached by a tout at the station, airport or sometimes outside one of the agencies. Most offers are genuine, but make sure you ask for a receipt before you pass over any money. Again, check exactly how far out of the centre you're going to be (and preferably see the room) before committing yourself.

Hotels and pensions

Pre-1989, Prague's **hotels** were much of a muchness: 1950s decor, a radio permanently tuned to the state news channel (very 1984) and sporadically hot showers. Matters have improved enormously since then, with almost all hotels now modernized to some degree, and more and more guaranteeing en-suite bathrooms, TVs and breakfast. Although standards still vary, Czechs generally run clean establishments. **Pensions** are a totally new phenomenon and tend to be much smaller outfits; however, there's no strict rule about this, and no specific price range into which all fit. On the whole, prices are pretty steep compared with those for everything else in the Czech Republic. Demand still exceeds supply, so unless you're here off season there's really no point in trekking around any of the hotels listed below on the off chance that they will have vacancies. Besides, Prague's cheaper hotels and pensions are scattered throughout the city, with very few in the older quarters of Hradčany, Malá Strana and Staré Město. The best policy is to contact the hotel by fax or phone before you leave for Prague and attempt to make a reservation.

Accommodation

Hradčany and Malá Strana

Previously a no-go area for hotels, the left bank is still really only for those with some serious financial clout. The nearest metro is Malostranská, unless otherwise stated.

Hotel pod věží, Mostecká, Malá Strana; ☎53 37 10. Tiny hotel right by the Charles Bridge with just twelve rooms at over 4000kč a double. ⑥.

Hotel Sax, Jánský vršek 3, Malá Strana; ☎53 84 22. A relative bargain in the

---

Accommodation

backstreets off Tržiště, run by the Nkoda car empire. ⑤.

Kampa − Stará zbrojnice, Všehrdova 16, Malá Strana; ☎24 51 04 09. Backstreet location on Kampa Island, close to the Charles Bridge − the rooms' lack of soul is reflected in the price. ⑤.

Pension Dientzenhofer, Nosticova 2, Malá Strana; ☎53 16 72. Birthplace of its namesake, and one of the few reasonably priced places (anywhere in Prague) to have wheelchair access. Just seven rooms on offer. ④.

Pension U raka, Černínská 10, Hradčany; ☎35 14 53; tram #22 from metro Malostranská. The perfect hideaway, six rooms in a little half-timbered cottage in Nový Svět, for just under 4000kč each. No children or dogs. ⑥.

U páva, U lužického semináře 32, Malá Strana; ☎24 51 09 22. An eight-room hotel in a quiet part of Malá Strana for around 4000kč a double. ⑥.

U tří pštrosů, Dražického náměstí 12, Malá Strana; ☎54 37 10. Exquisite Renaissance house adjacent to the Charles Bridge, with rooms for around 4000kč a double, some with original ceiling frescoes and views across the river. ⑥.

Around Betlemské náměstí

Just a few options here, right in the heart of Staré Město. The nearest metro is Národní třída.

Betlém Club, Betlémské náměstí 9; ☎24 21 68 72. Small rooms, perfect location and a Gothic cellar for breakfast. ⑤.

Pension Unitas, Bartolomějská; ☎232 77 00. Gloomy doubles, triples and quads in converted prison cells and rooms once used by the secret police (Havel stayed in P6), now owned by Fransiscan nuns. No smoking, no drinking and a 1am curfew, but unbelievably cheap. ①.

U klenotníka, Rytířská 3; ☎24 21 16 99. Ten small rooms on offer in a former jewellery factory for 3000kč a double. ⑥.

U krále Jiřího, Liliova 10; ☎24 22 20 13. Just eight attic rooms above an Irish pub, hidden in the network of lanes which characterize this part of Staré Město. ③.

Around Wenceslas Square

There's no question that these hotels are right in the centre of things, though it's worth bearing in mind that Wenceslas Square (Václavské náměstí) doubles as Prague's red-light district and nightclub zone by night. The nearest metros are Můstek and Muzeum unless otherwise stated.

Grand Hotel Evropa, Václavské náměstí 25; ☎24 22 81 17. Without doubt, the most beautiful hotel in Prague, built in the 1900s and sumptuously decorated in Art Nouveau style; the rooms are slowly being modernized, as are the prices. ④.

Juliš, Václavské náměstí 22; ☎24 21 70 92. Tired-looking 1930s functionalist hotel, halfway down Wenceslas Square, with surprisingly pleasant rooms. ④.

Around náměstí Republiky

There are a whole range of hotels within spitting distance of náměstí Republiky, which lies on the edge of Staré and Nové Město. The nearest metro is náměstí Republiky unless otherwise stated.

Albatros, nábřeží Ludvíka Svobody, Nové Město; ☎24 81 05 47. Double cabins for rent on a moored boat at the end of Revoluční. Not quite as romantic or cheap as it sounds, but the best of the city's three floating "botels" − watch out for the on-board disco which keeps going until the early hours. ③.

Atlantic, Na poříčí 9, Nové Město; ☎24 81 10 84. Modern but fairly soulless with reasonable facilities. ⑤.

Axa, Na poříčí 40, Nové Město; ☎24 81 25 80; metro Florenc. Partially refurbished hotel with adjacent swimming pool and gym, just five minutes' walk from náměstí Republiky − make sure you see your room before booking in, as standards in each can vary. ③−⑥.

Central, Rybná 8, Staré Město; ☎24 81 20 41. One of the very few reasonably priced hotels in Staré Město − no work of art, but true to its name and surprisingly cheap. ④.

Harmony, Na poříčí 31, Nové Město; ☎232 07 20; metro Florenc. Directly opposite the *Axa*, more thoroughly refurbished but pricier. ⑥.

Meteor, Hybernská 6, Nové Město; ☎24 22 06 64. Completely refurbished since Emperor Josef II stayed here, and now run by the *Best Western* hotel chain; around 5000kč a double. ⑥.

Opera, Těšnov 13, Nové Město; ☎231 56 09; metro Florenc. Moderately priced nineteenth-century hotel and remarkably pleasant considering it's right by the flyover. ④.

Paříž, U Obecního domu 1, Staré Město; ☎24 22 21 51. Elegantly refurbished interior to this turn-of-the-century hotel, where Hrabal set *I Served the King of England* – currently over 5000kč a double. ⑥.

Ungelt, Štupartská 1, Staré Město; ☎24 81 13 30. Unbelievable location in the backstreets of Staré Město, but over 5000kč for one of its ten suites. ⑥.

Southern Nové Město, Vinohrady and Žižkov

Southern Nové Město is only a metro stop or short stroll from the centre of things, though in parts blighted by heavy traffic flow; Vinohrady is rather quieter and more appealing; Žižkov is a run-down nineteenth-century neighbourhood, though still within easy access of the city centre by tram.

Ametyst, Jana Masaryka 11, Vinohrady; ☎24 24 76 20; metro náměstí Míru. Refurbished, purple (though not quite the right purple), neo-Rennaissance pile with a wonderful view overlooking the Botič valley. ⑥.

Hlávkova kolej, Jenštynská 1, Nové Město; ☎29 21 39; metro Karlovo náměstí. Spartan but clean former student hostel one block south of Resslova. ③.

Junior, Žitná 12, Nové Město; ☎24 22 28 11; metro Karlovo náměstí. Formerly the rather plush official youth hostel, now a

not so spectacular hotel on a busy road. ③.

Kafka, Cimburkova 24, Žižkov; ☎27 31 01; tram #5, #9 or #26 from metro Hlavní nádraží. Cheap but more cheerful than you'd expect in Prague 3. ②.

Koruna, Opatovická 16, Nové Město; ☎24 81 31 34; metro Národní třída. Great location in the backstreets just south of Národní, though the hotel itself is no great shakes. ④.

Luník, Londýnská 50, Vinohrady; ☎691 13 34; metro I. P. Pavlova. Fairly peaceful location, just a short walk from Wenceslas Square. ③.

Ostaš, Orebitská 8, Žižkov; ☎627 93 86; tram #5, #9 or #26 from metro Hlavní nádraží. Right in the heart of Žižkov – a mixed blessing – but walking distance from the centre. ④.

Pension Březina, Legerova 41, Nové Město; ☎291 36 16; metro Muzeum. Seven truly cheap rooms with minimal facilities, within walking distance of Wenceslas Square. ①.

Pension City, Belgická 10, Vinohrady; ☎691 13 34; metro náměstí Míru. Quiet locale, cheap, clean rooms, within walking distance of Wenceslas Square. ②.

VZ Hotel, Sokolská 33, Nové Město; ☎29 11 18; metro I. P. Pavlova. Former military R-and-R centre, just one stop or a short stroll from Wenceslas Square. ②.

Holešovice, Dejvice and Střešovice

These hotels are spread over a wide area ranging from the nineteenth-century tenements of Holešovice to the leafy garden suburbs of Dejvice and beyond.

International, Koulova 15, Dejvice; ☎24 39 31 11; tram #20 or #25 from metro Dejvická. Classic 1950s Stalinist hotel with plenty of dour social realist friezes and large helpings of marble, now somewhat unbelievably part of the *Holiday Inn* hotel chain. ④.

Parkhotel, Veletržní 20, Holešovice; ☎380 71 11; tram #5, #12 or #17. Fairly professionally run hotel from the 1960s, just a short distance from the Výstaviště fairground. ⑤.

Accommodation

Accommodation

Pension Digital, Na Petynce 106, Střešovice; ☎35 50 71; bus #108 or #174 from metro Hradčanská. Nine cheap rooms, with shared facilities only, but a great location in the villa quarter just ten minutes' walk from the Hrad. ①.

Pension Petynka, Na Petynce 100, Střešovice; ☎35 31 12; bus #108 or #174 from metro Hradčanská. Five rooms, again with shared facilities, just a few doors down from the *Digital*. ②.

Pension Větrník, U Větrníku 40, Střešovice; ☎351 96 22; tram #1 or #18 from metro Hradčanská. Six rooms in a converted eighteenth-century windmill, with private tennis courts and nice proprietor – book early. ③.

Praha, Sušická 20, Dejvice; ☎24 34 11 11; tram #2, #20 or #26 from metro Dejvická. The old Party VIP hotel, where Gorbachev, Ceaușescu and the like once stayed; an appropriately grotesque concrete palace with doubles for just under 5000kč and wonderful views over to the Hrad. ⑥.

Splendid, Ovenecká 33, Bubeneč; ☎37 33 51; tram #1, #8, #25 or #26; stop Letenské náměstí. Situated in a pleasant part of town, right by the Stromovka park. ⑤.

Smíchov

Smíchov is one of the poorer, traditionally working-class parts of Prague – hence the moderate price range – but it's just a step away from Malá Strana and Petřín Hill. The nearest metro is Anděl.

Admirál, Hořejší nábřeží; ☎24 51 16 97. The largest of Prague's floating "botels", perversely positioned the wrong side of the river for a really good view of the Hrad. ④.

Balkán, Svornosti 28; ☎54 07 77. One of the cheapest hotels in Prague; like Smíchov itself, reassuringly run-down. ②.

Bonaparte, Radlická 38; ☎543 80 09. Eleven rooms with all the requisite mod cons and very close to the metro. ③.

Gay Vila David, Holubova 5; ☎54 98 20; tram #14 from metro Anděl. Friendly gay/

lesbian pension (complete with sauna) in the hills above Smíchov. ③.

Mepro, Victora Huga 3; ☎561 81 21. The sort of hotel you'd expect to find in Smíchov. ④.

Petr, Drtinova 17; ☎54 08 44. Nothing fancy but pleasant enough, situated at the foot of Petřín Hill, close to Malá Strana. ③.

Hostels

There are scores of **hostels** in Prague which cater for the large number of back-packers who hit the city all year round – these are supplemented further by more transient high-season-only hostels. **Prices** in hostels range between 150kč to 250kč for a bed, usually in a dormitory.

Cestovní kancelář mládeže (CKM) lets out cheap **student accommodation** in July and August, though you don't neces-sarily need to be a student to stay in one of their hostels. Addresses change from year to year, so to check out the current locations, go to the *CKM* head office in Prague, at Žitná 12, Nové Město (☎24 91 57 67; Mon–Fri 9am–noon & 1–6pm). Although these hostels are often heavily booked in advance by groups, they will try their best to squeeze you in.

Many hostels operate **curfews** – it's worth asking before you commit yourself – and, although some rent out blankets and sheets, it's as well to bring your own sleeping bag. Note that some of the accommodation agencies in Prague also deal with hostels, see p.185 for details.

Domov mládeže, Dykova 20, Vinohrady; ☎25 06 88; metro Jiřího z Poděbrad. Big nineteenth-century mansion with eighty beds separated into dorms sleeping up to five people.

ESTEC kolej Strahov, Vaníčkova 5, Strahov; ☎52 73 44; tram #22 from metro Malostranská; open July & Aug. Lots of hostels and lots of beds to be found in the student dorms next to the Olympic stadium, a short walk from Hradčany.

Hostel Ostrov, Střelecký ostrov, Nové Město; ☎20 12 43; metro Národní třída;

open July & Aug. Summer-only dorm situated across most Legií on an island in the Vltava, outside toilets but otherwise okay.

Hostel Sokol, Helichova 1, Malá Strana; ☎24 51 06 07; metro Malostranská. Great central location, eighty-five beds, no-smoking and a small surcharge for entry after 12.30am curfew.

TJ Sokol Karlín, Malého 1, Karlín; ☎22 20 09; metro Florenc. Situated in the unsalubrious locale of the Praha-Florenc bus station. Reception opens at 6pm and you'll be turfed out at 8am the next morning – a definite last resort.

Campsites

Prague abounds in **campsites** – there's a whole rash of them in Troja (see below) – and most are relatively easy to get to by public transport. Facilities, on the whole, are rudimentary and badly maintained, but the prices reflect this, starting at around 200kč for a tent and two people.

Note that most Prague campsites are closed from October to March.

Džbán, Nad lávkou 3, Vokovice; ☎39 60 06; tram #20 or #26 from metro Dejvická; open May–Sept. Large field with tent pitches, bungalows and basic facilities, 4km west of the centre, near the Šárka valley.

Kotva, U ledáren 55, Braník; ☎46 17 12; tram #3 or #17 from metro Karlovo náměstí; open April–Oct. Prague's oldest campsite (and one of its nicest) situated beside the River Vltava in the far south of the city. Bike rental available.

Trojská & **Hájek**, Trojská 375/377, Troja; ☎66 41 60 31 or 66 41 60 36; bus #112 or tram #5, #17 or #25 from metro Nádraží Holešovice; open mid-June to Oct. Good location, 3km north of the centre, on the road to the Troja chateau. These are two of a whole series of sites which have sprung up in people's back gardens on Trojská; facilities are basic.

Accommodation

Chapter 10

Eating and Drinking

Every **restaurant** (*restaurace*) in Prague has either closed down or been privatized at some point in the last five years, so it's not surprising that the culinary scene is currently a bit unpredictable, with enormous variations in price and quality. A few authentic ethnic outfits have started up, though traditional Czech food still predominates (for more on which see below). New western-style restaurants have taken hold in many downtown areas, charging prices that westerners find very reasonable but few Czechs can afford – while traditional, informal Czech pubs or *pivnice*, where you can fill yourself up with cheap, basic fare, are becoming harder to find.

The biggest mistake most first-time visitors make is to confine their eating and drinking to the obvious sightseeing areas, where prices are generally much higher, quality lower, and, in summer, spare tables a real find. It's worth venturing, instead, into the backstreets of Staré Město and Nové Město, where good-value restaurants tend to hide; or to suburbs like Vinohrady and Holešovice, just ten minutes' travel by metro from the centre.

What you eat and how much you pay also depends very much on the type of place you go. For a full meal, you can go to a *restaurace*, a *pivnice* or a *vinárna* (wine bar or cellar). A **pivnice** is primarily a beer hall for serious (predominantly male) drinkers, but most also serve food, and some even have separate (generally more mixed) dining areas (*jídelna*). **Restaurace** span the range from glorified

pivnice to extremely posh affairs, run by tuxedoed waiters with Viennese airs and graces. A **vinárna** is traditionally a more intimate affair, perhaps with a little live music, a longer wine list, and later opening hours. Having said all that, the differences between all three can be very vague indeed. At the budget end of the scale, you can eat very cheaply indeed at a stand-up **bufet** or *lahůdky*, along with the local working population, or in one of the increasingly popular fast-food joints that have hit Prague in recent years (not all of them *McDonalds*).

It's as well to remember that traditionally Czechs eat their main meal of the day at lunchtime, between noon and 2pm. In *pivnice* and other more traditional Czech restaurants, you'll get the widest choice of dishes around this time of day, with progressively fewer available as the day goes on – kitchens in pubs can close as early as 9pm. Restaurants cater for more international habits, with the evening sitting just as important as the lunchtime slot.

Czech cuisine

Forty years of culinary isolation under the Communists introduced few innovations to the Germanic-influenced **Czech cuisine**, with its predilection for big slabs of meat served with lashings of gravy, dumplings and pickled gherkins, not to mention a good helping of pickled cabbage. Fresh vegetables (other than potatoes) are still a rare sight in Czech restaurants, and salads are still waiting for their day. On the plus side, Prague ham is justly famous, and Czech beer is among the best in the world.

Most menus start with **soup** (*polévka*), one of the country's culinary strong points, served mainly at lunchtimes. Posher joints will have a serious selection of starters such as *uzený jazyk* (smoked tongue), *tresčí játra* (cod's liver) or perhaps *kaviárové vejce* (hard-boiled eggs with caviar on top). *Šunková rolka* is another favourite, consisting of ham topped with whipped cream and horseradish, but you're more likely to find yourself skipping the starters, which are often little more than a selection of cold meats.

Main courses are overwhelmingly based on **meat** (*maso*), usually pork, sometimes beef. The Czechs are experts on these meats, and although the quality could often be better, the variety of sauces and preparative techniques beats traditional Anglo-American cooking hands down. The difficulty lies in decoding names such as *klašterny tajemství* ("mystery of the monastery") or even a common dish like *Moravský vrabec* (literally "Moravian sparrow", but actually just roast pork).

Fish (*ryby*) are generally listed, along with chicken and other fowl like duck, under a separate heading. Trout and carp (the traditional dish at Christmas) are the cheapest and most widely available fish, and although their freshness may be questionable, they are usually served, grilled or roasted, in delicious buttery sauces.

Dumplings (*knedlíky*), though German in origin and name, are now the mainstay of Bohemian cooking. The term itself is misleading for English-speakers, since they resemble nothing like the English dumpling – more like a heavy white bread. *Houskové knedlíky* are made from flour and come in large slices (four or five to a dish), while *bramborové knedlíky* are smaller and made from potato and flour. Occasionally, you may be treated to *ovocné knedlíky* (fruit dumplings), the king of Czech dumplings. **Fresh salads** rarely rise above lettuce, tomato or cucumber, often swimming in a slightly sweet, watery dressing.

With the exception of *palačinky* (pancakes) filled with chocolate or fruit and cream, **desserts**, where they exist at all, can be pretty unexciting. Often the ice cream and cakes on offer in restaurants aren't really up to the standards of the stuff sold on the street, so go to a *cukrárna* (confectioners) if you want a dose of sugar; for more on *cukrárna* see p.199.

Vegetarians

Prague is still no place for **vegetarians** or health freaks, since Czech meat consumption remains one of the highest in the world – around half a kilo a day per head. If you eat fish but not meat you won't have too hard a time, since most Czech menus usually feature either trout or carp. Many also have a section called *bezmasa* (literally "without meat") – don't take it too literally, though, for it simply means the main ingredient is not dead animal; dishes like *omeleta se šunkou* (ham omelette) regularly appear under these headings, so always check first. Emergency standbys which most Czech chefs will knock up for you without too much fuss include *knedlíky s vejci* (dumplings and egg) or *smažený sýr*, a slab of melted cheese (and, more often than not, ham) deep-fried in breadcrumbs.

Vegetarian phrases

As a serious meat-eating nation, many Czechs simply can't conceive of anybody going through even a small portion of their life without eating meat (unless they're critically ill or clinically insane). So simply saying you're a vegetarian or that you don't eat meat or fish may instil panic and/or confusion in the waiter – it's often better to ask what's in a particular dish you think looks promising.

The phrases to remember are *"jsem vegeterián/vegeteriánka. máte nejaké bezmasa?"* (I'm a vegetarian. Is there anything without meat?); for emphasis, you could add *"nejím maso nebo ryby"* (I don't eat meat or fish).

Eating and Drinking

Before you despair, however, there is some good news. Czechs are becoming more aware of health issues, including vegetarianism (the first-ever Czech vegetarian cookbook has now been published) and the situation in Prague is better than the rest of the country. On a more practical note, the huge Anglo-American ex-pat community has had a positive effect on the situation. In addition to the two *Country Life* outlets, several exclusively veggie options exist (listed on p.208 below) and most ex-pat hang-outs tend to offer at least one veggie alternative. Pizza places are also now extremely popular, with outlets in most districts of Prague, and *falafel* takeaways are pretty ubiquitous.

Alcohol

Alcohol consumption among Czechs has always been high, and in the decade following the events of 1968 it doubled. A whole generation found solace in drinking, mostly beer. It's a problem which seldom spills out onto the streets; violence in pubs is uncommon and you won't see that many drunks in public. Nevertheless, it's not unusual to see someone legless in the afternoon, on their way home from work.

The Czechs came top of the world league table of beer consumption in 1992, even beating the Germans into a poor second place – hardly surprising since its **beer** ranks among the best in the world. Although unable to boast the variety of its western neighbour, The Czech Republic remains the true home of most of the lager drunk around the world today. It was in the Bohemian city of Plzeň (Pilsen) that the first **bottom-fermented** beer was introduced in 1842, after complaints from the citizens about the quality of the top-fermented predecessor. The new brewing style quickly spread to Germany, and is now blamed for the bland rubbish served up in the English-speaking world as lager or Pils.

Whether due to lack of technological know-how or through positive choice, brewing methods in the Czech Republic have remained stuck in the old ways, eschewing chemical substitutes. The

distinctive flavour of Czech beer comes from the famous Bohemian hops, Žatec (Saaz) Red, still hand-picked and then combined with the soft local water and served with a high content of absorbed carbon dioxide – hence the thick, creamy head. Even if you don't think you like lager, you must try at least a *malé pivo* (0.3 litre). The average jar is medium strength, usually about 1050 specific gravity or 4.2% alcohol. To confuse matters further, the Czechs class their beers using the Balling scale, which measures the original gravity, calculated according to the amount of malt and dissolved sugar present before fermentation. The most common varieties are 10° (*desítka*), which are generally slightly weaker than 12° (*dvanáctka*). Light beer (*světlé*) is the norm, but many pubs also serve a slightly sweeter dark variety (*černé*) – or, if you prefer, you can have a mixture of the two (*řezané*).

The most famous Czech beer is **Pilsner Urquell**, know to the Czechs as *Plzeňský Prazdroj*, the original bottom-fermented Pils from Plzeň (Pilsen), a city 80km southwest of Prague. Plzeň also boasts the **Gambrinus** brewery, whose domestic sales actually topped those of *Pilsner Urquell* in 1994. The other big Bohemian brewing town is České Budějovice (Budweis), home to the country's biggest-selling export beer, **Budvar**, a mildly flavoured brew for Bohemia but still leagues ahead of *Budweiser*, the German name for *Budvar* that was adopted by American brewers, Anheuser Busch, in 1876.

The biggest brewery in the country, however, is in the Smíchov suburb of Prague where **Staropramen** (meaning "ancient spring") is produced, a typical Bohemian brew with a mild hoppy flavour. Prague also produces some of the country's best strong, special beer: **Flek**, a dark caramel concoction brewed and served exclusively at a pub called *U Fleků* in Prague's Nové Město since 1399; and **Braník**, a light, malty beer from south Prague, creamy even by smooth Bohemian standards. Other beers to look out for include **Radegast**, a very popular brew from North Moravia, the award-winning, slightly bitter

Velkopopovický kozel, and the smooth, hoppy *Krušovice* beer.

Czech **wine** will never win over as many people as its beer, but since the import of French and German vines in the fourteenth century, it has produced a modest selection of medium-quality wines. More and more are being exported, and labelling – previously notoriously imprecise – is undergoing something of a revolution, which may help boost the profile of Czech wines in the rest of the world. The two main wine regions are in the hills of south Moravia, and around the town of Mělník, which produces at least one good red, *Ludmila*, and a couple of passable whites. Suffice to say that most domestic wine is pretty drinkable – *Frankovka* is a perfectly respectable, though slightly sweet, red; *Tramín* a good, dry white – and rarely much more than £1/$1.60 a bottle in shops, while the best stuff can only be had from the private wine cellars, hundreds of which still exist out in the regions. A Czech speciality to look out for is *burčák*, a very young, misty wine of varying (and often very strong) alcoholic content, which appears on the streets in the vine harvest season in September.

All the usual **spirits** are on sale and known by their generic names, with rum and vodka dominating the market. Domestic brands originate mostly from east Moravia: the home-production of brandies is a national pastime, which results in some almost terminally strong liquors. The most renowned of the lot is *slivovice*, a plum brandy originally from the border hills between Moravia and Slovakia but now available just about everywhere. You'll probably also come across *borovička*, a popular firewater from the Slovak Spiš region, made from pine trees; *myslivec* is a rough brandy with a firm following. There's also a fair selection of intoxicating herbal concoctions: *fernet* is a dark-brown bitter drink, known as *bavorák* (Bavarian beer) when it's mixed with tonic, while *becherovka* is a supposedly healthy herbal spirit from the Bohemian spa town of Karlovy Vary, with a very unusual, almost medicinal taste.

Last of all, aside from western imports, the country has several idiosyncrasies when it comes to **non-alcoholic drinks**. If you ask for a lemonade (*limonáda*), you're just as likely to get orangeade, and vice versa if you ask for *oranž*. Unless you long for a cross between cherryade and dandelion and burdock, avoid the variety of vivid fizzy drinks that go under the promising name of *džus* (pronounced "juice"). Real fruit juice has only recently become available in supermarkets. The safest bet for those without a sweet tooth is to ask for *soda* or *tonic*. *Minerální voda* (mineral water) is everywhere, always carbonated, and a lot more "tasty" than western brands – try *Mattoni* for a milder option.

Breakfast, Snacks and fast Food

Many Czechs get up so early in the morning (often around 5 or 6am) that they don't have time to start the day with anything more than a quick cup of coffee. As a result, the whole concept of **breakfast** as such is alien to the Czechs. Most hotels will serve the "continental" basics, but it's cheaper and often more enjoyable to go hunting for your own. Bear in mind, too, that if you get up much past 10am, you might as well join Prague's working population for lunch.

Pastries (*pečivo*) are available from Prague's bakeries (*pekářství* or *pekárna*), but rarely in bars and cafés, so you'll most likely have to eat them on the go. Traditional Czech pastry (*koláč*) is more like sweet bread, dry and fairly dense with only a little condiment to flavour it, such as almonds (*oříškový*), poppy seed jam (*mákový*), plum jam (*povidlový*) or a kind of sour-sweet Slovak curd cheese (*tvarohový*). Recently, French- and Viennese-style bakeries have started to appear in Prague, selling croissants (*loupáky*) and lighter cream cakes.

Czech **bread** (*chléb*) is some of the tastiest around when fresh. The standard loaf is *šumava*, a dense mixture of wheat and rye, which you can buy whole, in halves (*půl*) or quarters (*čtvrtina*). *Český chléb* is a mixture of rye, wheat and

Eating and Drinking

A food and drink glossary

Basics

chléb	bread
chlebíček	(open) sandwich
cukr	sugar
hořčice	mustard
houska	round roll
jídla na objednávku	main dishes to order
knedlíky	dumplings
křen	horseradish
lžíce	spoon
maso	meat
máslo	butter
med	honey
mléko	milk
moučník	dessert
nápoje	drinks
nůž	knife
oběd	lunch
obloha	garnish
ocet	vinegar
ovoce	fruit
pečivo	pastry
pepř	pepper
polévka	soup
předkrmy	starters
přílohy	side dishes
rohlík	finger roll
ryby	fish
rýže	rice
sklenice	glass
snídaně	breakfast
sůl	salt
šálek	cup
talíř	plate
tartarská omáčka	tartare sauce
večeře	supper/dinner
vejce	eggs
vidlička	fork
volské oko	fried egg
zeleniny	vegetables

Soups

boršč	beetroot soup
bramborová	potato soup
čočková	lentil soup
fazolová	bean soup
hovězí vývar	beef broth
hrachová	pea soup
kapustnica	sauerkraut, mushroom and meat soup
kuřecí	thin chicken soup
rajská	tomato soup
zeleninová	vegetable soup

Fish

kapr	carp
losos	salmon
makrela	mackerel
platys	flounder
pstruh	trout
rybí filé	fillet of fish
sardinka	sardine
štika	pike
treska	cod
zavináč	herring/rollmop

Meat dishes

bažant	pheasant
biftek	beef steak
čevapčiči	spicy meat balls
dršťky	tripe
drůbež	poultry
guláš	goulash
hovězí	beef
husa	goose
játra	liver
jazyk	tongue
kachna	duck
klobásy	sausages
kotleta	cutlet
kuře	chicken
kýta	leg
ledvinky	kidneys
řízek	steak
roštěná	sirloin
salám	salami
sekaná	meat loaf
skopové maso	mutton
slanina	bacon
svíčková	fillet of beef
šunka	ham
telecí	veal
vepřový	pork
vepřové řízek	breaded pork cutlet or schnitzel
žebírko	ribs

Vegetables

brambory	potatoes
brokolice	brocoli
celer	celery
cibule	onion
česnek	garlic
chřest	asparagus
čočka	lentils
fazole	beans
houby	mushrooms
hranolky	chips, french fries
hrášek	peas
karot	carrot

květák	cauliflower	urda	soft, fresh, whey cheese
kyselá okurka	pickled gherkin		
kyselé zelí	sauerkraut	uzený sýr	smoked cheese
lečo	ratatouille	vlašské ořechy	walnuts
okurka	cucumber		
pórek	leek	**Common terms**	
rajče	tomato	čerstvý	fresh
ředkev	radish	domácí	home-made
řepná bulva	beetroot	dušený	stew/casserole
špenát	spinach	grilovaný	roast on the spit
zelí	cabbage	kyselý	sour
žampiony	mushrooms	na kmíně	with caraway seeds

Fruit and cheese and nuts

banán	banana	na roštu	grilled
borůvky	blueberries	na zdraví	cheers!
broskev	peach	nadívaný	stuffed
bryndza	goat's cheese in brine	nakládaný	pickled
		(za)pečený	baked/roast
citrón	lemon	plněný	stuffed
grejp	grapefruit	s.m. (s máslem)	with butter
hermelín	Czech brie	sladký	sweet
hrozny	grapes	slaný	salted
hruška	pear	smažený	fried in breadcrumbs
jablko	apple		
jahody	strawberries	studený	cold
kompot	stewed fruit	syrový	raw
maliny	raspberries	sýrový	cheesey
mandle	almonds	teplý	hot
meruňka	apricot	uzený	smoked
niva	semi-soft, crumbly, blue cheese	vařený	boiled
		znojmský	with gherkins
oříšky	peanuts		
ostružiny	blackberries	**Drinks**	
oštěpek	heavily smoked, curd cheese	čaj	tea
		destiláty	spirits
parenica	rolled strips of lightly smoked, curd cheese	káva	coffee
		koňak	brandy
		láhev	bottle
		led	ice
pivní sýr	cheese flavoured with beer	minerální (voda)	mineral (water)
		mléko	milk
pomeranč	orange	pivo	beer
rozinky	raisins	suché víno	dry wine
švestky	plums	svařené víno	mulled wine
třešně	cherries	vinný střik	white wine with soda
tvaroh	fresh, curd cheese		
		víno	wine

whey, with distinctive slashes across the top; kmínový chléb is the same loaf packed full of caraway seeds. Moskva is a national favourite, despite the name – a moist, heavy, sour dough loaf that lasts for days. Rolls come in two basic varieties: rohlík, a plain white finger roll, and houska, a rougher, tastier round bun.

Prague's stand-up **bufets** are open from as early as 6am and offer everything from light snacks to full meals. They're usually self-service (samoobsluha) and non-smoking, and occasionally have rudimentary seats. The cheapest of the tired-looking meat sausages on offer is sekaná, bits of old meat and bread

Eating and Drinking

Ice cream

Whatever the season, Czechs have to have their daily fix of **ice cream** (*zmrzlina*), dispensed from window kiosks in the sides of buildings, and, more frequently now, from more substantial outlets, some with seating.

Dánská zmrzlina, Spálená 49, Nové Město; metro Národní třída. None-too-cheap option, but you're paying for the delicious cones, baked fresh on the premises. *Open daily 10am–8pm.*

Dolce Vita, Vězeňská, 15, Staré Město; metro Staroměstská. A real sit-down café in the old town, which also serves excellent ice cream. *Open daily 10am–11pm.*

Gelatí Italská, Na poříčí 39, Nové Město; metro Florenc. Over thirty varieties of

real Italian ice cream and ten types of sundae at knock-down prices. *Open Mon–Fri 9am–6pm, Sat 9am–1pm.*

Ovocný bar, Václavské náměstí, Nove Město; metro Můstek/Muzeum. Very Czech, very *Clockwork Orange* milk bar serving ice cream and huge fruit salads; located on the first floor above a grocery store on the corner of Štěpánská. *Open Mon–Sat 10am–8pm.*

Světozor, Vodičková 39, Nové Město; metro Můstek. Sit-down or takeaway, this reasonably priced *lahůdky* has over twenty varieties of ice cream, plus pastries, cakes, the lot; it's situated in the *Světozor* cinema passage. *Open Mon–Sat 8.30am–8.30pm, Sun noon–8.30pm.*

---

squashed together to form a meat loaf – for connoisseurs only. *Guláš* is popular – stew that may bear little relation to the original of that name – usually *Szegedinský* (pork with sauerkraut) but sometimes *special* (with better meat and a creamier sauce). Less substantial fare boils down to *chlebíčky* – artistically presented **open sandwiches** with combinations of gherkins, cheese, salami, ham and aspic – and mountains of mayonnaise-type **salad**, bought by weight (200 grammes is a medium-sized portion).

The ubiquitous Czech street **takeaway** is the hot dog or *párek*, a dubious-looking frankfurter (traditionally two – *párek* means a pair), dipped in mustard and served with a white roll (*v rohlíku*). A greasier option is *bramborák*, a thin potato pancake with little flecks of bacon or salami in it; *felafal* is another popular takeaway, usually with pitta bread and salad. And, of course, there are now numerous western-style fast food joints (most notably McDonalds) all over Prague.

Staré Město and Josefov

Bona Vita, Dlouhá 4; metro Staroměstská. Antiseptic self-service restaurant with daily soya-based specialities, plus some meaty dishes. *Open Mon–Fri 10am–10pm, Sat & Sun 11am–10pm.*

Bonal, Staroměstské náměstí 4; metro Staroměstská. Flash Czech-German joint venture selling sandwiches, pastries and some of the best coffee in Prague. Stand-up only. *Open daily 9am–9pm.*

Country Life, Melantrichova 15; metro Můstek. Cramped, popular stand-up buffet within a health food shop, which serves vegan snacks – though you'll have to buy a lot to fill yourself up. *Open Mon–Fri until 7pm; Sun until 1pm.*

Frank's Bistro, Na můstku (right by the bottom end of Wenceslas Square); metro Můstek. A convenient but uninspiring stomach filler, run by an LA ex-pat, serving pizza, pasta and other snacks. *Open daily 7am–10pm.*

Nové Město

Adonis, Jungmannova 21; metro Národní třída. Cheap Middle Eastern fare – stuffed vine leaves, *felafal*, *taboule* and a salad bar – sit-in or takeaway. *Open daily 10am–8pm.*

Cornucopia, Jungmannova 10; metro Národní třída. Simple, cheap sandwich bar with a few hot dishes on offer, soup of the day and seating inside. *Open Mon–Fri 9.30am–11pm, Sat 10am–11pm, Sun 10am–10pm.*

Country Life, Jungmannova 1; metro Národní třída. Larger branch of the vegetarian chain with seating inside. *Open Mon–Thurs 9.30am–6.30pm, Fri 10am–3pm.*

Lucerna, Štěpánská 61; metro Můstek. A real pre-1989 *bufet* in the Lucerna arcade, serving cheap Czech slops on aluminium table tops with funky 1950s seating. *Mon–Fri 8am–8pm, Sat 10am–4pm.*

McDonald's, Vodičková 15; metro Národní třída. The first in the country, on the site of an old school dining hall, its main virtue is that it sells draught beer and has a children's play area. *Open daily 8am–11pm.*

Palace, Panská 12; metro Můstek. Situated in the basement of the most expensive hotel in Prague, on the corner with Jindřišská, this is no place to linger (there are no tables, only counters), but a good spot to binge on fresh produce and the self-service salad bar. *Open daily 10am–10pm.*

Poříčská pekárna, Na poříčí 30; metro náměstí Republiky. One of the new-style Viennese bakeries, selling coffee and pastries. *Open Mon–Fri 7am–7pm, Sat until 1pm.*

Rybarská bufet, Václavské náměstí 43; metro Můstek/Muzeum. Stand-up buffet with fish in batter and fishy salads on offer. *Open daily until 8pm.*

U české koruny, Vodičkova 30; metro Národní třída. Classic Czech stand-up *bufet*, inside the arcade at no. 30, with a cosier restaurant section tacked on. *Open Mon–Fri 10am–11pm, Sat & Sun 11am–8pm.*

Cafés and Bars

Prague can no longer boast a café society to rival the best in Europe, as it could at the beginning of this century and between the wars, though a few of the classic haunts survive. Nevertheless, many Praguers still spend a large part of the day smoking and drinking in the cafés, particularly in the summer, when the tables spill out onto the streets and squares. The cafés and bars listed below are a mixed bunch. The majority serve just coffee and cakes, and more often

than not, alcohol; others also serve up cheap and filling (though by no means gourmet) meals.

Like the Austrians who once ruled over them, the Czechs have a grotesquely sweet tooth, and the coffee-and-cake hit is part of the daily ritual. Many cafés offer a wide range of cakes, but the **cukrárna** is the place to go for cake-eating. There are two main types of **cake**: *dort*, like the German *Torte*, consist of a series of custard cream, chocolate and sponge layers, while *řez* are lighter, square cakes, usually containing a bit of fruit. A *věneček*, filled with "cream", is the nearest you'll get to an éclair; a *větrník* is simply a larger version with a bit of fresh cream added. One speciality to look out for is *rakvička*, which literally means "little coffin", an extended piece of sugar with cream, moulded vaguely into the shape of a coffin.

Coffee is drunk black and described rather hopefully as *turecká* (Turkish) – it's really just hot water poured over coffee grains. Downmarket *bufets* sell *ledová káva*, a weak, cold black coffee, while at the other end of the scale *Vídeňská káva* (Viennese coffee) is a favourite with the older generation, not quite as refined as the Austrian original, but still served with an adequate dollop of whipped cream. Another rather rich option is a mix with advocaat, *Alžírská káva*. Espresso coffee (*presso*) is becoming trendy in Prague, though its quality varies considerably compared to the Italian version. **Tea** is drunk weak and without milk, although you'll usually be given a glass of boiling water and a tea bag so you can do your own thing.

Hradčany and Malá Strana

Bílý orel (The White Eagle), Malostranské náměstí 17; metro Malostranská. A deep, dark dive on Malá Strana's main square that is to grungeful Czechs what *Jo's Bar* (see below) is to homesick Americans. *Open daily 8.30am–4am.*

Jo's Bar, Malostranské náměstí 7; metro Malostranská. A narrow bar in Malá Strana that is a perennially popular ex-pat/backpacker hang-out. Tex-Mex food served all day, bottled beer only and a

Eating and Drinking

Eating and Drinking

heaving crowd guaranteed most evenings. *Open daily 11am–2am.*

Malostranská kavárna, Malostranské náměstí 28; metro Malostranská. A time-honoured café founded in 1874 in a late eighteenth-century palace, currently closed due to litigation over ownership – worth checking to see if it's reopened.

Savoy, Vítězná 5; tram #12 or #22 from metro Malostranská. Renovated nineteenth-century café with high, gilded ceiling, but rather unfortunate modern fittings and little atmosphere. *Open daily 9am–midnight.*

U zeleného café (The Green Café), Nerudova 19; metro Staroměstská. Tiny vegetarian café with just four tables (almost invariably occupied), serving herbal teas, pizzas, salads, coffee and cakes, but no alcohol. *Open daily 10am–7pm.*

Staré Město and Josefov

Blatouch, Vězenská 7; metro Staroměstská. Smoky, literary café, frequented mostly by Czech trendies rather than ex-pats. Olives, snacks and alcoholic/non-alcoholic cocktails available. *Open Mon–Fri 11am–midnight, Sat 2pm–midnight, Sun 2–11pm.*

Café Milena, Staroměstské náměstí 22; metro Staroměstská. Nice attempt at a 1920s' style café, situated opposite the astronomical clock, named after Kafka's famous and talented lover, Milena Jesenská (see p.129), and by far the nicest café in this part of the old town. *Open daily 10am–10pm.*

Dolce Vita, Vězenská 15; metro Staroměstská. Ice cream and espresso bar popular with Prague's large Yugoslav contingent. *Open daily 10am–11pm.*

Hogo Fogo, Salvátorská 4; metro Staroměstská. Monochrome café tucked into the backstreets off Pařížská serving cheap and filling Czech pasta and meat dishes – very popular with young Czech trendies. *Open Mon–Thurs & Sun noon–midnight, Fri & Sat noon–2am.*

Konírna, Anenská 11; metro Staroměstská. Very popular vaulted stable

building, with cheap drinks and salad bar. *Open Mon–Fri noon–midnight, Sat & Sun 6pm–midnight.*

Lávka, Novotného lávka; metro Staroměstská. Tiny, trendy and lively riverside café, with tables outside in summer. Superb view of the castle; occasional theatre and music gigs inside. *Open daily noon–2am.*

Paříž, U obecního domu 1; metro náměstí Republiky. The prices are sky-high for Prague, but there's a certain faded elegance about this hotel *kavárna. Open daily until 1am.*

Rudolfinum, Alšovo nábřeží 12; metro Staroměstská. Gloriously ornate nineteenth-century café on the first floor of the old parliament building. *Open daily 10am–6pm.*

UPM, 17 listopadu; metro Staroměstská. Great place to relax after surveying the treasures of the Applied Art Museum. *Open Mon–Fri 10.30am–10.30pm, Sat & Sun 10.30am–6pm.*

Nové Město

Adria palác, Národní 40; metro Můstek. Large dining hall on the first floor of the Rondo-Cubist Adria Palace, with a summer terrace overlooking Národní; great location, avoid the food. *Open daily 8am–1am.*

Archa, Na poříčí 26; metro náměstí Republiky. Designer café belonging to the avant-garde venue of the same name, with big fishbowl windows for street-watching. *Open daily 10am–midnight.*

Café Bunkr, Lodecká 2; metro náměstí Republiky. Posey (but cheap) café attached to the grunge club of the same name. *Open daily 9am–3am.*

Dobrá čajovna, Václavské náměstí 14; metro Můstek/Muzeum. A small Buddhist tea house set back from the square, with world music wafting through it, floor seating and a vast range of teas – altogether a very un-Czech ambience (no smoking, no alcohol), but a great place to chill out. *Open daily 10am–11.30pm.*

Gany's, Národní 20; metro Národní třída. High ceiling, mirrors, daily papers, a billiard hall and window seats overlooking Národní make this a popular re-fuelling spot for tourists and shoppers alike. *Open daily 8am–11pm.*

Grand Hotel Evropa, Václavské náměstí 25; metro Můstek/Muzeum. To truly appreciate the sumptuous Art Nouveau decor, you'll have to forsake the terrace and step inside – worth it even if the music, coffee and staff are below par. *Open daily 7am – midnight.*

Institut Français, Štěpánská 35; metro Muzeum. Housed in the French cultural centre – great coffee and superb French pastries, plus of course the chance to pose with a French newspaper, make this one of Prague's best cafés. *Mon–Fri 9am–6pm.*

Mánes, Masarykovo nábřeží 250; metro Karlovo náměstí. Pristine white functional-ist café, one floor above the gallery that spans a small channel of the Vltava, with a view onto the island. The entrance is around the side from the gallery. *Open daily noon–1am.*

Obecní dům, náměstí Republiky; metro náměstí Republiky. The *kavárna*, with its famous fountain, is in the more restrained south hall of this huge Art Nouveau complex, which is currently undergoing a massive face-lift – check to see if it's re-opened.

Paris-Praha, Jindřišská 7; metro Můstek. Small café serving good French coffee, adjacent to the French delicatessen of the same name. *Open Mon–Fri 8.30am–7pm, Sat 8.30am–1pm.*

Praha-Roma, V jámě 5; metro Muzeum. Small *pasticceria* with dubious pink decor, serving authentic Italian pastries, coffee and ice cream. *Open Mon–Fri 8.30am–7pm, Sat 8.30am–1pm.*

Růžovná čajovna, Růžová 8; metro Můstek/Muzeum. Another ambient tea house to chill out in. *Open Mon–Fri 7.30am–9pm, Sat & Sun 11am–10pm.*

Slavia, Národní 1; metro Národní třída. An enduring and endearing Prague institution (see p.123), that has been closed for several years now, while the American lease-holders slowly get round to refurbishing it – worth checking to see if it's reopened.

Sports Bar, Ve Smečkách 30; metro Muzeum. Pool tables and live sports on TV are the attractions here – be prepared to pay through the nose for big match days. *Open daily 11am–2am.*

U sv Vojtěcha, Vojtěšská 14; metro Karlovo náměstí. Nice coffee place not far from the National Theatre and Žofín, with big windows that open out on to the street in summer. *Open Mon–Fri 8am–10pm, Sat 10am–10pm, Sun 10am–8pm.*

Velryba (The Whale), Opatovická 24; metro Národní třída. One of the most determinedly cool cafés in Prague, not intended as an ex-pat joint (though it attracts a fair few), serving cheap, post-revolutionary Czech food (several veggie options) and a stunning range of malt whiskies. *Open daily 11am–2am.*

Further out

The Globe, Janovského 14, Holešovice; metro Vltavská. This laid-back café – like the adjoining bookstore of the same name – is one big ex-pat hang-out, but enjoyable nevertheless. *Open daily 10am–midnight.*

Medúza, Belgická 17, Vinohrady; metro náměstí Míru. Trendy young crowd hang out in this deliberately faded, inexpensive café, which serves breakfast until 3pm and gets packed out most evenings. *Open daily 11am–2am.*

Radost FX Café, Bělehradská 120, Vinodrady; metro I. P. Pavlova. Without doubt the best vegetarian restaurant in town (okay so there's not much competi-tion), with imaginative dishes using fresh produce that draw in a large ex-pat posse, particularly for the Sunday brunch. *Open daily 11.30am–5am.*

Terasy na Barrandově, Hlubočepy; bus #105, #120, #128, #246, #247, #248 from metro Smíchovské nádraží. Pre-war functionalist classic perched above the Vltava close to the famous Barrandov film studios. Once a very trendy place to be seen, now just a little too far out to draw any kind of crowd – still worth a trip though. *Open daily 11am–11pm.*

Eating and Drinking

Eating and Drinking

The nearest metro is Malostranská, unless otherwise stated.

U knihomola, Mánesova 79, Vinohrady; metro Jiřího z Poděbrad. Basement café in Prague's other main ex-pat bookstore, with foreign papers to browse and art exhibitions to admire. *Open Mon–Fri 9am–midnight, Sat 10am–midnight, Sun 11am–6pm.*

U panáků, Letohradská 44, Holešovice; tram #1 from metro Vltavská. Puppet theatre café hung with marionettes, close to the National Technical Museum. *Open Tues, Thurs & Fri 4pm–midnight, Wed 3pm–midnight, Sat & Sun 2pm–midnight.*

Pubs

Traditional Czech *pivnice* are smoky, male-dominated places, where ninety-nine percent of the customers are drinking copious quantities of Czech beer by the half-litre. Pubs with a more youthful clientele, and ex-pat joints, tend to be a bit more mixed, but if you're not interested in drinking (and preferably smoking), you're going to have a hard time having a good time. Still, as with British pubs, whatever their faults, they remain deeply embedded in the local culture, and to sample that, you'll need to sample the amber nectar. Food is almost always of the traditional Czech variety (for more on Czech cuisine, see p.192), cheap and filling, but ultimately it could shorten your life by a couple of years.

Hradčany and Malá Strana

Baráčnická rychta, Na tržiště 22 (down a narrow passageway leading south off Nerudova). A real survivor – a small back-street *pivnice* squeezed in between the embassies, with a cheap and filling menu. *Open daily 11am–11pm.*

U bílé kuželky (The White Bowling Pin), Míšeňská 12. Not a bad pub considering its prime location right by the Charles Bridge; reasonably priced *Pilsner Urqeull* and Czech pub food. *Open daily noon–midnight.*

U černého orla (The Black Eagle), Újezd 33; tram #12 or #22 from metro Malostranská. Popular student pub with exceptionally cheap *Staropramen* 10°, across the bridge from the National Theatre. *Open Mon–Fri 10am–10pm, Sat & Sun 11am–10pm.*

U černého vola (The Black Bear), Loretánské náměstí 1; tram #22 from metro Malostranská. Does a brisk business providing the popular light beer *Velkopopovický kozel* in huge quantities to thirsty local workers. *Open daily 10am–10pm.*

U dvou sluncŭ (The Two Suns), Nerudova 47. Recently resurrected old pub on Nerudova, serving *Krušovice* beer and cheap Czech grub. *Open daily 11am–11pm.*

U hrocha (The Hippo), Thunovská 10. A real Czech pub in the heart of Malá Strana, difficult to believe but true – *Pilsner Urquell* and cheap grub. *Open daily 10am–11pm.*

U kocoura (The Cat), Nerudova 2. One of the few surviving pubs on Nerudova, owned by the Beer Party, but, for the most part, abandoned by its old clientele. Some of the best *Pilsner Urquell* in town; but little to eat beyond sausages. *Open 10am–11pm.*

Czech etiquette

It's common practice in Prague to share a table with other eaters or drinkers; *je tu volno*? (Is this seat free?) is the standard question. Waiter-service is the norm even in pubs, where if you sit tight a beer should come your way. You may have to ask for the menu (*jídelní lístek*) in pubs – and some cafés – to indicate that you wish to eat. When food arrives for your neighbours, it's common prac-tice to wish them bon appetit (*dobrou chut*). When you want to leave, simply say *zaplatím, prosím* (literally "I'll pay, please"), and your tab will be totted up; a modest form of **tipping** exists in all establishments, generally done by rounding up the bill to the nearest few crowns, though beware that the waiters haven't already done this for you. On leaving, bid your neighbours farewell (*na shledanou*).

Staré Město

Chapeau Rouge, Malá Štupartská; metro náměstí Republiky. Loud, posey, ex-pat boozer with wooden floorboards and red hat on door. *Open daily noon–midnight.*

James Joyce, Liliova 10; metro Staroměstská. A soulless and expensive recreation of an Irish pub, with prices that only businessmen think are reasonable – go to *Molly Malone's* instead. *Open Mon–Sat 10.30am–1am, Sun noon–midnight.*

Konvikt Klub, Konviktská 22; metro Staroměstská. Popular vaulted *pivnice* in the backstreets of the old town, with a mixed clientele of hard-drinking ex-pats and Czechs. *Open Mon–Fri 11am–1am, Sat 2pm–1am, Sun 5–11pm.*

Krušovická pivnice, Široká 20, Josefov; metro Staroměstská. Jewish Quarter watering hole, with dubious modern art, and a less than raucous ambience, but lashings of the great *Krušovice* beer, one of Bohemia's finest lagers. Cold food only. *Open daily 10am–10pm.*

Molly Malone's, U obecního dvora 4; metro Staroměstská. Real Irish pub with real Irish staff (who speak very little Czech), an open fire and draught *Kilkenny* and *Guinness* (neither of them very cheap). *Daily 11am–1am.*

Na Ovocném trhu, Ovocný trh 17; metro náměstí Republiky. New pub behind the Stavovské divadlo – perfect for a pre-theatre bite and a jar of *Velkopopovický kozel. Daily 10am–10pm.*

Rotunda, Karoliny Světlé 12; metro Národní třída. Czech beer cellar with cheap *Velkopopovický kozel* and the occasional live band. *Open daily 10am–5am.*

Taz-Pub, U obecního domu 3; metro náměstí Republiky. The latest in a series of rough and rowdy pubs in the vicinity of the *Hotel Paříž*, though this one is less fun than its predecessors. *Open daily 10am–midnight.*

U medvídků (The Little Bears), Na Perštýně 7; metro Národní třída. A Prague institution going back to the thirteenth century. Nowadays, the food is not great,

and the beer, *Budvar* (the original Budweiser), not always what it should be, but it's central, unpretentious and roomy. *Open Mon–Sat 11am–11pm.*

U staré školy (The Old School), Kozí; metro Staroměstská. Aggressively Czech spit-and-floorboard *pivnice*, filled with cigarette smoke and locals swilling down *Staropramen. Open Mon–Fri 9am–10pm, Sat & Sun 10am–10pm.*

U Vejvodů, Jilská 4; metro Národní třída. Classic medieval *pivnice* in the warren of streets south of Karlova. The usual filling Czech dishes on offer, washed down with *Smíchov* beer. *Open Mon–Fri until 10pm.*

U zlatého tygra (The Golden Tiger), Husova 17; metro Staroměstská. Beery *pivnice* once frequented by Prague's literary in-crowd – it's a bit too near Karlova for comfort, though the pub's erstwhile permanent resident, writer and bohemian, Bohumil Hrabal, still pops in occasionally. *Open daily 3–11pm.*

Nové Město

Branický sklípek, Vodičkova 26; metro Můstek. One of the few places where you can down the lethal *Braník 14°* brew. *Open daily until 11pm.*

Hlavní nádraží, Wilsonova; metro Hlavní nádraží. Sleazy, beery place on the first floor of the main train station, decorated with huge Art Nouveau murals – architectural (and sociological) curiosity value only. *Open daily 10am–10pm.*

Jáma (The Hollow), V jámě 7; metro Můstek/Muzeum. Loud, rock 'n' roll pub with *Regent* and *Samson* beer from south Bohemia and a strange mixture of food on offer, from Chinese to Tex-Mex, for a predominantly ex-pat posse. *Open Mon–Fri 11am–1am, Sat & Sun 1pm–1am.*

John Bull, Senovážná 8; metro náměstí Republiky. Yes, a real imitation British pub, serving *John Bull* ale and cheap Czech food – it even keeps to English licensing laws. *Open daily 11am–11pm.*

Novoměstský pivovar, Vodičkova 20; metro Můstek. New micro-brewery, which serves up its own misty home brew, plus

Eating and Drinking

Eating and Drinking

solid Czech food, in a series of bright, sprawling modern beer halls. *Open daily 11am–11pm.*

U bubeníčků, Myslíkova 8; metro Karlovo náměstí. Great place to down a few beers and eat some simple Czech cuisine, after visiting the Mánes gallery. *Open daily until 11pm.*

U Fleků, Křemencova 11; metro Karlovo náměstí. Famous medieval *pivnice* where the unique dark 13° beer, *Flek*, has been exclusively brewed and consumed since 1499. Despite seats for over five hundred – and beer served in 0.4 litre glasses or around 40kč – you may still have to fight with hundreds of Germans for a bench. You'll either love it or hate it – either way it's best to get there during the day. *Open daily 9am–11pm.*

U Pešků, Sokolská 50; metro I. P. Pavlova. Large and lively beer hall on one of Prague's most unhealthy streets, plus a smaller, more sedate *jídelna* serving some interesting Czech dishes – look out for the goose (*husa*). *Open daily until 11pm.*

U Pinkasů, Jungmannovo náměstí 15; metro Můstek. Famed as the first *pivnice* in Prague to serve *Pilsner Urquell* (which it still does). Despite its proximity to Wenceslas Square, it still manages to keep a few Czech regulars. *Open daily until 11pm.*

U zpěváčků (The Choir Boy), Na struze 7; metro Národní třída. A loud, smoky work-ers/musicians' pub just around the corner from the National Theatre, with an ironic line in Marxist-Leninist tracts, and the local *Staropramen* on tap. *Open daily 11am–10pm.*

The eastern suburbs

Hostinec pod Vyšehradem, Vratislavova 4, Vyšehrad; tram #3, #7 or #17 from metro Karlovo náměstí. Neo-Gothic building, with a modern marine theme inside, serving cheap mugs of *Staropramen* light and dark beer. *Open Mon–Sat 11am–11pm.*

Na zvonařce (The Bell), Šafaříkova, Vinohrady; tram #6 or #11 from metro I. P. Pavlova. Cheap Czech cuisine, *Pilsner Urquell*, billiards and great views from the terrace over the Nuselské schody

and Botič valley. *Open daily 4pm–midnight.*

U Bergnerů, Slezská 134, Žižkov; metro Flora. For beer connoisseurs: one of the few pubs serving the slightly bitter beer from the recently resurrected brewery in Kacov; good, simple Czech food available, too. *Open daily 11am–midnight.*

U Bulinů, Budečská 2, Vinohrady; metro náměstí Míru. Fine Czech pub with equally good pub food on offer, situated on the corner of Francouzská. *Open daily 10am–10pm.*

U koleje (The College), Slavíkova 24, Vinohrady; metro Jiřího z Poděbrad. Pubs have been closing down in droves since privatization, but this one has survived and thrived since. Cigarette smoke, beer, meat and dumplings all guaranteed. *Open daily 11am–10pm.*

U růžového sadu (The Rose Garden), Mánesova 89, Vinohrady; metro Jiřího z Poděbrad. New pub simply decorated with old shop signs and the like, perfectly situated if you're visiting the Plečnik Church or the Bookworm booktore; *Zubr* beer from Přerov in Moravia on tap. *Open Mon–Fri 10.30am–12.30am, Sat & Sun 11am–12.30am.*

U vystřeleýcho oka (The Shot-Out Eye), U božích bojovníků, Žižkov; metro Florenc. Big, smoky pub just south of the Žižkov Hill, with (unusually) good music playing and lashings of *Radegast* beer. *Open daily until midnight.*

U zlaté kotvy, Vratislavova 19, Vyšehrad; tram #3, #7 or #17 from metro Karlovo náměstí. New pub with dubious colour scheme, but excellent, cheap *Gambrinus*, *Pilsner* and *Punkmistr* dark beer. *Open Mon–Fri 9am–10pm, Sat & Sun 10am–10pm.*

The northern and western suburbs

The Derby, Dukelských hrdinů 20, Holešovice; tram #12 or #17 from metro Malostranská. A spacious, lively, British-style urban pub that lays on chess, draughts and backgammon, plus big, fill-ing pizzas and a wide range of Czech and foreign beers on draught. *Open daily 11am–2am.*

Late-night eating and drinking

At any of the late-opening restaurants and bars listed below you should be able to get something to eat and/or drink at least half an hour before the closing times given.

Adria palác, Národní 40; metro Můstek. Until 1am (see p.200).

Bílý orel (The White Eagle), Malostranské náměstí 17; metro Malostranská. Until 4am (see p.199).

Café Bunkr, Lodecká 2; metro náměstí Republiky. Until 3am (see p.200).

The Derby, Dukelských hrdinů 20, Holešovice; tram #12 or #17 from metro Malostranská. Until 2am (see p.204).

Hogo Fogo, Salvátorská 4; metro Staroměstská. Until 2am on weekends (see p.200).

Jama (The Hollow), V jámě 7; metro Můstek/Muzeum. Until 1am (see p.203).

Jo's Bar, Malostranské náměstí 7; metro Malostranská. Until 2am (see p.199).

Lávka, Novotného lávka; metro Staroměstská. Until 2am (see p.200).

Letenský zámeček, Kostelní, Holešovice; tram #1 from metro Vltavská. Until 2am (see p.210).

Mánes, Masarykovo nábřeží 250; metro Karlovo náměstí. Until 1am (see p.201).

U Mecenáše, Malostranské náměstí 10; ☎53 38 81; metro Malostranská. Until 1am; closed Saturday (see p.207).

Medúza, Belgická 17, Vinohrady; metro náměstí Míru. Until 2am (see p.201).

Molly Malone's, U obecního dvora 4; metro Staroměstská. Until 1am (see p.203).

Paříž, U obecního domu 1; metro náměstí Republiky. Until 1am (see p.200).

U pastýřky, Bělehradská 15, Vinohrady; ☎43 40 93; metro I. P. Pavlova. Until 1am (see p.210).

Pizzeria Kmotra, V jirchářích 12; ☎24 91 58 09; metro Národní třída. Until 1am (see p.208).

Radost FX Café, Bělehradská 120, Vinodrady; metro I. P. Pavlova. Until 5am (see p.201).

Rotunda, Karoliny Světlé 12; metro Národní třída. Until 5am (see p.203).

U Sixtů, Celetná 2; ☎236 79 80; metro Staroměstská. Until 1am (see p.208).

Sports Bar, Ve Smečkách 30; metro Muzeum. Until 2am (see p.201).

Velryba (The Whale), Opatovická 24; metro Národní třída. Until 2am (see p.201).

U zlatého rožně, Československé armády 22, Bubeneč; ☎31 11 61; metro Dejvická. Until 1am (see p.211).

Na slamníku (The Straw Bed), Schwaigrova 7, Bubeneč; bus #131 from metro Hradčanská. The perfect place to end up after a stroll in Stromovka: a *pivnice* serving good Czech grub and wonderful *Krušovice* beer. *Open daily 4pm–midnight.*

Nad královskou oborou (The Royal Game Preserve), Nad královskou oborou 31, Bubeneč; bus #1255 from the northern end of Revoluční. Another place to head for after a stroll in Stromovka; good Czech food, *Punkmistr* dark and *Gambrinus* light beers on tap, the world's cheapest pint of *Guinness*, and an impressive range of liquors, including *Bushmill's*, plus live bands on Fri & Sat. *Open daily noon–11pm.*

U buldoka (The Bulldog), Preslova 1, Smíchov; metro Anděl. A half-decent

Smíchov pub is hard to find, so here's one, serving the local *Staropramen* of course. *Open Mon–Fri 11am–midnight, Sat & Sun 1pm–midnight.*

Restaurants and Wine Bars

The restaurant scene has greatly improved in the last few years. Authentic ethnic places have opened up, pizza parlours continue to get better and there are some restaurants now serving Czech specialities way above the average. The down side is that prices have rocketed out of the reach of many Czechs, who tend more than ever to stick to pubs when eating out. Service is gradually becoming more sophisticated, though surly staff are still no rarity, nor are unscrupulous waiters who exercise

Eating and Drinking

The listings are divided into geographical areas, and into price categories, too – inexpensive, moderate and expensive. As a rough guide, you'll be able to get a three-course meal with drinks for:

Inexpensive under 200kč a head
Moderate 200–400kč a head
Expensive 400kč and upwards

While 400kč for a meal is hardly extravagant to a westerner, it still is for most Czechs – you're unlikely to share your table with any locals. Note that at restaurants where we have included phone numbers, it is advisable to book beforehand.

For a glossary of Czech terms for food and drink, see p.196.

some dubious arithmetics when totting up the bill. Fresh salads and fresh produce remain confined to the upper echelons of the catering industry; but overall the quality of the food being served is improving.

Away from the big hotels, the **menu** (*jídelní lístek*), which should be displayed outside, is often in Czech only and deciphering it without a grounding in the language can be quite a feat. Just bear in mind that the general rule is for the right-hand column to list the prices, while the far left column usually gives you the estimated weight of every dish in grammes; if what you get weighs more or less, the price alters accordingly.

Some Prague restaurants insist, with varying degress of coercion, that you leave your coat and bags in the **cloakroom** (*šatna*). It's another leftover of Austrian airs and graces, but also provides a meagre employment for the pensioners who generally run them.

Hradčany and Malá Strana

The nearest metro is Malostranská, unless otherwise stated.

INEXPENSIVE

Bar Bar, Všehrdova 17; tram #12 or #22 from metro Malostranská. Arty *crêperie* with cheap salads, sweet and savoury *crêpes* and Jamaican *palačinky* on offer. *Open Mon-Fri 11am-midnight, Sat & Sun noon-midnight.*

Český rybářský svaz (Czech Fishermen's Club), U Sovových mlýnů; ☎ 53 02 23. Worth the trouble to get to – it's hidden away in the park on Kampa Island. The manager has an appropriately sailor-like beard, and the fish is fresh from the Sázava river. *Open Mon-Sat 1-9pm.*

Saté Grill, Pohořelec 3; tram #22 from metro Malostranská. There isn't really a better place to fill your belly for very little, in the vicinity of the Hrad. Veggie and non-veggie noodle dishes prepared, all with a vaguely Indonesian bent. *Open daily 12.30-10pm.*

MODERATE

Čertovka, U lužického semináře 24. Small place down an alleyway, with a great summer terrace overlooking Charles Bridge; food's okay, but overpriced. *Open daily 11.30am-midnight.*

Faros, Šporkova 5; ☎ 53 34 82. Cosy little Greek restaurant in the backstreets of Malá Strana; a nice change but no gourmet experience. *Open daily noon-11pm.*

U Lorety, Loretánské náměstí 8; ☎ 53 13 95. Familiar Czech menu, bang next door to the Loreto chapel, and facing the monster Černín Palace – a great place to eat outside in summer. *Open daily 11am-11pm.*

U maltézských rytířů, Prokopská 10; ☎ 53 63 57. One of the cheapest gourmet spots in Prague, serving faultless local cuisine and excellent apple strudel. *Open daily 11am-11pm.*

Nebozízek (Little Auger), Petřínské sady 411; ☎ 53 79 05; funicular from Újezd to first stop. You used to go here for the view, not the food; now you can enjoy both as long as you stick to the traditional Czech dishes. *Open daily 11am-6pm & 7-11pm.*

Palffy palác, Valdštejnská 14; ☎ 513 24 18. Grand candle-lit room on the first floor of the conservatoire, with great salads, good desserts and a wonderful outdoor terrace from which to survey the red rooftops of Malá Strana. *Open daily 10am-11pm.*

U tří housliček (The Three Violins), Nerudova 10. Pleasant art-loving ambience to this Czech restaurant which boasts a good handful of veggie dishes. Just one of a number of small wine bars that line the climb up to the castle. *Open daily 11am–midnight.*

EXPENSIVE

Avalon, Malostranské náměstí 12; ☎53 02 76. Big Hockney mural as a backdrop and an imaginative menu with everything from burgers to fresh salads, but particularly strong on shellfish and the finned variety. *Open daily noon–midnight.*

David, Tržiště 17; ☎53 93 25. Czech cuisine and therefore much more together on the meat dishes than the accompanying veg – around 700kč a head. *Open daily 11.30am–3pm & 6–11pm.*

Kampa Park, Na Kampě 8b; ☎53 30 71. Pink house exquisitely located right by the Vltava on Kampa Island with a Swedish chef and a European menu that includes salmon and venison. *Open daily 11.30am–11.30pm.*

Lobkovická vinárna, Vlašská 17; ☎53 01 85. A pre-revolution institution in embassy land that's managed to keep up with the times (and raise its prices accordingly). *Open daily noon–3pm & 6.30pm–midnight.*

U malířů (The Artist's), Maltézské náměstí 11; ☎24 51 02 69. Prague's finest and most expensive French restaurant is a converted sixteenth-century house that used to belong to an artist called Jiří Šic (pronounced "Shits"). Fresh produce flown in daily from Paris means you won't get away for less than 1000kč a head. *Open daily 11am–11pm.*

U Mecenáše, Malostranské náměstí 10; ☎53 38 81. Vaulted Gothic *vinárna* where Václav IV used to drink (a lot). The menu features the usual Czech favourites, all superbly prepared. *Open 5pm–1am; closed Sat.*

U modré kachničky (The Blue Duck), Nebovidská 6; ☎53 97 51. Lurid murals somewhat overwhelm this cosy little restaurant, which serves up a mouth-watering selection of international dishes, including many Czech favourites, given the gourmet treatment. *Open noon–4pm & 6.30pm–midnight.*

U ševce Matouše (The Cobbler), Loretánské náměstí 4; ☎53 35 97. The cobbler's been made redundant and the prices have quadrupled, but this is still the best steak house in Prague. *Open daily noon–4pm & 6–11pm.*

U zlaté hrušky (The Golden Pear), Nový Svět 3 ☎53 11 33. Romantic, exclusive, intimate, the setting is perfect, the menu is game-heavy, and the bill (after careful massaging by the management) should come to around 800kč a head. *Open daily 6.30pm–midnight.*

Staré Město and Josefov

INEXPENSIVE

V Blatnici, Michalská 6; metro Můstek. Popular basement *vinárna* in the heart of the old town, serving Moravian wines and cheap Czech food. *Open Mon–Sat noon–10pm.*

Pizzeria Mikuláš, Benediktská 16; ☎231 57 27; metro náměstí Republiky. Stuck in a backstreet off Revoluční, which no doubt contributes to the fact that this is one of the best pizza-places in Prague; try the *krabí* (crab). *Open Mon–Sat 11.30am–10pm.*

U supa (The Vulture), Celetná 22; metro náměstí Republiky. Lively fourteenth-century pub serving cheap Czech meals and very strong, dark *Braník* beer, either inside or on the cobbles of its cool, vaulted courtyard. *Open Mon–Sat 11am–9pm.*

MODERATE

Pizzeria Rugantino, Dušní 4; ☎22 38 2; metro Staroměstská. This is the real thing: an oak-fired oven, gargantuan thin bases and nineteen toppings to choose from, *Bernard* beer on tap. *Open Mon–Sat 11am–11pm, Sun 4–11pm.*

Red, Hot & Blues, Jakubská 12; ☎231 46 39; metro náměstí Republiky. Laid-back ex-pat joint serving chilli hot Tex-Mex – *burritos*, *étoufées* and Creole food

Eating and
Drinking

Eating and Drinking

– to the sound of jazz and blues. *Open daily 10am-11pm.*

Reykjavik, Karlova 20; metro Staroměstská. The owners really are Icelandic, though the cuisine is pretty international. The soups and starters are definitely worth going for, but the best feature is the wonderful variety of fresh (ish) fish, flown in from you know where. *Open daily 11am-11pm.*

Zlatá ulička (Golden Lane), Masná 9; ☎ 232 08 84; metro náměstí Republiky. Confusing name, since it's located nowhere near the Golden Lane, but a friendly little place nevertheless, serving excellent veal dishes, run by Yugoslav expats, and decorated with a slightly surrealist touch. *Open daily 10am-midnight.*

EXPENSIVE

Au Saint Esprit, Elisky Krásnohorské 5; ☎ 231 00 39; metro Staroměstská. A dressy and expensive place serving steaks and superbly prepared fish, for no less than 600kč a head. *Open Mon-Fri 11.30am-2pm & 7-10.30pm, Sat & Sun 7-10.30pm.*

Bellevue, Smetanovo nábřeží 18; ☎ 235 95 99; metro Národní třída. The view of the Charles Bridge and Prague Castle is outstanding, and the food's not bad either. Anywhere that serves fresh vegetables and crispy French fries is a cut above most Prague outfits. *Open daily 11am-11pm.*

Parnas, Smetanovo nábřeží 2; ☎ 24 22 76 14; metro Národní třída. Prime location on the Vltava embankment by the National Theatre, classic 1920s' decor, a masterpiece on the wall and imaginative Czech-centred cuisine – hardly surprising then that it's around 1000kč a head. *Open daily noon-3pm & 5.30-11.30pm.*

Praha Tamura, Havelská 6; ☎ 236 79 80; metro Můstek. Authentic Japanese *sashimi* and *sushi* at authentic Japenese prices; fixed menus at 1200kč and 1900kč. *Open daily 11am-midnight.*

U Sixtů, Celetná 2; ☎ 236 79 80; metro Staroměstská. Beautiful setting under-

Vegetarian places

At the moment, these are the only exclusively vegetarian eateries in Prague:

Country Life
Jungmannova 15,
Nové Město   p.198

U Góvindy
Na hrázi 5,
Libeň   p.210

Radost FX Café
Bělehradská 120,
Vinohrady   p.201

U zeleného café
Nerudova 19,
Malá Strana   p.200

neath Gothic vaults, and an unusually varied menu, featuring fresh salmon, rabbit, veal and venison. Spoiled only by slow service, disappointing desserts and prices that approach 750kč per person. There's a café on the ground floor. *Open daily noon-1am.*

U zátiší (Still Life), Liliova 1; ☎ 24 22 89 77; metro Národní třída. Exquisitely prepared international cuisine with fresh vegetables and regular non-meat dishes, all served in *nouvelle cuisine* sized portions by professional waiters. Expect to pay around 500kč a head. *Open noon-3pm & 5.30-11pm.*

Nové Město

INEXPENSIVE

Buffalo Bill's, Vodičkova 9; ☎ 24 21 54 79; metro Můstek. Tex-Mex that's more like Czech-Mex, but still spicy and filling enough for all that. *Open daily 11am-11pm.*

Pezinok, Purkyňova 4; ☎ 29 19 96; metro Národní třída. Good place to sample cheap Slovak cuisine. *Open daily 11am-11pm.*

Pizzeria Kmotra, V jirchářích 12; ☎ 24 91 58 09; metro Národní třída. This sweaty basement pizza place is currently Prague's most popular, so be sure to book a table in advance. *Open daily 11am-1am.*

Pizzeria Mamma Mia, Na poříčí 13; ☎231 47 26; metro náměstí Republiky. The main feature is the restaurant's very own in-house tree. Otherwise it's easier to get a seat here than at *Kmotra* and not quite so stiflingly hot. *Open Mon–Sat 11am–11pm, Sun 5–10pm.*

Vltava, Rašínovo nábřeží; ☎29 49 64; metro Karlovo náměstí. A tasty and little-known Czech fish restaurant right by the water's edge, below the main road close to Palackého most – stick to carp or trout and you can't go wrong. *Open daily 11am–10pm.*

MODERATE

Cerberus, Soukenická 19; ☎231 09 85; metro náměstí Republiky. Cosy pristine little joint serving pasta and Czech favourites including plenty of imaginative pork dishes. *Open daily noon–midnight.*

Fregata, Ladova 3 ☎231 17 67; metro Karlovo náměstí. Stick to the trout and carp, washed down with a bottle of *Tramín* and you can't go far wrong. *Open Mon–Fri 11.30am–3.30pm, Sat & Sun 6pm–midnight.*

Na rybárně (The Fishmonger's), Gorazdova 17; ☎29 97 95; metro Karlovo náměstí. Cosy fish restaurant tucked away in the backstreets behind Havel's old riverside flat – as ever the trout and carp are your best bet for freshness; *Pilsner Urquell* on tap. *Open daily noon–midnight.*

Salammbo, Vyšehradská; ☎29 94 01; metro Karlovo náměstí. Tunisian restaurant that makes a few concessions to the Czech palate – ask for the spicier dishes if you want a hotter hit. *Open Mon–Sat 11am–3pm & 6pm–midnight, Sun 6pm–midnight.*

U bílého slona (The White Elephant), Soukenická 4; ☎231 17 67; metro náměstí Republiky. Toned-down Thai cuisine at moderate prices – don't go upstairs where the food is the same but the prices are higher. *Open Mon–Sat 11am–11pm.*

U čížků, Karlovo náměstí 34; ☎29 88 91; metro Karlovo náměstí. Cosy little restaurant on the the east side of the square, dishing

up a seriously meaty menu of beef, pork, goose, duck and anything else that moves, washed down with *Gambrinus*. *Open daily noon–3.30pm & 5–11pm.*

EXPENSIVE

Fakhreldine, Klimentská 48; ☎232 79 70; metro Florenc. Lebanese restaurant that charges a high price for its albeit fairly authentic Middle Eastern cuisine – not great for veggies either. *Open daily noon–11.30pm.*

Obecní dům, náměstí Republiky; metro náměstí Republiky. Superb Art Nouveau decor in this cavernous hall, but currently undergoing restoration; it's worth checking to see if it has reopened.

U šuterů, Palackého 4; ☎26 10 17; metro Můstek. Authentic French and Belgian cooking at this intimate, suave little restaurant where you can cook your own dishes on hot stones – the bill is unlikely to be less than 800kč, significantly more if you drink some of the ridiculously marked-up wine. *Open daily 11.30am–3pm & 6.30–11.30pm.*

Vinohrady and the eastern suburbs

INEXPENSIVE

Záhřeb, Záhřebská 24, Vinohrady; metro náměstí Míru. Plain, cheap restaurant serving fish and meat dishes, expertly cooked, plus the odd Chinese-style dish, too. *Open daily 11am–11pm.*

Zdar, Vinohradská 164, Vinohrady; metros Flora/Želivského. Situated opposite the big Olšany cemetery, this place specializes in serious game dishes. *Open daily 11am–10pm.*

MODERATE

Dolly Bell, Neklanova 20, Vyšehrad; tram #3, #7, #17, #18 or #24 from metro Karlovo náměstí. Yugoslav restaurant (named after a film – it probably sounds more promising in Serbo-Croat), which serves up excellent Balkan grub, and features upside-down tables stuck to the ceiling. *Open daily 11am–11pm.*

Fenix, Vinohradská 88, Žižkov; ☎25 03 64; metro náměstí Míru. One of Prague's

Eating and Drinking

Eating and Drinking

better Chinese restaurants, with loads of veggie dishes on offer. *Open daily 11.30am–3pm & 5.30–11pm.*

Il Ritrovo, Lublaňská 11, Vinohrady; ☎29 65 29; metro I. P. Pavlova. Italian-run outfit with a wide range of pasta dishes and salads, a great *antipasti* bar in the centre of the restaurant and *tiramisu* for dessert. *Open daily noon–3pm & 6pm–midnight.*

Kongzi, Seifertova 18, Žižkov; ☎27 50 26; tram #5, #9 or #26 from metro Hlavní nádraží. Very reasonable, very hot Chinese restaurant in deepest Žižkov. *Open daily 11.30am–3pm & 5.30–11pm.*

Myslivna (The Hunting Lodge), Jagellonská 21, Žižkov; ☎627 02 09; metro Flora. One of Prague's best game restaurants, serving up excellent venison and quail. *Open daily noon–4pm & 5pm–midnight.*

Pravěk (Prehistoric Times), Francouzská 30, Vinohrady; ☎786 33 14; metro náměstí Míru. Perfectly okay Czech restaurant, with the added bonus of fresh fish, unusual meats and a changing monthly menu from cuisines around the world – the dinosaur theme decor is less easy to stomach. *Open daily 11am–10pm.*

Thrakia, Rubešova 12, Vinohrady; ☎24 22 34 90; metro Muzeum. Bulgarian restaurant behind the National Museum which serves spicy yoghurty food, with a familiar Mediterranean feel to it. *Open daily 11am–11pm.*

U pastýřky (The Shepherdess), Bělehradská 15, Vinohrady; ☎43 40 93; metro I. P. Pavlova. Unashamedly touristy Slovak log cabin, great for charcoal-grilled meat dishes and other Slovak specialities. *Open daily 6pm–1am.*

EXPENSIVE

Principe, Anglická 23, Vinohrady; ☎25 96 14; metro náměstí Míru. A swish Italian restaurant with the airs, graces and prices of the real thing, though the food is not always what it could be and it's not difficult to blow 750kč or more per person here. *Open noon–2.30pm & 6–11.30pm.*

Taj Mahal, Škrétova 10, Vinohrady; ☎22 04 38; metro Muzeum. Basement Indian restaurant, serving the real thing: *poppadums, bhajees, samosas* and an excellent *chicken korma* but not so hot on veggie dishes. *Open daily noon–3pm & 6–11.30pm.*

The northern and western suburbs

INEXPENSIVE

Letenský zámeček, Kostelní, Holešovice; tram #1 from metro Vltavská. The *Ullman* restaurant on the ground floor serves cheap Czech food, including some veggie options, with *Velkopopvický kozel* on draught and a summer terrace with a wonderful view over Prague. *Open daily 10am–2am.*

U Góvindy, Na hrázi 5, Libeň; metro Palmovka. Newly opened Hare Krishna (*Haré Kršna* in Czech) restaurant serving organic veggie slop. Operates a pay-what-you-can system. *Open Mon–Fri noon–6pm.*

U Matouše, Matoušova 6, Smíchov; metro Anděl. Unpretentious restaurant serving Czech cuisine as it should be. The menu regularly contains a few surprises, aside from the staples: *smažený Olomoucký sýr*, a pungent deep-fried cheese and *špekové knedlíky*, bacon and onion dumplings, to name but two. *Open daily 11am–11pm.*

MODERATE

Bella Napoli, Na hrázi 5, Libeň; metro Palmovka; ☎24 22 73 15; metro Palmovka. One of the better Italian restaurants in Prague hidden away in the northeastern suburb of Libeň, and offering a range of pasta and pizza dishes, plus a great *antipasti* buffet. *Open daily noon–3pm & 6pm–midnight.*

U cedru (The Cedar), Na hutích 13, Dejvice; ☎312 29 74; metro Dejvická. If you can't afford the prices at *Fakhreldine* in town, try the more reasonable, but equally delicious Lebanese fare from this joint. *Open daily 11am–11pm.*

EXPENSIVE

Hanavský pavilón, Letenské sady 173; ☎32 57 92; tram #18 or #22 from metro Malostranská. Highly ornate Art Nouveau pleasure pavilion high above the Vltava, with stunning views and a bill that is unlikely to be less than 800kč per person. *Open daily noon–midnight.*

U zlatého rožně (The Golden Spit), Československé armády 22, Bubeneč; ☎31 11 61; metro Dejvická. Deep in the heart of ambassador-land, this exclusive new restaurant serves a startling variety of delicious Czech, Chinese and fishy and seafood dishes. *Open daily noon–1am.*

Eating and Drinking

Chapter 11

Clubs and Live Venues

Although there's infinitely more choice than there was prior to 1989, Prague still has nothing like the number of **clubs** you'd expect from a European capital. The dance craze has yet to hit Prague in any significant way; pure dance clubs are the exception away from the tacky meat markets around Wenceslas Square. The **live music** scene is a bit more promising, and many nightclubs double as live music venues; however, Czech reggae or skinhead punk may not suit everyone's tastes.

One good thing about going clubbing in Prague is that, compared to the West, it's phenomenally cheap. Admission to live gigs or nightclubs is rarely much more than 40kč, and drinks are only slightly more expensive than pub prices. And, if you can handle it, a few places stay open until 5 or 6am. To find out the latest on the city's up-and-coming events, scour the fly posters around town, or check the listings sections in *Prague Post*, or the Czech listings weekly *Program*.

Rock, Pop and Dance Music

Major western bands are beginning to include Prague in their European tours and, to be sure of a full house, many offer tickets at a fraction of their price in the West. There are gigs by Czech bands almost every night in the city's clubs and discos – a selection of the better ones is listed below.

Alterna Komotovka, Seifertova 3, Žižkov; tram #5, #9 or #26 from metro Hlavní nádraží. Occasionally puts on interesting gigs, but it's not a place to come on a slow night. *Open daily until 5am.*

Bar Club, Hybernská 10, Nové Město; metro náměstí Republiky. Incredibly uninspiring name for one of the city's best nightspots. A very mixed crowd, including many of Prague's African students, goes down to the basement ballroom for the club's nightly *Reggae Sound System* – loud, proud and very early 1980s. *Open daily until 5am.*

Belmondo Revival Club, Bubenská 1, Holešovice; metro Vltavská. Regular gigs at recently relocated club – hence the name – plus cheap beer and a couple of pool tables. *Doors open 7.30pm.*

Bunkr, Lodecká 2, Nové Město; metro náměstí Republiky. Prague's first real club, *Bunkr* is, as you might guess, a converted wartime bunker, painted black, and fitted with the longest bar (and slowest service) in Prague. *Open until 5am; live music from 9pm.*

Jam, Štefánikova 44, Smíchov; metro Anděl. New club housed in a Smíchov cellar playing everything from REM to acid jazz. Tiny dance floor and occasionally a bit dead, but still worth a trip. *Open daily 10pm–4am.*

Junior Klub, Koněvova 219, Žižkov; tram #16 from metro Želivského. An unprepossessing building in an equally unprepossessing neighbourhood, this was the venue that launched a thousand

Gay and Lesbian Nightlife

Prague Post does the occasional update on gay and lesbian nightlife in Prague, otherwise you'll need to get hold of the Czech listings tabloid *Program*, the monthly gay magazine *SOHO Revue*, or the monthly freebie *GAY Service*. In the meantime, check out the places listed below (for more on gay life, see p.231).

Drake's, Petřínská 5, Smíchov; tram #6 or #9 from metro Národní třída. Expensive, almost exclusively male hang-out, which bills itself as a "really big cruise facility"; twenty private video booths are the biggest draw. *Open 24 hours a day.*

G & L Club, Lublaňská 48, Vinohrady; metro I. P. Pavlova. Mixed lesbian/gay crowd at this restaurant, which turns into a disco after 10pm. *Open daily 7pm–4am.*

Mercury, Kolínská 11, Žižkov; metro Flora. A mixed gay/lesbian crowd enjoy this camp but classy place where you can eat, dance and watch strip shows and drag on the weekend. Occasional

lesbian-only nights. *Open daily until 6am.*

Riviera, Národní 20, Nové Město; metro Národní třída. The most popular and centrally located gay/lesbian club in Prague, packed out most nights. *Open daily until 5am.*

Tom's Bar, Pernerova 4, Karlín; metro Florenc. Small but popular restaurant and club frequented almost exclusively by Czech gay men. *Open daily until 5am.*

U dubu, Záhřebská 14, Vinohrady; metro náměstí Míru. Typical, cheap Czech pub with an almost exclusively gay male clientele. *Open daily 6pm–midnight.*

U Petra Voka, Na bědlidle 40, Smíchov; metro Anděl. Pre-1989 gay nightspot that's recently re opened, refurbished and regenerated. *Open daily 8pm–late.*

U střelce, Střelecký ostrov, Nové Město; tram #6, #9 or #12 from metro Národní třída. Sweaty cellar club with drag nights on Fridays and Saturdays. *Open Mon–Sat until 6am.*

Clubs and Live Venues

domestic indie bands. *Doors open at 7.30pm.*

Lucerna, Vodičkova, Nové Město; metro Můstek/Muzeum. Without doubt the best gig venue in Prague, a gilded turn-of-the-century hall with balcony, but open only when there's an event booked in – check the listings.

Music Park, Francouzská 4, Vinohrady; metro náměstí Míru. Prague's high-tech club is the city's premier meat market away from Wenceslas Square, with naff theme nights and plenty of mafiosi. *Open Mon–Sat until 7am.*

Radost, Bělehradská 120, Vinohrady; metro I. P. Pavlova. This is still by far the best dance club in Prague, with successfully whacky decor and a healthy mix of real clubbers and despots; great veggie café upstairs, too. *Open daily until 5am.*

Rock Café, Národní 22, Nové Město; metro Národní třída. The Rock Café has had its day. It made its name in the early days of

post-Communist euphoria, but is now considered passé in the fickle world of Prague clubbing, though it still puts on the odd worthwhile gig. *Open daily until 3am.*

Roxy, Dlouhá 33, Staré Město; metro náměstí Republiky. The Roxy is a great little venue: mellow decor and an interesting programme of events from arty films and exhibitions to live acts. *Open Thurs–Sat until 4am.*

Újezd (aka Borát), Újezd 18, Malá Strana; tram #6, #9 or #22 from metro Národní třída. A dark and dingy post-punk den which sprawls across three floors of a knackered old building close to the funicular railway, and happily allows any band whatsoever to play. *Open Tues–Thurs 6pm–2am, Fri & Sat 6pm–6am.*

Uzi, Legerova 44, Nové Město; metro I. P. Pavlova. Strange mixed crowd – from grunge to skinhead – flocks to this biker-themed club with its in-house tattooist. *Open Mon–Sat until 6am.*

Clubs and Live Venues

Jazz

Despite a long indigenous tradition, Prague these days has just a handful of good jazz clubs, and audiences remain predominantly foreign. With little money to attract acts from abroad, however, the artists are almost exclusively Czech, and do the entire round of venues each month. The one exception to all this is the annual **international jazz festival** in October, which attracts at least one big name; previous greats have included Wynton Marsalis, B. B. King and Jan Garbarek. More often than not, it's a good idea to book a table at the jazz clubs listed below – this is particularly true of *AghaRTA* and *Reduta*.

AghaRTA Jazz Centrum, Krakovská 5, Nové Město; metro Muzeum; ☎ 24 21 29 14. Probably the best jazz club in Prague, with a good mix of Czechs and foreigners and a consistently good programme of gigs; situated in a side street off the top end of Wenceslas Square. *Open daily until 1am.*

Highlander – Blue Note, Národní 28, Nové Město; metro Národní třída; ☎24 21 35 55. New jazz restaurant situated underneath the Lucerna concert hall. *Open daily until 2am.*

Malostranská beseda, Malostranské náměstí 21, Malá Strana; metro Malostranská; ☎ 53 90 24. Ramshackle venue, by no means exclusively jazz, but worth checking out nevertheless. *Open daily until 1am.*

Metropolitan Jazz Club, Jungmannova 14, Nové Město; metro Můstek; ☎24 21 60 25. Small jazz restaurant that tends to stick to a traditional menu, on stage and in the kitchen. *Open daily until 1am.*

Press Jazz Club, Pařížská 9, Staré Město; ☎53 18 35. Large former conference hall, with poor acoustics, but you're pretty well guaranteed a seat, and the acts are as good (or bad) as anywhere else. *Open until 2am.*

Reduta, Národní 20, Nové Město; metro Národní třída; ☎24 91 22 46. Prague's best-known jazz club – Bill Clinton played his sax here in front of Havel (but presumably didn't inhale). *Open Mon–Sat until 2am.*

Chapter 12

The Arts

Alongside the city's numerous cafés, pubs and clubs, there's a rich **cultural life** in Prague. Music is everywhere in the city: especially in the summer, when the streets, churches, palaces, opera houses and concert halls and even the gardens are filled with the strains of classical music. Czech theatre and film are in a state of turmoil at the moment as the industry tries to come to terms with the loss of state subsidy and diminishing audiences – not to mention freedom of expression. Even if you don't speak Czech, there are theatre performances worth catching – Prague has a strong tradition of mime, "black theatre" and puppetry, and many cinemas show films in their original language. Rock, pop and jazz gigs are covered in the previous chapter.

Tickets

By far the best way to obtain **tickets** is from the box office (*pokladna*) of the venue concerned. In addition, there are several **ticket agencies**, though they tend to cater for foreigners and hike up their prices accordingly. *Ticketpro* sells tickets for most events and has the largest number of branches in the city, including one in the *PIS* at Na příkopě 20 and one at *Melantrich* in the Rokoko pasáž, Václavské náměstí; *BTI* (*Bohemia Ticket International*) sells tickets only for the big venues and has several offices including one at Na příkopě 16. Ticket **prices**, with a few notable exceptions, are still extremely cheap for westerners, rarely

more than 300kč for a concert or theatre performance, and absolute peanuts for the cinema (usually around 40kč). And don't despair if everything is officially sold out (*vyprodáno*), as standby tickets are often available at the venue's box office on the night.

Listings and information

The English-language **listings** in *Prague Post* are selective, but they do at least pick out the events which may be of particular interest to the non-Czech speaker, and list all the major venues and their addresses. Also in English is the monthly handout, *The Arts In Prague*, currently priced at 30kč, which, along with the Czech monthly listings booklet *Přehled* (10kč), is available from any *PIS* office. For a truly comprehensive rundown of the week's events, buy a copy of *Program*, which is in Czech but easy enough to decipher. Any additional **information** you might need can usually be obtained from one of the *PIS* offices around town: at Na příkopě 20, or in the Staroměstská radnice.

Classical Music, Opera and Ballet

Folk songs lie at the heart of Czech music and have found their way into much of the country's **classical music**, of which the Czechs are justifiably proud, having produced four composers of international stature – Dvořák, Janáček, Smetana and Martinů – and, a fifth, Mahler, though

The Arts

German-speaking, was born in Bohemia. The music of Mozart also puts in a regular appearance in the city's monthly concert programme, partly because of his popularity, but also because of his special relationship with Prague (for more on which see p.69). The city boasts three large-scale theatres where opera is regularly staged, and has three resident orchestras, the most famous of which is the Czech Philharmonic (*Česká filharmonie*), which is based at the Rudolfinum. The country has also produced a host of singers, like the late Ema Destinová, and virtuoso violinists, the latest of whom play with the much praised Suk Quartet.

By far the biggest annual event is the *Pražské jaro* (Prague Spring), the country's most prestigious **international music festival**. It traditionally begins on May 12, the anniversary of Smetana's death, with a performance of *Má vlast* and finishes on June 2 with a rendition of Beethoven's Ninth Symphony. Tickets for the festival sell out fast – try your luck at the festival box office at Hellichova 18, Malá Strana. The main venues are listed below, but keep an eye out for concerts in the city's churches and palaces, gardens and courtyards (the main ones are listed separately below); note that evening performances tend to start fairly early, either at 5 or 7pm.

The main opera houses

Tickets for all three of the city's opera houses can be bought from the official box office at Stavovské divadlo (see below).

Národní divadlo (National Theatre), Národní 2, Nové Město; ☎24 91 34 37; metro Národní třída. Prague's grandest nineteenth-century theatre is the living embodiment of the Czech national revival movement, and continues to put on a wide variety of mostly, though by no means exclusively, Czech plays, opera and ballet. Worth visiting for the decor alone. *Box office open Mon–Fri 10am–6pm, Sat & Sun 10am–12.30pm & 3–6pm.*

Státní opera Praha (Prague State Opera), Wilsonova 4, Nové Město; ☎26 53 53; metro Muzeum. A sumptuous nineteenth-century opera house, built by the city's German community, and now the number-two venue for opera, with a repertoire that tends to focus on Italian pieces. *Box office open Mon–Fri 10am–5.30pm, Sat & Sun 10am–noon & 1–5.30pm.*

Stavovské divadlo (Estates Theatre), Ovocný trh 1, Staré Město; ☎24 21 50 01; metro Můstek. Prague's oldest opera house, which witnessed the première of Mozart's *Don Giovanni*, puts on a mixture of opera, ballet and straight theatre (with simultaneous headphone translation available). *Box office open Mon–Fri 10am–6pm, Sat & Sun 10am–12.30pm & 3–6pm.*

The main concert venues

Rudolfinum, Alšovo nábřeží 12, Staré Město; ☎24 89 31 11; metro Staroměstská. A truly stunning Neo-Renaissance concert hall from the late nineteenth century, and home base for the Czech Philharmonic. *Box office open Mon–Fri 10am–12.30pm & 1–6pm, plus Sat & Sun when concerts are scheduled.*

Smetanova síň, Obecní dům, náměstí Republiky 5, Nové Město; metro náměstí Republiky. Fantastically ornate Art Nouveau concert hall which usually kicks off the Prague Spring festival, but is currently closed for restoration until at least 1996.

Other concert venues

Basilika sv Jakuba (St James), Malá Štupartská, Staré Město; metro náměstí Republiky. Choral church music, sung mass and Prague's finest organ used for regular recitals (see p.94).

Bertramka, Mozartova 169, Smíchov; ☎54 38 93; metro Anděl. Occasional concerts given at the Mozart Museum (see p.159), though not necessarily of the composer's own music.

Chrám sv Mikuláše (St Nicholas), Malostranské náměstí, Mala Strána; metro Malostranská. Prague's most sumptuous Baroque church is the perfect setting for choral concerts and organ recitals (see p.69).

Dům U kamenného zvonu (House at the Stone Bell), Staroměstské náměstí 13, Staré Město; ☎24 81 00 36; metro Staroměstská. An adventurous programme of modern and classical concerts is staged at this contemporary art gallery, housed in an old building on Old Town Square (see p.92).

Klášter sv. Anežký České (Convent of sv Anežka), U milosrdiných 17, Staré Město; ☎24 21 50 18; metro náměstí Republiky. Regular Czech chamber concerts given in the convent's Gothic chapel (see p.95).

Klementinum, Mariánské náměstí, Staré Město; metro Staroměstská. Regular chamber and organ concerts held in the pink Baroque Zrcadlová kaple (Mirrored Chapel – see p.87).

Lichtenštejnský palác (Liechtenstein Palace), Malostranské náměstí 13, Malá Strana; metro Malostranská. The university music department lives here and puts on mostly Baroque music by chamber orchestras and string quartets.

Lobkovický palác (Lobkovic Palace), Jiřská 3, Hradčany; ☎53 73 06; metro Malostranská. Concerts held in the palace's main be-frescoed hall at the eastern edge of Prague Castle (see p.56).

Míčovna, U prašného mostu, Hradčany; tram #22 from metro Malostranská. Renaissance ball game court in the Royal Gardens of Prague Castle (see p.57).

Nostický palác (Nostic Palace), Maltézské náměstí 1, Malá Strana; metro Malostranská. Chamber concerts here start at the civilized hour of 8pm, and include a glass of champagne as part of the ticket price.

Pražský Hlahol, Masarykovo nábřeží 16, Nové Město; ☎232 98 38; Karlovo náměstí. Home to the Hlahol Choir, the hall holds regular concerts on Wednesday evenings and is decorated by, among others, the Art Nouveau artist Alfons Mucha.

Valdštejnská zahrada (Valdštejn Gardens), Letenská, Malá Strana; metro Malostranská. Probably the finest of the summer-only outdoor venues (see p.73).

Theatre

The Arts

Theatre has always had a special place in Czech culture, one which the events of 1989 only strengthened. Not only did the country end up with a playwright as president, but it was the capital's theatres that served as information centres during those first few crucial weeks. The opulent *kamenná divadla* or "stone theatres", still stage serious drama, but the whole scene, for so long heavily subsidized – and censored – by the authorities, is currently going through a difficult patch. Czech audiences have dropped considerably and tourists have become a lucrative source of income at a time when money is desperately needed – there are four or five English-language theatre companies now based in Prague. Ticket prices have risen dramatically, though you can still get into most theatres for less than 100kč; tickets are available from the venues themselves, or for considerably more from the ticket agencies listed on p.215.

Prague also has a strong tradition of **mime** and "**black theatre**" (visual trickery created by "invisible" actors dressed all in black) ranging from the classical style of the late Ladislav Fialka and his troupe to the more experimental work of Boris Polívka. Czechs and foreigners alike turn up to see these shows, whereas Prague's long-running multimedia company, *Laterna magika*, deliberately gears its programme towards tourists. **Puppet theatre** (*loutkové divadlo*) also has a long folk tradition, and is currently enjoying something of a renaissance, thanks to its accessibility to non-Czech audiences. That said, few companies maintain the traditional puppets-only set-up, and most now feature live actors in their productions, many of which can be very wordy making the shows less accessible if you don't speak the language.

Straight theatres

The Stavovské divadlo and the Národní divadlo both put on plays as well as opera and ballet, and are listed on p.216. Below is a selection of Prague's other straight theatres; the phone numbers given are for box offices.

The Arts

Činoherní klub, Ve Smečkách 26, Nové Město; ☎24 21 68 12; metro Muzeum. Regularly puts on good repertoire stuff from ancient to modern literary classics. *Box office open Mon–Sat from 3pm.*

Divadlo Kolowrat, Ovocný trh 6, Staré Město; ☎24 21 50 01; metro Můstek. The National Theatre puts on its more adventurous productions in its studio theatre, situated in a sweaty attic in a newly renovated Baroque palace. *Box office open Mon–Fri 10am–6pm, Sat & Sun 10am–12.30pm & 3–6pm.*

Divadlo na Vinohradech, náměstí Míru 7, Vinohrady; ☎24 25 52; metro náměstí Míru. An ornate nineteenth-century theatre that puts on anything from the classics to comedy (in Czech), and even the occasional concert. *Box office open Mon–Sat 10am–7pm.*

Divadlo na zábradlí, Anenské náměstí 5, Staré Město; ☎24 22 19 33; metro Staroměstská. Havel's old haunt and a centre of absurdist theatre back in the 1960s, it's now a provocative rep theatre, with a wide variety of shows (in Czech). *Box office open Mon–Fri 2–7pm.*

Divadlo v Celetné, Celetná 17, Nové Město; ☎24 81 27 62; metro náměstí Republiky. Student drama venue, which also puts on shows by visiting foreign companies and other tourist-friendly productions (including puppetry). *Box office open one hour before performance.*

Divadlo za branou III, Národní 40, Nové Město; ☎26 00 33; metro Národní třída. Headquarters of Civic Forum during the Velvet Revolution, and once the venue for *Laterna magika*, now in its third reincarnation as a straight theatre venue. *Box office open daily 10am–8pm.*

Labyrint, Štefánikova 57, Smíchov; ☎54 50 27; metro Anděl. One of Prague's main arty fringe theatres, with an excellent basement studio theatre, which stages English-language productions in the summer months. *Box office open Mon–Sat 10am–1pm & 1.30–7pm.*

Studio Ypsilon, Spálená 16, Nové Město; ☎29 22 55; metro Národní třída. One of the city's leading repertoire theatres, with music as well as straight drama (in

Czech). *Box office open Mon–Thurs 2–6pm, Fri 10am–noon & 1–5pm.*

Multimedia, black theatre, music and mime

Archa, Na poříčí 26, Nové Město; ☎232 88 00; metro Florenc. By far the most innovative venue in Prague, with two very versatile spaces, an art gallery and a café. The programming includes music, dance and theatre with an emphasis on the avant-garde. *Box office open Mon–Fri 10am–6pm.*

Branické divadlo (Braník Theatre), Branická 63, Braník; ☎46 27 79; tram #3 or #17, stop Modřanská. Puts on a strange mixture of music, mime and theatre, and hosts an international festival of mime every June.

Divadlo Image, Pařížská 4, Staré Město; ☎24 22 90 78; metro Staroměstská. "Black theatre" and mime productions, unashamedly aimed at the tourist market. *Box office open daily from 1pm.*

Hudební divadlo v Karlíně, Křižíkova 10, Karlín; ☎24 21 07 10; metro Florenc. Puts on a wide range of musicals and operettas, plus mime and the like in its studio. *Box office open Mon–Sat 10am–1pm & 2–6pm.*

Laterna magika (Magic Lantern), Nová scéna, Národní 4, Nové Město; ☎24 91 41 29; metro Národní třída. The National Theatre's *Nová scéna*, one of Prague's most modern and versatile stages, is now the main base for *Laterna magika*, founders of multimedia theatre way back in 1958, now content just to pull in crowds of tourists. *Box office open Mon–Fri 10am–8pm, Sat & Sun 3–8pm.*

Ta Fantastika, Karlova 8, Staré Město; ☎24 22 90 78; metro Staroměstská. A "black theatre" venue, strategically located close to the Charles Bridge, which puts on dialogue-free shows specifically aimed at tourists. *Box office open daily 1–9pm.*

Puppet theatre

Divadlo minor, Senovážné náměstí 28, Nové Město; ☎24 21 32 41; metro náměstí Republiky. The former state puppet theatre puts on children's puppet shows most days, plus adult shows on Thursday evenings. *Box office open Mon–Fri 2–5pm.*

Divadlo Spejbla a Hurvínka, Římská 45, Vinohrady; ☎25 16 66; metro náměstí Míru. Features the indomitable puppet duo, Spejbl and Hurvínek, created by Josef Skupa earlier this century and still going strong at one of the few puppets-only theatres in the country. *Box office open Mon–Fri 3–6pm, Sat 1–5pm.*

Národní divadlo marionet (National Marionette Theatre), Žatecká 1, Staré Město; ☎232 34 29; metro Staroměstská. This company's traditional all-string marionette version of Mozart's *Don Giovanni* has proved extremely popular and has been running without a break for several years now. *Box office open one hour before performance.*

Film

The **cinema** (*kino*) remains a cheap and popular form of entertainment, though since 1989 the majority of films on show have tended to be the standard Hollywood blockbusters. More and more foreign films are being shown in their original language with subtitles (*titulky*) – these are listed in *Prague Post*, but for a comprehensive rundown of the week's films, check out the poster, *Program pražských kin*, pinned up outside most cinemas. Titles are nearly always translated into Czech, so you'll need to have your wits about you to identify films such as *Umělcova smlouva* as *The Draughtsman's Contract*. A film which is dubbed into Czech is indicated by a small white square on the poster. For more on the history of Czech cinema, see *Contexts*. The city's main central screens are either on or just off Wenceslas Square. The **cinemas** listed below include some of the better screens in this area, as well as all that's left of Prague's once vast array of art house film clubs, where you'll need to buy a membership card (*legitimace*) in order to purchase tickets, plus the city's remaining café cinemas (known as *kino-kavárna*). Keep a look out, too, for films shown at the various foreign cultural insti-

tutions around town (see p.230 for addresses). A new event, *Zlatý golem*, has recently been established, and is set to replace Karlovy Vary's annual bash as the country's leading film festival.

Alfa, Václavské náměstí 28, Nové Město; ☎22 07 24; metro Můstek. A sadly underused 70mm screen that is, without doubt, the best place to see new releases.

DIF Centrum, Václavské náměstí 43, Nové Město; ☎24 22 88 14; metro Můstek. Two screens here, including one of the few *kinokavárna* left in Prague.

Dlabačov, Bělohorská 24, Střešovice; ☎311 53 28; tram #22 from metro Malostranská. Film club (membership 25kč) on the ground floor of the Hotel Pyramid, showing a discerning selection of new releases and plenty of other art house classics.

Lucerna, Vodičkova 36, Nové Město; ☎24 21 69 72; metro Můstek/Muzeum. Without doubt the most ornate film theatre in Prague, decked out in Moorish style by Havel's grandfather.

Ponrepo, Národní 40, Nové Město; metro Národní třída. Really old classics from the black-and-white era, dug out from the National Film Archives. Membership cards (120kč) can only be bought Mon–Fri 1–3pm.

Pražský filmový klub, Václavské náměstí 17, Nové Město; ☎26 20 35; metro Můstek. *Kino Praha* runs a very popular film club (membership 25kč) in its second screen, showing some seriously offbeat and unusual material from the archives.

Výstaviště, U výstaviště, Holešovice; ☎871 91 11; tram #5, #12 or #17 from metro Nádraží Holešovice. There are two open-air screens which show films after dark in the summer months, and a multiplex and IMAX screen planned for the future.

The Visual Arts

Prague's permanent art collections are described in detail in the guide section, but the city also boasts a good selection of galleries where **temporary exhibitions** are held. *Prague Post* has full listings, and

The Arts

The Arts

there's a list of foreign cultural institutes, which also put on regular exhibitions on p.230. After years of fairly dull state-approved art, there have been some illuminating and challenging exhibitions in recent years: on previously ignored topics such as Czech Cubism, on relatively "undiscovered" artists such as Josef Váchal, on artists such as Jiří Kolář, who are better known in the West than in their own country, and even reappraisals of socialist realism and the like. Dozens of **commercial galleries** have also sprung up, though few can be relied on regularly to show interesting stuff; below is a selection of the best (the "galerie a výstavy" section of *Přehled* will have a full rundown).

Exhibitions spaces

Belvedér, Mariánské hradby 1, Hradčany; tram #22 from metro Malostranská. One of the most beautiful Renaissance buildings in Prague (see p.58), which usually shows works by contemporary artists, but was closed for restoration work at the time of going to print. *Open Tues–Sun 10am–6pm.*

České muzeum výtvarných umění (Museum of Czech Fine Art), Husova 19–21, Staré Město; metro Staroměstská. Showcases retrospectives of twentieth-century Czech and foreign artists. *Open Tues–Sun 10am–noon & 1–6pm.*

Císařská konírna (Imperial Stables), druhé nádvoří, Hradčany; tram #22 from Malostranská. Temporary exhibition space in Rudolf II's stables, situated in the second courtyard of Prague Castle. *Open Tues–Sun 10am–6pm.*

Dům U černé Matky boží, Ovocný trh, Staré Město; metro náměstí Republiky. First two floors of this new Cubist museum are given over to exhibitions of modern Czech artists. *Open Tues–Sun 10am–6pm.*

Dům U kamenného zvonu, Staroměstské náměstí 13, Staré Město; metro Staroměstská. A real range from Baroque to avant-garde sees the light of day in the small Gothic rooms and courtyard of this ancient building (see p.92). *Open Tues–Sun 10am–6pm.*

Galerie Hollar, Smetanovo nábřeží 6, Nové Město.; metro Národní třída. The main exhibition space for Czech graphic artists. *Open Tues–Sun 10am–1pm & 2–6pm.*

Galerie Jaroslav Fragnera, Betlémské náměstí, Staré Město; metro Národní třída. Gallery space next door to the Bethlehem Chapel used for architectural exhibitions. *Open Tues–Sun 10am–6pm.*

Jízdárna pražkého hradu (Prague Castle Riding School), U prašného mostu, Hradčany; tram #22 from Malostranská. One of the National Gallery's main exhibition spaces, used mostly to display twentieth-century Czech art. *Open Tues–Sun 10am–6pm.*

Karolinum, Ovocný trh 3, Staré Město; metro Můstek. Gothic vaulted room in Prague's Charles University which puts on shows by Czech and foreign artists. *Open daily 10am–6pm.*

Mánes, Masarykovo nábřeží 250, Nové Město; metro Karlovo náměstí. White functionalist building spanning a channel in the Vltava, with an open-plan gallery and a tradition of excellent exhibitions. *Open Tues–Sun 10am–6pm.*

Palác Kinských (Goltz-Kinsky Palace), Staroměstské náměstí 12, Staré Město; metro Staroměstská. Prints and drawings from the National Gallery's collection. *Open Tues–Sun 10am–6pm.*

Rudolfinum, Alšovo nábřeží 12, Staré Město; metro Staroměstská. One of the few galleries which can take large-scale international exhibitions. *Open Tues–Sun 10am–6pm.*

UPM, 17 listopadu 2, Staré Město; metro Staroměstská. The UPM, the city's museum of applied art (see p.111), owns some of finest Czech art in the world, much of which is hidden away in the vaults due to lack of space – be sure to catch their generally excellent temporary exhibitions. *Open Tues–Sun 10am–6pm.*

Valdštejnská jízdárna, Valdštejnská 3, Malá Strana; metro Malostranská. Another National Gallery exhibitions space. *Open Tues–Sun 10am–6pm.*

Commercial galleries

Galerie Behémot, Elišky Krásnohorské 6, Josefov; metro Staroměstská. Avant-garde installations by up-and-coming Czech and Slovak contemporary artists. *Open daily 10am–6pm.*

Galerie Böhm, Anglická 1, Vinohrady; metro I. P. Pavlova. Czech glassmakers lead the world, and more than twenty major contemporary artists exhibit their work here. *Open Tues–Fri 2–6pm, Sat & Sun 10am–3pm.*

Galerie jednorožec s harfou, Průchoní 4, Staré Město; metro Staroměstská. The "Unicorn with a Harp" gallery is located in an alleyway off Konviktská, and show-cases works in a variety of media by contemporary disabled artists. *Open daily 11am–10pm.*

Galerie mladých, Vodičkova 10, Nové Město; metro Můstek. Gothic vaulting and Baroque figurines provide the backdrop for this artists' co-op, which displays works by contemporary young Czech artists (under 35 years of age). *Open Tues–Sun 10am–1pm & 2–6pm.*

Galerie MXM, Nosticova 6, Malá Strana; metro Malostranská. Prague's pioneering and highly influential private gallery puts on consistently good shows by contemporary Czech artists in its one, small vaulted room. *Open Tues–Sun noon–7pm.*

Galerie Pallas, Náprstkova 10, Staré Město; metro Staroměstská. The gem of Prague's private galleries with works by all the greats of the Czech modern art movements of the twentieth century: Alfons Mucha, Cubists Emil Filla and Bohumil Kubišta, plus contemporary artists' works. *Open Mon–Sat 10am–6pm.*

Galerie Petra Brandla, Na slupi 17, Nové Město; metro Vyšehrad. This is where the country's recently returned aristocrats sell off the family silver, or in this case, their Czech and foreign masters – anything from Monet to Mucha – to raise a bit of capital. *Open Mon noon–6pm, Tues–Fri 10am–noon & 12.30–6pm.*

Gambra-surrealisticka galerie, Černínská 5, Hradčany; tram #22 from metro Malostranská. The gallery of Prague's small, but persistent surrealist movement, past and present, hidden in the enchanted backstreets of Hradčany, also provides a window for the works of animator extraordinaire, Jan Švankmajer, and his wife, the artist Eva Švankmajerová. *Open Wed–Sun noon–6pm.*

Pražský dům fotografie, Husova 23, Staré Město; metro Staroměstská. Prime loca-tion on the corner of busy Karlova, and without doubt the best photographic gallery in Prague. *Open daily 11am–6pm.*

Středoevropská galerie, Husova 10 & 21, Staré Město; metro Staroměstská. Czech and foreign artists' works are exhibited in two separate galleries: one, at no. 10, focuses on graphic works, while the other, at no. 21, concentrates on oil paint-ings. *Open daily 10am–6pm.*

The Arts

Chapter 13

Kids' Activities

Being a (nominally) Catholic country, the Czech attitude to kids is generally very positive. That said, you'll see few Czech babies out in the open, unless snuggled up in their giant old-fashioned perambulators, and almost no children in pubs, cafés or even most restaurants. Czechs generally expect children to be unreasonably well behaved and respectful to their elders, and many of the older generation may frown at over-boisterous behaviour. Nevertheless, most kids will enjoy Prague, with its hilly cobbled streets and trams, especially in the summer, when the place is positively alive with buskers and street performers. If you've tried the patience of your offspring with too many Baroque churches and art galleries, any of the suggestions below should head off a rebellion. Most have been covered in the text, so you can get more information by turning to the relevant page; for **sporting** suggestions, see the next section.

Castles Many of the castles outside Prague are at least as much fun for children as adults – try especially Křivoklát (see p.178) and Kokořín (see p.166).

Museums Some which might be of particular interest to children include the National Technical Museum (see p.153); the National Museum (see p.119); the Toy Museum (p.55); the Police Museum (see p.135); and the Military museums (see pp.59 & 148). Another possibility – not covered in the main text – is the **City Transport Museum**, Patočkova 4, Střešovice (tram #1 or #8 from metro Hradčanská), which houses a collection of historic trams and trolleybuses and runs a tram service from the museum to the centre in the summer. *Open April–Oct Sat & Sun 9am–5pm.*

Parks and gardens Playgrounds in parks tend to be rusty (and often potentially dangerous) places, but there are several gardens in which kids can happily expend excess energy. Try any of the following: Valdštejnská zahrada (see p.73), the Royal Gardens (see p.57), Petřín Hill (see below), Letná (see p.152), Vojanovy sady (see p.74), Vyšehrad (see p.137) and Žižkov Hill (see p.147).

Petřín Hill Take the funicular railway to the top for a spectacular view of Prague, followed by a visit to the observatory, the Bludiště (Mirror Maze) and a climb up the miniature Eiffel Tower. See p.78.

Puppet theatre See theatre section of the previous chapter for details about puppet theatre for children in Prague.

Restaurants Czech restaurants do nothing whatsoever to accommodate children. The one exception is, it has to be said, *McDonalds*, which provides a kids' play area in its Vodičkova branch. See p.199.

Swimming Whether the weather's hot or cold, there are plenty of pools to choose from – for more details, see p.225.

Toys There's a list of toy shops given in the shopping chapter, on p.229.

Trams Any tram will do, but, for preference, the regular #22 goes round some great hairpins, across the river and past a fair few city landmarks. In the summer a historic tram (#91) also criss-crosses the city; tickets are more expensive than normal and they run less frequently.

Výstaviště Large turn-of-the-century funfair and a dancing fountain in the summer, as well as a planetarium and adventure playground, *Dětský svět*, open all year. See p.154.

Zoo All the usual beasts and birds in a rather sad and inaccessible locale, plus a children's train, swings and slides. See p.155.

Kids'
Activities

Chapter 14

Sports

The Czech Republic is probably most famous for its world-class tennis players and for its national ice hockey team, but the sport which actually pulls the biggest crowds is soccer. Getting tickets to watch a particular sport is easy (and cheap) enough on the day – even big matches rarely sell out. If you want to check forthcoming sports events, get hold of the Czech weekly, *Program*, or ask at a *PIS* office. Taking part is more difficult – Czechs who do so all belong to local clubs and there are still remarkably few rental facilities for the general public.

Spectator Sports

Prague is a great place to catch live and exciting sports action, especially soccer and ice hockey; and – somewhat unbelievably given the recent spate of football violence – you can still drink inexpensive and delicious beer on the terraces.

Soccer

The break-up of Czechoslovakia may have cut transport costs for clubs in half, but it has had nothing but a detrimental effect on the quality of the country's football league. The most predictable development is that the best home-grown players have, almost without exception, chosen to seek fame and fortune abroad. Another small tragedy was the demise of the old army team, Dukla Praha – immortalized in the pop song *All I Want for Christmas is a Dukla Prague Away-Kit* by British band Half Man Half Biscuit – which

was forced into the amateur league due to financial difficulties.

For years cosseted by state backing, all the county's clubs are having to learn fast how to survive in the market. Big money is being pumped into certain clubs by local entrepreneurs, accompanied by the odd scandal – the owner of Švarc Benešov was arrested on embezzlement charges – and wrangling over TV rights for the new Czech league. Nevertheless, true to form, Prague's, and the Czech Republic's, top soccer team, Sparta Praha, won the first all-Czech league title, though they lost out to Viktoria Žižkov, in the first-ever Czech-Moravian Cup Final. The season runs from September to December and March to June, and matches are usually held on a Sunday afternoon.

Prague is dominated by four main teams, including the country's top club, **Sparta Praha**, now owned by Opel car dealer Petr Mach, who have won over twenty league titles and look set to maintain their hold over Czech football for some time to come. They play at the country's finest, and newly renovated Sparta stadium, by the Letná plain (five minutes' walk from metro Hradčanská); international matches are also regularly played there. Traditionally Sparta's closest rivals, **Slavia Praha** are used to coming second in everything; their ground is in Vršovice, just off U Slavie (tram #4 or #22 from metro náměstí Míru). Slavia are having to look over their shoulder though, for coming up behind them, backed by big bucks, are **Viktoria Žižkov**, a previously little-known club now owned by self-made man, Vratislav Čekan. Viktoria's ground is on Seifertova (tram #5, #9 or #26 from metro Hlavní nádraží). Prague's fourth and least successful professional side, **Bohemians Praha**, play just south of Vršovické náměstí (tram #4 or #22 from metro náměstí Míru).

Ice hockey

Ice hockey runs soccer a close second as the nation's most popular sport. It's not unusual to see kids playing their own form of the game in the street, rather than kicking a football around. As with soccer, the break-up of the Republic has affected the quality of the game, but ice hockey received an unexpected boost with the return of several exiled stars from North America's National Hockey League. Their arrival gave the game some badly needed media attention, and halted the slide in attendances, though they are unlikely to stay in the Czech league for good.

Games are fast and physical, cold but compelling viewing, and can take anything up to three hours; they take place on Tuesday and Friday at around 6pm, and sometimes Sunday afternoon. The season starts at the end of September and culminates in the annual World Championships the following summer, when the fortunes of the national side are subject to close scrutiny, especially if pitched against the old enemy Russia, not to mention their former-bed-mate and new rival, Slovakia. A double victory against the Soviets in 1969 precipitated riots in towns across the country, culminating in the torching of the Soviet airline *Aeroflot's* offices in Prague.

Unlike in football, **Sparta Praha** are only one of a number of successful teams, and the league is usually hotly contested. Sparta's *zimní stadión* (winter stadium) is next door to the Výstaviště exhibition grounds in Holešovice (metro nádraží Holešovice). Prague's only other first division team are the newly promoted **Slavia Praha**, who play at the *zimní stadión* to the south of the Havlíčkovy sady in Vršovice (tram #4 or #22 from metro náměstí Míru).

Tennis

Tennis has been one of the country's most successful exports, although the country holds no major international events and its national Davis Cup team have a fairly poor record. Martina Navrátilová, now in retirement, has been the most consistent Czech player on the circuit, although she became a naturalized American some years ago. On the men's side, Ivan Lendl, also now retired, has been a towering figure in world tennis since the mid-1980s, even though a Wimbledon title always eluded him. These two are a difficult double act to follow, and although Jana Novotná and Karel Nováček are both promising young stars, neither has managed to take a Grand Slam title as yet. Any home-grown talent there is will be on display in the Czech Open, held every August in Prague on Štvanice ostrov, the island on the Hlávkův most (metro Florenc).

Horse racing

Prague's main racecourse is at **Velká Chuchle**, 5km or so south of the city centre; bus #129, #172, #241, #243, #244, #255 or *osobní* train from metro Smíchovské nádraží. Steeplechases and hurdles take place on Sunday afternoons from May to October; trots all year round on Thursdays. There's a smaller trot course on **Císařský ostrov** (May–Oct only); walk through the Stromovka park and across the river to the island from metro Nádraží Holešovice.

Participatory Sports

At present there isn't a great deal to choose from, but the situation is improving; the big drawback remains the lack of facilities for renting equipment. However, anyone keen on working out will have no problems as there are numerous public gyms.

Swimming

The waters of the Vltava, Beroun and Labe are all pretty polluted – the Sázava is marginally better – so for a clean swim it's best to head for one of the city's

Sports

Sports

swimming pools, though these, too, can be of varying water quality.

Hotel Axa, Na poříčí 20, Nové Město; metro Florenc. A 25m indoor pool – the oldest and largest of the hotel pools in Prague. *Open Mon–Fri 5–10pm, Sat 9am–6pm, Sun 9am–8pm.*

Koupaliště Divoká Šárka, Divoká Šárka, Vokovice; tram #20 or #26 from metro Dejvická. Idyllically located in a craggy valley to the northwest of Prague, with two small oudoor pools filled with cold but fresh and clean water – great for a full, hot day out. Food and drink and plenty of shade available, too. *Open daily 9am–7pm.*

Koupaliště Oáza, Novodvorská, Lhotka; bus #106, #121, #139 or #170 from metro Kačerov. Deep pool with sandy borders set in a park; wading pool and bouncy castle for children. Food, beer and ice cream available. *Open daily 9am–7pm.*

Plavecký stadión Podolí, Podolská, Podolí; tram #3, #17 or #21 from metro Karlovo náměstí, stop Kublov. Well-heated 50m indoor pool, plus two smaller outdoor ones and a childrens' wading pool and water slide. *Open daily 6am–9.45pm.*

Plavecký stadión Slavia, Vladivostocká 2, Vršovice; tram #7 from metro Strašnická. Clean, indoor pool in winter; outdoor only in summer. *Open Mon–Fri 6am–7.45pm, Sat & Sun 9am–6.45pm.*

Ice skating

Given the nation's penchant for ice hockey, it's not surprising that **ice skating** (*bruslení*) is Prague's most popular winter activity. There's no shortage of rinks (*zimní stadión*) in the city, although public opening hours are limited, and of course there are the city's two reservoirs, Hostivař and Šárka, which regularly freeze over in winter. Most rinks don't rent out skates, and those that do have only a limited selection. Your best bet is to buy a pair from shops like *Bílá labuť* or *Sport YMCA*, both on Na poříčí, Nové Město (metro

Florenc); men's skates tend to be for ice hockey, women's for figure skating – either will set you back around £25/$40.

Štvanice, Štvanice ostrov, Holešovice; five-minute walk on to the island from metro Florenc. Skate rental is available but the rink is only open to the public for a very limited period. *Open Fri 7.30–10pm, Sat 1–3.30pm, Sun 8.30–11am.*

USK (University Sports Club), Sámova, Vršovice; tram #7 or #24 from Karlovo náměstí. Located just below the Havlíčkovy sady, with long weekend opening hours but no skate rental. *Open Sat & Sun 8.30am–4.45pm.*

Výstaviště, U výstaviště, Holešovice; metro Nádraží Holešovice. Skating takes place in the *malá hala* behind the big ice hockey stadium; rental is from the basement. *Open Fri 3–6pm, Sat & Sun 1–6pm.*

Gyms and saunas

There's no shortage of fitness centres and hotels in Prague with good gyms, saunas and masseurs – rates are generally very low compared to the West, but hours are erratic so check before you go.

Body and Fitness Club, Bolzanova 7, Nové Město; ☎24 22 73 96; metro Hlavní nádraží. Small weight-training gym with modern equipment and air-con; massage also available. *Open Mon–Fri 2–9.30pm, Sat & Sun 4–8pm.*

Hotel Axa, Na poříčí 20, Nové Město; ☎232 39 67; metro Florenc. Very reasonably priced gym, sauna, first-rate massage and 25m indoor pool (see above for swimming times). *Gym open Mon–Fri 8am–10pm, Sat & Sun 9am–6pm; sauna open Mon–Fri 8am–11pm, Sat 9am–6pm & Sun 9am–8pm; massage Mon–Fri 9am-10pm, Sat 9am–noon, Sun 9am–8pm.*

Hotel Forum, Kongressová 4, Nusle; ☎61 19 13 26; metro Vyšehrad. Pool, sauna, weights, solarium and massage – pricey, but luxurious, with an amazing view over Prague. *Open Mon–Fri 7am–9pm, Sat & Sun 9am–8pm.*

Chapter 15

Shopping

Consumer goods always had a low priority under the centralized state-run economy of the Communist system, and the country is only now beginning to develop a significant consumer culture. Despite enormous improvements over the past few years, service is still surly, and the variety and quality of the goods suspect.

Even bargains are becoming harder to track down, as factories across the country close. In their place the market has been flooded with goods from multinationals like *Benetton*, charging prices the same as in the West. The few bargains that still exist are in goods like glass, ceramics, wooden toys, cutlery, CDs, cassettes, LPs and books and, of course, smoked meats, salamis and alcohol, all of which the Czechs continue to produce at a fraction of western prices.

Department Stores

For most basic goods, you're best off heading for one of Prague's three department stores, which stock most things – including toiletries, stationery and usually an extensive food and drink selection. The prices are low, but so, generally, is the quality.

Bílá labuť, Na poříčí 23, Nové Město; metro Florenc. Built in the 1930s, when its functionalist design turned more than a few heads, but nowadays in need of serious renovation. *Open Mon–Fri 8am–7pm, Sat 8am–6pm.*

Kmart, Národní 26, Nové Město; metro Národní třída. Neo-functionalist store on

four floors, selling everything from food to hi-fi goods, now owned by cheap and cheerful American company. *Open Mon–Wed 6.30am–7pm, Thurs & Fri 6.30am–8pm, Sat 7am–6pm, Sun 10am–5pm.*

Kotva, náměstí Republiky 8, Nové Město; metro náměstí Republiky. Ugly, Swedish-built store, spread over five floors, with a food section in the basement, now run by *Kmart. Open Mon–Wed & Fri 8am–7pm, Thurs 8am–8pm, Sat 8am–2pm.*

Markets and Food Stores

Prague is chronically short of good **markets** of all types, despite the introduction of free enterprise. For bread, butter, cheese, wine and beer, you can simply go to the nearest *potraviny* or supermarket. These have changed enormously since 1989 in terms of what they stock, but are still a long way from the superstores of the western world. Again, low prices are the main draw. For health-food-starved visitors, a few outlets now stock some basic items, as listed below.

Markets

Havelská, Staré Město; metro Můstek. Food, flowers and wooden toys are sold in the only open-air fruit and veg market in central Prague. *Open Mon–Fri 8am–6pm, Sat & Sun 8am–2pm.*

Pražská tržnice, Bubenské nábřeží, Holešovice; metro Vltavská. Prague's largest market, a sprawling mass of cheap stalls housed in a disused abattoir. *Open Mon–Fri 6am–6pm, Sat 6am–2pm.*

Shopping

Sparta, Milady Horákové, Holešovice; five minutes' walk from metro Hradčanská. Seedy flea market resembling a giant car-boot sale, held in Sparta Praha football stadium. *Open Sat & Sun 8am–12.30pm.*

Specialist food stores

Country Life, Melantrichova 15, Staré Město; metro Můstek. All the health food staples from dried bananas to seaweed, plus freshly baked wholemeal bread. *Open Mon–Thurs 8.30am–6.30pm, Fri 8.30am–3pm, Sun noon–6pm.*

Fruits de France, Jindřišská 9, Nové Město; metro Můstek. Unusually good selection of fruit and vegetables, plus various other longer-lasting delights flown in fresh from France. *Open Mon–Wed & Fri 9.30am–6.30pm, Thurs 11.30am–6.30pm, Sat 9.30am–1pm.*

Hisho, Havelská 6, Staré Město; metro Můstek. Expensive Japanese deli. *Open daily 11am–midnight.*

J & J Mašek, Karmelitská 30, Malá Strana; tram #12 or #22 from metro Malostranská. Prague's number one deli, which stocks excellent game and fish. *Open Mon–Fri 8am–6pm, Sat 8am–noon.*

Košer potraviny, Břehová, Josefov; metro Staroměstská. Disappointing kosher grocery for the strict adherent only. *Open Mon–Fri 10am–6pm.*

Moby Dick, Strossmajerovo náměstí 11, Holešovice; metro Vltavská. Fresh fish and seafood arrives Tuesdays and Fridays at this fishmongers, which sells mostly to wholesalers – check out the cheap Russian caviar. *Open Mon–Fri 9.30am–6pm, Sat 9am–4pm.*

Books, Maps and Graphics

Prague is now home to numerous English-language bookstores, which thrive on the large ex-pat community. The city is also replete with second-hand bookstores (*antik-variát*), though these are often pricey antiquarian-type places rather than cheap, rambling stores; however, many also stock a goodly selection of old prints and posters.

Antikvariát Galerie Můstek, 28 října, Nové Město; metro Můstek. Centrally located *antikvariát* with one of the largest selection of old maps, prints and paintings in town. *Open Mon–Fri 10am–5pm, Sat 10am–1pm.*

Big Ben Book Shop, Rybná 2, Staré Město; metro náměstí Republiky. Small, soulless bookstore with cheap paperbacks and lots of language courses. *Open Mon–Thurs 9am–6pm, Fri 9.30am–6.30pm, Sat 10am–3pm.*

Bohemian Ventures, náměstí Jana Palacha, Staré Město; metro Staroměstská. Located on the ground floor of the university's philosophy faculty, this shop specializes in new English-language books, including cheap Penguin classics and heaps of dictionaries. *Open Mon–Fri 9am–5pm.*

Dušní, Dušní 6, Staré Město; metro Staroměstská. *Antikvariát* with big selection of second-hand Czech, German, French and English books. *Open Mon–Fri 10am–6pm, Sat 10am–1pm.*

The Globe, Janovského, Holešovice; tram #1, #8, #25 or #26 from metro Hradčanská. The ex-pat bookstore *par excellence*: both a social centre and superbly well-stocked ramshackle store, with an adjacent café and friendly staff. *Open daily 10am–midnight.*

Karel Křenek, Celetná 32, Staré Město; metro náměstí Republiky. High-quality second-hand and antiquarian dealer, with a handful of English books, and lots of old maps, graphics and art books. *Open Mon–Fri 10am–6pm, Sat 10am–2pm.*

U knihomola (The Bookworm), Mánesova 79, Vinohrady; metro Jiřího z Poděbrad. Much larger selection of art and coffee-table books (some at extortionate prices) and a classier range all round, than its rival, *The Globe*; the café in the basement is quiet and relaxed. *Open Mon–Fri 9am–midnight, Sat 10am–midnight, Sun 11am–6pm.*

Music

Czech CDs are no longer the bargain they once were, though they are still priced a tad lower than in the West; cassettes and LPs are significantly cheaper. Classical buffs will fare best of all, not just with the Czech composers, but cheap copies of Mozart, Vivaldi and other favourites.

Karel Schuss, Národní 25, Nové Město; metro Národní třída. The best second-hand record store in Prague, particularly good for jazz and folk, but also rock/pop – not much in the way of classical. *Open Mon–Sat 11.30am–7.30pm.*

Maximum Underground, Dlouhá 36, Staré Město; metro náměstí Republiky. The best indie record shop in town, very strong on new wave and punk, and even some ragga, rave and world music. *Open Mon–Fri 10am–7pm, Sat noon–7pm.*

Music Word CD, Benediktská 9, Staré Město; metro náměstí Republiky. Zero browsability, but something of a mecca for Czech pop and rock fans – CDs only. *Mon–Fri 8am–7pm, Sat 8am–4pm.*

Popron, Jungmannova 30, Nové Město; metro Můstek. Calls itself a "megastore" – strongest on pop and rock CDs, though it does stock jazz and classical (not to mention video games). *Open Mon–Sat 9.30am–7pm, Sun 10am–6pm.*

Studio Matouš, Staroměstské náměstí, Staré Město; metro Staroměstská. Excellent selection of classical CDs on the ground floor of the Goltz-Kinsky Palace. *Open daily 10.30am–6pm.*

Supraphon, Jungmannova 20, Nové Město; metro Můstek. Classical CDs, cassettes and LPs. *Open Mon–Fri 9am–7pm, Sat 9am–1pm.*

Souvenirs, Toys and Antiques

Tacky tourist gifts – Kafka T-shirts, Mucha merchandise and Gorby/Yeltsin matrioshka dolls – are mostly sold from market stalls set up along the main tourist thoroughfares. For better quality goods and more specialist gifts, try some of the shops listed below.

Amor, Václavské náměstí 40, Nové Město; metro Muzeum. Czech garnets are among the best in the world, and this shop has some unusually interesting pendants and brooches. *Open Mon–Fri 9am–8pm, Sat & Sun 9am–6pm.*

Antikva Nova Praga, Štěpánská 24, Nové Město; metro Muzeum. Lithographs, drawings, acrylic and oil paintings mostly by Czech artists. *Open Mon–Fri 10am–1pm & 2–6pm.*

Art Deco Galerie, Michalská 21, Staré Město; metro Můstek. Clothes, shoes, coffee sets, lamps and accessories all dating from the turn of the century or between the wars. *Open Mon–Fri 2–6pm.*

Cristallino, Celetná 12, Staré Město; metro náměstí Republiky. Good selection of crystal and glass in fairly traditional designs. *Open daily 9am–8pm.*

Furalo, Václavské náměstí 60, Nové Město; metro Muzeum. Eclectic range of Czech crystal from trad to modern. *Open daily 9am–6pm.*

Lidová řemesla, Jilská 22, Staré Město; metro Staroměstská. Good selection of Czech folk art from painted eggshells and linen to straw and corn dolls. *Open Mon–Sat 10am–7.30pm.*

Loutkami, Nerudova 47, Malá Strana; metro Malostranská. Quite the widest selection of puppets, old and new, for sale anywhere in Prague: hand, glove and rod puppets, plus marionettes. *Open daily 9.30am–8pm.*

Manhartský dům, Celetná 12, Staré Město; metro náměstí Republiky. Performance-quality marionettes at high prices. *Open daily 10am–6pm.*

Senior bazar, Senovážné náměstí; Nové Město; metro náměstí Republiky. One of the best second-hand clothes stores in the city, with men's and women's clothing at knock-down prices. *Open Mon–Thurs 8.30am–3.30pm.*

U Šaška, Jilská 7, Staré Město; metro Staroměstská. One of the country's most successful exports has always been its simple wooden toys for kids – this store stocks some of the best at very reasonable prices. *Open Mon–Fri 9.30am–9pm, Sat & Sun 10.30am–9.30pm.*

Zlatá koruna, Pařížská 8, Josefov; metro Staroměstská. Heaps of old coins and medals. *Open Mon–Fri 10am–7pm, Sat 10am–6pm.*

Shopping

Chapter 16

Directory

AIRLINES *Aeroflot*, Pařížská 28, Josefov; ☎ 24 81 26 82; metro Staroměstská. *Alitalia*, Revoluční 5, Nové Město; ☎ 24 81 00 79; metro náměstí Republiky. *British Airways*, Staroměstské náměstí 10, Staré Město; ☎ 232 90 20; metro Staroměstská. *Czechoslovak Airlines*, Kotva, Revoluční 1, Nové Město; ☎ 24 80 61 11; metro náměstí Republiky. *Delta*, Národní 32, Nové Město; ☎ 26 85 21; metro Národní třída. *KLM*, Václavské náměstí 37, Nové Město; ☎ 24 22 86 80; metro Můstek/ Muzeum. *Lufthansa*, Pařížská 28, Josefov; ☎ 24 81 10 07; metro Staroměstská.

AMERICAN EXPRESS *Amex*, Václavské náměstí 56, Nové Město; ☎ 24 22 98 83; metro Muzeum. *Open Mon–Fri 9am–6pm, Sat 9am–noon; slightly longer hours in summer.*

BIKE RENTAL *Rent-A-Bike*, Školská 12, Nové Město; metro Národní třída; *Landa*, Šumavská 33, Vinohrady; metro náměstí Míru.

BOTTLES The Czech Republic has yet to become a fully paid-up member of the throw-away culture and many drinks still come in glass bottles with a deposit on them. For non-deposit bottles, there are now numerous bottle banks scattered around Prague.

ČEDOK offices within the Republic are even less useful than their foreign branches. The only office you may need to use is at Na příkopě 18, Nové Město, which sells international train, bus and boat tickets, and organizes guided tours.

CIGARETTES Loosely packed and lethal, the only virtue of Czech cigarettes is their cheapness. Top of the domestic range is *sparta*, named after the country's leading soccer team. The workers smoke *mars* or *start*, while the rest smoke *petra*. Havel switched from the latter to *Marlboro* once he became president – all other western brands are available at standard continental prices. *Duma* rolling tobacco is widely available; domestic brands and their cigarette papers are worth avoiding. Matches are *sirky* or *zápalky*.

CONTRACEPTIVES Condoms (*kondom* or *prezervativ*) are now available in metro stations in the centre of Prague from machines marked *Men's Shop*, *Easy Shop* or some such euphemism. They're also on sale from pharmacies.

CULTURAL INSTITUTES

American Centre for Culture and Commerce, Hybernská 7a, Nové Město; ☎ 24 23 10 85; metro náměstí Republiky. Exhibitions and video showings, plus an excellent library with books, papers and magazines. *Exhibitions open Mon–Fri 9am–4pm; library open Mon, Tues & Thurs 11am–5pm, Wed noon–5pm, Fri 11am–3pm.*

British Council, Národní 10, Nové Město; ☎ 24 91 21 79; metro Národní třída. A window gallery for temporary exhibitions; newspapers and magazines in the foyer and the top floor reading room; Sky TV in the auditorium and various events during the year. There's an English-language teaching library and resources centre in the basement. *Open Mon–Fri 9am–4pm; closed July & Aug.*

French Institute, Štěpánská 35, Nové Město; ☎24 21 66 30; metro Muzeum. Great exhibitions and a great café, with croissants and *journeaux*; also puts on more or less daily screenings of classic French films, plus lectures and even the odd concert. *Open Mon–Fri 9am–6pm.*

Goethe Institute, Masarykovo nábřeží 32, Nové Město; ☎24 91 57 25; metro Národní třída. Weekly film showings and more frequent lectures; small exhibition space and café. *Open Mon–Fri 9am–6pm.*

Hungarian Cultural Centre, Rytířská 25, Staré Město; ☎24 22 24 24; metro Můstek. Weekly film showings and regular exhibitions. *Open Mon–Fri 10am–6pm.*

Polish Cultural Centre, Václavské náměstí 19, Nové Město; ☎24 21 47 08; metro Můstek. Weekly film showings, occasional concerts and lectures. *Open Mon–Fri 9am–5pm, Sat 9am–noon.*

ELECTRICITY This is the standard continental 220 volts AC. Most European appliances should work as long as you have an adaptor for European-style two-pin round plugs. North Americans will need this plus a transformer.

EMBASSIES/CONSULATES

Belgium, Valdštejnská 6, Malá Strana; ☎24 51 05 32; metro Malostranská.

Britain, Thunovská 14, Malá Strana; ☎24 54 04 39; metro Malostranská.

Canada, Mickiewiczova 6, Hradčany; ☎24 31 11 08; metro Hradčanská.

Denmark, U páté baterie, Střešovice; ☎24 31 19 19; tram #1 or #18 from metro Hradčanská.

France, Velkopřevorské náměstí 2, Malá Strana; ☎24 51 04 02; metro Malostranská.

Finland, Dřevná 2, Nové Město; ☎24 91 35 94; metro Karlovo náměstí.

Germany, Vlašská 19, Malá Strana; ☎24 51 03 23; metro Malostranská.

Hungary Badeniho 1, Hradčany; ☎36 50 41; metro Hradčanská.

Norway, Na Ořechovce 69, Střešovice; ☎35 45 26; tram #1, #8 or #18 from metro Hradčanská.

Sweden, Úvoz 13, Malá Strana; ☎24 51 04 36; metro Malostranská.

USA, Tržiště 15, Malá Strana; ☎24 51 08 47; metro Malostranská.

EXCHANGE OFFICES 24-hour service at Staroměstské náměstí 21, Staré Město, metro Staroměstská; 28 října 13, Nové Město, metro Můstek; Vodičkova 41, Nové Město, metro Můstek.

GAY/LESBIAN There is no great "scene" in Prague as such, but there are a few bars and clubs that have become an established part of Prague nightlife (details on p.213) and even a gay-friendly hotel (see p.190). For information and help with accommodation, go to the *Gay Information Centre*, Krakovská 3, Nové Město; ☎26 44 08; metro Muzeum; *open April–Oct only*. Another good source of information is the *Mercury Club*, Kolínská 11, Vinohrady; ☎67 31 06 03; metro Flora. Alternatively, pick up a copy of the *SOHO revue*, a monthly Czech gay magazine, with a brief section in English and some useful listings. *Lambda* (Zborovská 22, Smíchov; ☎54 91 27; metro Anděl), the organization for Czech gays and lesbians, which started up in 1989, holds meetings at the *Mercury Club*: every other Thurs for gay men, Wed for lesbians. *Promluv*, (Volšinách 50, Strašnice; ☎781 71 58; metro Strašnická) is a more radical lesbian organization, who held the first gay festival in 1995. The age of consent in the Czech Republic is 15 whatever your sexual orientation.

KIDS/BABIES Hotels and private landlords are generally very accommodating, but you'll rarely see any children in restaurants. Kids under ten travel free on public transport within Prague, while those under five go free on trains; five- to ten-year olds pay half-fare. Disposable nappies are available in most department stores, but convenience food for babies is thin on the ground. Some private landlords will baby-sit by prior arrangement. For a list of specific places to take children in Prague, see pp.222–223.

Directory

Directory

LANGUAGE SCHOOLS *Angličtina expres,* Vodičkova 39, Nové Město, charges around 3000kč a month for eight hours of Czech lessons a week; *Jazyková škola,* Národní 20, Nové Město, charges around 4000kč a year for three lessons a week. All-inclusive month-long beginners' courses in Czech cost around £400/$640 for the month, which includes half-board accommodation. For further details (and possible financial assistance), contact the British Council in Prague (see previous page).

LAUNDRIES Most Czechs still wash their clothes by hand or leave them at a *čistírna,* where they are washed, dried, ironed and neatly folded. If time isn't a problem, try *Čistírna oděvů,* Opletalova 16, Nové Město; metro Muzeum/Hlavní nádraž.; open Mon–Fri 8am–6pm. Ex-pats tend to head for self-service launderettes: *Laundry Kings,* Dejvická 16; ☎312 37 43; metro Hradčanská; open daily 8am–10pm, is very much part of the ex-pat scene. The other American-style launderette is *Laundryland,* Londýnská 71, Vinohrady; ☎25 11 24; metro náměstí Míru/I. P. Pavlova; open daily 8am–10pm.

LEFT LUGGAGE Most bus and train stations have lockers and/or a 24-hour left-luggage office, which officially only take bags under 15kg. If your bag is very heavy, say *promiňte, je těžký* and offer to carry it to the locker yourself – *já to vezmu.* To work the lockers, put a crown in the slot on the inside of the door and set the code (choose a number you can easily remember and make a note of it), then shut the door. To re-open it, set the code on the outside and wait a few seconds before trying the door. The lockers are usually checked every night, and the contents of any still occupied are taken to the 24-hour left-luggage office.

LIBRARIES The following libraries all stock English-language books and are open to the general public – the *CEU* has the largest selection.

American Centre for Culture and Commerce, Hybernská 7a, Nové Město; ☎24 23 10 85; metro náměstí Republiky; open Mon, Tues & Thurs 11am–5pm, Wed noon–5pm, Fri 11am–3pm.

British Council, Národní 10, Nové Město; ☎24 91 21 79; metro Národní třída; open Mon–Fri 9am–4pm.

Central European University (CEU) Táboritská 23, Žižkov; ☎27 97 31; tram #5, #9 or #26 from metro Hlavní nádraží; open Mon–Fri 9am–11pm, Sat & Sun 1–8pm.

PHARMACIES Late-night pharmacies include Na příkopě 7, Nové Město; open daily until 8pm, Sat & Sun 24-hr emergency service; metro Můstek: Štefánikova 6, Smíchov; open daily 7pm–7am; metro Anděl: and Volšinách 41, Strašnice; open daily 8pm–7am; metro Strašnická.

RACISM It is a sad fact that racism in the Czech Republic is a casual and common phenomenon, the country's 250,000-strong Romany minority bearing the brunt of the nation's ignorance and prejudice. Another alarming development is the rise of right-wing extremism and the skinhead movement, who have been responsible for attacks on Romanies, Vietnamese and even foreign black tourists. That said, the most you're likely to experience on a short visit is a certain amount of curiosity, understandable from a country which remains for the most part, monocultural.

RELIGIOUS SERVICES Anglican, sv Kilment, Klimentská 5, Nové Město; *Sun 11am*; metro náměstí Republiky. **Baptist** Vinohradská 68, Vinhorady; Sun 11am; metro Jiřho z Poděbrad. **Catholic** (in English), sv Josef, Josefská, Malá Strana; Sun 10.30am; metro Malostranská. **Interdenominational,** Czech Brethren, Vrázova 4, Smíchov; Sun 11.15am; metro Anděl. **Jewish Orthodox,** Old-New Synagogue, Červená, Josefov; Mon & Thurs 8am, Sat 9am; metro Staroměstská. **Jewish Reform,** Jerusalem Synagogue, Jeruzalemská, Nové Město; May–Sept Fri 4pm, Sat 8.45am and Oct–April Fri 7.30pm, Sat 8.45am; metro Hlavní nádraží.

TAMPONS Tampons (*tampóny*) and sanitary towels (*dámské vložky*) are cheap and easy to get hold of in major department stores (see p.227).

THOMAS COOK Václavské náměstí 47, Nové Město; ☎26 31 06; metro Můstek;

open Mon–Fri 9am–9pm, Sat 9am–4pm, Sun 10am–2pm.

TIME The Czech Republic is generally one hour ahead of Britain and six hours ahead of EST, with the clocks going forward as late as May and back again some time in September – the exact date changes from year to year. Generally speaking, Czechs use the 24hr clock.

TOILETS Apart from the automatic ones in central Prague, toilets (*záchody, toalety* or *WC*) are few and far between. In most, you can buy toilet paper (by the sheet) from the attendant, whom you will usually have to pay as you enter. Standards of hygiene are generally fairly low.

WOMEN The Czech Republic remains a conservative and patriarchal society, despite the upheaval of 1989. The atmosphere in Prague is slightly more liberated than in the rest of the country, however, and street-level sexual harassment rarely approaches levels experienced in some western countries. Pubs are about the only places where men always predominate; the usual commonsense precautions apply here and elsewhere. Feminism and women's issues keep a very low profile in the Czech Republic. The city's only feminist organization is the *Centre for Gender Studies*, Legerova 39, Vinohrady; metro Muzeum/I. P. Pavlova.

Directory

Metric Weights and Measures	
1 ounce = 28.3 grammes	1 pint = 0.47 litres
1 inch = 2.54 centimetres (cm)	1.09 yards = 1m
1 pound = 454 grammes	1 quart = 0.94 (l.)
1 foot = 0.3 metres (m)	1 mile = 1.61 kilometres (km)
2.2 pounds = 1 kilogramme	1 gallon = 3.78 (l.)
1 yard = 0.91 m	0.62 miles = 1km

The Contexts

A History of Prague

The famous pronouncement (attributed to Bismarck) that "he who holds Bohemia holds mid-Europe" gives a clear indication of the pivotal role the region has played in European history. As the capital of Bohemia, Prague has been fought over and occupied by German, Austrian, French and even Swedish armies. Consequently, it is virtually impossible to write a historical account of the city without frequent reference to the wider events of European history. One of the constant themes that runs throughout Prague's history, however, has been the conflicts between the city's Germans and Czechs, Protestants and Catholics. The history of Prague as the capital of, first Czechoslovakia, and now the Czech Republic, is less than a hundred years old, beginning with the foundation of the country in 1918. Since then, the country's numerous tragedies, mostly focused on Prague, have been exposed to the world at regular intervals – 1938, 1948, 1968 and, most recently (and most happily), 1989.

Beginnings

According to Roman records, the area now covered by Bohemia was inhabited as early as 500 BC by a Celtic tribe – the **Boii**, who gave their name to the region. Very little is known about the Boii except that around 100 BC they were driven from their territory by a Germanic tribe, the **Marcomanni**, who occupied Bohemia.

The Marcomanni were a semi-nomadic people and later proved awkward opponents for the Roman Empire, which wisely chose to use the River Danube as its natural eastern border.

The disintegration of the Roman Empire in the fifth century AD corresponded with a series of raids into central Europe by eastern tribes: firstly the **Huns,** who displaced the Marcomanni, and later the **Avars,** who replaced the Huns around the sixth century, settling a vast area including the Hungarian plains and parts of what is now Slovakia. Around the same time, the **Slav tribes** entered Europe from somewhere east of the Carpathian mountains. To begin with, at least, they appear to have been subjugated by the Avars. The first successful Slav rebellion against the Avars seems to have taken place in the seventh century, under the Frankish leadership of **Samo**, though the kingdom he created, which was centred on Bohemia, died with him around 658 AD.

The Great Moravian Empire

The next written record of the Slavs in the region isn't until the eighth century, when East Frankish (Germanic) chroniclers report a people known as the **Moravians** as having established themselves around the River Morava, a tributary of the Danube. It was an alliance of Moravians and Franks (under Charlemagne) which finally expelled the Avars from central Europe in 796 AD. This cleared the way for the establishment of the **Great Moravian Empire**, which at its peak included Slovakia, Bohemia and parts of Hungary and Poland. Its significance in terms of Czech-Slovak relations is that it was the first and last time (until the establishment of Czechoslovakia, for which it served as a useful precedent) that the Czechs and Slovaks were united under one ruler.

The first attested ruler of the empire, **Mojmír**, found himself at the political and religious crossroads of Europe under pressure from two sides: from the west, where the Franks and Bavarians (both Germanic tribes) were jostling for position with the papacy; and from the east, where the Patriarch of Byzantium was keen to extend his influence across eastern Europe. Mojmír's successor, **Rastislav** (850–870), plumped for Byzantium, and invited the missionaries Cyril and Methodius to introduce Christianity, using the Slav liturgy and Eastern rites. Rastislav, however, was ousted by his nephew, **Svätopluk** (871–894), who captured and blinded his uncle, allying himself with the Germans instead. With the death of Methodius in 885, the Great Moravian Empire fell decisively under the influence of the Catholic Church.

Svätopluk died shortly before the **Magyar invasion** of 896, an event which heralded the end of the Great Moravian Empire and a significant break in Czecho-Slovak history. The Slavs to the west of the River Morava (the Czechs) swore allegiance to the Frankish Emperor, Arnulf; while those to the east (the Slovaks) found themselves under the yoke of the Magyars. This separation, which continued for the next millennium, is one of the major factors behind the distinct social, cultural and political differences between Czechs and Slovaks, which culminated in the separation of the two nations in 1993.

The Přemyslid Dynasty: legends and history

The Czechs have a **legend** for every occasion and the founding of Bohemia and Prague are no exception. The mythical mound of Říp, the most prominent of the pimply hills in the Labe (Elbe) plain, north of Prague, is where **Čech**, the leader of a band of wandering Slavs, is alleged to have founded his new kingdom, Čechy (Bohemia). His brother Lech, meanwhile, headed further north to found Poland.

Some time in the seventh or eighth century AD, **Krok** (aka Pace), a descendant of Lech, moved his people south from the plains to the rocky knoll that is now Vyšehrad (literally "High Castle"). Krok was succeeded by his youngest daughter, **Libuše**, the country's first and last female ruler, who, handily enough, was endowed with the gift of prophecy. Falling into a trance one day, she pronounced that the tribe should build a city "whose glory will touch the stars", at the point in the forest where they found an old man constructing the threshold of his house. He was duly discovered on the Hradčany hill, overlooking the Vltava, and the city was named Praha, meaning threshold. Subsequently, Libuše was compelled to take a husband, and again she fell into a trance, this time pronouncing that they should follow her horse to a ploughman, with two oxen, whose descendants (the ploughman's, that is) would

rule over them. Sure enough, a man called **Přemysl** (which means ploughman) was discovered, and became the mythical founder of the Přemyslid dynasty which ruled Bohemia until the fourteenth century.

So much for the legend. **Historically**, Hradčany, and not Vyšehrad, was where the first Slav settlers established themselves. The Vltava was relatively shallow at this point, and it probably seemed a safer bet than the plains of the Labe. The earliest recorded Přemyslid was Prince **Bořivoj**, the first Christian ruler of Prague, baptized in the ninth century by the Slav apostles Cyril and Methodius (see above). Other than being the first to build a castle on Hradčany, nothing very certain is known about Bořivoj, nor about any of the other early Přemyslid rulers, although there are numerous legends, most famously that of **Prince Václav** (Saint Wenceslas), who was martyred by his pagan brother Boleslav the Cruel in 929 (see p.49).

Bohemia under the Přemyslids

Cut off from Byzantium by the Hungarian kingdom, Bohemia lived under the shadow of the **Holy Roman Empire** from the start. In 950, Emperor Otto I led an expedition against Bohemia, making the kingdom officially subject to the empire and its king one of the seven electors of the emperor. In 973, under Boleslav the Pious (967–999), a bishopric was founded in Prague, subordinate to the archbishopric of Mainz. Thus, by the end of the first millennium, German influence was already beginning to make itself felt in Bohemian history.

The **thirteenth century** was the high point of Přemyslid rule over Bohemia. With Emperor Frederick II preoccupied with Mediterranean affairs and dynastic problems, and the Hungarians and Poles busy trying to repulse the Mongol invasions from 1220 onwards, the Přemyslids were able to assert their independence. In 1212, Otakar I (1198–1230) managed to extract a **"Golden Bull"** (formal edict) from the emperor, securing the royal title for himself and his descendants (who thereafter became kings of Bohemia). Prague prospered too, benefiting from its position on the central European trade routes. Merchants from all over Europe settled there, and in 1234 the first of Prague's historic five towns, **Staré Město**, was founded to accommodate them.

As a rule, the Přemyslids welcomed **German colonization**, none more so than Otakar II

(1253–78), the most distinguished of the Přemyslid kings, who systematically encouraged German craftsmen to settle in the kingdom. The switch to a monetary economy and the discovery of copper and silver deposits heralded a big shift in population from the countryside to the towns. German immigrants founded whole towns in the interior of the country, where German civic rights were guaranteed them, for example Kutná Hora, Mělník and, in 1257, **Malá Strana** in Prague. At the same time, the territories of the Bohemian crown were expanded to include not only Bohemia and Moravia but also Silesia and Lusatia to the north (now divided between Germany and Poland).

The beginning of the fourteenth century saw a series of dynastic disputes – messy even by medieval standards – beginning with the death of Václav II from consumption and excess in 1305. The following year, the murder of his son, the heirless, teenage Václav III, marked the **end of the Přemyslid dynasty** (he had four sisters, but female succession was not recognized in Bohemia). The nobles' first choice of successor, the Habsburg Albert I, was murdered by his own nephew, and when Albert's son, Rudolf I, died of dysentery not long afterwards, Bohemia was once more left without any heirs.

The Luxembourg Dynasty

The crisis was finally solved when the Czech nobles offered the throne to **John of Luxembourg** (1310–46), who was married to Václav III's youngest sister. German by birth, but educated in France, King John spent most of his reign participating in foreign wars, with Bohemia footing the bill, and John himself paying for it first with his sight, and finally with his life, on the field at Crécy in 1346. His son, **Charles IV** (1346–78), was wounded in the same battle, but thankfully for the Czechs lived to tell the tale.

It was Charles who ushered in Prague's **golden age**. Although born and bred in France, Charles was a Bohemian at heart (his mother was Czech and his real name was Václav): he was also extremely intelligent, speaking five languages fluently and even writing his own autobiography. In 1344, he had wrangled an archbishopric for Prague, independent of Mainz, and two years later he became not only king of Bohemia, but also, by election, Holy Roman Emperor. In the thirty years of his reign, Charles transformed Prague into the new capital of the empire, and one of the most impor-

tant cities in fourteenth-century Europe. He established institutions and buildings that still survive today – the university, St Vitus Cathedral, the Charles Bridge, a host of monasteries and churches – and founded an entire new town, **Nové Město**, to accommodate the influx of students and clergy. Artists and architects from all over the continent were summoned to work in his new capital, while Charles himself cobbled together a vast collection of art and relics. As emperor, Charles was also entitled to issue the all-important Golden Bull edicts, which helped to strengthen Bohemia's position. He promoted Czech as the official language alongside Latin and German and, perhaps most importantly of all, presided over a period of peace in central Europe while western Europe was tearing itself apart in the Hundred Years' War.

Charles' son, **Václav IV**, who assumed the throne in 1378, was no match for such an inheritance. Stories that he roasted an incompetent cook alive on his own spit, shot a monk whilst hunting, and tried his own hand at lopping off people's heads with an axe, are almost certainly myths. Nevertheless, he was a legendary drinker, prone to violent outbursts, and so unpopular with the powers that be that he was imprisoned twice – once by his own nobles, and once by his brother, Sigismund. His reign was also characterized by religious divisions within the Czech Lands and in Europe as a whole, beginning with the **Great Schism** (1378–1417), when rival popes held court in Rome and Avignon. This was a severe blow to Rome's centralizing power, which might otherwise have successfully combated the assault on the Church that was already under way in the Czech Lands towards the end of the fourteenth century.

The Czech Reformation

Right from the start, Prague was at the centre of the Czech reform movement. The increased influence of the Church, and the independence from Mainz established under Charles, led to a sharp increase in debauchery, petty theft and alcoholism among the clergy – a fertile climate for militant reformers like Jan Milíč of Kroměříž, whose fiery sermons drew crowds of people to hear him at Prague's Týn Church. In Václav's reign, the attack was led by the peasant-born preacher **Jan Hus**, who gave sermons at Prague's Bethlehem Chapel, and in 1403 became the first Czech to hold the influential position of Rector of Prague University.

Hus's main inspiration was the English reformist theologian John Wycliffe, whose heretical works found their way to Bohemia via Václav's sister, Anne, who married King Richard II. Worse still, as far as Church traditionalists were concerned, Hus began to preach in the language of the masses (ie Czech) against the wealth, corruption and hierarchical tendencies within the Church at the time. A devout, mild-mannered man himself, as Rector he became embroiled in a dispute between the conservative German archbishop and clergy and the Wycliffian Czechs at the university. Václav backed Hus, for political and personal reasons – Hus was the confessor to his wife, Queen Sophie – and in 1409 issued the **Kutná Hora Decree**, which rigged the voting within the university in the Czechs' favour. The Germans, who made up the majority of the students, immediately left the university in protest.

The scene was set for an international showdown – and a civil war. Widening his attacks on the Church, Hus began to preach against the sale of religious indulgences to fund the inter-papal wars, thus incurring the enmity of Václav, who received a percentage of the sales. In 1412 Hus and his followers were expelled from the university then excommunicated, and spent the next two years as itinerant preachers spreading their reformist gospel throughout Bohemia. In 1414 Hus was summoned to the **Council of Constance** to answer charges of heresy. Despite a guarantee of safe conduct from Emperor Sigismund, Hus was condemned to death and, having refused to renounce his beliefs, was burned at the stake on July 6, 1415.

Hus's martyrdom sparked off **widespread riots** in Prague, initially uniting virtually all Czechs – clergy and laity, peasant and noble (including many of Hus's former opponents) – against the decision of the council, and, by inference, against the Catholic Church and its conservative, mostly German, clergy. The Hussites immediately set about reforming church practices, most famously by administering communion *sub utraque specie* ("in both kinds", ie bread and wine) to the laity, as opposed to the Roman Catholic practice of reserving the wine for the clergy.

The Hussite Wars: 1419–34

In 1419, Václav inadvertently provoked further large-scale rioting by endorsing the readmission of anti-Hussite priests to their parishes. In the ensuing violence, several Catholic councillors (including the mayor) were thrown to their death from the windows of Prague's Novoměstská radnice, in Prague's **first defenestration** (see p.130). Václav himself was so enraged (not to say terrified) by the mob that he suffered a stroke and died, "roaring like a lion", according to a contemporary chronicler. The pope, meanwhile, declared an international crusade against the Czech heretics, under the leadership of Emperor Sigismund, Václav's brother and, since Václav had failed to produce an heir, next in line for the Bohemian throne.

Already, though, cracks were appearing in the Hussite camp. The more radical reformers, who became known as the **Táborites**, broadened their attacks on the Church hierarchy to include all figures of authority and privilege. Their message found a ready audience among the oppressed classes in Prague and the Bohemian countryside, who went around eagerly destroying church property and massacring Catholics. Such actions were deeply disturbing to the Czech nobility and their supporters who backed the more moderate Hussites – known as the **Utraquists** (from the Latin *sub utraque specie*) – who confined their criticisms to religious matters.

For the moment, however, the common Catholic enemy prevented a serious split developing amongst the Hussites, and under the inspirational military leadership of the Táborite **Jan Žižka**, the Hussites' (mostly peasant) army enjoyed some miraculous early victories over the numerically superior "crusaders", most notably at the Battle of Vítkov in Prague in 1420. The Bohemian Diet quickly drew up the **Four Articles of Prague**, a compromise between the two Hussite camps, outlining the basic tenets about which all Hussites could agree, including communion "in both kinds". The Táborites, meanwhile, continued to burn, loot and pillage ecclesiastical institutions from Prague to the far reaches of the kingdom. At the **Council of Basel** in 1433 Rome reached a compromise with the Utraquists over the Four Articles, in return for ceasing hostilities. The peasant-based Táborites rightly saw the deal as a victory for the Bohemian nobility and the status quo, and vowed to continue the fight. However, the Utraquists, now in cahoots with the Catholic forces, easily defeated the remaining Táborites at the **Battle of Lipany**, outside Kolín, in 1434. The Táborites were forced to withdraw to the fortress town from which they took their name, Tábor.

Poor old Sigismund, who had spent the best part of his life fighting the Hussites, died only three years later.

By the end of the Hussite Wars, the situation for the majority of the population – landless serfs, and as such virtual slaves to the local feudal lords – had changed very little. The most significant development in terms of **social structure** was in the balance of power between the Czechs and Germans of Bohemia. Temporarily, at least, the seemingly inexorable German immigration had been checked. The merchant class was still predominantly German and the peasantry mostly Czech, but now, for the first time, there were additional religious differences between the two communities which only increased the mutual distrust.

Compromise and Counter-Reformation

Despite the agreement of the Council of Basel, the pope refused to acknowledge the Utraquist church in Bohemia. The Utraquists nevertheless consolidated their position, electing the gifted **George of Poděbrady** first as Regent and then King of Bohemia (1458–71). The first and last Hussite king, George (Jiří to the Czechs) is remembered primarily for his commitment to promoting religious tolerance and for his far-sighted efforts in trying to establish some sort of "Peace Confederation" in Europe.

On George's death, the Bohemian Estates handed the crown over to the **Polish Jagiellonian dynasty**, who ruled in absentia, effectively relinquishing the reins of power to the Czech nobility. In 1526, the last of the Jagiellonians, King Louis, was decisively defeated by the Turks at the Battle of Mohács, and died shortly afterwards, leaving no heir to the throne. The Roman Catholic Habsburg, Ferdinand I, was elected king of Bohemia – and what was left of Hungary – in order to fill the power vacuum, marking the **beginning of Habsburg rule** over what is now the Czech Republic. Ferdinand adroitly secured automatic hereditary succession over the Bohemian throne for his dynasty, in return for which he accepted the agreement laid down at the Council of Basel back in 1433.

In 1546, the Utraquist Bohemian nobility provocatively joined the powerful Protestant Schmalkaldic League in their (ultimately successful) war against the Holy Roman Emperor, Charles V. When armed conflict broke out in Bohemia, however, victory fell to Ferdinand, who took the opportunity to extend the influence of Catholicism in the Czech Lands, executing several leading Protestant nobles, persecuting the reformist Unity of Czech Brethren, who had figured prominently in the rebellion, and inviting Jesuit missionaries to establish churches and seminaries in the Czech Lands.

Like Václav IV, **Emperor Rudolf II** (1576–1611), Ferdinand's eventual successor, was moody and wayward, and by the end of his reign Bohemia was once more rushing headlong into a major international confrontation. But Rudolf also shared characteristics with Václav's father, Charles, in his genuine love of the arts, and in his passion for Prague, which he re-established as the royal seat of power, in preference to Vienna, which was then under threat from the Turks. He endowed Prague's galleries with the best Mannerist art in Europe, and, most famously, invited the respected astrologists Tycho de Brahe and Johannes Kepler, and the infamous English alchemists John Dee and Edward Kelley, to Prague (see p.55).

Czechs tend to regard Rudolfine Prague as a second golden age, but as far as the Catholic Church was concerned, Rudolf's religious tolerance and indecision were a disaster. In the early 1600s, Rudolf's melancholy began to veer dangerously close to insanity, a condition he had inherited from his Spanish grandmother, Joanna the Mad. And in 1611, the heirless Rudolf was forced to abdicate by his brother **Matthias**, to save the Habsburg house from ruin. Ardently Catholic, but equally heirless, Matthias proposed his cousin **Ferdinand II** as his successor in 1617. This was the last straw for Bohemia's mostly Protestant nobility, and the following year conflict erupted again.

The Thirty Years' War: 1618–48

On May 23, 1618, two Catholic governors appointed by Ferdinand (and their secretary) were thrown out of the windows of Prague Castle – the country's **second defenestration** (see p.51) – an event that's now taken as the official beginning of the complex religious and dynastic conflicts collectively known as the **Thirty Years' War**. Following the defenestration, the Bohemian Diet expelled the Jesuits and elected the youthful Protestant "Winter King", Frederick of the Palatinate, to the throne. In the first decisive set-to of the war, on November 8, 1620, the Czech Protestants were utterly defeated at the **Battle of Bílá hora** or Battle of the White

Mountain (see p.158) by the imperial Catholic forces under Count Tilly. In the aftermath, twenty-seven Protestant nobles were executed on Prague's Staroměstské náměstí, and the heads of ten of them displayed on the Charles Bridge.

It wasn't until the Protestant Saxons occupied Prague in 1632 that the heads were finally taken down and given a proper burial. The Catholics eventually drove the Saxons out, but for the last ten years of the war, Bohemia became the main battleground between the new champions of the Protestant cause – the Swedes – and the imperial Catholic forces. In 1648, the final battle of the war was fought in Prague, when the Swedes seized Malá Strana, but failed to take Staré Město, thanks to the stubborn resistance of Prague's Jewish, and newly Catholicized student populations on the Charles Bridge.

The Dark Ages and the Enlightenment

The Thirty Years' War ended with the **Peace of Westphalia**, which, for the Czechs, was as disastrous as the war itself. An estimated five-sixths of the Czech nobility went into exile, their properties handed over to loyal Catholic families from Austria, Spain, France and Italy. Bohemia had been devastated, towns and cities laid waste, and the total population reduced by almost two-thirds. On top of all that, Bohemia was now decisively within the Catholic sphere of influence, and the full force of the **Counter-Reformation** was brought to bear on its people. All forms of Protestantism were outlawed, the education system was handed over to the Jesuits and, in 1651 alone, more than two hundred "witches" were burned at the stake in Bohemia.

The next two centuries of Habsburg rule are known to the Czechs as the **dark ages**. The focus of the empire shifted back to Vienna, Austria's absolutist grip over the Czech Lands catapulted the remaining nobility into intensive Germanization, while fresh waves of German immigrants reduced Czech to a despised dialect spoken only by peasants, artisans and servants. The situation was so bad that Prague and most other urban centres became practically all-German cities. By the end of the eighteenth century, the Czech language was on the verge of dying out, with government, scholarship and literature carried out exclusively in German. For the newly ensconced Germanized aristocracy, and for the Catholic Church, of course, the good times rolled and Prague was endowed

with numerous Baroque palaces, churches, monasteries and monuments, many of which still grace the city today.

After a century of iron-fisted Habsburg rule, dispute arose over the accession of Charles VI's daughter, **Maria Theresa** (1740–80), to the Habsburg throne. In the course of the ensuing war, Prague was briefly occupied by the Bavarian and French armies, though ultimately the Empress retained hold of Bohemia. Later, during the Seven Years' War, Prague was once more captured, this time by the Prussians, in 1757; though it was Silesia, not Bohemia, that was the price of this defeat. Maria Theresa's reign also marked the beginning of the **Enlightenment** in the Habsburg Empire. Despite her own personal attachment to the Jesuits, the empress acknowledged the need for reform, and followed the lead of Spain, Portugal and France in expelling the order from the empire in 1773.

But it was her son, **Joseph II** (1780–90), who, in the ten short years of his reign, brought about the most radical changes to the social structure of the Habsburg lands. His 1781 Edict of Tolerance allowed a large degree of freedom of worship for the first time in over 150 years, and went a long way towards lifting the restrictions on Jews within the empire. The following year, he ordered the dissolution of the monasteries, and embarked upon the abolition of serfdom. Despite all his reforms, Joseph was not universally popular. Catholics – some ninety percent of the Bohemian population – viewed him with disdain, and even forced him to back down when he decreed that Protestants, Jews, unbaptized children and suicides should be buried in consecrated Catholic cemeteries. His centralization and bureaucratization of the empire placed power in the hands of the Austrian civil service, and thus helped entrench the **Germanization** of Bohemia. He also offended the Czechs by breaking with tradition and not bothering to hold an official coronation ceremony in Prague.

The Czech National Revival

The Habsburgs' enlightened rule inadvertently provided the basis for the economic prosperity and social changes of the **Industrial Revolution**, which in turn fuelled the Czech national revival of the nineteenth century. The textile, glass, coal and iron industries began to grow, drawing ever more Czechs from the countryside and swamping the hitherto mostly Germanized towns and cities, including Prague. A Czech working class, and even an embryonic Czech bourgeoisie emerged, and, thanks to Maria Theresa's reforms, new educational and economic opportunities were given to the Czech lower classes.

For the first half of the century, the Czech **national revival** or *národní obrození* was confined to the new Czech intelligentsia, led by philologists like Josef Dobrovský and Josef Jungmann at the Charles University or *Karolinum* in Prague. Language disputes (in schools, universities and public offices) remained at the forefront of Czech nationalism throughout the nineteenth century, only later developing into demands for political autonomy from Vienna. The leading figure of the time was the historian **František Palacký**, a Protestant from Moravia who wrote the first history of the Czech nation, rehabilitating Hus and the Czech reformists in the process. He was in many ways typical of the early Czech nationalists – pan-Slavist, virulently anti-German, but not yet entirely anti-Habsburg.

1848 and all that

The fall of the French monarchy in February 1848 prompted a crisis in the German states and in the Habsburg Empire. The new Bohemian bourgeoisie, both Czech and German, began to make political demands – freedom of the press, of assembly, of religious creeds. In Prague, liberal opinion became polarized between the Czech- and German-speakers. Palacký and his followers were against the dissolution of the empire and argued instead for a kind of multinational federation. Since the empire contained a majority of non-Germans, Prague's own Germans were utterly opposed to Palacký's scheme, campaigning for unification with Germany to secure their interests. So when Palacký was invited to the Pan-German National Assembly in Frankfurt in May, he refused to go. Instead, he convened a **Pan-Slav Congress** the following month, which met on Prague's Slovanský ostrov, an island in the Vltava. Meanwhile, the radicals and students (on both sides) took to the streets of Prague, barricades went up, and the local Austrian commander, Prince Windischgrätz (whose famous dictum was "Man begins with Baron") declared martial law. On June 16, Windischgrätz bombarded Prague; the following morning the city capitulated – the counter-revolution in Bohemia had begun. The upheavals of 1848 left the absolutist Habsburg Empire shaken but

fundamentally unchanged and served to high-light the sharp differences between German and Czech aspirations in Bohemia.

Dualism

The Habsburg recovery was, however, short-lived. In 1859, and again in 1866, the new emperor, Franz Joseph II, suffered humiliating defeats at the hands of the Italians and Prussians respectively. In order to buy some more time, the compromise or *Ausgleich* of 1867 was drawn up, establishing the so-called **Dual Monarchy** of Austria-Hungary – two independent states united by one ruler.

For the Czechs, the *Ausgleich* came as a bitter disappointment. While the Magyars became the Austrians' equals, the Czechs remained second-class citizens. The Czechs' failure in bending the emperor's ear was no doubt partly due to the absence of a Czech aristocracy that could bring its social weight to bear at the Viennese court. Nevertheless, the *Ausgleich* did mark an end to the absolutism of the immediate post-1848 period, and, compared to the Hungarians, the Austrians were positively enlightened in the wide range of civil liberties they granted, culminating in universal male suffrage in 1907.

The industrial revolution continued apace in Bohemia, bringing an ever-increasing number of Czechs into the newly founded suburbs of Prague, such as Smíchov and Žižkov. Thanks to the unfair voting system, however, the German minority managed to hold onto power in the Prague city council until the 1880s. By the turn of the century, Germans made up just five percent of the city's population – fewer than the Czechs in Vienna – and of those more than half were Jewish. Nevertheless, German influence in the city remained considerable, far greater than their numbers alone warranted; this was due in part to economic means, and in part to overall rule from Vienna.

Under Dualism, the Czech *národní obrození* flourished. Towards the end of the century, Prague was endowed with a number of symbolically significant Czech monuments, like the National Theatre (built by private subscription), the National Museum and the Rudolfinum. Inevitably, the movement also began to splinter, with the liberals and conservatives, known as the **Old Czechs**, advocating working within the existing legislature to achieve their aims, and the more radical **Young Czechs** favouring a policy of non-cooperation. The most famous political figure to emerge from the ranks of the Young Czechs was the Prague university professor **Tomáš Garrigue Masaryk**, who founded his own Realist Party in 1900 and began to put forward the (then rather quirky) concept of closer cooperation between the Czechs and Slovaks.

The Old Czechs, backed by the new Czech industrialists, achieved a number of minor legislative successes, but by the 1890s, the Young Czechs had gained the upper hand and conflict between the Czech and German communities became a daily ritual in the boulevards of the capital – a favourite spot for confrontations being the promenade of Na příkopě. Language was also a volatile issue, often fought out on the shop and street signs of Prague. In 1897 the **Badeni Decrees**, which put Czech on an equal footing with German in all dealings with the state, drove the country to the point of civil war, before being withdrawn by the cautious Austrians.

World War I

At the outbreak of **World War I**, the Czechs and Slovaks showed little enthusiasm for fighting alongside their old enemies, the Austrians and Hungarians, against their Slav brothers, the Russians and Serbs. As the war progressed, large numbers defected to form the **Czechoslovak Legion**, which fought on the Eastern Front against the Austrians. Masaryk travelled to the USA to curry favour for a new Czechoslovak state, while his two deputies, the Czech Edvard Beneš and the Slovak Milan Štefánik, did the same in Britain and France.

Meanwhile, the Legion, which by now numbered some 100,000 men, became embroiled in the Russian revolutions of 1917, and, when the Bolsheviks made peace with Germany, found itself cut off from the homeland. The uneasy cooperation between the Reds and the Legion broke down when Trotsky demanded that they hand over their weapons before heading off on their legendary **anabasis**, or march back home, via Vladivostok. The soldiers refused and became further involved in the Civil War, for a while controlling large parts of Siberia and, most importantly, the Trans-Siberian Railway, before arriving back to a tumultuous reception in the new republic.

In the summer of 1918, the Slovaks finally threw in their lot with the Czechs, and the Allies recognized Masaryk's provisional Czechoslovak government. On October 28, 1918, as the Habsburg Empire began to collapse, the first **Czechoslovak Republic** was declared in Prague. In response, the German-speaking border regions (later to become known as the Sudetenland) declared their own *Deutsch-Böhmen* (German-Bohemian) government, loyal to the Austrians. Nothing came of the latter, and by the end of the year Czechoslovak troops had gained control of the Sudetenland with relatively little resistance.

Last to opt in favour of the new republic was **Ruthenia** (officially known as Sub-Carpatho Ruthenia), a rural backwater of the old Hungarian Kingdom which became officially part of Czechoslovakia by the Treaty of St Germain in September 1919. Its incorporation was largely due to the campaigning efforts of Ruthenian emigrés in the USA. For the new republic the province was a strategic bonus, but otherwise a huge drain on resources.

The First Republic

The new nation of Czechoslovakia began post-war life in an enviable economic position – **tenth in the world industrial league table** – having inherited seventy to eighty percent of Austria-Hungary's industry intact. Prague regained its position at the centre of the country's political and cultural life, and in the interwar period was embellished with a rich mantle of Bauhaus-style buildings. Less enviable was the diverse make-up of the country's population – a melange of minorities which would in the end prove its downfall. Along with the six million Czechs and two million Slovaks who initially backed the republic, there were more than three million Germans and 600,000 Hungarians, not to mention sundry other Ruthenians (Rusyns), Jews and Poles.

That Czechoslovakia's democracy survived as long as it did is down to the powerful political presence and skill of **Masaryk**, the country's president from 1918 to 1935, who shared executive power with the cabinet. It was his vision of social democracy that was stamped on the nation's new constitution, one of the most liberal of the time (if a little bureaucratic and centralized), aimed at ameliorating any ethnic and class tensions within the republic by means of universal suffrage, land reform and, more specifically, the Language Law, which ensured bilinguality to any area where the minority exceeded twenty percent.

The elections of 1920 reflected the mood of the time, ushering in the left-liberal alliance of the **Pětka** (The Five), a coalition of five parties led by the Agrarian, Antonín Švehla, whose slogan "We have agreed that we will agree" became the keystone of the republic's consensus politics between the wars. Gradually all the other parties (except the Fascists and Communists) – including even Hlinka's Slovak People's Party and most of the Sudeten German parties – began to participate in (or at least not disrupt) parliamentary proceedings. On the eve of the Wall Street Crash, the republic was enjoying an economic boom, a cultural renaissance and a temporary *modus vivendi* among its minorities.

The Thirties
The 1929 Wall Street Crash plunged the whole country into crisis. Economic hardship was quickly followed by **political instability**. In Slovakia, Hlinka's People's Party fed off the anti-Czech resentment that was fuelled by Prague's manic centralization, consistently polling around thirty percent, despite its increasingly nationalist/separatist position. In Ruthenia, the elections of 1935 gave only 37 percent of the vote to parties supporting the republic, the rest going to the Communists, pro-Magyars and other autonomist groups.

But without doubt the most intractable of the minority problems was that of the Sudeten Germans, who occupied the heavily industrialized border regions of Bohemia and Moravia. Nationalist sentiment had always run high in the Sudetenland, whose German-speakers resented having been included in the new republic, but it was only after the Crash that the extremist parties began to make significant electoral gains. Encouraged by the rise of Nazism in Germany, and aided by rocketing Sudeten German unemployment, the proto-Nazi **Sudeten German Party** (SdP), led by a gym teacher called Konrad Henlein, was able to win over sixty percent of the German-speaking vote in the 1935 elections.

Although constantly denying any wish to secede from the republic, after 1935 Henlein and the SdP were increasingly funded and directed from Nazi Germany. To make matters worse, the Czechs suffered a severe blow to their morale with the death of Masaryk late in 1937, leaving the country in the less capable hands of his Socialist deputy, Edvard Beneš. With the Nazi annexation of Austria (the

Anschluss) on March 11, 1938, Hitler was free to focus his attention on the Sudetenland, calling Henlein to Berlin on March 28 and instructing him to call for outright autonomy.

The Munich Crisis
On April 24, 1938, the SdP launched its final propaganda offensive in the **Karlsbad Decrees**, demanding (without defining) "complete autonomy". As this would clearly have meant surrendering the entire Czechoslovak border defences, not to mention causing economic havoc, Beneš refused to bow to the SdP's demands. Armed conflict was only narrowly avoided and, by the beginning of September, Beneš was forced to acquiesce to some sort of autonomy. On Hitler's orders, Henlein refused Beneš's offer and called openly for the secession of the Sudetenland to the German Reich.

On September 15, as Henlein fled to Germany, the British prime minister, Neville Chamberlain, flew to Berchtesgaden on his own ill-conceived initiative to "appease" the Führer. A week later, Chamberlain flew again to Germany, this time to Bad Godesburg, vowing to the British public that the country would not go to war (in his famous words) "because of a quarrel in a faraway country between people of whom we know nothing". Nevertheless, the French issued draft papers, the British Navy was mobilized, and the whole of Europe fully expected war. Then, in the early hours of September 30, in one of the most treacherous and self-interested acts of modern European diplomacy, prime ministers Chamberlain (for Britain) and Deladier (for France) signed the **Munich Diktat** with Mussolini and Hitler, agreeing – without consulting the Czechoslovak government – to all of Hitler's demands. The British and French public were genuinely relieved, and Chamberlain flew back to cheering home crowds, waving his famous piece of paper that guaranteed "peace in our time".

The Second Republic

Betrayed by his only Western allies and fearing bloodshed, Beneš capitulated, against the wishes of most Czechs. Had Beneš not given in, however, it's doubtful anything would have come of Czech armed resistance, surrounded as they were by vastly superior hostile powers. Beneš resigned on October 5 and left the country. On October 15, **German troops occupied Sudetenland**, to the dismay of the forty percent of Sudeten Germans who hadn't voted for Henlein (not to mention the half a million Czechs and Jews who lived there). The Poles took the opportunity to seize a sizeable chunk of North Moravia, while in the short-lived "rump" **Second Republic** (officially known as Czecho-Slovakia), the one-eyed war veteran Jan Sýrový became prime minister and Emil Hácha became president, Slovakia and Ruthenia electing their own autonomous governments.

The Second Republic was not long in existence before it too collapsed. On March 15, 1939, Hitler informed Hácha of the imminent Nazi occupation of what was left of the Czech Lands, and persuaded him to demobilize the army, again against the wishes of many Czechs. The Germans encountered no resistance (nor any response from the Second Republic's supposed guarantors, Britain and France) and swiftly set up the Nazi **Protectorate of Bohemia and Moravia**. The Hungarians effortlessly crushed Ruthenia's brief independence, while the Slovak People's Party, backed by the Nazis, declared **Slovak independence**, under the leadership of the clerical fascist and Catholic priest, Jozef Tiso.

World War II

In the first few months of the occupation, left-wing activists were arrested, and Jews were placed under the infamous Nuremberg Laws, but Nazi rule in the Protectorate was not as harsh as it would later become – the economy even enjoyed something of a mini-boom. In late October and November 1939, Czech students in Prague began a series of demonstrations against the Nazis, who responded by closing down all institutions of higher education. In 1941 a leading SS officer, **Reinhard Heydrich**, was put in charge of the Protectorate. Arrests and deportations followed, reaching fever pitch after Heydrich himself was assassinated by the Czech resistance in June 1942 (see pp.130–131). The "final solution" was meted out on the country's remaining Jews, who were transported first to the ghetto in Terezín (see p.167), and then on to the extermination camps. The rest of the population were frightened into submission – very few acts of active resistance being undertaken in the Czech Lands until the Prague Uprising of May 1945 (see below).

By the end of 1944, Czechoslovak and Russian troops had begun to liberate the country, starting with Ruthenia, which Stalin decided to take as war booty despite having guaranteed to maintain Czechoslovakia's pre-Munich borders. On April 4, 1945, under Beneš's leadership, the provisional National Front or **Národní fronta** government – a coalition of Social Democrats, Socialists and Communists – was set up in Košice. On April 18, the US Third Army, under General Patton, crossed the border in the west, meeting very little German resistance. The people of Prague finally rose up against the Nazis on May 5, many hoping to prompt an American offensive from Plzeň, which the Third Army were on the point of taking. In the end, the Americans made the politically disastrous (but militarily wise) decision not to cross the demarcation line that had been agreed between the Allies at Yalta. Two crack German armoured divisions, not to mention some extremely fanatical SS troops, remained in position near the capital. Some 1600 barricades were erected, and around 30,000 Praguers held out against the numerically superior German troops, backed up by tanks and artillery, until they finally capitulated on May 8. The Russians entered the city the following day.

The Third Republic

Violent reprisals against suspected collaborators and the German-speaking population in general began as soon as the country was liberated. All Germans were immediately given the same food rations as the Jews had been given during the war. Starvation, summary executions and worse resulted in the deaths of thousands of ethnic Germans. With considerable popular backing and the tacit approval of the Red Army, Beneš began to organize the forced **expulsion of the German-speaking population**, referred to euphemistically by the Czechs as the *odsun* (transfer). Only those Germans who could prove their anti-Fascist credentials were permitted to stay – the Czech community was not called on to prove the same – and by the summer of 1947, nearly 2.5 million Germans had been expelled or had fled in fear. On this occasion, Sudeten German objections were brushed aside by the Allies, who had given Beneš the go-ahead for the *odsun* at the postwar Potsdam Conference. Attempts by Beneš to expel the Hungarian-speaking minority in similar fashion, however, proved unsuccessful.

On October 28, 1945, in accordance with the leftist programme thrashed out at Košice, sixty percent of the country's industry was nationalized. Confiscated Sudeten German property was handed out by the largely Communist-controlled police force, and in a spirit of optimism and/or opportun-ism, people began to join the Communist Party (KSČ) in droves; membership more than doubled in less than a year. In the **May 1946 elections**, the Party reaped the rewards of their enthusiastic support for the *odsun*, of Stalin's vocal opposition to Munich, and of the recent Soviet liberation, emerging as the strongest single party in the Czech Lands with up to forty percent of the vote (the larg-est ever for a European Communist Party in a multi-party election). In Slovakia, however, they achieved just thirty percent, thus failing to push the Democrats into second place. President Beneš appointed the KSČ leader, **Klement Gottwald**, prime minister of another *Národní fronta* coalition, with several strategically important cabinet portfo-lios going to Party members, including the minis-tries of the Interior, Finance, Labour and Social Affairs, Agriculture and Information.

Gottwald assured everyone of the KSČ's commitment to parliamentary democracy, and initially at least even agreed to participate in the Americans' Marshall Plan (the only Eastern Bloc country to do so). Stalin immediately summoned Gottwald to Moscow, and on his return the KSČ denounced the Plan. By the end of 1947, the Communists were beginning to lose support, as the harvest failed, the economy faltered and malpractices within the Communist-controlled Ministry of the Interior were uncovered. In response, the KSČ began to up the ante, constantly warning the nation of imminent "coun-ter-revolutionary plots", and arguing for greater nationalization and land reform as a safeguard.

Then in February 1948 – officially known as **"Victorious February"** – the latest in a series of scandals hit the Ministry of the Interior, prompting the twelve non-Communist cabinet ministers to resign en masse in the hope of forcing a physi-cally weak President Beneš to dismiss Gottwald. No attempt was made, however, to rally popular support against the Communists. Beneš received more than 5000 resolutions supporting the Communists and just 150 opposing them. Stalin sent word to Gottwald to take advantage of the crisis and ask for military assistance – Soviet troops began massing on the Hungarian border. It was the one time in his life when Gottwald disobeyed Stalin; instead, by exploiting the divi-sions within the Social Democrats he was able to maintain his majority in parliament. The KSČ took to the streets (and the airwaves), arming "workers' militia" units to defend the country against coun-ter-revolution, calling a general strike and finally, on February 25, organizing the country's biggest-ever demonstration in Prague. The same day Gottwald went to an indecisive (and increasingly ill) Beneš with his new cabinet, all Party members or "fellow travellers". Beneš accepted Gottwald's nominees and the most popular Communist coup in Eastern Europe was complete, without blood-shed and without the direct intervention of the Soviets. In the aftermath of the coup, thousands of Czechs and Slovaks fled abroad.

The People's Republic

Following Victorious February, the Party began to consolidate its position, a relatively easy task given its immense popular support and control of the army, police force, workers' militia and trade unions. A **new constitution** confirming the "lead-ing role" of the Communist Party and the "dictat-orship of the proletariat" was passed by parliament on May 9, 1948. President Beneš refused to sign it, resigned in favour of Gottwald, and died (of natural causes) shortly afterwards. Those political parties that were not banned or forcibly merged with the KSČ were prescribed fixed-percentage representation within the so-called "multi-party" *Národní fronta*.

With the Cold War in full swing, the **Stalinization** of Czechoslovak society was quick to follow. In the Party's first Five Year Plan, ninety percent of industry was nationalized, heavy indus-try (and in particular the country's defence indus-try) was given a massive boost and compulsory collectivization forced through. Party membership reached an all-time high of 2.5 million, and "class-conscious" Party cadres were given positions of power, while "class enemies" (and their children) were discriminated against. It wasn't long, too, before the Czechoslovak mining "gulags" began to fill up with the regime's political opponents – "kulaks", priests and "bourgeois oppositionists" – numbering more than 100,000 at their peak.

Having incarcerated most of its non-Party opponents, the KSČ, with a little prompting from Stalin, embarked upon a ruthless period of inter-nal blood-letting. As the economy nose-dived, calls for intensified "class struggle", rumours of impending "counter-revolution" and reports of economic sabotage by fifth columnists filled the press. An atmosphere of fear and confusion was created to justify **large-scale arrests of Party members** with an "international" background – those with a wartime connection with the West,

Spanish Civil War veterans, Jews and Slovak nationalists for the most part.

In the early 1950s, the Party organized a series of Stalinist **show trials** in Prague, the most spectacular of which was the trial of Rudolf Slánský, who had been second only to Gottwald in the KSČ before his arrest. He and thirteen other leading Party members (eleven of them Jewish, including Slánský) were sentenced to death as "Trotskyist-Titoist-Zionists". Soon afterwards, Vladimír Clementis, the former KSČ foreign minister, was executed along with other leading Slovak comrades (Gustáv Husák, the post-1968 president, was given life imprisonment).

After Stalin

Gottwald died in mysterious circumstances in March 1953, nine days after attending Stalin's funeral in Moscow (some say he drank himself to death). The whole nation heaved a sigh of relief, but the regime seemed as unrepentant as ever. The arrests and show trials continued. Then, on May 30, the new Communist leadership announced a drastic currency devaluation, effectively reducing wages by ten percent, while raising prices. The result was a wave of isolated **workers' demonstrations** and rioting in Plzeň and Prague. Czechoslovak army units called in to suppress the demonstrations proved unreliable, and it was left to the heavily armed workers' militia and police to disperse the crowds and make the predictable arrests and summary executions.

So complete were the Party purges of the early 1950s, so sycophantic (and scared) was the surviving leadership, that Khrushchev's 1956 thaw was virtually ignored by the KSČ. An attempted rebellion in the Writers' Union Congress was rebuffed and an enquiry into the show trials made several minor security officials scapegoats for the "malpractices". The genuine mass base of the KSČ remained blindly loyal to the Party for the most part; Prague basked under the largest statue of Stalin in the world; and in 1957, the dull, unreconstructed neo-Stalinist **Antonín Novotný** – recently alleged to have been a spy for the Gestapo during the war – became First Secretary and President.

Reformism and Invasion

The first rumblings of protest against Czechoslovakia's hardline leadership appeared in the official press in 1963. At first, the criticisms were confined to the country's worsening economic stagnation, but soon developed into more generalized protests against the KSČ leadership. Novotný responded by ordering the belated release and rehabilitation of victims of the 1950s purges, permitting a slight cultural thaw and easing travel restrictions to the West. In effect, he was simply buying time. The half-hearted economy reforms announced in the 1965 **New Economic Model** failed to halt the recession, and the minor political reforms instigated by the KSČ only increased the pressure for greater changes within the Party.

In 1967, Novotný attempted a pre-emptive strike against his opponents. Several leading writers were imprisoned, Slovak Party leaders were branded as "bourgeois nationalists" and the economists were called on to produce results or else forego their reform programme. Instead of eliminating the opposition, though, Novotný unwittingly united them. Despite Novotný's plea to the Soviets, Brezhnev refused to back a leader whom he saw as "Khrushchev's man in Prague", and on January 5, 1968, the young Slovak leader **Alexander Dubček** replaced Novotný as First Secretary. On March 22, the war hero Ludvík Svoboda dislodged Novotný from the presidency.

1968: The Prague Spring

By inclination, Dubček was a moderate, cautious reformer – the perfect compromise candidate – but he was continually swept along by the sheer force of the reform movement. The virtual **abolition of censorship** was probably the single most significant step Dubček took. It transformed what had been until then an internal Party debate into a popular mass movement. Civil society, for years muffled by the paranoia and strictures of Stalinism, suddenly sprang into life in the dynamic optimism of the first few months of 1968, the so-called **"Prague Spring"**. In April, the KSČ published their Action Programme, proposing what became popularly known as "socialism with a human face" – federalization, freedom of assembly and expression, and democratization of parliament.

Throughout the spring and summer, the reform movement gathered momentum. The Social Democrat Party (forcibly merged with the KSČ after 1948) re-formed, anti-Soviet polemics appeared in the press and, most famously of all, the writer and lifelong Party member Ludvík Vaculík published his personal manifesto entitled **"Two Thousand Words"**, calling for radical de-Stalinization within the Party. Dubček and the moderates denounced the manifesto and reaffirmed the country's support for the Warsaw Pact military alliance. Meanwhile, the Soviets and their hardline allies – Gomulka in Poland and Ulbricht in the GDR – viewed the Czechoslovak developments on their doorstep very gravely, and began to call for the suppression of "counter-revolutionary elements" and the reimposition of censorship.

As the summer wore on, it became clear that the Soviets were planning military intervention. Warsaw Pact manoeuvres were held in Czechoslovakia in late June, a Warsaw Pact conference (without Czechoslovak participation) was convened in mid-July and, at the beginning of August, the Soviets and the KSČ leadership met for **emergency bilateral talks** at Čierná nad Tisou on the Czechoslovak–Soviet border. Brezhnev's hardline deputy, Alexei Kosygin, made his less than subtle threat that "your border is our border", but did agree to withdraw Soviet troops (stationed in the country since the June manoeuvres) and gave the go-ahead to the KSČ's special Party Congress scheduled for September 9.

In the early hours of August 21, fearing a defeat for the hardliners at the forthcoming KSČ Congress, and claiming to have been invited to provide "fraternal assistance", the Soviets gave the order for the **invasion of Czechoslovakia** to be carried out by all the Warsaw Pact forces (only Romania refused to take part). Dubček and the KSČ reformists immediately condemned the invasion before being arrested and flown to Moscow for "negotiations". President Svoboda refused to condone the formation of a new government under the hardliner Alois Indra, and the people took to the streets in protest, employing every form of non-violent resistance in the book. Individual acts of martyrdom, like the self-immolation of **Jan Palach** on Prague's Wenceslas Square, hit the headlines, but casualties were light compared to the Hungarian uprising of 1956 – the cost in terms of the following twenty years was much greater.

Normalization

In April 1969, there were anti-Soviet riots during the celebrations of the country's double ice hockey victory over the Soviets. On this pretext, another Slovak, **Gustáv Husák**, replaced the broken Dubček as First Secretary, and instigated his infamous policy of **"normalization"**. More than 150,000 fled the country before the

borders closed, around 500,000 were expelled from the Party, and an estimated one million people lost their jobs or were demoted. Inexorably, the KSČ reasserted its absolute control over the state and society. The only part of the reform package to survive the invasion was **federalization**, which gave the Slovaks greater freedom from Prague (on paper at least), though even this was severely watered down in 1971. Dubček, like countless others, was forced to give up his job, working for the next twenty years as a minor official in the Slovak forestry commission.

An unwritten social contract was struck between rulers and ruled during the 1970s, whereby the country was guaranteed a tolerable standard of living (second only to that of the GDR in Eastern Europe) in return for its passive collaboration. Husák's security apparatus quashed all forms of dissent during the early 1970s, and it wasn't until the middle of the decade that an organized opposition was strong enough to show its face. In 1976, the punk rock band *The Plastic People of the Universe* was arrested and charged with the familiar "crimes against the state" clause of the penal code. The dissidents who rallied to their defence – a motley assortment of people ranging from former KSČ members to right-wing intellectuals – agreed to form **Charter 77** (*Charta 77* in Czech), with the purpose of monitoring human rights abuses in the country. One of the organization's prime movers and initial spokespeople was the absurdist Czech playwright **Václav Havel**. Havel, along with many others, endured relentless persecution (including long prison sentences) over the next decade in pursuit of Charter 77's ideals. The initial gathering of 243 signatories had increased to more than 1000 by 1980, and caused panic in the moral vacuum of the Party apparatus, but consistently failed to stir a fearful and cynical populace into action.

The Eighties

In the late 1970s and early 1980s, the inefficiencies of the economy prevented the government from fulfilling its side of the social contract, as living standards began to fall. Cynicism, alcoholism, absenteeism and outright dissent became widespread, especially among the younger (post-1968) generation. The **Jazz Section** of the Musicians' Union, who disseminated "subversive" western pop music (like pirate copies of "Live Aid"), highlighted the ludicrously harsh nature of the regime when they were arrested and imprisoned in the mid-1980s. Pop concerts, religious pilgrimages and, of course, the anniversary of the Soviet invasion all caused regular confrontations between the security forces and certain sections of the population. Yet still a mass movement like Poland's Solidarity failed to emerge.

With the advent of **Mikhail Gorbachev**, the KSČ was put in an extremely awkward position, as it tried desperately to separate *perestroika* from comparisons with the reforms of the Prague Spring. Husák and his cronies had prided themselves on being second only to Honecker's GDR as the most stable and orthodox of the Soviet satellites – now the font of orthodoxy, the Soviet Union, was turning against them. In 1987, **Miloš Jakeš** – the hardliner who oversaw Husák's normalization purges – took over from Husák as General (First) Secretary and introduced *přestavba* (restructuring), Czechoslovakia's lukewarm version of *perestroika*.

The Velvet Revolution

Everything appeared to be going swimmingly for the KSČ as it entered 1989. Under the surface, however, things were becoming more and more strained. As the country's economic performance worsened, divisions were developing within the KSČ leadership. The protest movement was gathering momentum: even the Catholic Church had begun to voice dissatisfaction, compiling a staggering 500,000 signatures calling for greater freedom of worship. But the 21st anniversary of the Soviet invasion produced a demonstration of only 10,000, which was swiftly and violently dispersed by the regime.

During the summer, however, more serious cracks began to appear in Czechoslovakia's staunch hardline ally, the GDR. The trickle of East Germans fleeing to the West turned into a mass exodus, forcing Honecker to resign and, by the end of October, prompting nightly mass demonstrations on the streets of Leipzig and Dresden. The opening of the Berlin Wall on November 9 left Czechoslovakia, Romania and Albania alone on the Eastern European stage still clinging to the old truths.

All eyes were now turned upon Czechoslovakia. Reformists within the KSČ began plotting an internal coup to overthrow Jakeš, in anticipation of a Soviet denunciation of the 1968

invasion. In the end, events overtook whatever plans they may have had. On Friday, **November 17**, a 50,000-strong peaceful demonstration organized by the official Communist youth organization was viciously attacked by the riot police. More than 100 arrests, 500 injuries and one death were reported (the fatality was later retracted) in what became popularly known as the *masakr* (massacre). Prague's students immediately began an occupation strike, joined soon after by the city's actors, who together called for an end to the Communist Party's "leading role" and a general strike to be held for two hours on November 27.

Civic Forum and the VPN

On Sunday, November 19, on Václav Havel's initiative, the established opposition groups, like Charter 77, met and agreed to form *Občanské fórum* or **Civic Forum**. Their demands were simple: the resignation of the present hardline leadership, including Husák and Jakeš; an enquiry into the police actions of November 17; an amnesty for all political prisoners; and support for the general strike. In Bratislava, a parallel organization, Veřejnosť proti nasiliu or **People Against Violence** (VPN), was set up to coordinate protest in Slovakia.

On the Monday evening, the first of the really big **nationwide demonstrations** took place – the biggest since the 1968 invasion – with more than 200,000 people pouring into Prague's Wenceslas Square. This time the police held back and rumours of troop deployments proved false. Every night for a week people poured into the main squares in towns and cities across the country, repeating the calls for democracy, freedom and an end to the Party's monopoly of power. As the week dragged on, the Communist media tentatively began to report events, and the KSČ leadership started to splinter under the strain, with the prime minister, **Ladislav Adamec**, alone in sticking his neck out and holding talks with the opposition.

The end of one-party rule

On Friday evening, Dubček, the ousted 1968 leader, appeared alongside Havel, before a crowd of 300,000 in Wenceslas Square, and in a matter of hours the entire Jakeš leadership had resigned. The weekend brought the largest demonstrations the country had ever seen – more than 750,000 people in Prague alone. At the invitation of Civic Forum, Adamec addressed the crowd, only to be booed off the platform. On Monday, November 27, eighty percent of the country's workforce joined the two-hour **general strike**, including many of the Party's previously stalwart allies, such as the miners and engineers. The following day, the Party agreed to an end to one-party rule and the formation of a new "coalition government".

A temporary halt to the nightly demonstrations was called and the country waited expectantly for the "broad coalition" cabinet promised by Prime Minister Adamec. On December 3, another Communist-dominated line-up was announced by the Party and immediately denounced by Civic Forum and the VPN, who called for a fresh wave of demonstrations and another general strike for December 11. Adamec promptly resigned and was replaced by the Slovak Marián Čalfa. On December 10, one day before the second threatened general strike, Čalfa announced his provisional **"Government of National Understanding"**, with Communists in the minority for the first time since 1948 and multi-party elections planned for June 1990. Having sworn in the new government, President Husák, architect of the post-1968 "normalization", finally threw in the towel.

By the time the new Čalfa government was announced, the students and actors had been on strike continuously for over three weeks. The pace of change surprised everyone involved, but there was still one outstanding issue: the election of a new president. Posters shot up all round the capital urging **"HAVEL NA HRAD"** (Havel to the Castle – the seat of the presidency). The students were determined to see his election through, continuing their occupation strike until Havel was officially elected president by a unanimous vote of the Federal Assembly, and sworn in at the Hrad on December 29.

The 1990 Elections

Czechoslovakia started the new decade full of optimism for what the future would bring. On the surface, the country had a lot more going for it than its immediate neighbours (with the possible exception of the GDR). The Communist Party had been swept from power without bloodshed, and, unlike the rest of Eastern Europe, Czechoslovakia had a strong interwar democratic tradition with which to identify – Masaryk's First Republic. Despite Communist economic mismanagement, the country still had a relatively high standard of living, a skilled workforce and a manageable foreign debt.

In reality, however, the situation was somewhat different. Not only was the country economically in a worse state than most people had imagined, it was also environmentally devastated, and its people were suffering from what Havel described as "post-prison psychosis" – an inability to think or act for themselves. The country had to go through the painful transition "from being a big fish in a small pond to being a sickly adolescent trout in a hatchery". As a result, it came increasingly to rely on its new-found saviour, the humble playwright-president, Václav Havel.

In most people's eyes, "Saint Václav" could do no wrong, though he himself was not out to woo his electorate. His call for the rapid withdrawal of Soviet troops was popular enough, but his apology for the postwar expulsion of Sudeten Germans was deeply resented, as was his generous amnesty which eased the country's overcrowded prisons. The amnesty was blamed by many for the huge **rise in crime** in 1990. Every vice in the book – from racism to homicide – raised its ugly head in the first year of freedom.

In addition, there was still a lot of talk about the possibility of "counter-revolution", given the thousands of unemployed StB (secret police) at large. Inevitably, accusations of previous StB involvement rocked each political party in turn in the run-up to the first elections. The controversial **lustrace** (literally "lustration" or cleansing) law, which barred all those on StB files from public office for the following five years, has ended the career of many a politician and public figure, often on the basis of highly unreliable StB reports.

Despite all the inevitable hiccups and the increasingly vocal Slovak nationalists, Civic Forum/VPN remained high in the opinion polls. The **June 1990 elections** produced a record-breaking 99 percent turnout. With around sixty percent of the vote, Civic Forum/VPN were clear victors (the Communists got just thirteen percent) and Havel immediately set about forming a broad "Coalition of National Sacrifice", including everyone from Christian Democrats to former Communists.

The main concern of the new government was how to transform an outdated command-system economy into a **market economy** able to compete with its EU neighbours. The argument over the speed and model of economic reform eventually caused Civic Forum to split into two main camps: the centre-left *Občánské hnutí* or Civic Movement (OH), led by the foreign minister and former dissident Jiří Dienstbier, who favoured a more gradualist approach; and *Občánská democratická strana*, the right-wing **Civic Democratic Party** (ODS), headed by the finance minister **Václav Klaus**, whose pronouncement that the country should "walk the tightrope to Thatcherism" sent shivers up the spines of those familiar with the UK in the 1980s.

One of the first acts of the new government was to pass a **restitution law**, handing back small businesses and property to those from whom it had been expropriated after the 1948 Communist coup. This proved to be a controversial issue, since it excluded Jewish families driven out in 1938 by the Nazis, and, of course, the millions of Sudeten Germans who were forced to flee the country after the war. A law has since been passed to cover the Jewish expropriations, but the Sudeten German issue remains a tricky one, and a possible stumbling block in negotiations over entry into the EU.

The Slovak Crisis

One of the most intractable issues facing post-Communist Czechoslovakia turned out to be the **Slovak problem**. Having been the victim of Prague-inspired centralization from Masaryk to Gottwald, the Slovaks were in no mood to suffer second-class citizenship any longer. In the aftermath of 1989, feelings were running high in Slovakia, and more than once the spectre of a "Slovak UDI" was threatened by Slovak politicians, who hoped to boost their popularity by appealing to voters' nationalism. Despite the tireless campaigning and negotiating by both sides, a compromise failed to emerge.

The **June 1992 elections** soon became an unofficial referendum on the future of the federation. Events moved rapidly towards the break-up of the republic after the resounding victory of the Movement for a Democratic Slovakia (HZDS), under the wily, populist politician Vladimir Mečiar, who, in retrospect, was quite clearly seeking Slovak independence, though he never explicitly said so during the campaign. In the Czech Lands, the right-wing ODS emerged as the largest single party, under Václav Klaus, who – ever the economist – was clearly not going to shed tears over

losing the economically backward Slovak half of the country.

Talks between the two sides got nowhere, despite the fact of opinion polls in both countries consistently showing majority support for the federation. The HZDS then blocked the re-election of Havel, who had committed himself entirely to the pro-federation cause. Havel promptly resigned, leaving the country president-less and Klaus and Mečiar to talk over the terms of the divorce. On January 1, 1993, after seventy-four years of troubled existence, Czechoslovakia was officially divided into two new countries: the Czech Republic and Slovakia.

The Outlook

Generally speaking, the past few years since the country split in two have been much kinder to the Czechs than the Slovaks. While the latter have seen their currency depreciate, unemployment rise, and their government lurch from one crisis to another, the Czechs have enjoyed political stability, jumped to the front of the queue for the EU and are now held up as a shining example to all other former Eastern Bloc countries. After a slow start, millions of people took up the offer to buy 2000kč worth of privatization coupons, in what is the most radical privatization programme in eastern Europe. The Czech crown is, if anything, currently undervalued, and looks set to move towards full convertibility in the next few years. In macroeconomic terms, the situation is looking very healthy: unemployment remains very low – suspiciously so, some might argue – as does inflation.

Klaus himself remains extremely popular, despite a series of corruption scandals, and would doubtless win any future elections. In any case, the left-wing opposition is small, weak and divided, and continues to be dominated by former Communists, who have themselves now divided into two separate parties. The only consistently dissenting voice is that of Havel, who was elected as the first Czech president in 1993, and enjoys a less than warm relationship with premier Klaus. That said, the Czech presidency is by and large a ceremonial post with little real power, and Havel has been unforgivably silent on one or two highly controversial issues. The most important of these is the new citizenship law, which has left an estimated 100,000 Romanies stateless within their own country.

Princes, Kings, Emperors and Presidents

The Přemyslid dynasty

Princes

Bořivoj I d. 895
Spytihněv I 895–905
Vratislav I 905–921
Václav I 921–929
Boleslav I 929–972
Boleslav II 972–999
Boleslav III 999–1002
Vladivoj 1002–1003
Jaromir 1003–1012
Ulrich 1012–1034
Břetislav I 1034–1055
Spytihněv II 1055–1061
Vratislav II (king from 1086) 1061–1092
Břetislav II 1092–1110
Bořivoj II 1110–1120
Vladislav I 1120–1125
Soběslav I 1125–1140
Vladislav II (as king, I) 1140–1173
Soběslav II 1173–1189
Otho 1189–1191
Václav II 1191–1192
Otakar I (king from 1212) 1192–1230

Kings

Václav I 1230–1253
Otakar II 1253–1278
Václav II 1278–1305
Václav III 1305–1306

Habsburgs

Rudolf I 1306–1307
Henry of Carinthia 1307–1310

The Luxembourg dynasty

John 1310–1346
Charles I (as emperor, IV) 1346–1378
Václav IV 1378–1419
Sigismund 1436–1437

Habsburgs

Albert 1437–1439
Ladislav the Posthumous 1439–1457

Czech Hussite

George of Poděbrady 1458–1471

The Jagiellonian dynasty

Vladislav II 1471–1516
Louis I 1516–1526

The Habsburg dynasty

Ferdinand I 1526–1564
Maximilian 1564–1576
Rudolf II 1576–1612
Matthias 1612–1619
Ferdinand II 1619–1637
Ferdinand III 1637–1657
Leopold I 1657–1705
Joseph I 1705–1711
Charles II (as emperor, VI) 1711–1740
Maria Theresa 1740–1780
Joseph II 1780–1790
Leopold II 1790–1792
Franz 1792–1835
Ferdinand IV (I) 1835–1848
Franz Joseph 1848–1916
Charles III 1916–1918

Presidents

Tomáš Garrigue Masaryk 1918–1935
Edvard Beneš 1935–1938 & 1945–1948
Klement Gottwald 1948–1953
Antonín Zápatocký 1953–1957
Antonín Novotný 1957–1968
Ludvík Svoboda 1968–1975
Gustáv Husák 1975–1989
Václav Havel 1989–1992 & 1993–

Life after the Revolution

HOW IT HAS CHANGED....

A group of western tourists emerge from a privately owned vegetarian restaurant where the latest grunge hit from the States is playing on the sound system. A tram passes advertising a sale of German cars at a Czech department store. The waiter says good night (in English) and directs them to the late-night exchange office. To a first time visitor to Prague in 1995, this could be an unremarkable start to an evening on the town; to anyone who knew the Czech capital before the fall of Communism, the incident would be almost inconceivable. Coming from the West, it is easy to take for granted many aspects of life that barely existed before the revolution. Advertising, late-night venues, vegetarian food, Czechs speaking English could only be found before 1989 with persistent searching. But the main aim of the revolution was not just to make life easier for tourists.

It's hard for an outsider to comprehend how much more open **Czech society** has become in the last five years. Young people have seized on western fashions, opportunities for contact with foreigners and travel with enormous enthusiasm. Unburdened by guilt for compromises with the previous regime and untainted by nostalgia for pre-Communist Czechoslovakia, young Czechs have flung themselves into international youth culture with a vengeance; lead-

ing bands sing in English, popular slang is laced with English expressions, and (sometimes ill-deserving) foreigners are welcomed with curiosity and respect. Apologists for the former regime are quick to point out openness has led to an influx of the worst of western pornography, drugs and criminality, but in fact these imports have made remarkably little impact on Czech life as a whole.

More serious is the suspicion that openness to **foreign influence** may mean standardization rather than diversity, a replacement of one uniformity with another; grey concrete and drab Communist corridors for pink neon and antiseptic new interiors. Czech culture has been slow to find any distinctive voice because both the orthodox state-sponsored arts and the counter-culture of the underground have been rendered obsolete. The novelist Ivan Klíma has eloquently expressed the difficulty of finding a new readership; the popular musician Michal Kocáb gave up writing songs, and, after a spell in politics, has gone into business – and of course, Havel himself has written no plays since before the revolution.

Economically, life has changed dramatically. There used to be only a handful of private businesses and a mass of bureaucracy. The bureaucracy has not gone away – new regulations are still being implemented at a bewildering pace – yet despite this, the Czech model of privatization, and the massive restitution of property confiscated by the Communists, has been held up as a model for other Eastern Bloc countries. In theory, private ownership should bring better service and more choice and indeed the formerly ubiquitous stores looking like warehouses and offering anonymous paper packaging are now few and far between, but for Czechs economic readjustment has been extremely protracted.

In **agriculture**, for instance, the Communist system was based entirely around huge state-owned co-operatives. It has been hard to break their monopoly on machinery and distribution, or even to find private farmers willing to take on the responsibility of farming for themselves. In the **property market**, private landlords eager to improve neglected properties, and western firms hungry for offices and accommodation, have sent rents and prices spiralling beyond the reach of most Czechs. While the city centre is being modernized and repaired, people living in tower blocks or dependent on moribund housing co-operatives have faced a decline in services and maintenance.

Most Czechs cannot afford the foreign holidays or luxury goods now tantalizingly promoted on commercial television. Some commentators have detected the emergence of a twin-track society. For those running the new businesses or with access to western-style incomes, the post-revolutionary years have been a boom time. For the sick, elderly or those finding themselves unemployed, as defunct industries close down, it has been much harder to maintain living standards. Some **public services**, like crèches for working mothers, have almost entirely disappeared, and private medicine is now regarded as the only way to secure decent health care. Nevertheless, the widely predicted public outcry has not materialized; unlike other countries in eastern Europe, there is little sign in the Czech Republic of a Communist revival. Coupon privatization has convinced Czechs they have a stake in the changes, and the scale of incompetence and corruption under the previous regime has completely discredited notions of public welfare or state assistance.

The key change since 1989, however, is **psychological**. For the first time people can contemplate actually fulfilling their personal dreams. Not everyone can adjust to this, and, of course, not all the private businesses have succeeded – for example, only a handful of the private publishers or antique shops that emerged in 1990–91 have survived, but the idea of determining one's own life, for the young especially, is a revolution indeed. One should not underestimate the insecurity that has accompanied the first five years since the revolution; the very absence of a determined "plan", the memory of what happened to the reformist government of 1989, pressure of mounting nationalism throughout Europe, and the secession of Slovakia, have all undermined the euphoria of the fall of Communism. But the sight of Czech companies competing successfully abroad, and the continuing tide of western investment, are beginning to shift the deep Czech inferiority complex, born of years of foreign domination.

.....AND HOW IT HASN'T

Some scars of forty years of a paternalist system have proved hard to erase, and some of the perks of the former system are still yearned for. Personal computers may have been few and far between before the revolution, but at least beer cost only a couple of crowns. Many families had a country house (the ubiquitous Czech *chata*) to compensate for their lack of foreign travel. With friends in the right places, one could comfortably find time to work for oneself alongside one's official job. These cosy features of the old system are still deeply ingrained in **Czech attitudes to work**.

Western employers often complain about the lack of initiative and responsibility amongst their Czech staff, and anyone trying to deal with officialdom on a Friday afternoon will testify to the difficulties in understanding the Czech work ethic. The popular saying under the Communists was "we pretend to work and you pretend to pay us". For foreign visitors, the impact of such a system is all too apparent whenever they come into contact with the remnants of the state apparatus. Castles mysteriously closed "for technical reasons", peculiar beeping sounds instead of a telephone connection, inadequate maintenance in hotels and trains, perplexing timetables and meaningless bureaucracy designed above all to justify its own existence, are enough to reduce any supplicant to impotent fury.

There are now more insidious **relics of the Communist system**. The infamous yellow and white of the Communist police have been replaced by the green and white of the new *Policie*, but the Czech attitude towards authority cannot be changed so swiftly. Deprived of the vicious menace of the totalitaran security apparatus, the police have done little to gain moral authority amongst Czechs. Many have kept their posts (and their uniforms) from the old regime and are now hopelessly isolated from fellow citizens in a battle with ever-more sophisticated criminals. More generally, few Czechs respect their own tax or traffic laws and government initiatives are usually regarded with disinterest or mistrust. Corruption scandals involving public officials are widely seen in a self-fulfilling prophecy as confirming the absence of morals in public life. Politics has moved a long way from when Václav Havel seemed about to inaugurate an era of integrity and public service.

Czechs find it hard to agree on how life has changed since 1989. They rarely speak now of how life was *před* ("before" – not "before the revolution", but simply "before"). It is not just the foreign visitor who takes the fall of Communism for granted. The enthusiasm of the first days of freedom, the election of a parliament of former dissidents, when hundreds of Russian teachers had to be retrained to teach English, all sound like ancient history even to those who lived through it. (A very few) Czechs talk of the need for a new revolution to rejuvenate society, about the need for deeper objectives than material prosperity and about the need to salvage the environment. The emergence of such groups is perhaps the greatest testimony to how life has changed since 1989: before, getting rid of the Communist regime seemed a worthy and sufficient goal, now Czech idealism has a more complex and equally daunting agenda.

David Charap

Czech Cinema

The Czechs are undoubtedly proud of their cinema. The cities may be polluted, the economy might be bankrupt, but everybody knows that, certainly in the 1960s, the country produced some of the finest films – and some of the finest film-makers – in the world.

Pessimists maintain that the weight of that "golden age" is a factor dragging down Czech cinema today. A generation of film-makers have returned from exile or emerged from obscurity to produce films that are no longer exciting or innovative. Not only do they dominate the film-making institutions, but as idol figures they dominate the thinking of younger film-makers, whose contemporary works are pale imitations of forgotten classics. More charitably, the "New Wave" of the 1960s can be seen as a high point in a long and distinguished cinematic tradition, which – although it may now be in the form of television or co-productions – shows every sign of continuing.

Interwar cinema: Avante-garde to erotic

From the early days, the Czech contribution to European cinema has not been just great films and outstanding directors. Even in the 1920s, foreign companies were coming to use the facilities at the Barrandov **studios** in Prague – built by Václav Havel's architect grandfather –

or the Baťa documentary studios in Zlín; and Czech film technicians, like the cameramen Jan Roth and Otto Heller, were much in demand abroad.

With around thirty films produced annually, the Czech **avant-garde** were excited by the possibilities of cinema. In pioneering articles, the leading theoretician of the *Devětsil* group, Karel Teige, saw not only the possibility of an art for the masses, but what he called "pure cinematography", an opportunity to escape from (bourgeois) objective realism. The Czech public was perhaps less discerning. The most famous prewar film, *Extase* (1933), was notorious not for the Devětsil motifs of circles, trains and picture poem montages from the director **Gustáv Machatý**, but for the (briefly naked) appearance of a young Slovak actress, later to become known the world over as Hedy Lamarr. Machatý never recovered from his initial success and his career was dogged by proposals to make a pornographic sequel.

There were initially strong ties with early **German cinema**. Paul Wagner's expressionist classic *The Golem* (1920) was based on the Prague legend. Karl Junghans made *Such is Life* (1929) with a Czech cast, and Přemsyl Pražský's silent classic *Battalion* (1927) showed the extent of German influence. However, the coming of sound and the rise of fascism propelled Czech film-makers in different directions.

Czech theatre contributed an important influence on film, with **E.F. Burian** switching from directing for the stage to the screen and Voskovec and Werich bringing their successful blend of comedy and politics from the Liberated Theatre in Prague (now the ABC Theatre, just off Wenceslas Square) to films like *Your Money or Your Life* (1932) and *The World is Ours* (1937). Their domestic popularity was enormous, comparable to that of Chaplin in the West, and Werich in particular remained a powerful figure in Czech culture long after the war. He continued writing and making films and records well into the 1970s, ceasing only when the authorities threatened to prevent him receiving vital throat surgery.

Nazi Occupation and Nationalization

The **Nazi takeover** did not spell the end of Czech film production. Although many people in the film industry took their talents into exile – notably the director Karel Lamač, and actors Hugo Haas and Jiří Voskovec – others managed to continue working, albeit on more lyrical and less controversial themes. Frič, Vávra and Burian, all of whom were to be major figures in Czech cinema, continued working during the occupation.

One reason they were able to do so was that the Germans envisaged a major role for the film industry in Czechoslovakia. The Barrandov studios were greatly expanded and produced more than a hundred features for the Reich. In 1945, Czechoslovakia found itself with the largest undamaged film complex in Europe and the surviving community of film-makers had already decided how best to manage it. As President Beneš put it, "If there is anything in our country ripe for nationalization, it is film!"

Public support for the arts was not unknown in Czechoslovakia (theatre had been subsidized since the 1880s) but after the war cinema acquired a new prominence. In October 1945 the **Prague film academy (FAMU)** was founded and film students started to gather in the *Café Slavia*. A surge of movie-making began, under the direction of Vítězslav Nezval, once *Devětsil* poet, then Minister of Information. With other studios badly damaged, Barrandov again became an international production centre, whilst Vávra, Frič and Weiss (fresh back from his spell at the British Crown Film Unit) demonstrated the strength of domestic talent.

Meanwhile, freed from commercial pressures and advertising fashions by nationalization, Czech **animation** began to bloom. **Jiří Trnka**, a master of puppet animation, produced *The Czech Year* in 1947, while Hermína Týrlová and Karel Zeman experimented with combining filters, live action and cut-out cartoons at the Baťa studios at Zlín.

Under the Communists

When the Communists took power, they inherited a centralized film industry and quickly began implementing the new orthodoxy of **social realism** that had been laid down in Moscow by Zhadnov two years earlier. Vávra, Frič, Trnka – even Burian – were all curbed by the new bureaucracy, and bright talents, such as student directors Vojtěch Jásny and Karel Kachyňa, were prevented from making feature films.

The authorities were not consistent, however. While for most of the 1950s Czech cinema produced an unappetizing diet of girls in love with tractors, war epics and uninspiring biographies, some unusual gems emerged. The sentimental fairy tales and old Czech legends produced by Zeman and others then appealed to basic Czech instincts and have remained perennially popular. Of more universal interest, **Alfred Radok** (founder of the *Laterna magika* theatre company) made *The Longest Journey* (1950), a striking portrait of the Terezín ghetto, and **Martin Frič** made a two-part intellectual comedy about the limits of absolute power, based on the golem myth and starring Jan Werich: *The Emperor's Baker* and *The Baker's Emperor* (1951). Zeman managed his surreal *The Invention of Destruction* in 1957 and Trnka produced *The Cybernetic Grandma* in 1962 – demonstrating that animation is perhaps harder to control politically than normal film.

After the ideological savaging of the Stalinist era, when feature film production dropped as low as eight films a year, a slightly more relaxed attitude prompted a series of questioning and often elegant films from directors like Ladislav Helge (*The Great Solitude*, 1959 – on the difficulty of being a rural party official), and Zdeněk Brnych (whose *Local Romance*, 1957, produced the term "dingy realism").

The Czech New Wave

Although there was a sudden freeze – with the conference on Czechoslovak cinema in 1959 at Banská Bystrica ending the promising careers of Krska and Svitaček – production reached 35 films a year in the early 1960s and a trend away from predictable conformity became apparent. The great partnerships of Czech cinema between directors **Jan Kadar** and **Elmar Klos**, and between scriptwriter **Jan Procházka** and director **Karel Kachyňa** got under way. Vojtěch Jásny and Štefan Uher both found their way past the censor and inspired a new and bolder generation. One of the most original films of Czech cinema was the historical epic *Markéta Lazarska* (1960), directed by Vlacil. When it was recently reissued with a new print, it stunned audiences with its arresting images and ravishing camerawork.

Assisting these film-makers were various young students from FAMU. They were not only directors, but cameramen like Jan Kučera and

Miroslav Ondříček, and editors such as Miroslav Hájek. As economic sluggishness produced turmoil within the Communist Party, these students were to find a new contemporary voice and lead the Czech **New Wave**.

Their teachers showed the way. Jásný's *Cassandra Cat* (1963) starred Werich in a fairy tale about a cat who saw people in their true colours; Kadar and Klos's *The Shop on Main Street* (1964) described the fascist puppet state of wartime Slovakia; and Kachyňa's *Long Live the Republic* looked at the liberation from the Nazis with a new objectivity (1964).

The student directors took the contemporary feel and the flexibility modern cameras allowed to produce stunning low-budget films. **Věra Chytilová** completed her *Something Different* (a woman's point of view) in 1963. **Miloš Forman** was filming his first feature, *Black Peter*, out on the streets in the same year. **Jan Němec** took Arnošt Lustig's autobiographical story of boys fleeing from the Nazis and turned it into a terrifying vision of youth in a hostile world with *Diamonds of the Night* (1964). **Pavel Juráček** brought Kafka back to Prague with *Josef Kilian* (1964), a nightmare tale of a man trying to find the shop from which he had borrowed a cat. A number of young directors were brought together to produce a series of short films, *Pearls at the Bottom* (1965), each based on a short story by the surrealist writer Bohumil Hrabal.

The New Wave was characterized by energetic and innovative camera work, a brazen questioning of assumptions and a darkly humorous accuracy in observing contemporary mores. As the political uncertainty in the Party deepened, the films became more daring: in *Daisies* (1966) Chytilová showed two girls having a food fight at an official banquet; in *The Fireman's Ball* (1967) Forman hilariously satirized bureaucratic incompetence; and in *The Report on the Party and the Guests* (1966), Němec depicted a chilling party where the guests couldn't leave. Trnka contributed the blatantly allegorical *The Hand* (1966), and in the same year **Jiří Menzl** won an Oscar for his delightfully irreverent look at wartime resistance – *Closely Observed Trains*, again based on a Hrabal story.

By the time the tanks rolled in, a number of even stronger films were already in production. Jaromír Jireš' version of Milan Kundera's mournful novel about the 1950s, *The Joke*, came out – briefly – in 1969, as did Evald Schorm's bitterly

funny *End of the Priest* (with a script by Josef Škvorecký). Menzl's *Larks on the String* (1969) had the same lead (Vlastimil Brodský) in a Hrabal tale of love and politics amongst the labour gangs at a Kladno steel works. Most terrifying, in *The Ear* (1970), Kachyňa and Procházka produced an image of an entire society under surveillance.

All these films were **banned**, along with Vojtěch Jásny's lyrically melancholy *All My Good Countrymen* (1969), arguably the finest film of the period, and *The Uninvited Guest*, which starred a youthful Landovsky as a mysterious visitor who arrives one night and refuses to leave.

Post-1968: normalization and exile

The era of normalization blighted the burgeoning Czech film industry. While Chytilová and Menzl, in particular, produced some interesting work in the 1970s, and Ondříček became one of the world's most valued cameramen, little of note emerged from Czechoslovakia in the drab decades after 1969. Dozens of film-makers fled, including Kadar and Němec, while many of those who stayed found themselves excluded from regular film-making and isolated from international film trends.

The most successful **director in exile** has undoubtedly been **Miloš Forman**. His most famous films, *Amadeus* (which was filmed in Prague) and *One Flew Over The Cuckoo's Nest*, had a particular relevance to Czechoslovakia, where artists still suffered the vagaries of official patronage, and mental hospitals were just one of numerous institutions used to curb individual will. These films only secured public release in full after the revolution of 1989.

Several major **foreign films** were made in Czechoslovakia throughout the seventies and early eighties, including *A Bridge Too Far* (which turns out to be the railway bridge over the Vltava near Dobříš), *Slaughterhouse 5* and *Yentl* (a picture of Barbra Streisand still hangs proudly in Prague's main kosher restaurant). However, domestic production plummeted.

One outstanding Czech film-maker who just about continued to function was **Jan Švankmajer**, although he had to move to Bratislava for a while to evade official restrictions. He was not associated with the New Wave, partly because he had not been at FAMU, and partly because he saw himself as primarily a surrealist rather than solely a film-maker. He used an enforced break from film-making to conduct "touch experiments", exploring the nature of objects. When he returned to animation, he produced a series of stunning films including *Dimensions of a Dialogue, Down to the Cellar* and the feature-length *Alice*. In recent years he has been acknowledged in the West as one of the giants of contemporary animation, and he continues to work with his dedicated team in his studio in Nový Svět. His latest masterpiece combines live action, puppets, animation and opera to produce a devastating version of *Faust* (1994).

The Velvet Revolution and after

The revolution, in which FAMU students played a prominent part, raised enormous expectations of Czech cinema. These were further encouraged when Czech audiences for the first time had an opportunity to view some of the finest films that had been buried in the archives. However, the **post-revolutionary films** of Němec (*In the Heat of Royal Love*, 1990) and Menzl (*Threepenny Opera*, 1991 – using Havel's script) and Chytilová's depiction of Mozart in Prague have all been disappointing. Like all art forms, cinema suffered a loss of direction when both Communist and opposition orthodoxies vanished.

Tank Division (Wit Olmer, 1990) was the first privately financed Czech film since the 1940s. It recouped its budget, but its script (based on a Škvorecký story) is typical of the films from the immediate post-revolution era; a mildly amusing tale of boys growing up, full of cheap anti-Communist gibes, awash with nostalgia and laced with tedious sexism. It was clear that the years of isolation and restriction had taken their toll, less in terms of a depletion of technology and skills, but more in their impact on creative thinking. During the revolution, Švankmajer had painted a banner calling for "More Imagination Please", but there was little sign of film-makers heeding his call.

Meanwhile, foreign crews began flocking to use cheap Czech **facilities** and **locations**. Productions included the TV series, *Young Indie* (based on the youthful adventures of fictional archeologist, Indiana Jones) and the BBC's version of *The Trial*. But the foreign films gener-

ated insufficient revenue to finance local productions. The privatization of the huge Barrandov film studios, mass lay-offs and threats of turning the place into a theme park or a vast supermarket complex provoked enormous controversy. Reluctantly, the government was forced to concede that Czech cinema is a vital national asset and has set up grants to fund it.

A new generation of film-makers is now benefiting from this system, producing a mixture of slick commercial and ambitiously creative material (but rarely in the same film). In 1992, Jan Svěrak secured an Oscar nomination for best foreign-language film with the sentimental *Elementary School*. In the same year, the Caban brothers bewildered audiences with a dazzling mixture of menace and farce, *Don Gio*, that used a contemporary revival of Mozart's opera as an ironic commentary on the arrival of rapacious capatalism. Han Hrejbeik directed the first Czech musical for decades with *Big Beat* (1993) about the arrival of rock 'n' roll in Dejvice, and Jiří Brabec used grotesque tales and illustrations by Váchal from the 1930s to make *The Bloody Novel* (1993), a very Czech horror film and a technical masterpiece including a whirlwind history of cinematography. Similarly inventive was Kotek's realization of *Rychlé sipy* (1993), with camerawork by Miro Gabor, based on the classic children's books by Jaroslav Foglar.

Although the country has a loyal and remarkably sophisticated film audience, it is simply too small (especially now Czechoslovakia has split in two) to support a major domestic film industry. Inevitably, cinemas are now filled with the latest offerings from Hollywood (or with uniformly dire local imitations). There are, nevertheless, real prospects for a revival of Czech cinema, probably in collaboration with other European partners. Government grants, however small and haphazardly administered, coupled with private production companies and broadcasting interest from both Czech TV and the new commercial station *Nova*, mean there is now a serious attempt to foster domestic production. The pressures for international standardization are familiar throughout Europe, but the Czechs have a better chance than most.

David Charap

Books

The recent upsurge of interest in all things eastern European has had a number of positive repercussions in the publishing world. In the immediate aftermath of 1989, several eye-witness accounts of the "Velvet Revolution" appeared, and there's now a much wider choice of Czech fiction than ever before, including some previously untranslated women writers. If you encounter any difficulties, the best source of specialist books on all things Czech in the UK is *Zwemmer Central & East European Books*, 28 Denmark Street, London WC2H 8NJ (☎0171/379 6253). A list of English-language bookstores in Prague can be found on p.228. Where two publishers are given in the selection below, the first is the UK publisher, the second the US.

History, Politics and Society

Karel Kaplan *Report on the Murder of the General Secretary* (I. B. Tauris/Ohio State University Press). Detailed study of the most famous of the anti-Semitic Stalinist show trials, that of Rudolf Slánský, number two in the Party until his arrest.

Jaroslav Krejčí *Czechoslovakia at the Crossroads of European History* (I. B. Tauris/St Martin's Press). Fairly breezy, lacklustre account of Czechoslovakia's history by a 1968 Czech emigré. Despite its recent publication, it contains only the briefest summary of the events of November 1989.

Callum MacDonald *The Killing of SS Obergruppenführer Reinhard Heydrich* (Papermac/ Macmillan). Gripping account of the build-up to the most successful and controversial act of wartime resistance, which took place in May 1942, and prompted horrific reprisals by the Nazis on the Czechs.

R. W. Seton-Watson *The History of the Czechs and Slovaks* (Shoe String Press in US, o/p). Seton-Watson's informed and balanced account, written during World War II, is hard to beat. The Seton-Watsons were lifelong Slavophiles but maintained a scholarly distance in their writing, rare amongst emigré historians.

Elizabeth Wiskemann *Czechs and Germans* (Macmillan, o/p /AMS Press). Researched and written in the build-up towards Munich, this is the most fascinating and fair treatment of the Sudeten problem. Meticulous in her detail, vast in her scope, Wiskemann manages to suffuse the weighty text with enough anecdotes to keep you gripped. Unique.

Essays, Memoirs and Biography

After the Velvet Revolution – Václav Havel & the New Leaders of Czechoslovakia Speak Out ed. by Tim D. Whipple (Freedom House in US). An account of the Velvet Revolution, plus interviews with and articles by, members of the first post-Communist government, some of whom are still leading players in Czech politics.

Stephen Brook *The Double Eagle: Vienna, Budapest and Prague* (Hamish Hamilton, o/p / published as *Vanished Empire: Vienna, Budapest and Prague* by Morrow, o/p in US). Taking their shared Habsburg tradition as a starting point, Brook's readable, personal foray gives an illuminating picture of dissident life in Prague in the late 1980s before the neo-Stalinist bubble finally burst.

Margarete Buber-Neumann *Milena* (Schocken). A moving biography of Milena Jesenská, one of interwar Prague's most beguiling characters, who befriended the author while they were both interned in Ravensbrück concentration camp.

Neil Butterworth *Dvořák* (Omnibus Press). An extremely accessible illustrated biography of the country's best-known composer.

Jana Cerná *Kafka's Milena* (Souvenir Press/ Northwestern University Press). Another biography of Milena Jesenská, this time written by her daughter, a surrealist poet, whose own works were banned under the Communists.

Timothy Garton Ash *The Uses of Adversity* (Granta/Random House). A collection of Garton Ash's journalistic pieces on Eastern Europe, written mostly in the 1980s, including several informative pieces on Czechoslovakia. *We The People: The Revolutions of 89* (Penguin in UK). A personal, anecdotal, eye-witness account of the Velvet Revolution (and the events in Poland, Berlin and Budapest) – by far the most compelling of all the post-1989 books.

■ *Goodbye, Samizdat: Twenty Years of Czechoslovak Underground Writing*, ed. by Marketa Goetz-Stankiewicz (Northwestern University Press in US). Political essays and short pieces of fiction by the country's leading post-68 dissidents, from Václav Havel to Egon Bondy.

Patrick Leigh Fermor *A Time of Gifts* (Penguin). The first volume of Leigh Fermor's trilogy based on his epic walk along the Rhine and Danube rivers in 1933–34. In the last quarter of the book he reaches Czechoslovakia, indulging in a quick jaunt to Prague before crossing the border into Hungary. Written forty years later in dense, luscious and highly crafted prose, it's an evocative and poignant insight into the culture of *Mitteleuropa* between the wars.

Václav Havel *Living in Truth* (Faber); *Letters to Olga* (Faber/Holt); *Disturbing the Peace* (Faber/Random House), *Open Letters: Selected Prose* (Faber/Random House); *Summer Meditations* (Faber/Random House). The first essay in *Living in Truth* is "Power of the Powerless", Havel's lucid, damning indictment of the inactivity of the Czechoslovak masses in the face of "normalization". *Letters to Olga* is a collection of Havel's letters written under great duress (and heavy censorship) from prison in the early 1980s to his wife, Olga – by turns philosophizing, nagging, effusing, whingeing. *Disturbing the Peace* is probably Havel's most accessible work yet: a series of autobiographical questions and answers in which he talks interestingly about his childhood, the events of 1968 when he was in Liberec, and the path to Charter 77 and beyond (though not including his reactions to being thrust into the role of president). *Summer Meditations* is Havel's most recent collection of essays.

Václav Havel et al *Power of the Powerless* (M. E. Sharp). A collection of essays by leading Chartists,

kicking off with Havel's seminal title-piece. Other contributors range from the dissident Marxist Petr Uhl to devout Catholics like Václav Benda.

Miroslav Holub *The Dimension of the Present Moment* (Faber). A series of very short philosophical musings/essays by this unusual and clever scientist-poet.

Heda Margolius Kovaly *Prague Farewell* (Gollancz, o/p in UK) . An autobiography that starts in the concentration camps of World War II, ending with the author's flight from Czechoslovakia in 1968. Married to one of the Party hacks executed in the 1952 Slánský trial, she tells her story simply, and without bitterness. The best account there is on the fear and paranoia whipped up during the Stalinist terror.

Nikolaus Martin *Prague Winter* (Peter Halban Publishers in UK). Brought up in Prague in the 1930s, Martin ended up in Terezín, Czechoslovakia's most notorious ghetto and concentration camp, because of his mother's Jewish background. This autobiography follows his life up to and including the 1948 Communist coup, after which he escaped to Canada.

Jan Patočka – Philosophy and Selected Writings (University of Chicago Press). A collection of essays by one of the first of Charter 77's spokespeople, on subjects ranging from Charter 77 itself to Husserl and phenomenology.

Angelo Maria Ripellino *Magic Prague* (Picador/University of California Press). A wide-ranging look at the bizarre array of historical and literary characters who have lived in Prague, from the mad antics of the court of Rudolf II to the escapades of Jaroslav Hašek. Scholarly, rambling, richly and densely written – unique and recommended.

William Shawcross *Dubček and Czechoslovakia 1918–1990* (Hogarth Press/Simon & Schuster, o/p). Biography of the most famous figure of the 1968 Prague Spring, updated to include Dubček's role in the 1989 Velvet Revolution.

Michael Simmons *The Reluctant President* (Methuen, o/p in UK). The definitive (and so far the only) biography of Václav Havel, by the longtime *Guardian* reporter.

Phyllis Myrtle Clarke Sisperova *Not Far From Wenceslas Square* (The Book Guild, o/p in UK). Autobiography of an English woman who married a Czech airman in World War II, and afterwards settled in Prague, only to be arrested during the 1950s "terror". She was released and finally returned to England in 1955 amid a blaze of publicity in the West.

Josef Škvorecký *Talkin' Moscow Blues* (Faber/ Ecco Press). Without doubt the most user-friendly of Škvorecký's works, containing a collection of essays on his wartime childhood, Czech jazz, literature and contemporary politics, all told in his inimitable, irreverent and infuriating way.

The Spirit of Thomas G. Masaryk 1850–1937 (Macmillan/St Martin's Press). An anthology of writings on philosophy, religion, Czech history and politics by the country's founder and first president, affectionately known as TGM.

Ludvík Vaculík *A Cup of Coffee with My Interrogator* (Readers International). A Party member until 1968, and signatory of Charter 77, Vaculík revived the *feuilleton* – a short political critique once much loved in central Europe. This collection dates from 1968 onwards.

Zbyněk Zeman *The Masaryks – The Making of Czechoslovakia* (I. B. Tauris/St Martin's Press). Written in the 1970s while Zeman was in exile, this is a very readable, none too sentimental biography of the country's founder Tomáš Garrigue Masaryk, and his son Jan Masaryk, the postwar Foreign Minister who died in mysterious circumstances shortly after the 1948 Communist coup.

Czech Fiction

Karel Čapek *Towards a Radical Centre* (Catbird Press); *The War with the Newts* (Pan/Catbird Press); *Nine Fairy Tales* (Northwestern University Press in US). Čapek was the literary and journalistic spokesperson for Masaryk's First Republic, but he's better known in the West for his plays, some of which feature in the anthology, *Towards a Radical Centre*.

Ladislav Fuks *The Cremator* (Marion Boyars); *Mr Theodore Mundstock* (Four Walls Eight Windows). Two readable novels – the first about a man who works in a crematorium in occupied Prague, and is about to throw in his lot with the Nazis when he discovers that his wife is half-Jewish. The second is set in 1942 Prague, as the city's Jews wait to be transported to Terezín.

Jaroslav Hašek *The Good Soldier Švejk* (Penguin); *The Bachura Scandal* (Angel Books/Dufour). The former, by Bohemia's most bohemian writer, is a rambling, picaresque tale of Czechoslovakia's famous fictional fifth columnist, Švejk, who wreaks havoc in the Austro-Hungarian army during World War I. The latter is a collection of zany short stories on life in prewar Prague.

Václav Havel *The Memorandum* (Eyre-Methuen/ Grove-Atlantic, o/p in UK and US); *Three Vaněk Plays* (Faber & Faber in UK); *Temptation* (Grove-Atlantic in US). Havel's plays are not renowned for being easy to read (or watch). *The Memorandum* is one of his earliest works, a classic absurdist drama that, in many ways, sets the tone for much of his later work, of which the *Three Vaněk Plays*, featuring Ferdinand Vaněk, Havel's *alter ego*, are perhaps the most successful.

Bohumil Hrabal *Closely Observed Trains* (Abacus/ Northwestern University Press); *I Served the King of England* (Picador/Random House); *Too Loud a Solitude* (Deutsch/Harcourt Brace); *The Little Town Where Time Stood Still* (Macdonald/ Pantheon). A thoroughly mischievous writer, Hrabal's slim but superb *Closely Observed Trains* is a postwar classic, set in the last days of the war and relentlessly unheroic; it was made into an equally brilliant film by Jiří Menzl. *I Served the King of England* follows the antihero Dítě, who works at the *Hotel Paříž*, through the decade after 1938. *Too Loud a Solitude*, about a wastepaper disposer under the Communists, is also being made into a film, again by Menzl.

Alois Jirásek *Old Czech Legends* (Forest Books/ Dufour). A major figure in the nineteenth-century Czech *národní obrození*, Jirásek popularized Bohemia's legendary past. This collection includes all the classic texts, including the story of the founding of the city by the prophetess Libuše.

Franz Kafka *The Collected Novels of Franz Kafka*; *Letters to Felice*; *Diaries* (all Minerva/Schocken). A German-Jewish Praguer, Kafka has drawn the darker side of central Europe – its claustrophobia, paranoia and unfathomable bureaucracy – better than anyone else, both in a rural setting, as in *The Castle*, and in an urban one, in one of the great novels of the twentieth century, *The Trial*.

Eva Kantůrková *My Companions in the Bleak House* (Quartet, o/p /Overlook Press). Kantůrková spent a year in Prague's Ruzyně prison, and *Companions* is a well-observed novel based around the characters within the prison's women's wing, their kindness, violence and despair mirroring the outside world.

Ivan Klíma *A Summer Affair* (Penguin in UK); *My Merry Mornings* (Readers International); *First Loves* (Penguin/Norton); *Love and Garbage* (Penguin/ Random House); *Judge on Trial* (Vintage/Random

House); *My Golden Trades* (Penguin/Macmillan); *Waiting for the Dark*, *Waiting for the Light* (Granta/ Grove-Atlantic); *The Spirit of Prague* (Granta in UK). A survivor of Terezín, Klíma is another writer in the Kundera mould as far as sexual politics goes, but his stories are a lot lighter. *Judge on Trial*, written in the 1970s, is one of his best, concerning the moral dilemmas of a Communist judge. *Waiting for the Dark*, *Waiting for the Light* is Klíma's first post-89 novel and deals with the issues thrown up in the aftermath of those events. *The Spirit of Prague* is a very readable collection of biographical and more general articles and essays on subjects ranging from Klíma's childhood experiences in Terezín to the current situation in Prague.

Milan Kundera *Laughable Loves*; *The Farewell Party*; *The Joke*; *The Book of Laughter and Forgetting*; *The Unbearable Lightness of Being*; *The Art of the Novel*; *Immortality* (all Faber/ HarperCollins); *Life is Elsewhere* (Faber/Penguin). Milan Kundera is the country's most popular writer – at least with non-Czechs. His books are very obviously "political", particularly *The Book of Laughter and Forgetting*, which led the Communists to revoke Kundera's citizenship. *The Joke*, written while he was still living in Czechoslovakia and in many ways his best work, is set in the very unfunny era of the Stalinist purges. Its clear, humorous style is far removed from the carefully poised posturing of his most famous work, *The Unbearable Lightness of Being*, set in and after 1968, and successfully turned into a film some twenty years later.

Arnošt Lustig *Diamonds of the Night*; *Night and Hope* (both Quartet/Northwestern University Press); *Darkness Casts No Shadow* (Quartet/Avon, o/p); *A Prayer for Kateřina Horovitová* (Overlook Press in US); *Indecent Dreams* (Northwestern University Press in US). A Prague Jew exiled since 1968, Lustig spent World War II in Terezín, Buchenwald and Auschwitz, and his novels and short stories are consistently set in the Terezín camp.

Gustav Meyrink *The Golem* (Dedalus/Dover); *The Angel of the West Window* (Dedalus/Ariadne). Meyrink was another of Prague's weird and wonderful characters who started out as a bank manager, but soon became involved in cabalism, alchemy and drug experimentation. His *Golem*, based on Rabbi Löw's monster, is one of the classic versions of the tale, set in the Jewish quarter. *The Angel at the West Window* is a historical novel about John Dee, an English

alchemist invited to Prague in the late sixteenth century by Rudolf II.

Jan Neruda *Prague Tales* (Chatto in UK). Not to be confused with the Chilean Pablo Neruda (who took his name from the Czech writer), these are short, bitter-sweet snapshots of life in Malá Strana at the close of the last century.

Leo Perutz *By Night Under the Stone Bridge* (Harvill/Arcade Publishing, o/p). A Jewish-German Praguer who emigrated to Israel and wrote a series of historical novels. This one is set in Rudolfine Prague, and, among other things, tells the story of the emperor's love affair with the wife of Mordecai Maisl.

Karel Poláček *What Ownership's All About* (Catbird Press). A darkly comic novel set in a Prague tenement block, dealing with the issue of fascism and appeasement, by a Jewish-Czech Praguer who died in the camps in 1944.

Prague – A Traveler's Literary Companion (Whereabouts in US). A series of extracts about Prague from all the leading Czech and Czech-German writers of the last hundred years from Neruda to to Klíma.

Prague – Chronicles Abroad (o/p in UK and US). Prettily packaged and pocketish, this is a short anthology of predictable fictional extracts about Prague by Havel, Kundera, Chatwin, Škvorecký and Kafka.

Rainer Maria Rilke *Two Stories of Prague* (University Press of New England). Both tales deal with the artificiality of Prague's now defunct German community, whose claustrophobic parochialism drove the author into self-imposed exile in 1899 (for more on Rilke see *Poetry*, p.264).

Peter Sís *The Three Golden Keys* (Doubleday in US). A short, hauntingly illustrated children's book set in Prague, by Czech-born American Sís.

Josef Škvorecký *The Cowards* (Faber/Ecco Press); *The Swell Season* (Vintage/Ecco Press); *The Bass Saxophone* (Vintage/Ecco Press); *Miss Silver's Past* (Vintage/Ecco Press); *Dvořák in Love* (Vintage/Norton); *The Engineer of Human Souls* (Vintage/Pocket Books); *The Miracle Game* (Faber & Faber/Norton); *The Republic of Whores* (Faber & Faber/Ecco Press). A relentless anti-Communist, Škvorecký is typically Bohemian in his bawdy sense of humour and irreverence for all high moralizing. *The Cowards* (which briefly saw the light of day in 1958) is the tale of a group of irresponsible young men in the last days of the war, an antidote to the lofty prose from official authors at the time, but hampered by its dated Americanized translation.

Josef Škvorecký *The Mournful Demeanor of Lieutenant Boruvka; Sins for Father Knox; The Return of Lieutenant Boruvka* (all Faber & Faber/ Norton). Less well known (and understandably so) are Škvorecký's detective stories featuring a podgy, depressive Czech cop, which he wrote in the 1960s at a time when his more serious work was banned. The later book, *The Return of Lieutenant Boruvka,* is set in Škvorecký's new home, Canada.

Zdena Tomin *Stalin's Shoe* (Dent, o/p in UK); *The Coast of Bohemia* (Dent o/p in UK). Although Czech-born, Tomin writes in English (the language of her exile since 1980); she has a style and fluency all her own. *Stalin's Shoe* is the compelling and complex story of a girl coming to terms with her Stalinist childhood, while *The Coast of Bohemia* is based on Tomin's experiences of the late 1970s dissident movement, when she was an active member of Charter 77.

Ludvík Vaculík *The Guinea Pigs* (Northwestern University Press in US). Vaculík was expelled from the Party in the midst of the 1968 Prague Spring; this novel, set in Prague, catalogues the slow dehumanization of Czech society in the aftermath of the Soviet invasion.

Jiří Weil *Life With a Star; Mendelssohn is on the Roof* (Collins, o/p in UK/Penguin). A novel written just after the war and based on Weil's experiences as a Czech Jew in Prague under Nazi-occupied Czechoslovakia.

Poetry

Jaroslav Čejka, Michal Černík and Karel Sýs *The New Czech Poetry* (Bloodaxe/Dufour). Slim, but interesting volume by three Czech poets; all in their late forties, all very different. Čejka is of the Holub school, and comes across simply and strongly; Černík is similarly direct; Sýs the least convincing.

Child of Europe – A New Anthology of East European Poetry (Penguin). This collection contains many hitherto untranslated Czech poets, including Ivo Šmoldas, Ewald Murrer and Jana Štroblová.

Sylva Fischerová *The Tremor of Racehorses: Selected Poems* (Bloodaxe/Dufour). Poet and novelist, Fischerová is one of the new generation of Czech writers, though in many ways she is

continuing in the Holub tradition. Her poems are by turns powerful, obtuse and personal, as was necessary to escape censorship during the late 1980s.

Josef Hanzlík *Selected Poems* (Bloodaxe/Dufour). Refreshingly accessible collection of poems written over the last thirty-five years by a poet of Havel's generation.

Miroslav Holub *The Fly; The Jingle Bell Principle* (both Bloodaxe/Dufour); *Poems Before & After; Vanishing Lung Syndrome* (both Faber/Oberlin College Press). Holub is a scientist and scholar, and his poetry reflects this unique fusion of master poet and chief immunologist. Regularly banned in his own country, he is the Czech poet *par excellence* – classically trained, erudite, liberal and westward-leaning. *Vanishing Lung Syndrome* is his latest volume; the other two are collections.

Rainer Maria Rilke *Selected Poems* (Penguin/ Routledge, Chapman and Hall). Rilke's upbringing was unexceptional, except that his mother brought him up as a girl until the age of six. In his adult life, he became one of Prague's leading Jewish-German authors of the interwar period.

Jaroslav Seifert *The Selected Poetry of Jaroslav Seifert* (Andre Deutsch/Macmillan, o/p in UK and US). Czechoslovakia's only author to win the Nobel prize for literature, Seifert was a founder-member of the Communist Party and the avant-garde arts movement *Devětsil,* later falling from grace and signing the Charter in his old age. His longevity means that his work covers some of the most turbulent times in Czechoslovak history, but his irrepressible lasciviousness has been known to irritate.

Literature by Foreign Writers

Bruce Chatwin *Utz* (Picador/Viking Penguin, o/p). Chatwin is one of the "exotic" school of travel writers, hence this slim, intriguing and mostly true-to-life account of an avid crockery collector from Prague's Jewish quarter.

Lionel Davidson *The Night of Wenceslas* (Mandarin/Penguin, o/p). A Cold War thriller set in pre-1968 Czechosloavkia.

Martha Gellhorn *A Stricken Field* (Virago, o/p / Penguin). The story of an American journalist who arrives in Prague just as the Nazis march into Sudetenland. Based on the author's own experiences, this is a fascinating, if sentimental, insight into the panic and confusion in "rump"

Czecho-Slovakia after the Munich Diktat. First published in 1940.

Zina Rohan *The Book of Wishes and Complaints* (Flamingo/Hutchinson). Rohan is a British-born writer of German-Jewish and Russian-Yugoslav origin, who married a Czech. The story revolves around a young country girl, Hana, who moves to Prague and embarks upon a voyage of self-discovery against the backdrop of the 1968 Prague Spring.

Philip Roth *Prague Orgy* (Cape in UK). A novella about a world-famous Jewish novelist (ie Roth) who goes to Prague to recover some unpublished Jewish stories. Prague "is the city I imagined the Jews would buy when they had accumulated enough money for a homeland", according to Roth.

Art, Photography and Film

The Castle of Prague and its Treasures (Vendome in US). Heavy, coffee-table book with excellent colour photos of all the main sights, plus exclusive coverage of the castle interiors – many by Plečnik – which remain closed to the public.

Czech Modernism 1900–1945 (Bullfinch Press in US, o/p). Wide-ranging and superbly illustrated, this American publication records the journey of the Czech modern movement through Cubism and Surrealism to Modernism and the avant-garde. The accompanying essays by leading art and film critics cover fine art, architecture, film, photography and theatre.

Devětsil – Czech Avant-Garde Art, Architecture and Design of the 1920s and 30s (Museum of Modern Art, Oxford in UK). Published to accompany the 1990 Devětsil exhibition at Oxford, this is the definitive account of interwar Czechoslovakia's most famous left-wing art movement, which attracted artists from every discipline.

Disorientations – Eastern Europe in Transition (Thames & Hudson in UK). A self-explanatory book of photos accompanied by Pavel Kohout's text.

Peter Hames *The Czechoslovak New Wave* (Californian University Press in US, o/p). An intelligent and detailed history of the golden age of Czechoslovak cinema during the 1960s, but a bit short on the stills.

Josef Koudelka (o/p in UK and US). Without doubt the most original Czech photographer and purveyor of fine Prague Spring photos. This pocket-size monograph is occasionally available in second-hand art bookshops.

Miroslav Lamač *Osma a skupina 1907–1917* (Szwede Slavic in US). Czech text, but with a good selection of colour reproductions (mostly of paintings) of the Cubist phase in Czech art.

Ivan Margolius *Prague – A guide to twentieth-century architecture* (Artemis in UK). Dinky little pocket guide to all the major modern landmarks of Prague (including a black and white photo of each building), from the Art Nouveau Obecní dům, through functionalism and cubism, to the Fred & Ginger building, currently in construction.

Prague – Passages et Galeries (o/p in UK and US). Superb photos of the remarkable series of shopping arcades (*pasáž* in Czech) built, for the most part, in the first half of this century on and around Wenceslas Square. Text in French.

Josef Sudek – A Photographer's Life (John Murray, o/p /published as *Josef Sudek: A Life's Work* by Aperture in US). Hauntingly beautiful set of sepia photos of Prague by the old man of Czech photography, who died in the 1970s.

Petr Wittlich *Prague – Fin de Siècle* (Flammarion/ Abbeville Press). Big coffee-table book, richly illustrated with colour photos of every Art Nouveau detail and building in Prague.

Language

The official language of the Czech Republic is Czech (český), a highly complex western Slav tongue. Any attempt to speak Czech will be heartily appreciated, though don't be discouraged if people seem not to understand, as most will be unaccustomed to hearing foreigners stumble through their language. If you don't know any Czech, brush up on your German, since, among the older generation at least, this is still the most widely spoken second language. Russian, once the compulsory second language, has been practically wiped off the school curriculum, and the number of English-speakers has been steadily increasing especially among the younger generation.

Pronunciation

English-speakers often find Czech impossibly difficult to pronounce. In fact, it's not half as daunting as it might first appear from the traffic jams of

The Alphabet

In the Czech alphabet, letters which feature a **háček** (as in the č of the word itself) are considered separate letters and appear in Czech indexes immediately after their more familiar cousins. More confusingly, the consonant combination *ch* is also considered as a separate letter and appears in Czech indexes after the letter *h*. In the index in this book, we use the English system, so words beginning with *c*, *č* and *ch* all appear under *c*.

consonants which crop up on the page. Apart from a few special letters, each letter and syllable is pronounced as it's written – the trick is always to **stress the first syllable** of a word, no matter what its length; otherwise you'll render it unintelligible.

Short and long vowels

Czech has both short and long vowels (the latter being denoted by a variety of accents). The trick here is to lengthen the vowel without affecting the principal stress of the word, which is invariably on the first syllable.

a like the u in cup
á as in father
e as in pet
é as in fair
ě like the ye in **yes**
i or y as in pit
í or ý as in seat
o as in not
ó as in door
u like the oo in book
ů or ú like the oo in fool

Vowel combinations and diphthongs

There are very few diphthongs in Czech, so any combinations of vowels other than those below should be pronounced as two separate syllables.

au like the ou in foul
ou like the oe in foe

Consonants and accents

There are no silent consonants, but it's worth remembering that r and l can form a syllable if standing between two other consonants or at the end of a word, as in Brno (Br–no) or Vltava (Vl–ta–va). The consonants listed below are those which differ substantially from the English. Accents look daunting – particularly the háček, which appears above c, d, l, n, r, s, t, and z – but the only one which causes a lot of problems is ř,

probably the most difficult letter to say in the entire language – even Czech toddlers have to be taught how to say it.

c like the **ts** in boats
č like the **ch** in chicken
ch like the **ch** in the Scottish loch
ď like the **d** in duped
g always as in goat, never as in general
h always as in have, but more energetic

BASIC WORDS AND PHRASES

Yes	*ano*
No	*ne*
Excuse me/don't mention it	*prosím/není zač*
Sorry	*pardon*
Thank you	*děkuju*
Bon appétit	*dobrou chuť*
Bon voyage	*šťastnou cestu*
Hello/goodbye (informal)	*ahoj*
Goodbye (formal)	*na shledanou*
Good day	*dobrý den*
Good morning	*dobré ráno*
Good evening	*dobrý večer*
Good night (when leaving)	*dobrou noc*
How are you?	*jak se máte?*
Today	*dnes*
Yesterday	*včera*
Tomorrow	*zítra*
The day after tomorrow	*pozítří*
Now	*hnet*
Later	*později*
Leave me alone	*dej mi pokoj*
Go away	*jdi pryč*
Help!	*pomoc!*
This one	*tento*
A little	*trochu*
Large/small	*velký/malý*
More/less	*více/méně*
Good/bad	*dobrý/špatný*
Hot/cold	*horký/studený*
With/without	*s/bez*

GETTING AROUND

Over here	*tady*
Over there	*tam*
Left	*nalevo*
Right	*napravo*
Straight on	*rovně*
Where is . . .?	*kde je . . .?*
How do I get to Prague?	*jak se dostanu do Prahy ?*

How do I get to the university?	*jak se dostanu k univerzitě?*
By bus	*autobusem*
By train	*vlakem*
By car	*autem*
On foot	*pěšky*
By taxi	*taxíkem*
Ticket	*jízdenka/lístek*
Return ticket	*zpateční*
Railway station	*nádraží*
Bus station	*autobusové nádraží*
Bus stop	*autobusová zastávka*
When's the next train to Prague?	*kdy jede další vlak do Prahy?*
Is it going to Prague?	*jede to do Prahy?*
Do I have to change?	*musím přestupovat?*
Do I need a reservation?	*musím mít místenku?*

QUESTIONS AND ANSWERS

Do you speak English?	*mluvíte anglicky?*
I don't speak German	*nemluvím německy*
I don't understand	*nerozumím*
I understand	*rozumím*
Speak slowly	*mluvte pomalu*
How do you say that in Czech?	*jak se tohle řekne česky?*
Could you write it down for me?	*mužete mí to napsat? .*
What	*co*
Where	*kde*
When	*kdy*
Why	*proč*
How much is it?	*kolík to stojí?*
Are there any rooms available?	*máte volné pokoje?*
I would like a double room	*chtěl bych dvou lůžkovy pokoj*
For one night	*na jednu noc*
With shower	*se sprchou*
Is this seat free?	*je tu volna?*

j like the **y** in yoke
kd pronounced as **gd**
ľ like the **lli** in colliery
mě pronounced as mnye
ň like the **n** in nuance
p softer than the English **p**

r as in rip, but often rolled
ř like the sound of r and ž combined
š like the **sh** in shop
ť like the **t** in tutor
ž like the **s** in pleasure; at the end of a word
   like the **sh** in shop

May we (sit down)?	*můžeme (se sednout)?*	Thursday	*čtvrtek*
The bill please	*zaplatím prosím*	Friday	*pátek*
Do you have . . .?	*máte . . .?*	Saturday	*sobota*
We don't have	*nemáme*	Sunday	*neděle*
We do have	*máme*	Day	*den*
		Week	*týden*
SOME SIGNS		Month	*měsíc*
Entrance	*vchod*	Year	*rok*
Exit	*východ*		
Toilets	*záchody/toalety*	**MONTHS OF THE YEAR**	

Many Slav languages have their own highly individual systems in which the words for the names of the month are descriptive nouns – sometimes beautifully apt for the month in question.

Men	*muži*		
Women	*ženy*		
Ladies	*dámy*		
Gentlemen	*pánové*		
Open	*otevřeno*		
Closed	*zavřeno*	January	*leden* – ice
Danger!	*pozor!*	February	*únor* – hibernation
Hospital	*nemocnice*	March	*březen* – birch
No smoking	*kouření zakázáno*	April	*duben* – oak
No bathing	*koupání zakázáno*	May	*květen* – blossom
No entry	*vstup zakázán*	June	*červen* – red
Arrival	*příjezd*	July	*červenec* – redder
Departure	*odjezd*	August	*srpen* – sickle
Police	*policie*	September	*zaří* – blazing
		October	*říjen* – rutting
DAYS OF THE WEEK		November	*listopad* – leaves falling
Monday	*pondělí*	December	*prosinec* – slaughter of pigs
Tuesday	*uterý*		
Wednesday	*středa*		

NUMBERS

1	*jeden*	14	*čtrnáct*	90	*devadesát*		
2	*dva*	15	*patnáct*	100	*sto*		
3	*tří*	16	*šestnáct*	101	*sto jedna*		
4	*čtyři*	17	*sedmnáct*	155	*sto padesát pět*		
5	*pět*	18	*osmnáct*	200	*dvě stě*		
6	*šest*	19	*devatenáct*	300	*tři sta*		
7	*sedm*	20	*dvacet*	400	*čtyři sta*		
8	*osm*	21	*dvacetjedna*	500	*pět set*		
9	*devět*	30	*třicet*	600	*šest set*		
10	*deset*	40	*čtyřicet*	700	*sedm set*		
11	*jedenáct*	50	*padesát*	800	*osm set*		
12	*dvanáct*	60	*šedesát*	900	*devět set*		
13	*třináct*	70	*sedmdesát*	1000	*tisíc*		
		80	*osmdesát*				

Prague's leading personalities – past and present

Beneš, Edvard (1884–1948). Hero to some, traitor to others, Beneš was president from 1935 until 1938 – when he resigned, having refused to lead the country into bloodshed over the Munich Crisis – and again from 1945 until 1948, when he aquiesced to the Communist coup.

Čapek, Karel (1890–1938). Czech writer, journalist and unofficial spokesperson for the First Republic. His most famous works are *The Insect Play* and *R.U.R.*, which introduced the word *robot* into the English language.

Dobrovský, Josef (1753–1829). Jesuit-taught pioneer in Czech philology. Wrote the seminal text *The History of Czech Language and Literature*.

Dubček, Alexander (1921–92). Slovak Communist who became First Secretary in January 1968, at the beginning of the Prague Spring. Expelled from the Party in 1969, but returned to become speaker in the federal parliament after 1989, before being killed in a car crash in 1992.

Dvořák, Antonín (1841–1904). Perhaps the most famous of all Czech composers. His best-known work is the *New World Symphony*, inspired by an extensive sojourn in the USA.

Fučik, Julius (1903–43). Communist journalist murdered by the Nazis, whose prison writings, *Notes from the Gallows*, were obligatory reading in the 1950s. Hundreds of streets were named after him, but doubts about the authenticity of the work, and general hostility towards the man have made him *persona non grata*.

Gottwald, Klement (1896–1953). One of the founders of the KSČ, General Secretary from 1927, Prime Minister from 1946 to 1948, and President from 1948 to 1953, Gottwald is universally abhorred for his role in the show trials of the 1950s.

Hašek, Jaroslav (1883–1923). Anarchist, dog-breeder, lab assistant, bigamist, cabaret artist and People's Commissar in the Red Army, Hašek was one of prewar Prague's most colourful characters,

who wrote the famous *Good Soldier Švejk* and died from alcohol abuse in 1923.

Havel, Václav (1936–). Absurdist playwright of the 1960s, who became a leading spokesperson of Charter 77 and, following the Velvet Revolution, the country's first post-Communist president.

Havlíček-Borovský, Karel (1821–56). Satirical poet, journalist and nationalist, exiled to the Tyrol by the Austrian authorities after 1848.

Hrabal, Bohumil (1936–). Writer and bohemian, whose novels were banned under the Communists, but revered worldwide. Hrabal is a regular at Prague's *U zlatého tygra*.

Hus, Jan (1370–1415). Rector of Prague University and reformist preacher who was burnt at the stake as a heretic by the Council of Constance.

Husák, Gustáv (died 1991). Slovak Communist who was sentenced to life imprisonment in the show trials of the 1950s, released in 1960, and eventually became General Secretary and President following the Soviet invasion. Resigned in favour of Havel in December 1989.

Jirásek, Alois (1851–1930). Writer who popularized Czech legends for both children and adults and became a key figure in the Czech national revival.

Jungmann, Josef (1773–1847). Prolific Czech translator and author of the seminal *History of Czech Literature* and the first Czech dictionary.

Kafka, Franz (1883–1924). German-Jewish Praguer who worked as an insurance clerk in Prague for most of his life, and also wrote some of the most influential novels of the twentieth century, most notably *The Trial*.

Kelley, Edward. English occultist who was summoned to Prague by Rudolf II, but eventually incurred the wrath of the emperor and was imprisoned in Kokořín castle.

Kepler, Johannes (1571–1630). German Protestant forced to leave Linz for Denmark because of the Counter-Reformation. Succeeded Tycho de Brahe as Rudolf II's chief astronomer.

His observations of the planets became the basis of the laws of planetary motion.

Kisch, Egon Erwin (1885–1948). German-Jewish Praguer who became one of the city's most famous investigative journalists.

Klaus, Václav. Known somewhat bitterly as "Santa Klaus". Prime Minister since 1992, confirmed Thatcherite, and driving force behind the country's present economic reforms.

Komenský, Jan Amos (1592–1670). Leader of the Protestant Czech Brethren. Forced to flee the country and settle in England during the Counter-Reformation. Better known to English-speakers as Comenius.

Mácha, Karel Hynek (1810–36). Romantic nationalist poet, great admirer of Byron and Keats and, like them, died young. His most famous poem is *Maj*, published just months before his death.

Masaryk, Jan Garrigue (1886–1958). Son of the founder of the republic (see below), Foreign Minister in the postwar government and the only non-Communist in Gottwald's cabinet when the Communists took over in February 1948. Died ten days after the coup in suspicious circumstances.

Masaryk, Tomáš Garrigue (1850–1937). Professor of Philosophy at Prague University, President of the Republic from 1918 to 1935. His name is synonymous with the First Republic and was removed from all street signs after the 1948 coup. Now back with a vengeance.

Mucha, Alfons (1860–1939). Moravian graphic artist and designer whose Art-Nouveau posters and artwork for Sarah Bernhardt brought him international fame. After the founding of Czechoslovakia, he returned to the country to design stamps, bank notes, and complete a cycle of giant canvases on Czech nationalist themes.

Němcová, Božena (1820–62). Highly popular writer who became involved with the nationalist movement and shocked many with her unorthodox behaviour. Her most famous book is *Grandmother*.

Neruda, Jan (1834–91). Poet and journalist for the *Národní listy*. Wrote some famous short stories describing Prague's Malá Strana.

Palacký, František (1798–1876). Nationalist historian, Czech MP in Vienna and leading figure in the events of 1848.

Purkyně, Jan Evangelista (1787–1869). Czech doctor, natural scientist and pioneer in experimental physiology who became professor of physiology at Prague and then at Wroctaw University.

Rieger, Ladislav (1818–1903). Nineteenth-century Czech politician and one of the leading figures in the events of 1848 and the aftermath.

Rilke, Rainer Maria (1876–1926). Despite having been brought up as a girl for the first six years of his life, Rilke ended up as an officer in the Austrian army, and wrote some of the city's finest German *fin-de-siècle* poetry.

Smetana, Bedřich (1824–84). Popular Czech composer and fervent nationalist whose *Má vlast* (My Homeland) traditionally opens the Prague Spring Music Festival.

Svoboda, Ludvík (1895–1979). Victorious Czech General from World War II, who acquiesced to the 1948 Communist coup and was Communist President from 1968 to 1975.

Tycho de Brahe (1546–1601). Ground-breaking Danish astronomer, who was summoned to Prague by Rudolf II in 1597, only to die from over-drinking in 1601.

Tyl, Josef Kajetán (1808–56). Czech playwright and composer of the Czech half of the national anthem, *Where is my Home?*

Werfel, Franz (1890–1945). One of the German-Jewish literary circle, which included Kafka, Kisch and Brod.

Žižka, Jan (died 1424). Brilliant, blind military leader of the Táborites, the radical faction of the Hussites.

A glossary of Czech words and terms

brána gate.

český Bohemian.

chata chalet-type bungalow, country cottage or mountain hut.

chrám large church.

divadlo theatre.

dóm cathedral.

dům house.

dům kultury generic term for local arts and social centre; literally "House of Culture".

hrad castle.

hřbitov cemetery.

hora mountain.

hospoda pub.

hostinec pub.

kaple chapel.

katedrála cathedral.

kavárna coffee house.

klášter monastery/convent.

kostel church.

koupaliště swimming pool.

Labe River Elbe.

lanovka funicular or cable car.

les forest.

město town.

most bridge.

muzeum museum.

nábřeží embankment.

nádraží train station.

náměstí square.

ostrov island.

památník memorial or monument.

pivnice pub.

radnice town hall.

restaurace restaurant.

sad park.

sál room or hall (in a chateau or castle).

schody steps.

svatý saint; often abbreviated to sv.

třída avenue.

ulice street.

věž tower.

vinárna wine bar or cellar.

Vltava River Moldau.

vrchy hills.

výstava exhibition.

zahrada garden.

zámek chateau.

An Architectural Glossary

Ambulatory Passage round the back of the altar, in continuation of the aisles.

Art Nouveau French term for the sinuous and stylized form of architecture dating from 1900 to 1910; known as the Secession in the Czech Republic and as *Jugendstil* in Germany.

Baroque Expansive, exuberant architectural style of the seventeenth and mid-eighteenth centuries, characterized by ornate decoration, complex spatial arrangement and grand vistas.

Chancel The part of the church where the altar is placed, usually at the east end.

Empire Highly decorative Neoclassical style of architecture and decorative arts, practised in the early 1800s.

Fresco Mural painting applied to wet plaster, so that the colours immediately soak into the wall.

Functionalism Plain, boxy, modernist architectural style, prevalent in the late 1920s and 1930s in Czechoslovakia, often using plate-glass curtain walls and open-plan interiors.

Gothic Architectural style prevalent from the fourteenth to the sixteenth century, characterized by pointed arches and ribbed vaulting.

Loggia Covered area on the side of a building, often arcaded.

Nave Main body of a church, usually the western end.

Neoclassical Late eighteenth- and early nineteenth-century style of architecture and design returning to classical Greek and Roman models as a reaction against Baroque and Rococo excesses.

Oriel A bay window, usually projecting from an upper floor.

Rococo Highly florid, fiddly though (occasionally) graceful style of architecture and interior design, forming the last phase of Baroque.

Romanesque Solid architectural style of the late tenth to thirteenth century, characterized by round-headed arches and geometrical precision.

Secession Linear and stylized form of architecture and decorative arts imported from Vienna as a reaction against the academic establishment.

Sgraffito Monochrome plaster decoration effected by means of scraping back the first white layer to reveal the black underneath.

Stucco Plaster used for decorative effects.

Trompe l'oeil Painting designed to fool the onlooker into believing that it is actually three-dimensional.

Index

Amsterdam	1-85828-086-9	£7.99	US$13.95	CAN$16.99
Andalucia	1-85828-094-X	8.99	14.95	18.99
Australia	1-85828-141-5	12.99	19.95	25.99
Bali	1-85828-134-2	8.99	14.95	19.99
Barcelona	1-85828-221-7	8.99	14.95	19.99
Berlin	1-85828-129-6	8.99	14.95	19.99
Brazil	1-85828-102-4	9.99	15.95	19.99
Britain	1-85828-208-X	12.99	19.95	25.99
Brittany & Normandy	1-85828-224-1	9.99	16.95	22.99
Bulgaria	1-85828-183-0	9.99	16.95	22.99
California	1-85828-181-4	10.99	16.95	22.99
Canada	1-85828-130-X	10.99	14.95	19.99
China	1-85828-225-X	15.99	24.95	32.95
Corsica	1-85828-089-3	8.99	14.95	18.99
Costa Rica	1-85828-136-9	9.99	15.95	21.99
Crete	1-85828-132-6	8.99	14.95	18.99
Cyprus	1-85828-182-2	9.99	16.95	22.99
Czech & Slovak Republics	1-85828-121-0	9.99	16.95	22.99
Egypt	1-85828-188-1	10.99	17.95	23.99
Europe	1-85828-159-8	14.99	19.95	25.99
England	1-85828-160-1	10.99	17.95	23.99
First Time Europe	1-85828-270-5	7.99	9.95	12.99
Florida	1-85828-184-4	10.99	16.95	22.99
France	1-85828-124-5	10.99	16.95	21.99
Germany	1-85828-128-8	11.99	17.95	23.99
Goa	1-85828-156-3	8.99	14.95	19.99
Greece	1-85828-131-8	9.99	16.95	20.99
Greek Islands	1-85828-163-6	8.99	14.95	19.99
Guatemala	1-85828-189-X	10.99	16.95	22.99
Hawaii: Big Island	1-85828-158-X	8.99	12.95	16.99
Hawaii	1-85828-206-3	10.99	16.95	22.99
Holland, Belgium & Luxembourg	1-85828-087-7	9.99	15.95	20.99
Hong Kong	1-85828-187-3	8.99	14.95	19.99
Hungary	1-85828-123-7	8.99	14.95	19.99
India	1-85828-200-4	14.99	23.95	31.99
Ireland	1-85828-179-2	10.99	17.95	23.99
Italy	1-85828-167-9	12.99	19.95	25.99
Kenya	1-85828-192-X	11.99	18.95	24.99
London	1-85828-231-4	9.99	15.95	21.99
Mallorca & Menorca	1-85828-165-2	8.99	14.95	19.99
Malaysia, Singapore & Brunei	1-85828-103-2	9.99	16.95	20.99
Mexico	1-85828-044-3	10.99	16.95	22.99
Morocco	1-85828-040-0	9.99	16.95	21.99
Moscow	1-85828-118-0	8.99	14.95	19.99
Nepal	1-85828-190-3	10.99	17.95	23.99
New York	1-85828-171-7	9.99	15.95	21.99
Pacific Northwest	1-85828-092-3	9.99	14.95	19.99

around the world

Paris	1-85828-235-7	8.99	14.95	19.99
Poland	1-85828-168-7	10.99	17.95	23.99
Portugal	1-85828-180-6	9.99	16.95	22.99
Prague	1-85828-122-9	8.99	14.95	19.99
Provence	1-85828-127-X	9.99	16.95	22.99
Pyrenees	1-85828-093-1	8.99	15.95	19.99
Rhodes & the Dodecanese	1-85828-120-2	8.99	14.95	19.99
Romania	1-85828-097-4	9.99	15.95	21.99
San Francisco	1-85828-185-7	8.99	14.95	19.99
Scandinavia	1-85828-039-7	10.99	16.99	21.99
Scotland	1-85828-166-0	9.99	16.95	22.99
Sicily	1-85828-178-4	9.99	16.95	22.99
Singapore	1-85828-135-0	8.99	14.95	19.99
Spain	1-85828-240-3	11.99	18.95	24.99
St Petersburg	1-85828-133-4	8.99	14.95	19.99
Thailand	1-85828-140-7	10.99	17.95	24.99
Tunisia	1-85828-139-3	10.99	17.95	24.99
Turkey	1-85828-242-X	12.99	19.95	25.99
Tuscany & Umbria	1-85828-243-8	10.99	17.95	23.99
USA	1-85828-161-X	14.99	19.95	25.99
Venice	1-85828-170-9	8.99	14.95	19.99
Vietnam	1-85828-191-1	9.99	15.95	21.99
Wales	1-85828-245-4	10.99	17.95	23.99
Washington DC	1-85828-246-2	8.99	14.95	19.99
West Africa	1-85828-101-6	15.99	24.95	34.99
More Women Travel	1-85828-098-2	9.99	14.95	19.99
Zimbabwe & Botswana	1-85828-186-5	11.99	18.95	24.99
Phrasebooks				
Czech	1-85828-148-2	3.50	5.00	7.00
French	1-85828-144-X	3.50	5.00	7.00
German	1-85828-146-6	3.50	5.00	7.00
Greek	1-85828-145-8	3.50	5.00	7.00
Italian	1-85828-143-1	3.50	5.00	7.00
Mexican	1-85828-176-8	3.50	5.00	7.00
Portuguese	1-85828-175-X	3.50	5.00	7.00
Polish	1-85828-174-1	3.50	5.00	7.00
Spanish	1-85828-147-4	3.50	5.00	7.00
Thai	1-85828-177-6	3.50	5.00	7.00
Turkish	1-85828-173-3	3.50	5.00	7.00
Vietnamese	1-85828-172-5	3.50	5.00	7.00
Reference				
Classical Music	1-85828-113-X	12.99	19.95	25.99
Internet	1-85828-198-9	5.00	8.00	10.00
Jazz	1-85828-137-7	16.99	24.95	34.99
Opera	1-85828-138-5	£16.99	24.95	34.99
Rock	1-85828-201-2	17.99	26.95	35.00
World Music	1-85828-017-6	16.99	22.95	29.99

Good Vibrations!

You are
A STUDENT

You travel
THE WORLD

You want
TO SAVE MONEY

Here's how

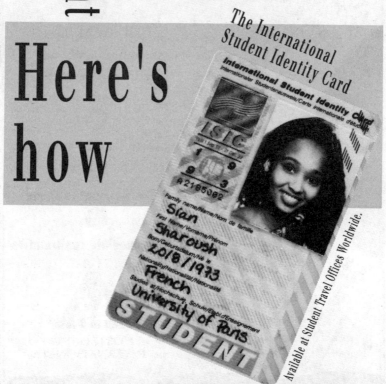

The International Student Identity Card

Available at Student Travel Offices Worldwide.

Entitles you to discounts and special services worldwide.